GENERAL HYLAN B. LYON

GENERAL HYLAN B. LYON

A Kentucky Confederate and the War in the West

Dan Lee

The University of Tennessee Press / Knoxville

Library of Congress Cataloging-in-Publication Data

Names: Lee, Dan, 1954– author.
Title: General Hylan B. Lyon : a Kentucky Confederate and the war in the West /
Dan Lee.
Description: First edition. | Knoxville : The University of Tennessee Press, [2019] |
Includes bibliographical references and index. |
Identifiers: LCCN 2018058790 (print) | LCCN 2018060328 (ebook) | ISBN
9781621904885 (Kindle) | ISBN 9781621904892 (pdf) | ISBN 9781621904878
(hardcover)
Subjects: LCSH: Lyon, Hylan B. (Hylan Benton), 1836–1907. | United States—
History—Civil War, 1861–1865—Biography. | United States—History—Civil War,
1861-1865—Campaigns. | Generals—Confederate States of America—Biography. |
Kentucky—Biography.
Classification: LCC E467.1.L896 (ebook) | LCC E467.1.L896 L44 2019 (print) | DDC
355.0092 [B] –dc23 LC record available at https://lccn.loc.gov/2018058790

This book is for Hazel

He was the biggest thing in their sight and in his own too; who went to war to protect it and lost the war and returned home to find that he had lost more than the war even, though not absolutely all; who said *At least I have life left.*

—William Faulkner in *Absalom, Absalom!*

CONTENTS

ILLUSTRATIONS

Figures

Maps

PREFACE

Many years ago, the *Courier-Journal Magazine* asked the question, "Is Kentucky Southern?" Geographers have occasionally tried to place the Bluegrass State in the Midwest. Those scholars who belong to the Midwest school of thought are persuasive. Kentucky grows corn, beans, and tobacco, not sugar cane, peanuts, and cotton. In the pre-settlement era, the Shawnee and other nations from north of the Ohio River had a traditional claim to Kentucky as a hunting ground that was as valid as that of the Southern Indians. Virginians who would become Kentuckians won Ohio, Indiana, Illinois, Wisconsin, and Michigan from the British in the American Revolution, and, after the war, great numbers of Kentuckians settled in the land between the Ohio River and the Great Lakes. In the War of 1812, feeling a paternalistic concern for what was then called the Northwest, Kentuckians volunteered by the hundreds to march north of the Ohio and fight the British and their native allies in Tecumseh's confederacy; many more fought in the North under William Henry Harrison than in the South with Andrew Jackson.

These geographers who advocate for a Midwestern identity for Kentucky regard the Ohio River not as a barrier between regions, but as a shared trade route, and they point to the vigorous trade that existed between Kentucky and the Midwest in both the antebellum and the post-Civil War periods. One need only look at the examples of the twin cities that looked across the river at one another, Covington and Cincinnati, Louisville and Jeffersonville, and Henderson and Evansville, to see that Kentucky had a natural and irreversible connection to the north. No such metropolitan areas of common economic bonds were found on the border with Tennessee. Neither did ancestry settle the issue in favor of the South. It was true that many Kentuckians traced their ancestry to Virginia and the Carolinas and equally true that many other Kentuckians traced their ancestry to Pennsylvania, New Jersey, New York, and even Vermont.

While these geographers make some excellent arguments, there *is* a case to be made for placing Kentucky in the South. It is well below the Mason-Dixon

Line, which would run just south of Columbus, Ohio, and Indianapolis, Indiana, if it were extended westward. In cuisine and regional accent, Kentucky is Southern, as well, and also in what Bill Ferris, director of the Center for the Study of Southern Culture at the University of Mississippi, called the commonwealth's "dichotomy." Ferris said, "The dichotomy, that tension which Kentucky symbolizes, Bourbon and poor white, Republican and Democrat, slave and abolitionist, old and new, all of which Kentucky is well known for, is Southern." Sociologist John Shelton Reed of the University of North Carolina approached the question by posing a single, pertinent question which he considered the "litmus test." He asked, "Where do the natives consider themselves Southerners?" The result? Kentucky was "firmly in the South."[1]

By all measures, this feeling of Southern-ness has not diminished in the years since the *Courier-Journal* first asked the question; if anything, Kentuckians have become more entrenched in their identification with the South. The fact that modern Kentuckians identify themselves so thoroughly as Southern loyalists would be a surprise to their ancestors. At the beginning of the Civil War, Kentucky held to the Union and did not secede. Historians Lowell H. Harrison and James C. Klotter point out that "between twenty-five thousand and forty thousand Kentuckians fought for the Confederacy, between ninety thousand and one hundred thousand for the Union," a difference of as much as four to one in the North's favor.[2]

Their state's stubborn adherence to the North put the Confederate officers who hailed from Kentucky in a peculiar situation, none more than the three dozen or so who became generals. They were foreigners in the new country whose gray uniform they wore, and they were enemies of the nation and the state where they were born. And because their state had not seceded, they usually found themselves leading men from states not their own. Often, their units were from the states to which these men had moved after leaving Kentucky. Several of them led with distinction in the Trans-Mississippi, particularly Missouri and Arkansas. There, General Joseph O. Shelby is the standout. Shelby was born in Kentucky and kept close ties to the state, but he lived most of his adult life in Missouri. Shelby was one of the great cavalry officers of the war, and when the war was lost he led a column of men to exile in Mexico; it was one of the legendary marches of American history.

Among the other Kentuckians in the Trans-Mississippi were Thomas J. Churchill and Samuel B. Maxey, both of whom attained the rank of general before the war was a year old. At the same time, some Kentuckians who were or who would become generals made names for themselves in the Eastern Theatre. Gustavus W. Smith commanded the Aquia District in the Department of Northern Virginia and led one wing at Seven Pines and briefly succeeded a wounded General J. E. Johnson. William T. Martin rode with J. E. B. Stuart, and Jerome Bonaparte Robertson served under James Longstreet. Some saw their first battles in the East, and then came to join the fighting west of the Appalachians. Richard Taylor was the son of the Mexican War General and 12th President Zachary Taylor and also the one-time brother-in-law of Jefferson Davis (another Kentuckian in service to the Confederacy). The Kentucky-born Taylor grew up in Louisiana and was there when the war began. Taylor led his Louisianans at the Battle of First Manassas, and he was in Stonewall Jackson's Valley Campaign as well as the Seven Days Before Richmond. Then he was transferred west. He became a district commander and ended the war in charge of the Department of Alabama, Mississippi, and East Louisiana. One of the highest ranked Kentuckians in the Confederacy, though by no means one of the most gifted, was General John Bell Hood. He, like Taylor, had seen his first fighting in the East. He commanded a division in Longstreet's Corps and came west with him during the Chickamauga Campaign of 1863. Longstreet eventually returned to the East; Hood stayed in the West. He became the commander of the Army of Tennessee, and hurled it forward to its destruction at the Battles of Franklin and Nashville.

However, as Harrison and Klotter point out, there *were* Kentucky Confederates in the rank and file, and in some instances there were Kentucky-born generals leading Kentuckians in battle. Kentucky's most famous Confederate unit was the First Kentucky Brigade, better known as the Orphan Brigade. An impressive list of prominent Kentucky generals led the Orphans through the war. They included Roger Hanson, Ben Hardin Helm, Joseph H. Lewis, and John C. Breckinridge. It was Breckinridge, now promoted to division command, who gave the brigade its name after the Battle of Stones River. The argument can be made that Breckinridge was the greatest Confederate from the Bluegrass State in talent, temperament, and accomplishments. He had been the Vice-President of the United States, a presidential candidate in 1860, and he was a U.S. Senator at the time the war began. He left the Union to become one of the South's most gallant battlefield commanders, and he ended the war as the Confederate Secretary of War. After Breckinridge had served for a time as Secretary of War and his qualities could be fairly judged, Robert E. Lee said of him, "He is a great man. I was acquainted with him as Congressman and Vice-President and as one of our Generals, but I did not know him until he was secretary of war, and he is a lofty, pure strong man." Another of the Orphans' commanders, Ben Hardin Helm, was Abraham Lincoln's brother-in-law. The President was desperately interested in enlisting Helm in the Northern cause. He offered Helm the position of Union paymaster, with the rank of major. Helm refused, and when he was killed on the second day at Chickamauga, the White House was thrown into a deep gloom. The Lincolns were criticized for their grief over the death of an enemy officer and for their courtesy to his widow.[3]

Besides the Orphans, there was another brigade of Kentuckians in the Confederate Army. It was the Third Brigade in General Abraham Buford's division of Nathan Bedford Forrest's cavalry corps. It was usually called simply the Kentucky Brigade. During some of the bloodiest epochs of the war, the brigade was commanded by Colonel Hylan B. Lyon of Eddyville. Nathaniel C. Hughes says, "Forrest did not possess a more professional, experienced brigade commander than this young, energetic Kentuckian." Lyon was a West Point graduate. He was a veteran of the Third Seminole War in Florida and of the Coeur d'Alene War in Washington Territory. He was back home in Lyon County, Kentucky, on a leave of absence when the trouble between North and South boiled over. He had returned to Kentucky with the desire to resign from the army, marry, and become a farmer. The firing on Fort Sumter followed by President Lincoln's call for 75,000 volunteers changed his plans. Although he had just received a promotion to 1st lieutenant, 3rd U.S. Artillery, he resigned his commission and immediately began to raise a company of Southern loyalists. Lyon and his men marched south to Tennessee where like-minded men were gathering. Lyon's Confederate career, during which he rose through the ranks from captain to brigadier general, was one of sacrifice and devotion to an insurgent nation that was the enemy to all he had known before 1861, to the country that had educated him and the state that had nurtured him.

Like so many of his fellow Confederate officers, Lyon hesitated to return to Kentucky when the war was lost. He and the others did not realize that Kentucky had changed in the four years of war. The harsh rule of the occupying Federals and the emancipation issue had made Kentucky more in sympathy with the South; so it was that the returning Confederate officers, like Lyon, were not ostracized; they were celebrated, and many of them went on to win political office and to serve Kentucky in other ways as if the "late unpleasantness" had never occurred. During the war, Lyon had been admired for his courage—he was called by one subordinate "amongst the bravest of the brave"—but there was little warmth in the admiration. He did not inspire the kind of affection that his fellow Kentuckians Simon Bolivar Buckner and John C. Breckinridge attracted. It was not until his later years, long after the war, that Lyon became the object of something approaching the devotion that men of a more accessible personality had enjoyed all along. His public service was no doubt responsible, at least in part, for his newfound popularity.[4]

This is the story of General Hylan B. Lyon, a West Point graduate, a respected soldier of the United States who renounced his nation, went to war, and returned in the end to serve his state honorably.

ACKNOWLEDGMENTS

The author wishes to thank:

Linda A. Lee

Steven L. Wright

Tammy Snook, City Historian/Curator/Interpretive Park Ranger, City of Yuma, Yuma Crossing National Heritage Area, & Yuma Quartermaster Depot State Historic Park, Yuma, CA

Lucas Griswold, Visitor Services Supervisor, Boston Harbor Islands National and State Park, MA Department of Conservation and Recreation

The staff at Mississippi's Last Stands Visitor & Interpretive Center, Baldwyn, MS

The staff at the Glenn E. Martin Genealogy Library, Princeton, KY

The staff of the Kentucky Museum and Library at Western Kentucky University, Bowling Green, KY

The staff of the Pogue Special Collections Library, Murray State University, Murray, KY

Sasha Jovanovic for the cartography.

General Lyon, c. 1864. MOLLUS Mass. Collection, United States Army Heritage and Education Center, Carlisle, PA.

I

FAR FROM HOME

Hylan Benton Lyon was born February 22, 1836, near Eddyville, Kentucky. His family was prosperous, the overseers of an impressive business and farming empire, but material wealth was not his most important birthright. What proved to be more important to H. B. Lyon was his family's century-long tradition of rebellion.

His great-grandfather was an Irish insurrectionist, the leader of a group called the White Boys. The White Boys opposed Ireland's British landlords. Government authorities captured and executed the elder Lyon about 1762. In 1765, his son, Matthew Lyon, boarded a ship for America. In the decade that followed, Lyon became increasingly involved with the rebellious colonials, particularly after 1771, when he married Mary Hosford, the niece of Ethan Allen. The young couple joined Allen's colony of settlers in the country west of the Green Mountains in what is now Vermont. Revolution was brewing in all of New England, and Allen became the leader of a rebel group called the Green Mountain Boys. Matthew Lyon was one of them.

In the first year of the Revolution, Lyon helped capture Fort Ticonderoga and Crown Point and later claimed that he worked the first cannon ever fired in the cause of American liberty. He took part in General Richard Montgomery's invasion of Canada, after which he was promoted to colonel. He left the army in 1778 to pursue a business and political career in Rutland County, Vermont. In 1782, Lyon's wife Mary died, leaving their son and daughters motherless. The next year, he married Beulah Chittenden Galusha, a widow. During their nearly forty years of marriage, Beulah Lyon would bear her husband eight more children. Six of them survived to adulthood.

In 1796, Lyon, a Jeffersonian, was elected to the U.S. House of Representatives. He served two turbulent terms before deciding to leave Vermont for the West. He dispatched a colony of friends and family members to a site at the mouth of Eddy Creek, a tributary of the Cumberland River, near the nascent village of Eddyville in present day Lyon County, Kentucky. He joined them there with another group of settlers in 1801, after the end of his second term in Congress. He called his farm Riverview.

The seventy people who accompanied Matthew Lyon from Vermont found themselves among a strange people in their new home on the Cumberland. They were mostly settlers from Virginia and the Carolinas, and while they possessed an abundance of hospitality, they were shockingly destitute of books. Even more disquieting to the Northern newcomers than the widespread illiteracy was the practice of slavery. The Lyons opposed slavery. Mrs. Lyon was particularly outspoken in her disapproval, and it nearly destroyed her satisfaction with Kentucky, but Matthew Lyon was undoubtedly more effective in his own rebellion against the peculiar institution. It is true that Lyon leased slaves from their masters for his various business and farming interests, but he became known in the slave community as a white man who could be trusted. Many runaway slaves came to beg him to buy their freedom, which he did. He set them free when they performed labor equal in dollars to what he had paid for them. Untold numbers of former slaves owed their freedom to Lyon's personal emancipation efforts.

In 1802, Matthew Lyon resumed his political career. He was elected to the Kentucky General Assembly, and, after only one year, he had become so well regarded that he was elected to the U.S. House of Representatives. He remained in office until his opposition to the War of 1812 cost him the support of his constituents, who failed to return him to office. The war ruined Lyon. Risky investments left him $28,000 in debt. His sons rescued him from defaulting and the disgrace of a bankruptcy, but his life in Kentucky came to an end. He finagled an appointment from President James Monroe as factor of the Cherokee Nation in Arkansas. From then on, his sons Chittenden and Matthew would be the important Lyons in Kentucky. Matthew Lyon, Sr. died in Arkansas on August 1, 1822, and was buried there, but his sons had the body disinterred in 1833 and returned to Kentucky for reburial in the Eddyville Cemetery overlooking the Cumberland River.

After Matthew Lyon's death, Chittenden Lyon became the acknowledged head of the extended clan. He was the oldest son of Matthew and Beulah Lyon and was in personality the spitting image of his father. Thompson A. Lyon, Chittenden's son, said that his father had been "a 'broth of a boy,' with so much of the blood of his father, that he was ever ready for a hand to hand fight on the shortest notice." Chittenden Lyon had also inherited old Matthew's charm, and he was "universally popular and greatly beloved" among his neighbors. Chittenden Lyon continued his father's mercantile and farming interests and, also like his father, rode his popularity to a successful political career. He was elected to the Kentucky House of Representatives in 1822, and he went on to serve in the Kentucky Senate and three terms in the U.S. House of Representatives. When Lyon County was formed as Kentucky's 102nd in 1854, it was not named in honor of the old Jeffersonian Matthew Lyon; it was in honor of his son the Jacksonian, Chittenden Lyon.[1]

Matthew Lyon Jr. was the fourth child and the second son of Matthew and Beulah Lyon. He was less flamboyant than his older brother "Chit," and less is known about him; a regrettable fact, for he became the father of the present subject, future General Hylan B. Lyon. While not as fond of the spotlight as his brother Chit, the record shows that Matthew Jr. possessed the Lyon talent for accomplishment. He was a captain in the local militia and served in the Kentucky Senate from 1834 to 1837, but he had less interest in a public life than his better-known brother. As Chittenden Lyon wrote to a friend, "My brother Matthew lives within two miles of my residence, (Eddyville, Ky.) and is doing very well—in fact, getting rich, for he minds the main chance and dabbles but little in politics."[2]

Nine-year-old Matthew Jr. had come to Eddyville with his father's colony in 1801 and, from the evidence, he became thoroughly absorbed with making a prosperous start on the Kentucky frontier. He was unusually slow to take a wife. It was not until 1821, when he was nearly thirty years old, that he married his fellow Vermonter, Elizabeth Maria Martin. The couple became the parents of eight children, but their marriage was brief. Matthew Lyon Jr. died in 1839 in Eddyville. The 1840 Federal Census shows that he did not leave his family destitute and reveals also that Matthew Jr. had not shared his parents' disapproval of slavery. The widow Elizabeth M. Lyon was the owner of eighteen slaves in addition to eight free white employees. The slave property of the Lyons placed them very near the top of the social pyramid, the planter class. Though they had suffered a grievous loss when Matthew died, they might still have survived had not Elizabeth Lyon followed him to the grave in 1844. The children were completely orphaned. Hylan B. Lyon was eight years old.

The parentless Lyon children went to live in the home of Frederick H. and Helen Skinner. Both Skinners were grandchildren of old Matthew Lyon, first cousins and, hence, also cousins to the orphans. F. H. Skinner kept a working man's hotel in Eddyville. His boarders included barkeeps, carpenters, grocers, brick masons, a constable, a telegrapher, and, now, his unfortunate young cousins. Skinner did not resent the unexpected burden. He proved to be a good guardian for the Lyon children and was their friend for life.

The extended Lyon family and their many enterprises made Eddyville a Lyon town, and the familiar faces and scenes of their surroundings must have eased, somewhat, the orphans' passage from grief to acceptance and from childhood to adolescence. Elizabeth Lyon Roe remembered Eddyville as an idyllic Southern town, "dotted all over with neat dwellings and good gardens, producing every variety of vegetables and flowers."[3]

However, the town was changing in a way that was not calculated to increase its charm. In 1849, the state repealed the law that forbade the importation of slaves. In Eddyville and the surrounding county, there was a resulting growth in the slave population, and there developed "a viable slave-based economy in need of more hands."[4]

The slaves that came in under the new law were destined for the corn and tobacco fields, primarily, or for work in the nearby iron furnaces, and their owners looked ahead to a long future of profitable slave ownership, for the imported were very young. A quarter of them were in their mid-teens. Furthermore, Christopher Waldrep finds in examining the pertinent documents from the 1850s that the nature of slavery in Lyon County was changing. He says, "While most Lyon County slaves were female [indicating house servants], males made up seventy-three percent of the imported population. Lyon County masters sought labor." If there was any redeeming aspect to this enthusiasm for importing slaves, it was found in the fact that Lyon Countians were not entering the deplorable business of slave breeding. Waldrep says that if they had been "breeding slaves for re-export South, they would have imported women and children at least as readily as men." Neither were they becoming slave traders. The new state law prohibited the imported slaves from being re-sold within five years. Importers were required "to swear that their human chattels were for their personal use, not for resale." Violators faced a $600 fine, which was stiff enough to encourage a high degree of compliance.[5]

The Lyons took advantage of the 1849 law to augment their work force with imported slave labor. As a boy, Hylan B. Lyon saw that his surviving blood kin believed in owning slaves and were eager to own even more. It was a part of his early education, as integral to his understanding as the reading, writing, and the rule of three that he learned in the village schools. By age fourteen, he had acquired all he could from a rustic education, and his guardian arranged to send him to attend classes at the Masonic University in La Grange, Kentucky, near Louisville. His schooling at La Grange cost him $12 per term for classes in mathematics, spelling, and Latin, and his books cost another $1.08. The young scholar showed an aptitude for the written word; algebra gave him trouble. He heard the abolitionist Cassius M. Clay speak at La Grange, but he was not persuaded of the evils of slavery or convinced of the benefits of ending it.

After eighteen months, Lyon returned to Western Kentucky to attend Cumberland College at Princeton, only a few miles from Eddyville. His term there was brief. In 1852, at age sixteen, he won an appointment to the U.S. Military Academy at West Point, New York. He was admitted to the academy on July 1, 1852, one of a class of ninety-four cadets. They included future Civil War notables Orlando M. Poe, Fitzhugh Lee, and his fellow Kentuckian, William P. Sanders.

If Lyon had been pampered in Eddyville as a child of one of the community's elite families, he soon learned at West Point that there was nothing considered exceptional about him. The upperclassmen tormented the plebes, or
freshmen, and "those plebes who were deviled most were the sons of wealthy
or prominent men. . . . The rich and the poor came here from all sections of
the country and of all classes and degrees of society; but after they reported,
wealth, or knowledge, or family reputation counted for nothing."[6]

Cadets spent the months of July and August camping on the Plain. At the
end of August, they moved into the Barracks, a new building in cadet Lyon's
time (it was built in 1851); a four-story edifice of red sandstone "castellated and
corniced . . . in the Elizabethan style." The cadets lived two to a room and the
space was barely adequate. The rooms were a cramped fourteen by twenty-
two feet, but they did feature a modern convenience previously unknown to
many of the young men, a hot water heating system. A power plant in the
basement kept the rooms comfortable in the coldest of New York winters.[7]

At least as prominent in the cadets' lives was the classroom building, built
in 1839. Its three stories contained the chemistry department, including a lab-
oratory; the fencing department, which included a gymnasium; the cabinet
of minerals and fossils; the mineralogical recitation room; the geographical
room; the engineering academy; the mathematical model room; the drawing
academy; and the artillery model room. Upon examination of West Point's
curriculum, Horace Mann, the great educator and head of the committee on
instruction, had said, "The committee would express the opinion that when
they consider the length of the course and the severity of the studies pursued
at the academy, they have rarely, if ever, seen anything that equaled either the
excellence of the teaching or the proficiency of the taught."[8]

The academic expectations were high, and many of those who enrolled
with high hopes for a career as an officer in the U.S. Army found, to their
surprise, that they had come poorly prepared for the challenge of West Point
classwork. Of the ninety-four who enrolled as Fourth Classmen with Lyon,
only forty-nine graduated. Beginning his classes, the cadet found that the
minimum standard of scholarship expected of him included being able to
"read and write well, and perform with facility and accuracy the various operations of the four ground rules of Arithmetic, of Reduction, of simple and
compound Proportion, and of vulgar and decimal Fractions." The cadet was
also expected to "write in a fair and legible hand, and without any material
mistakes in spelling." Incoming students must demonstrate all of this, while,
at the same time, trying to suppress the natural and nearly crippling homesickness suffered by so many and in addition to the daily drills that tested
their physical stamina between mid-March and the beginning of November.
Hylan B. Lyon measured up. At the end of his first year, he stood in about

the middle of his class, academically. He ranked forty-first in mathematics, forty-second in English studies, and twenty-third in French.[9]

In conduct, Lyon racked up a disappointing 126 demerits, which, from the available records, seem to be the most of his four years at the Academy. He improved as time went on, but at his best, he still fell far short of Superintendent Robert E. Lee, who had graduated in the class of 1829 without a single black mark against his name. Lee had assumed his duties as superintendent in September 1852, the same summer that Lyon came to West Point, and the dignified Virginian devoted himself to his work with high expectations of excellence from others, as well as from himself.

Lee felt that the "curriculum was overcrowded and some important subjects were being omitted" at the Academy. The reforms he recommended grew out of his experiences during the Mexican War, when he had the long opportunity to witness both the strengths and the shortcomings of a West Point education. Lyon may have been motivated to be more studious by the modern and more interesting classes that Lee instituted. They included Spanish, constitutional and international law, history, geography, and composition. The Kentucky cadet's marks improved during his second year at the academy, and his demerits dropped by a third. If Lyon was inspired by Lee to aim higher, he was not alone. The superintendent was idolized by many. Future Union General John M. Schofield, who graduated in 1853, later said that Lee "was the personification of dignity, justice and kindness, and was respected and admired as the ideal of a commanding officer."[10]

Lee took a personal interest in each cadet's successes or failures. Douglas Southall Freeman writes, "When he could praise a boy's work, Lee did not stint in his encomiums." The superintendent would send letters of praise to the parents, complimenting them on raising such a fine son. Conversely, if it was obvious that the cadet was faltering, Lee would urge the parents to allow their boy to resign before examinations. To persist when failure was certain would only lead to unnecessary humiliation. There is no record of Lee ever sending either form of letter to Lyon's guardians, and neither is there any record of Lee ever calling young Lyon into his office for a disciplinary talk. Lyon remained middling in both his grades and his deportment.[11]

Lee left West Point in 1855 to accept an assignment as lieutenant colonel of the 2nd U.S. Cavalry, Colonel Albert Sidney Johnston, commanding. He was succeeded at the academy on April 1, 1855, by Major Jonathan G. Bernard, a colorless administrator whose tenure lasted only until the summer of 1856. Bernard was the superintendent during Lyon's last year at West Point.

Lyon graduated on July 1, 1856. He ranked nineteenth among his forty-nine classmates. The best scholars among the graduates were assigned to the engineer corps. Lyon, now a brevet 2nd lieutenant, was assigned to the 2nd U.S.

Artillery, but in October, presumably after the traditional post-graduation visit home, he was reassigned to the 3rd Artillery. The assignment may have pleased him. He certainly had heard the stories handed down about his grandfather's service as one of the Revolution's first artillerymen, a claim based on his service as a gunner at Crown Point in 1775.

Lieutenant Lyon was ordered to report to Florida, where the 3rd Artillery was fighting in the Third Seminole War. He got only as far as New Orleans when his orders were countermanded, and he was ordered back to Fort Independence in the harbor of Boston, Massachusetts. He boarded a steamer from New Orleans to Boston, but upon reaching New York City he learned from a fellow officer that their respective companies of the 3rd Artillery were relieved from duty and were on their way from Florida. Consequently, he requested and received permission to wait on his company before proceeding to Boston. He waited for three weeks at Fort Columbus, Governors Island, New York, before learning that his company had been detained and would not come north until spring. He was ordered to remain in New York City until December 30, at which time he would turn about again and embark for Florida at the head of 294 recruits.

The United States had been fighting the Seminoles since 1817, when Andrew Jackson led excursions into West Florida in an attempt to capture runaway slaves who had found sanctuary with the tribe. The First Seminole War sputtered to an end in 1819, only to be resumed in 1835. The Second Seminole War ended in 1842 with the relocation of most of the Seminoles to a reservation west of the Mississippi. A few hundred fled deep into the Everglades and hid there under the leadership of Holata-Micco (Alligator Chief), who the whites called Billy Bowlegs.

In the next few years, there were intermittent clashes between the Seminoles and white settlers, and after each incident more soldiers were sent into the region to keep the peace. General David Twiggs was ordered to bring an end to these simmering hostilities. In January 1850, he was able to persuade a handful of Seminoles to relocate west of the Mississippi. The next month, they boarded a ship bound for New Orleans, and more Indians were said to be ready to accept General Twiggs's offer. Billy Bowlegs was not among them. He and his fellow resistors still roamed free in the swamps, and there they remained. Five more years of white efforts failed to force their surrender. Whites continued to push into Seminole land, occasional blood was shed, and the settlers demanded protection. Troops poured into the region.

In December 1855, Lieutenant George L. Hartsuff led an army surveying party of ten men and two wagons into the wilds south of Fort Myers. At Big Cypress Swamp, the Seminoles attacked them. Four whites were killed and five were wounded. The newspapers called it a massacre. War was declared on the Seminoles, and General William S. Harney was sent to command the troops. Escalating violence led to more deaths on both sides, but the Indians had the advantage, initially, as guerrillas always do. Harney was not discouraged. He called on the War Department for more soldiers, augmented them with Florida volunteers, and conducted a campaign that combined water and land forces. Troops in canoes and skiffs scoured the swamps, driving the Indians before them, while dragoons, or mounted infantry, patrolled the edges to catch any Seminoles who emerged to escape. This campaign was underway when Lieutenant Lyon arrived from New York in early 1857.

Harney's campaign appeared to be succeeding, but it was exceedingly slow work. By late February, it was clear to Harney that the campaign was going to extend into summer. Floridians were becoming impatient with the progress of the general's campaign, and they clamored to join the fight. They promised "if the government will offer a reward for every live Indians [sic] with a proportionate less sum for the scalps of those who may be killed, that the 'Crackers' of that region will bring them in in sixty days."[12]

The army persisted through the summer and fall. On November 19, 1857, the Alligator Chief's lair was found and destroyed, along with his animals, stores, and crops in the field. The Seminole resistors had suffered a disaster, one that was repeated time and again as other villages were discovered. Winter was a starving time for the war-weary Indians, and it broke them. On March 27, 1858, Billy Bowlegs accepted the terms of surrender. The next day, the chief and his remaining followers boarded the steamer *Grey Cloud* for the passage to New Orleans, the first leg of their journey west. The Third Seminole War was over.

Lieutenant Lyon was not there to see the end. On March 1, 1857, he was ordered to Fort Yuma, California. Lyon was an observant traveler, and throughout his military career he wrote long, newsy letters to his family back in Kentucky to tell them about his adventures. In a letter to his cousin Laura O'Hara, written from San Diego on April 27, 1857, he described his circuitous trip west. He traveled by open yacht for four days to reach Tampa, a "miserable place," where he spent four days before going on to Pensacola. From there he took a stagecoach to Mobile, thence to New Orleans. He enjoyed four days in the Crescent City and then made the three-day voyage to Havana, Cuba. He considered Havana a very pretty city but he felt that it had not reached its potential under the Spanish. "In the hands of the Americans it would be in a short time the Queen city of the world," he said.[13]

From Havana, Lyon crossed the Western Caribbean to Aspinwall, Isthmus of Panama. He continued to the Pacific coast of the isthmus by rail and caught a ship for San Francisco. The voyage took thirteen days, with stops at Acapulco and Manzanilla. He told Laura that the trip north was a pleasant one. The ship was not crowded and there were "a number of pretty and agreeable ladies on board, with one of whom, free as I am from all love affairs, I should most certainly have fallen in love had she not been a Spanish lady." The young army officer and the señorita could not overcome the language barrier, and the budding romance faded. Lieutenant Lyon spent nearly a week in San Francisco ("the handsomest men and ugliest women of any city I have ever visited"), before traveling south to San Diego. There, he wrote his letter. The next day, April 28, he set out for the ten-day trip to Fort Yuma, his new assignment.[14]

Fort Yuma was an open compound of adobe buildings located at the mouth of the Gila River, at the place where it entered the Colorado. The outpost owed its existence to the gold rush of 1849. Gila Crossing became an important landmark for the gold seekers coming west on the California Trail. The Yuma Indians saw an opportunity in providing the prospectors an easy way to get across the river. They opened a ferry. After a while, a gang of whites launched a hostile takeover of the little enterprise, and they added a new, violent twist. More than a few emigrants were robbed and killed at the crossing by this homicidal gang. One night, when the usurpers were lying drunk in their camp, the Yumas crept back and killed all but three of them. The Yumas burned the bodies and quietly went back to running their ferry. The three survivors spread the word of the attack. A small militia unit was raised to punish the Indians. The brave volunteers marched out, only to be defeated in one encounter after another. Responding to the need for a better armed, more professional force to bring peace to the region, Major Samuel P. Heintzelman and three companies of the 2nd U.S. Infantry moved east from San Diego and established Fort Yuma on the California side of the Gila. The Yuma War lasted three years, 1850 to 1853. A treaty finally brought peace to the region, but the soldiers stayed on as an occupying force to protect travelers against Indians and renegade whites and to keep a cautious eye on Mexico.

Fort Yuma sat on a rocky hill, eighty feet above the rivers. Major Heintzelman wrote a long report in July 1853, describing conditions in his desert outpost. Away from the rivers, he said, the land was barren from lack of rainfall. In 1852, there had been only two inches of rain at Fort Yuma. The rivers were the essential life givers for the Indians and the soldiers alike. Fort Yuma's garrison was primarily supplied by ships from San Francisco that came up the Sea of Cortez (the Gulf of California) to the mouth of the Colorado and then fought the hard current up to the mouth of the Gila. Heintzelman pointed out that Fort Yuma was made possible as a permanent installation only after navigation on the Colorado became a reliable source of supply. Fort Yuma's other connection to the West Coast was the overland route from San Diego, 220 miles long and brutal in the best of times. It was by this desert trail that Lieutenant Lyon came to Fort Yuma in the spring of 1857.

Captain Henry S. Burton was the commander at Fort Yuma during the time that Lyon was posted there. Lyon's immediate superior was 1st Lieutenant Robert O. Tyler. He led Company A, 3rd U.S. Artillery, and was often assigned to escort arriving parties of soldiers across the desert. When Captain Burton was absent, Tyler commanded Fort Yuma. At those times, Lyon took temporary command of Company A, but his regular assignment was as post adjutant, which meant a great deal of paperwork, especially in dealing with Captain Burton's official correspondence.

Not long after Lyon assumed his duties there, a correspondent for the Washington, [DC] *Union* called Fort Yuma "the most important post in California." The roving reporter went on to say, "Two ferries have heretofore found active employment in crossing emigrants and cattle at the Colorado River. . . . They are now, by purchase at a large amount, merged into one. I have known the receipts of the Colorado Company to be upwards of $2000 in one day." A stage line, the San Antonio and San Diego Stage Company, began service along the California Road in 1857, and when the company won the government contract to deliver mail from the east, Fort Yuma became more important than it had ever been. The resulting increase in travelers, the station manager and his crew, the blacksmiths and the wheelwrights, along with the local native population, the crews of the Gila River steamers, and the miners at the nearby mining operations who found their pleasures in the saloons and fleshpots of Arizona City (across the Gila from the fort)—all made Fort Yuma anything but lonely.[15]

Lyon rather liked it. The letter that he wrote home in mid-October was filled with interesting items. He told his cousin Laura O'Hara that it had taken him eight days to travel from San Diego to the fort, or, more accurately, four days and four nights, because the heat had been so fierce on four of those days that it was feasible only to travel at night. Now, in October, the weather was the "most pleasant I have experienced in a long time. It is something like Indian summer in Kentucky." The autumn mornings were sometimes foggy. The fort was on a hill, and the misty valleys gave one the impression of being "on an island in a vast sea." For daily amusement he had a pretty little dog with dark eyes and light brown spots. He called the dog "Dic" and went out with him frequently to hunt. Also, he told Miss O'Hara, there had been a recent dance. The ladies were Mexican, and a Mexican boy who played a comb covered by a sheet of paper provided the music. "We danced to our hearts content," Lieutenant Lyon said.[16]

However, despite the exotic desert scenery, his hunting excursions with Dic, and dancing with the Mexican girls, Lyon confessed to Laura that soldiering on the frontier could be monotonous; in fact, life was more monotonous "than it was at even West Point." He hoped that he might be transferred back east, to a post in Virginia. There may have been yet another reason that he wanted to return closer to home.[17]

In this letter appeared the first hint that there was something deeper than simple friendship developing between Lieutenant Lyon and Laura O'Hara. He told her that if she did not want him to love her and pester her with love letters, she "must be careful how you address me as Dear Cousin." He said, "it would require but little encouragement for me to love, as I have never loved before, one whose beauty I admire and whose friendship I esteem so much as yours."[18]

Laura replied on December 8, "Cousin, I feel much flattered by the high compliments you have paid me, for which I feel myself so unworthy. You may have been jesting, but as you know I never flatter and believe everyone else to be equally serious. . . . You must not flatter me again for fear it will turn my head." She commented on the approaching Christmas season and assured him that his friends and loved ones would miss him. "I think you had better persuade Uncle Sam to send your regiment out here for our sake," she said.[19]

In the winter of 1857–1858, the 3rd U.S. Artillery was scattered all over the Department of the Pacific. The headquarters was at Benicia, California, and there was one company there. There was another company at the Presidio in San Francisco, one at San Diego, one at Fort Miller, California, and one at Fort Cascades, Washington Territory. There were two companies at Fort Umpqua, Oregon Territory, and there were three companies at Fort Yuma. The outliers were the one company at Fort Leavenworth, Kansas Territory, and the one at Fortress Monroe, Virginia, where Lyon hoped to be reassigned.

It was not to be. Despite Laura O'Hara's wishes that he be sent to the East and his own desires in that direction, Lyon would not leave the West for some time to come. Hostilities had broken out in Washington Territory. A campaign was planned against the Indians, and the 3rd U.S. Artillery was on its way to take part. It was in the Pacific Northwest that Lyon would become fully acquainted with what his West Point education had only hinted at and what his time in Florida and California had only fleetingly revealed. In Washington, Lyon would learn what it meant to be a soldier.

2

THE COEUR D'ALENE WAR

The situation in Washington Territory had been tense for some time. There were small incidents between the Indians and the settlers and prospectors whose numbers multiplied year by year. The government responded to the whites' complaints by increasing the army's presence in the region, which only aggravated the situation. Colonel George Wright commanded in the field, and he soon demonstrated that he believed less in diplomacy and more in intimidation. Soon after taking the field in March 1856, Colonel Wright captured and hanged eight Chinook tribesmen. Wright's show of force did not subdue the Indians. They vowed "that no white settlements should be made in their country, nor should there be any roads through it." The miners and the settlers were frightened.[1]

In April 1858, forty Colville settlers signed a petition asking for army protection. They reported that two whites had been killed and some cattle had been stolen. Consequently, Lieutenant Colonel Edward Steptoe was dispatched from Fort Walla Walla at the head of a force numbering between 130 and 159 men. While accounts vary as to the exact number of men, they agree that the column was made up primarily of dragoons with two howitzer crews accompanying. At the Jesuit mission on the Coeur d'Alene River, Steptoe learned that the Indians were massing in his front. Father Peter Joset told Steptoe that the Indians were upset because they had learned that "the Government was fitting out an expedition to survey a military road from Fort Walla Walla to Fort Benton on the Missouri River, and that they would resist and prevent it."[2]

Steptoe decided to press on to the Spokane River. He found one thousand Spokans, Palouses, Coeur d'Alenes, and Yakimas waiting for him there. The brief skirmish that followed persuaded Steptoe that he could not fight his way across the river, and he decided to fall back to Walla Walla. On May 17, as the column retreated, the Indians attacked. Steptoe's soldiers kept moving, fighting off dashes against their supply wagons, until they reached Pine Creek.

The Indians were too many, and the soldiers could not cross. They dug in on a nearby hill. The soldiers' fire was accurate, but the Indians would not retire. The fighting continued through the day. Six soldiers were killed, eleven were wounded, the able bodied were exhausted, and those who could still fight were running critically low on ammunition. When full dark descended, Steptoe had the dead and his two howitzers buried, and the bluecoats slipped away. After a running skirmish of seventy-five miles, they reached Fort Walla Walla and reported the action that the press soon labeled as the Steptoe Massacre.

The Indians of the Northwest had the reputation of being "the most bold and warlike on the continent. Splendid specimens of physical humanity, they are skillful in the use of arms, and accustomed from childhood almost to live on horseback." Now these fearsome warriors had formed a confederacy, and they were emboldened by their victory over Steptoe. The campaign to regain their lands had begun. It was imperative that the army reassert its presence in the Northwest before conditions grew worse. Troops were summoned to the Columbia River from all over the Department of the Pacific. These included the companies of the 3rd U.S. Artillery from Fort Yuma.[3]

Lieutenant Lyon was ordered to report to San Bernardino, thence to San Francisco, and from there on June 13, 1858, he embarked for the Northwest aboard the steamer *Pacific*. A reporter for the New York *Herald* witnessed the departure. He wrote, "It was a lively scene at the wharf when the steamer sailed. The neat, soldierlike appearance of the troops from the Presidio; the bronzed, worn appearance of those who had crossed the desert from Fort Yuma, and the brilliant trappings of the officers, formed quite a contrast." The dispatch continued, "The steamer will leave these troops at Fort Vancouver on the Columbia river. Here they will remain for a few days to be fully fitted for the field, and then proceed to the fort at the Dalles. From there, they will march 200 miles across the Plains to Walla-Walla, where Colonel Steptoe is posted."[4]

The *Pacific* arrived at the mouth of the Columbia River on June 18. Captain Erasmus D. Keyes was in charge of the 3rd Artillery on board. By evening, Keyes and his men were at Fort Vancouver, "a picketed enclosure of about three hundred yards square, composed of roughly split pine logs." The buildings within the walled compound dated from the days of Dr. John McLoughlin and the Hudson Bay Company.[5]

On June 21, the artillerymen moved up the Columbia toward Fort Dalles. They arrived the next day and learned there, if they had not known before, that they were assigned to Colonel George Wright, who was leading one of the two punitive expeditions against the Indians for the Steptoe Massacre. Major Richard S. Garnett was going to lead the other punitive expedition

Ft. Vancouver, c. 1855. Library of Congress.

and march from Fort Simcoe to search for Indians further north. Lieutenant Lyon could have served comfortably under either Wright or Garnett. Garnett was a West Pointer and a Virginian, and Lyon shared his Southern sensibilities, but one can easily imagine that he thought himself lucky to have as his commander the more experienced Wright. Wright was fifty-five years old, a Vermonter by birth, and a West Point graduate, class of '22. He was a veteran of both the Second Seminole War in 1844 and the Mexican War. The brevet colonel was made full colonel in 1855. He recruited the 9th U.S. Infantry that same year and was ordered to Washington Territory. It was Colonel Wright who had hanged the eight Chinooks in 1856, an act that contributed to the further militancy of the Indians who defeated Steptoe in the so-called massacre, which, in turn, precipitated the punitive action that was now underway. In the spring of 1858, Wright built Fort Dalles on the site of an earlier camp, and it was from there that the 3rd Artillery marched as part of Wright's column on the afternoon of July 7, 1858.

The column made only six miles on the first day of the march, no great distance, but as Lieutenant Lawrence Kip of the 3rd Artillery explained in his campaign diary, "The length of each day's march will have to be regulated by the water, which in some places is not to be found for a distance of twenty miles. The country over which we passed during the afternoon is barren and desolate, unfit for culture." They camped at a place called Five Mile Creek.[6]

Marching some days as few as five miles and other days as much as twenty (and one day, a backbreaking thirty), the column reached Fort Walla Walla on July 19. The weather was blazing hot and the country barren except for a verdant strip right along the rivers, where plant and animal life abounded. Fort Walla Walla was in such a place, and the men found good water and abundant timber there.

Four companies of the 1st Dragoons and two companies of the 9th Infantry waited at the fort, and they joined the column when it resumed its march. Before then, there was business to attend to. All but one company of the 3rd Artillery spent the time drilling in light infantry tactics, and Colonel Wright held the first of his treaty councils when a band of sixty Nez Perce braves came in. By his negotiations with these representatives of their tribe, Wright was able to win over a sizable force of Indians—an estimated seventeen hundred warriors—who might otherwise have joined the hostile Coeur d'Alene confederacy. It was arranged that thirty of the Nez Perce braves would accompany Wright as scouts. They were placed under the command of Lieutenant John Mullan and given army uniforms. They had a dance to celebrate their new alliance with the whites.

Including the Nez Perce scouts, Wright's column now numbered about 720 men. All three branches of the army were represented, but, as Lieutenant Lyon recalled, it was mostly "artillerymen trained as infantry." On August 5, 1858, the 3rd Artillery moved out ahead of the other regiments in order to build a fort sixty miles away on the Snake River. The fort was named Fort Taylor. Beyond the Snake, baggage wagons would find it to be hard going, so Colonel Wright replaced the wagons with pack animals and hired additional men to tend them.[7]

A terrible storm delayed the expedition's planned departure on August 23. During the unanticipated four-day wait, a party of three Indians appeared across the river. One was brought into camp. He explained that they were Spokans and that they were seeking safety from attack. Wright told this messenger to bring in the women and children and turn over the weapons and they would be safe. The Indians complied, and as a sign of their friendship told Wright that he would find the hostiles waiting for him on the Spokane River. This confirmed the intelligence that the Nez Perce scouts had already brought in.

On August 25, the column moved out, led by the dragoons, and crossed the Snake River. There had only been glimpses of the hostiles before this and occasional exchanges of ineffective gunfire. Now the soldiers were in enemy territory, and clashes became more frequent and more serious. On the last day of August, Wright's men were passing through a pine woods when they heard gunshots ahead. The Nez Perce scouts and the hostiles were fighting. Wright ordered the dragoons to advance. When they heard the horse soldiers coming, the enemy faded back to just beyond gunshot range. The Indians continued to play this taunting game all day, and that evening they set fire to the grass and attacked the rear guard. The green grass did not burn well, and when the infantry went into battle formation the Indians once again fell back. They stopped on a hilltop where they could observe the soldiers' camp.

By the next morning, September 1, 1858, more Indians were seen on the hill. Colonel Wright ordered the dragoons, a rifle battalion of two infantry companies, and one of the howitzer gun crews to drive them away. The first major action of the campaign was about to commence. A detachment of dragoons, one of the field pieces, and fifty-four infantrymen were left behind to protect and defend the camp. Captain J. A. Hardie, the field officer of the day, was responsible for the camp; Lieutenant Lyon was in charge of the infantrymen there.

It took only a single volley for the dragoons to drive the Indians from the hilltop, but they only fell back to the base of the hill and there they turned to fight. Topping the hill, the pursuing soldiers could see "a vast plain, in a beautiful and exciting panorama. At the foot of the hill was a lake, and just beyond, three others surrounded by rugged rocks. Between them, and stretching to the northwest, as far as the eye could reach, was level ground; in the distance, a dark range of pine-covered mountains. A more desirable battle-field could not have been selected." And battle was what the Indians intended. Kip said, "On the plain below us we saw the enemy. Every spot seemed alive with the wild warriors we had come so far to meet. They were in the pines on the edge of lakes, in the ravines and gullies, on the opposite hillsides, and swarming over the plain. They seemed to cover the country for some two miles." They shook their Hudson Bay Company muskets and their bows and arrows while they shouted defiance at the soldiers. Wright ordered his men forward.[8]

The howitzer spoke, and the line of soldiers moving down the hillside began firing as soon as they came within range—about six hundred yards—and fired steadily as they advanced. The Indians had not seen rifled muskets before this, and they could not stand in the face of such heavy and accurate fire. They broke and ran. This was the moment the dragoons had been awaiting. Kip said, "In an instant we heard the voice of Major [William N.] Grier ringing over the plain, as he shouted, 'Charge the rascals!' and on the dragoons went at headlong speed." In his report of the battle, Colonel Wright wrote of the dragoons' charge in the present tense: "At a signal, they mount, they rush with lightning speed through the intervals of skirmishers, and charge the Indians on the plains, overwhelm them entirely, kill many, defeat and disperse them all." The Indians were driven from the plain.[9]

The Indians who survived the saber charge were making for the woods where the dragoons could not maneuver. It was again time for the infantry to make its strength felt, and they pushed the Indians out. The hostiles stopped in the distance, still within eyesight, and the howitzer sent a few rounds in their direction and scattered them. After four hours of fighting, the Battle of Four Lakes was over. Colonel Wright ordered the Nez Perce scouts to follow the hostiles while the rest of the men returned to camp. Passing again over the field where they had fought, the men collected souvenirs and reflected on their good luck. Not a man had been wounded and only one horse. That night, the Nez Perce scouts returned to camp with some scalps and captured horses. They had a victory dance that lasted into the wee hours. Hylan B. Lyon had played no major role in the victory, but Captain Keyes of the 3rd Artillery knew the importance of protecting the supply train in such barren country, and he trusted Lyon to carry out the infantry's role in the assignment. If Lyon felt chagrined that he and the defenders of the train had not been challenged by the hostiles, he did not mention it in his late life memoir.

Wright's victory was due in large part in the improved weapons the troops carried. A reporter for the San Francisco *Herald* said that "Col. Wright's command is the first one armed with Sharpe's and Minie's guns." And a reporter for the Washington [DC] *Union* told readers, "The recent improvement in fire-arms (the rifling of the musket and the use of the elongated ball) enabled the troops to reach the enemy at ranges hitherto not effective." Captain Keyes developed the theme further in his official report: "During the last two months it has been my ceaseless endeavor, seconded by my officers, to impress upon the men, by instruction and precept, the conviction that, with our long range arms, we could kill Indians in a fair fight, and not be killed ourselves. Our lessons have been well learned. The men fired at the gallant red rascals as they would have fired at targets, and all the movements during the action were as orderly as on a field day." The officers, the men, and the civilian members of the press had all seen what the rifled musket and the minié ball could do in the hands of trained men. What they could not foresee was what this improved weaponry would mean in the next decade, when white men would be fighting one another.[10]

Wright and his men rested in camp until September 5. The weather had turned from hot and dry to cold and damp. Their route took them along "the margin of a lake for about three miles, and thence for two miles over broken country thinly scattered with pines." After about two hours on the trail, the men began to see groups of hostiles in the distance, keeping parallel to their right flank. They did not charge, and they did not leave, they simply rode alongside, their numbers steadily growing until there were an estimated five to seven hundred. When the men emerged from the woods onto a wide prairie, the Indians came out to the edge of the plain and set fire to the grass. Kip the diarist wrote, "Under cover of the smoke, they formed around us in one third of a circle, and poured in their fire upon us, apparently each one on his own account."[11]

Wright ordered the pack train to close up, and the train guard took position while four companies of the 3rd Artillery "deployed on the right and left." The fire was approaching dangerously close, threatening the men and the pack train. Wright gave the order to advance. "The men," said Kip," dashed through the flames, charged and drove the enemy before them." One of the howitzers began to fire as the foot soldiers charged. The Indians fell back and dashed "from cover to cover, from behind trees and rocks, and through the ravines and cañons, till the woods for more than four miles, which lately seemed perfectly alive with their yelling and shouting, were perfectly cleared." The Indians were forced into the open where the dragoons charged into them. The horse soldiers scattered the hostiles, yet they fought on. "Groups [of Indians] gathered, and the flying stragglers again waited in the woods which surrounded us on every side." The soldiers charged these pockets of resistance and gouged the hostiles out of their hiding places. Still, the Indians were not finished. Even as they fell back, they reformed into determined groups and the soldiers had to charge repeatedly into the face of heavy fire to drive them away. In their retreat, the Indians finally came to one of their own villages. They set it afire rather than have it fall into the hands of the whites.[12]

The fighting continued for seven hours, all the way to the Spokane River, a distance of fourteen miles. There the exhausted soldiers camped. They had suffered only one man wounded. Lieutenant Hylan B. Lyon had had his first real taste of being under enemy fire, yet he does not seem to have reveled in it. As an old man in Eddyville, looking back over a span of fifty years and speaking of himself in the third person, Lyon wrote very sparingly of the event, saying only that he "engaged in one battle with the Indians on Spokane plains." He added that he was "complimented . . . for gallantry." His immediate commander, Captain Erasmus D. Keyes (who was himself described by Colonel Wright as "persevering, energetic, and gallant . . . always in the right place at the right time") had observed Lyon's conduct during the battle and was the source of the compliment. Keyes mentioned Lyon, among others, as being "particularly distinguished," and Colonel Wright repeated the praise in his report.[13]

Across the Spokane River, a large party of Indians had collected, perhaps as many as five hundred of them. They were led by Gearry, "one of the head chiefs of the Spokan." Gearry spoke English, and he let Colonel Wright know that he wanted a parley. The colonel agreed to council with him. At the meeting, Gearry played the victim, a chief who was powerless to control the rash young warriors of his tribe. Wright told him, "I have met you in two battles;

you have been badly whipped; you have had several chiefs and many warriors killed or wounded; I have not lost a man or animal." He told Gearry, "I did not come into your country to ask you to make peace; I came here to fight. Now, when you are tired of war and ask for peace, I will tell you what you must do. You must come to me with your arms, with your women and children, and everything you have, and lay them at my feet. You must put your faith in me and trust to my mercy. If you do this, I shall then tell you the terms upon which I will give you peace. If you do not do this, war will be made on you this year and the next, and until your nations shall be exterminated." He told Gearry to tell the other Spokan chiefs to come in the next morning. Other warriors appeared, individually or in groups, through the rest of the day, and the colonel arrested two of them, a Spokan and a Palouse, and held them as hostages.[14]

A watchful night passed. Wright did not linger in camp to meet with the hostile chiefs but set out at sunrise and marched up the Spokane. After about ten miles, the Nez Perce scouts announced, once again, that there was a war party ahead. The supply train guards assumed their posts and the rest moved out. They discovered that the Indians the Nez Perce had seen were moving their pony herd, about nine hundred head. The Nez Perce attacked the enemy herders and routed them. The pony herd was captured. The soldiers camped again that night on the Spokane River. The scouts reported finding some cattle nearby and some lodges filled with grain. Two companies of artillery and one company of dragoons went forward with orders to burn the lodges and bring back the stock. They found that the cattle were so wild that they could not be herded. The soldiers had to be content with burning the lodges before returning to camp. That night, Wright executed one of his two hostages. The colonel had become convinced that the Palouse prisoner was guilty of killing whites before the present campaign began, and for that reason the man was sentenced to death. One suspects that Wright had another motivation in executing the hostage; he wanted to demonstrate to the Indians that he had the power of life or death over them and that it was impossible for them to prevent his arbitrary use of it. In any case, Wright ordered the prisoner hanged.

The condemned Palouse warrior may have been guilty of crimes against the whites, and perhaps the taking of his life was justified, but the next morning, when Colonel Wright ordered the destruction of the herd of captured horses, the young soldiers learned a different kind of lesson in the wanton destruction and waste of war. Wright later explained, "I found myself embarrassed with these 800 [sic] horses. I could not hazard the experiment of moving with such a number of animals (many of them very wild) along with my large train. Should a stampede take place, we might not only lose our captured animals, but many of our own. Under these circumstances, I determined to kill them all, save a few for service in the quartermaster's department and to replace broken-down animals. I deeply regretted killing these poor creatures, but a dire necessity drove me to it."[15]

One hundred thirty of the horses were selected for army use. The rest were put into a makeshift corral and two companies of soldiers were detailed to carry out the execution. They lassoed the horses and brought them out one by one to be shot; the colts were bashed over the head. The slaughter was so immense that they could not finish it in one day. That night, the brood mares whinnied for their colts, and their frantic, unanswered cries disturbed the soldiers and they could not sleep. And they knew that the job was not done. The killing continued the next morning. To speed up the butchery, the executioners poured volleys of rifle fire into the corral. Captain Erasmus D. Keyes, who had trained his soldiers so well in the use of their weapons, said, "It was a cruel sight to see so many noble beasts shot down. They were all sleek, glossy, and fat." Keyes said that, toward the end of the killing, the soldiers, bleary from lack of sleep and drunk on excess, "seemed to exult in their bloody task; and such is the ferocious character of men." The bones of those nearly one thousand horses could still be seen a decade later and, one must think, even longer in the memories of the men who had seen and heard the slaughter.[16]

That same day, September 10, a runner came from Father Joset at the Coeur d'Alene Mission. The hostiles were gathering there and were desirous of peace, he said. The column did not move until the next morning. Fifteen miles brought them to Coeur d'Alene Lake, where they camped. Continuing on September 12, they "struck into the mountains with a forest on either hand and a trail which admitted only the passage of a single man or animal at a time." Even so, the column made twelve miles before stopping. The men resumed their march on September 13, "through a dense forest with an impenetrable undergrowth of bushes on both sides, and an almost continuous obstruction from fallen trees." The men were strung out single file over six or eight miles, and a perfect time for ambush presented itself whenever they stalled, waiting for the pioneers to chop through the downed trees. Yet, the Indians did not attack. They were defeated in spirit as well as in body. The soldiers proceeded without harassment. The head of the column began reaching the mission later that day; it was hours before the rear guard caught up. The men camped about a quarter of a mile away, and the priests sent out to them a wagonload of fresh vegetables.[17]

Colonel Wright said, "For the last eighty miles our route has been marked by slaughter and devastation. Nine hundred horses and a large number of cattle have been killed or appropriated to our own use; many houses with large quantities of wheat and oats, also many caches of vegetables, and dried berries, have been destroyed. A blow has been struck which they will never forget." He admitted that the Indians had suffered a severe "chastisement," but he insisted that it was "well merited, and absolutely necessary to impress them with our power." Now, he was ready to capitalize on the desolation he had inflicted on the Indian confederacy; he was about to realize the object of his campaign and make lasting peace with the tribes.[18]

The treaty council with the Coeur d'Alenes convened on September 17, and Colonel Wright laid out the conditions for peace. The Indians must deliver up those who had been in the attack on Steptoe, and all property taken in the Steptoe fight must be turned over; the Indians must select a chief and four warriors with their families to return with the soldiers to Fort Walla Walla; henceforth, they must not harass whites passing through their country; and, the Indians must not allow hostiles from outside to operate in their country or find sanctuary there. He added that they must make peace with the Nez Perce, whose tribesmen had been his scouts. Wright said, "I promise you, that if you will comply with all my requirements, none of your people will be harmed, but I will withdraw from your country and you shall have peace forever."[19]

It was a harsh peace that Wright offered the defeated, though not so harsh as continuing a war that they knew they had lost, and they accepted. The colonel and his officers, including Lieutenant Lyon, and the chiefs all signed the treaty, and a pipe was passed around to sanctify the occasion. The Indians left, taking with them the Spokan captive who had been with the soldiers for several days. He said that he would try to persuade his people to accept the terms. Wright called for a council with the Spokans to be held on September 23.

During the afternoon, the Indians began returning plunder from the Steptoe fight, and the priests sent over to the soldiers' camp more garden truck as well as some butter and milk, which Lieutenant Kip said were "two luxuries which we have not seen for a long time."[20]

On September 18, the soldiers left the mission for their return trip to Walla Walla. As they traveled, the Coeur d'Alene hostages and their families, which Wright had insisted on as a condition for peace, came to join them, and on September 23, the second treaty council, this one with the Spokans, occurred. The Pend d'Oreilles and some other small tribes also attended. Wright promised them peace on the same terms as he had offered to the Coeur d'Alenes, and they accepted. Another instrument of peace was signed by all, and the Spokan chief who was the spokesman for the former hostiles said, "I am sorry for what has been done and glad of the opportunity now offered to make peace with our Great Father. We promise to obey and fulfill these terms in every point."[21]

Not every Indian leader was so obsequious. The most influential chief among the tribes was the Yakima Kamiakin. He did not attend the treaty council. He sent a message to Wright in which he said that of all the "fighting chiefs," he was the only one left alive. "I will not disgrace their memory by surrendering to a hated race. With my few remaining horses, I will take my family and journey to find a different people." Kamiakin would not submit to the whites and was not interested in whatever threats or promises his enemy might make in council. Some of his kinsmen felt differently, however. That evening his relative by marriage, Owhi, came in to Wright's camp. Like Kamiakin, Owhi had been an intractable enemy to the whites, and, along with his son Qualchan, was one of the principal war leaders since 1855. He had been driven south by Major Garnett, and now, hemmed in by his enemies on either side, he was ready to make peace.[22]

Wright treated Owhi sternly. After a round of sharp questions, he told the Indian that he was going to send a message to his son Qualchan warning that if he did not come in within four days (that is, before the soldiers crossed the Snake River), then Owhi would be hanged. Wright told Owhi that he, too, must send Qualchan a message. Then, he clapped Owhi in irons and ordered him to be taken away.

The next day, September 24, 1858, Qualchan came in. From the statements of various witnesses, his arrival was pure coincidence; he did not know that his father was a prisoner in the camp and expressed great surprise when he did learn it. Even late into his life, Hylan B. Lyon remembered what happened that day, and it became one of the most detailed vignettes in his autobiographical notes. Lyon said that Qualchan, "a chief that had been seen by so few Americans that he was regarded almost a myth," rode into camp "mounted on a fine Indian horse, with a double barreled shot gun in his hands, and a six shooter buckled to his waist, followed by a handsome half-breed woman also well mounted." The warrior rode up to Lyon and asked, "Where does your chief live?" Lyon pointed to Colonel Wright's tent and then walked over and called inside, "Here is an Indian that wants to see you." Qualchan, still on horseback, came forward and Colonel Wright stepped out. Lyon remembered that Wright conversed with Qualchan in "Chinook," and also sent an orderly to the officer of the guard with instructions "to send him a detachment of soldiers." When they appeared, Qualchan handed over his weapons. The woman sensed the danger before Qualchan did, and when he surrendered his guns, she quickly turned and "galloped out of camp." Simultaneously, Wright ordered the guards to seize Qualchan and hang him without delay. Now, too late, Qualchan understood what was happening. He threw himself on the ground and would not rise. Six soldiers bound his hands and feet and carried him over to a tree. Lyon said, "No more mournful sounds were ever uttered, than those made by Qualshem [sic], in begging for his life." He threatened his executioners with the vengeful anger of his warriors, and he promised them "a great deal of money

[and] a great many horses" if they spared his life. Qualchan's cries were so loud that they were heard by Owhi, who was confined nearby.[23]

The soldiers pulled him up, and Qualchan kicked out his life at the end of a rope. He was quickly buried, but a rumor spread through the camp that he had a large amount of money in his clothes, so the next day he was dug up. His clothes were rifled, but no money was found. The summary execution of Qualchan disgusted Lyon. He called it "the basest piece of treachery on the part of the commander of the expedition ever charged against an intelligent American." What Lyon had witnessed was undoubtedly a factor in his increasing determination to leave the army.[24]

Colonel Wright's bloody mood continued the next day when he hanged six more Indians, Palouses who had come into his camp. They were believed to have been in the Steptoe fight. The march south continued without further incident until September 30, when a large band of Palouse Indians came in. Wright met with them and said through his interpreter that they were "a set of rascals and deserve to be hung; that if I should hang them all, I should not do wrong." He then told them that he had concluded written treaties with the Coeur d'Alenes and Spokans, "but I will not make a written treaty with them, and if I catch one of them on the other side of Snake River, I will hang him." He warned them to stay out of the other tribes' country and promised that if they behaved well he would make a written treaty with them next spring. Then he repeated the thread-bare threat, "If they do not submit to these terms, I will make war on them, and if I come here again to war, I will hang them all, men, women, and children." To prove to them his willingness to resort to the rope, he demanded that some warriors who were accused of killing miners and stealing cattle be turned over to him, and when the accused criminals were produced, he hanged four of them on the spot. Finally, he demanded from the Palouse (as he had done from the other tribes) a chief and four warriors and their families to accompany him as hostages to Fort Walla Walla.[25]

The weather had turned cold and rainy again. Autumn had caught them, but the soldiers knew they were nearly home when they began crossing the Snake River on October 1, 1858. One final killing awaited them. Just after crossing the Snake, Owhi attempted to escape on horseback. His guard shot him and he fell wounded. Kip wrote, "A private in the dragoons reached the spot and gave Owhi the *coup de grace* by shooting him through the head. He died in about two hours."[26]

On October 2, Colonel Wright and the rest of the column followed the vanguard, who had preceded them across the Snake River, to Fort Taylor. Their reception there was warm. The officers were met with a feast of beef, prairie chicken, and vegetables, and champagne was served. "The men were supplied with the same good cheer," Captain Keyes said.[27]

Wright's men did not have long to rest at Fort Taylor. The day after their arrival, they were ordered to proceed to Fort Vancouver, and they moved in that direction. They paused at Fort Walla Walla, where the officers were honored with another feast and this time the Nez Perce scouts were included. While at Walla Walla, Wright treated with the Indians. He told the Walla Walla tribesmen that because they had been "exceedingly troublesome," it was "necessary to teach them a lesson." He commanded every man who had been in the Battles of Four Lakes and Spokane Plains to stand. Thirty-five did so. Wright selected four and hanged them. By this time, Lawrence Kip had lost count of just how many Indians Wright had hanged during the campaign. "I believe that sixteen of the Indians have been executed in this way," said the diarist.[28]

On October 18, the column reached Fort Vancouver. Wright had brought peace to the region, and although the many executions he had ordered "exposed him to some criticism," at least one scholar has said that he had carried out the campaign "with a skill that stamped him as one of the Army's ablest regimental commanders." One of the most celebrated results of the expedition was the killing of Qualchan. The manner of it had filled Lyon with revulsion, but the nation at large seemed to have no interest in the details of Qualchan's death; only that the renegade was dead. The Washington [DC] *Union* had carefully reported the campaign, and in its summary of Wright's expedition it said that Qualchan's death "will be hailed with satisfaction by this whole country."[29]

The Army was certainly satisfied with Colonel Wright. Lieutenant General Winfield Scott wrote in his General Orders that Colonel Wright is much to be commended for the "zeal, perseverance and gallantry he has exhibited" in a campaign that resulted in the "unqualified submission" of the hostile tribes. Scott also praised Brigadier General Newman S. Clarke, head of the Department of the Pacific, for the "sound judgment shown in planning and organizing the campaign (including Major Garnett's simultaneous expedition), as well as for his promptness and energy in gathering, from remote points in his extended command, the forces, supplies, etc., necessary for its successful prosecution." Knowing that victory over a well-matched opponent is the only victory worth claiming, Scott even complimented the Indians for being "brave, well-armed, [and] confident in themselves."[30]

Scott was only partially correct in his assessment of the Indians. Brave they were, but their arms were an obsolete mismatch to the soldier's rifled muskets. Scott was most mistaken in his assertion that the Indians were "confident in themselves." They felt encouraged by their initial victory over Steptoe, it is true, and they remained determined to the end—the blue-coated enemy had invaded their country; what could they do except resist? Yet, from the beginning, the Indians fought under the conviction that they were destined to lose. The same summer as their war, an ominous celestial event began, a phenomenon that white men called Donati's Comet. Night after night it appeared. Its pale light shined down on them as they planned their attacks and groomed their ponies and readied their weapons for fighting. It illuminated the night sky through the duration of the hostilities and continued to shine through the rest of the year. One night in September, while engaged in his series of debates with Stephen A. Douglas, Abraham Lincoln sat up late in Jonesboro, Illinois, just to see the comet. The whole country was mesmerized, none so much as the Indians who were fighting for their homeland in Washington Territory. To the Coeur d'Alene, the Yakima, the Palouse, the Walla Walla and other tribes, the comet was layered with supernatural significance, and it was perceived by them to bring a sad intelligence: their way of life was about to be swept away and they could not prevent it. From the first, they were fighting for a lost cause.

3

THE MULLAN ROAD

On October 24, 1858, Brigadier General William S. Harney arrived at Fort
Vancouver to relieve General Newman S. Clarke as commander of the Department of the Pacific. Lieutenant Hylan B. Lyon had become a seasoned
campaigner since he served under Harney in Florida, and he may have expected to serve closely with him for the remainder of his time in the army,
especially in the effort to bring the fugitive Kamiakin to bay. It was not to be.
Now that the Coeur d'Alene War had ended, the long-delayed road between
the Columbia River and the Missouri River was to be built. Lieutenant John
Mullen of the 2nd U.S. Artillery led the expedition, and Lieutenant Lyon's assignment was to join him as "Quartermaster Commissary and Ordnance Officer of the Escort," the escort being a detachment of the 3rd U.S. Artillery.[1]

Mullan was a Virginian and an 1852 graduate of West Point. He had
spent practically his entire career in the West as a topographical engineer
and a road builder, most notably with the government survey supervised by
Isaac Stevens in 1853–54. Many surveys were underway at the time, search-
ing for the most favorable route for a transcontinental railroad. The Stevens
Survey between Fort Benton and Eastern Oregon proved not to be the best
route for a railroad, but it did suggest both the necessity and the feasibility of
a military road between Fort Benton and Fort Walla Walla. In March 1858,
the War Department authorized construction of the road, and Lieutenant
Mullan was ordered to supervise the work. At the time of the Steptoe fight,
Mullan was already in the planning stages of the road. The outbreak of the
war prevented his start. He offered the services of himself and his command
to Colonel Wright's punitive expedition. The chance to fight Indians under
Wright was not the young officer's only reason for volunteering to join the
campaign. By accompanying Colonel Wright, he would be able to examine
the country his road would traverse and to make a preliminary start on the
construction. Wright assigned Mullan to command the Nez Perce scouts. He
was often far ahead of the main column. His duties included those of a chief

of engineers. He had to prepare the way for the soldiers coming along be-hind, and he became so adept at laying spans across the streams that Captain Erasmus D. Keyes dubbed him the "Duke of Bridgewater."[2]

At the conclusion of the Coeur d'Alene War, Mullan went to Washington, DC, to report to Congress what he had seen and to argue the need for a larger appropriation. He secured $100,000 and returned to the West in April 1859. He was back at Fort Walla Walla in June, and it was there that Lieutenant Lyon joined him. The Kentuckian had spent the winter of 1858–59 at Fort Vancouver.

Before the main party left on July 1, 1859, Lyon went ahead to Fort Taylor to deliver a wagon train of quartermaster and commissary stores and to guard another cargo of supplies that came up the Snake River to that point aboard a small paddle wheeler. On July 4, the main column caught up with Lyon. The next day, the united party pushed forward up the Palouse Valley. There were 230 men in the expedition, both soldiers and civilians. One hundred of them were men picked from the various companies of the 3rd Artillery. The New York *Herald* reported, "They are all a fine looking set of men, and seem *au fait* to withstand the trials and hardships which must attend Lieutenant Mullan's party in the mountains during the coming winter." In addition, there were beef cattle, more than fifty ox and mule teams, and horses on the expedition.[3]

On July 14, they bivouacked at Hangman Creek. It brought back somber memories to Lyon and to Mullan, who said of the Indians whom Wright had hanged, "Poor creatures! their doom, although in this instance [Qualchan] a just one, is nevertheless pitiable; had the white men been to them more just, fate had proved less hard."[4]

Beyond Hangman Creek, Mullan found land which afforded "induce-ments for small farms . . . with rich grazing, fine timber in abundance, and water in creeks and springs of the most delicious purity." Some miles be-yond, the crew met a band of the Coeur d'Alene Indians who not long before had been the masters of this fine land, and they still kept a protective eye over it. Mullan said that they were "anxious to learn our mission, our line of direction, and plied us with many questions as to our ultimate ends and objects." He felt that "discretion and prudence directed our course towards them should be both frank and honest." He observed the etiquette of such occasions by inviting the Indians to his camp, where they feasted and smoked, and he answered all their questions. He believed that they left satisfied, but that did not make him complacent. "They are wily fellows, and great caution is necessary in all intercourse with them," he said.[5]

So far, the work had been over country that was largely familiar and not too hard. Then they reached the edge of the escarpment overlooking the

St. Joseph's River, where they faced a rugged descent of seven hundred feet. Mullan called it "our first work of difficulty." They could find no natural route that would place them on the valley floor, so the men had to make one down to "the juncture of the St. Joseph's river with the outlet of the Poun Lake." They spent eight days here making a sixty-foot long bridge. They also moved up the valley to a place where a ferry boat could operate. Crews went into the woods to whipsaw the timber into lumber while others burned tar, and they built two flatboats. Each was forty-two feet long and twelve feet wide. The first was for the St. Joseph's River. It was assigned to the artillery escort and Lieutenant Lyon's supply train for their use in crossing the river. The crossing took three and one-half hours but was completed without incident. The second boat was for use on the Coeur d'Alene. It was poled upstream to the point selected while a crew graded, filled, and corduroyed the road over the divide between the St. Joseph's and the Coeur d'Alene. They completed their work on this section on August 5. Mullan's men continued to labor in the area until the 16th, when they reached the Coeur d'Alene Mission. It was a welcome sight, as it had been during Colonel Wright's campaign. The mission was in a place of great natural beauty, and Mullan admired the Jesuits' improvements, the church and the barns and the mill, and he noted with approval the hundreds of acres of grain and potatoes that the fathers and their Indian acolytes had cultivated. Yet, he anticipated that the placement of his road so close to the mission would be its doom. He wrote, "I fear that the location of our road, and the swarms of miners and emigrants that must pass here year after year, will so militate against the best interests of the mission that its present site will have to be changed or abandoned. This, for themselves and the Indians, is to be regretted, but I can only regard it as the inevitable result of opening and settling the country."[6]

It is unlikely that Mullan shared with the fathers his doubts for their survival when he arranged with them for Lieutenant Lyon to make the mission his wagon park, supply depot, and pasture. They waited there while the survey and construction crews forged ahead to find the way into the foothills. The reports they brought back were not encouraging. No matter which route was selected, the way was going to involve one hundred miles of dense timber, winding water courses, and poor grazing for the animals.

As they plunged forward, another difficulty proved to be the Indians. The New York *Daily Tribune* reported, "The Coeur d'Alene Indians have been acting in a hostile manner lately toward Lieut. Mullan's wagon-road party. . . . Mr. [Gustav] Sohon of that party found the Indians sullen, insolent, and manifestly unfriendly and dangerous." The reporter admitted that they had committed no openly hostile acts against Mullan or his men; rather, they had "refused to serve as guides, sell him horses, or hire as expressmen." The most overt act of the Indians' hostility took the form of a mild vandalism. Every day, the workers discovered that the Indians behind had ripped up the markers that were so carefully placed every mile. This and other unspecified depredations made a correspondent assert "considerable doubt exists among the officers of the party as to the ultimate success of this gigantic work."[7]

If Mullan was one of those doubtful officers, he never revealed it in either his report or his 1865 book about the expedition. He did confess his disappointment that his party was unable to reach the Bitterroot River. Winter caught them on the western slope. The falling snow soon reached a depth of eighteen inches, and Mullan decided to cross the divide into the valley of the St. Regis Borgia River. He believed the winter would be milder there. By the time they topped the crest and began the descent, the snow was four feet deep. Lyon and his men sledded their wagons down to the campsite. Mullan ordered the beef cattle to be slaughtered and ordered that the surviving draft animals be driven one hundred miles ahead to the best available grazing, the Bitterroot Valley. While the drovers made this difficult trek and tried, largely in vain, to keep the animals alive, those who remained in the St. Regis Borgia Valley began building log cabins. Mullan named the compound Cantonment Jordan. One of the buildings erected was an office, and Mullan set regular office hours from 10:00 AM to 3:00 PM, and a shorter shift in the evening from 6:00 PM to 9:00 PM. Here the officers worked on their field notes and maps. The enlisted men performed those duties that were "incident to camp life," such as gathering fuel, and, even though the threat of Indian attack was slight, guard duty was continued as a matter of discipline.[8]

Everyone at Cantonment Jordan suffered from the frigid temperatures. Lyon remembered that the mercury dropped to forty degrees below zero and remained there. Cases of frostbite were common, and one hunter who became lost for four days and nights would have lost his life to gangrene spreading from his frozen limbs had Dr. James A. Mullan not amputated both his legs.

One thing that took their minds off of their suffering was the delivery of the mail twice a month by men on snowshoes. The New York *Herald* reported, "An express will ply between Walla-Walla and the Bitterwood [*sic*] Valley during the winter—so our friends in the States can continue to write us, sending their letters via Fort Walla Walla." Of course, the soldiers not only received mail; they also had mail for the expressmen to carry out. It was by one of these mail carriers that Lyon sent an intimate letter to Laura O'Hara, who by now had become his fiancée. Their engagement had led to his tentative decision to leave the army. He told Laura that he had seen how officers of low rank and their wives lived. He knew that Laura would not like it, and he would not like to subject her to it. Lyon said that his desire was to return home and be a farmer. He weighed the advantages of asking for a leave of absence against simply resigning, but he worried that resigning from the road building expedition before the assignment was done would hurt his reputation and reflect poorly on his honor. Finally, he said that he would see it through to completion, at which time he could return to Fort Walla Walla, "and then I shall hasten home."[9]

Lyon mentioned in the letter that he was going forward to the Bitterroot Valley in a few days to buy beef cattle and some oxen to replace the many that had died. He was included in the small group that Mullan led to the Flathead Agency at Fort Owen. While Lyon made the rounds of the settlers in the Bitterroot region, Mullan met with the Indians and explained why he had come. He wrote in his report, "I told them that I needed one hundred and seventeen horses, with pack saddles, and from fifteen to twenty of their men to accompany Mr. Sohon across the mountains." The Flathead chiefs thought about it for a day and then agreed to help. Mullan cited their "nobleness of character" and said, "I never had a want but which, when made known to them, they supplied . . . they always treated myself and my parties with a frank generosity and a continuous friendship."[10]

The Flatheads were paid, and they set out with "Mr. Sohon." Gustav Sohon was a civilian translator and guide. He was a talented artist who could speak multiple native tongues, among them the Flathead language. The Flatheads and the Prussian made a successful late winter crossing of the Rockies, reached Fort Benton, and when they returned they brought eleven thousand rations for Mullan and his men.

From Fort Owen, Mullan also sent a courier south to Salt Lake City to requisition fifty mules from the army post there. Lyon took advantage of the situation to post another letter to Laura O'Hara. He complained to her that the settlers of the Bitterroot Valley had not been willing to sell many oxen or cattle at the prices he offered; they were "desirous of making a fortune off the Government through me." At the same time, he refused to give them more than what he considered a fair price for their livestock. It was a frustrating predicament.[11]

On a more personal note, Lyon said to Miss O'Hara, "I hope more hopefully now than ever to be able to get home next fall." He believed the expedition would get to Fort Benton in late September, too late for him to return to Fort Walla Walla, so he would travel down the Missouri River, obtain a winter-long leave of absence when he arrived at Fort Leavenworth, and be home no later than mid-December. The time was soon coming when choices would have to be made. He reminded her that his ambition was to be a farmer but said that he would stay in the army if her decision was to "condemn" him to that "drudgery." To help ease his homesickness, he asked her to have either an ambrotype or a daguerreotype made and to send it to him. "Please have it taken in your everyday appearance, for it was at home that I ever admired you most," he said.[12]

From Fort Owen, Mullan and Lyon made a trip to the Pend d'Oreille Mission. Some of the men back at Cantonment Jordan were showing the symptoms of scurvy, and it was necessary to supplement their diet of beef with fresh vegetables. Mullan hoped the Pend d'Oreilles would have some produce to share. He and Lyon anticipated a hard trip, and they carried forage for their horses with them. They were pleasantly surprised to find that the country was open and that there was adequate grazing for the animals at each night's camp.

One wonders if the two Southerners, resting at night around the campfire, discussed the news from back East, especially the growing tensions between the North and the South. Letters were reaching Cantonment Jordan. There was going to be a presidential election later that year, and they must have known that in Lyon's own state in 1859 there had been a bitter gubernatorial election that split Kentuckians over the question of the process by which slavery should be allowed to expand into the Western territories. The Democrat, Beriah Magoffin, believed that territorial slaveholders should look to the Federal courts to protect their slave property. The opposition candidate, Joshua F. Bell, believed in a policy of affirmative Congressional intervention wherever Free Soilers contested the legality of slave property. (The opposition party had no official name; it was stitched together from the remnants of the Whig and Know-Nothing parties and was known simply as the opposition.) The name calling and finger pointing began early in the campaign. The opposition party branded the Democrats as secessionists and as the party of extravagance. The Democrats called the opposition abolitionists. Neither description was quite accurate, but accuracy was less important than finding a calumny that would stick to the other candidate. Magoffin and Bell debated in small towns across the state, including in Lyon's hometown of Eddyville. On election day, the Democrat Magoffin defeated his opponent by a margin of nine thousand votes. What did the Kentucky election mean for the fate of the nation? What did it mean for the future of the West? Mullan and Lyon were professional soldiers, graduates of the U.S. Military Academy; what did the deepening divide over slavery mean for them, personally, and for their comrades? These questions must have weighed on their minds as they rode toward the Pend d'Oreille Mission.

In his next letter home, Lyon told Laura that the Jesuits and the Indians treated them well. He considered the Flatheads and the Pend d'Oreilles to be the most intelligent, generous, and comely Indians he had known. He felt kindly toward them and hoped that they would be able to keep their reservation in the beautiful Bitterroot Valley. There was, however, a hint of the era's nativist anti-Catholic prejudice shown in his attitude toward the Jesuits at the mission. Mullan told them for a joke that Lyon believed in the doctrine of predestination. Lyon went along with it, and he said, "it amused me to see the fathers' attempts to point out the errors of my supposed belief. . . . I combatted their arguments, if not in words at least in my own mind, and am now as good a protestant as I have ever been."[13]

In the same letter, Lyon spoke once again of his engagement to Miss O'Hara. They had not yet announced to her parents their plan to wed, and Lyon said that he was going to wait until he got home to ask them for their consent to the marriage. They had been kind to him in the past, and he believed that they would not refuse him, and "if there should be any objection I can better answer them in person than by letter."[14]

He had learned, he told her, that he would not be included in the party that descended the Missouri from Fort Benton in the late summer or fall. He would have to return to Fort Walla Walla. The mid-December reunion in Eddyville that he longed for was not going to be possible. He now thought that he could be home by New Year's Day, 1861. When he came, he would try to bring his new dog, which he called "the ugliest, most ill-shapen dog I have ever seen, but a very intelligent one." If the ugly, intelligent dog had a name, Lyon did not reveal it in his letter.[15]

Mullan and Lyon were back at Cantonment Jordan by the end of the first week in April. The vegetables they brought, when consumed with a draught of vinegar, soon cured the scurvy-stricken men. They needed to be healthy, for the spring campaign began with an assault on Big Mountain, a "severe piece of work." Getting beyond Big Mountain would require a side hill cut six miles long. Mullan said, "My camps were formed at its west base, where a small creek and an abundance of timber afforded all the conveniences required. In order to obtain the practicable elevation, on account of the abrupt, rocky face of the spur, I carried the line up a ravine until, gaining 1,000 feet, I wound around mountain sides, making the re-entering angles by gentle curves, until the entire six miles was completed." It took 150 men six weeks to build the road around and over Big Mountain, and the work was not without accident. "Being rocky in most places," Mullan said, "we were compelled to blast, when, by a premature explosion, one of our men, Sheridan, lost one of his eyes, and another, Robert P. Booth, was severely stunned." However, after a month and a half the rugged mountain spur was crossed, and "all further difficulties as to location ceased."[16]

Sixty more miles brought the expedition to Hell's Gate. They made some small side-cuts and built a 150-foot long bridge, but the stretch was one of open timber and road building was much quicker work here. Between Hell's Gate and Mullan Pass, Lieutenant Mullan came to a winding creek that he called "Lyon's Creek" in honor of his quartermaster. They crossed the final range of the Rockies at Mullan Pass and emerged onto the "Missouri slopes," a region they saw at once was warmer, more rolling than steep, and less tim-bered. Mullan said, "Only light work was needed in this last section." Some days they made nineteen miles, and on July 28 they reached the Sun River. Mullan said, "At this point our proper work ceased, for the remaining dis-tance of fifty-five miles was over an easy and almost level prairie road, with no running streams." Leaving Sun River, Mullan divided his party into four groups and sent each one by a different route to Fort Benton. In this way, he could determine the best approach to the fort. None seems to have been mea-surably superior to the others; each of the four groups came into Fort Benton by August 1, and the Mullan Road was done. In slightly over a year's time, Mullan's crew had built 624 miles of graded road over some of the most chal-lenging terrain in America. It required 120 miles of "difficult timber-cutting" and thirty miles of "excavation." It was twenty to twenty-five feet wide, and it made a wagon trip from Fort Benton to Fort Walla Walla possible in only forty-seven days. A pack train could complete the journey in thirty-five days. It was a monumental accomplishment, and the men had earned a good rest.[17]

Mullan gave them only until August 5. On that day he released from further Western service those men who were going down the Missouri to St. Louis. Lyon was not among them. One can imagine how homesick he was, watch-ing them leave for the East where he longed to be, but he did not have time to brood. Six companies of the 1st U.S. Dragoons under Major George A. H. Blake had been at Fort Benton since July 3, waiting on Mullan to arrive before they began their march to Fort Walla Walla. They had come up the river aboard the *Chippewa* and the *Key West No. 2*, the first steamboats to reach Fort Benton. Now Mullan had come and the dragoons' journey was about to continue. They saw to their equipment and the condition of the horses, and the same day that the Mackinac boats shoved off down the Missouri, they took their place in the rear of Mullan's westbound column. Lyon, one of Mullan's most reliable officers, fixed his mind on his responsibilities and put thoughts of Kentucky out of his mind as the Rockies, once more, loomed ahead.

Mullan planned to move quickly and to make improvements and repairs to the winter-battered road as he went. Major Blake was given all of the wag-ons and Mullan and his reduced command traveled using only pack animals, until they reached Hell's Gate, where they had cached a few wagons in July. They recovered these and pushed on. No one had driven himself harder over the past year than Lieutenant Mullan, and it caught up with him in the Bitter-root Mountains. He said in his report that his health "seriously failed me, and I had to intrust the general work to Lieutenant Lyon and Mr. W. W. Johnson . . . On reaching the Coeur d'Alene Mission I divided my party into two por-tions, one under Lieutenant Lyon, to proceed towards Walla Walla."[18]

They made good time and arrived on October 4, almost a week earlier than they had expected. At Fort Walla Walla, Major Blake's command was divided, with some remaining there, some going on to Fort Colville, and the rest to Fort Dalles and Fort Vancouver. Mullan said, "Thus ended this military experiment via the upper Missouri and Columbia rivers; and the success that attended it, the good effects that it induced, the economy resulting, and the eulogistic manner in which every officer of the command referred to the trip all constitute a sufficient commentary upon its feasibility for future movements towards the north Pacific."[19]

While Mullan turned to the task of shaping his field notes into a finished report, Lieutenant Hylan B. Lyon obtained his leave of absence and prepared for his triumphal return to Kentucky and his pending marriage to Laura O'Hara.

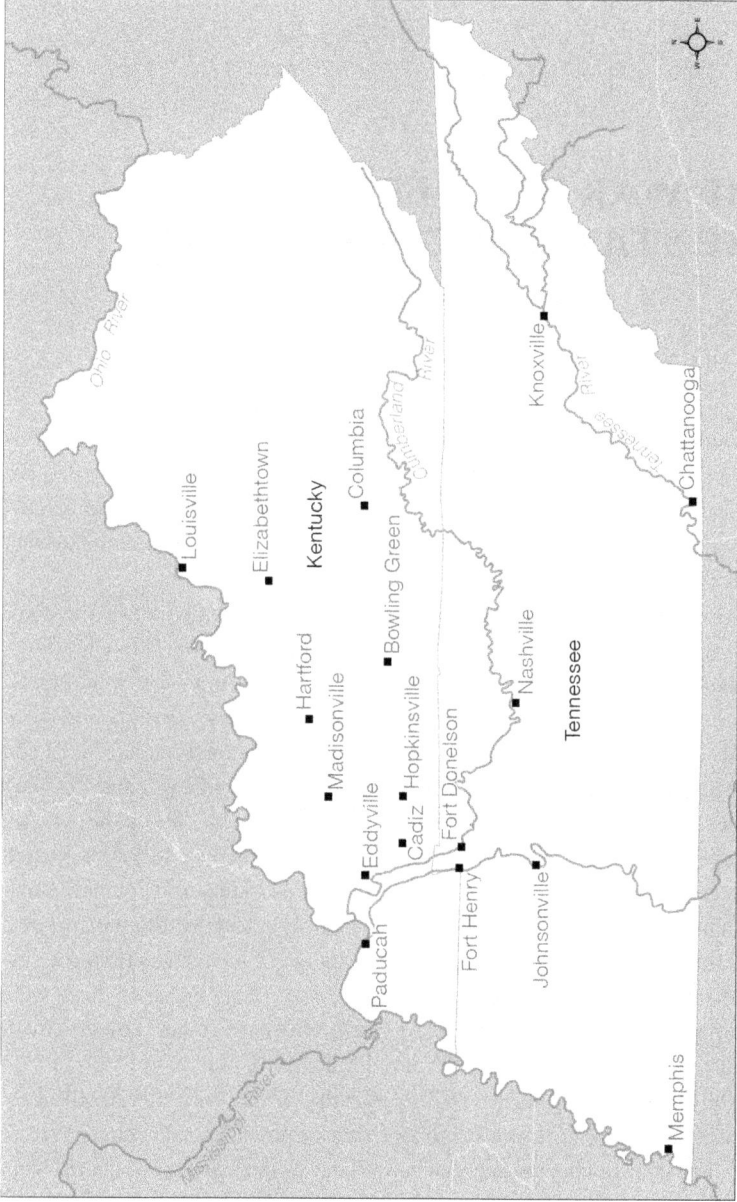

Lyon's Civil War: The Upper South. Map by Sasha Jovanovic.

4

THE WAR BETWEEN
THE STATES BEGINS

Lieutenant Hylan B. Lyon returned to a Kentucky in turmoil. The gubernatorial election was scarcely over before the 1860 presidential campaign began, and once again the slavery issue dominated. By the time Lyon arrived
in Eddyville, the nation had chosen as the new president the candidate that
Kentucky had almost universally rejected, Abraham Lincoln.

In 1860, slaves made up nearly one-fifth of the population of the commonwealth. The institution was not deep in Kentucky—there were few large
slaveholders such as one found in Alabama or Mississippi—but it was widespread, with many families owning a handful of house servants and farm
hands. The Lyons were among these. The 1860 Slave Schedule for Lyon
County, part of the Federal Census, shows that Hylan B. Lyon and his older
brother Matthew M. Lyon each owned ten slaves. This was above the average.
The statistical charts compiled by Kenneth H. Williams and James Russell
Harris reveal that there were 1094 slaves in Lyon County and 178 slave owners, making an average of 6.1 slaves per owner. Incidentally, the statistics also
show that Lyon County had a higher percentage of free blacks than the surrounding counties of Livingston, Caldwell, and Trigg. Some of them were
undoubtedly descendants of the many blacks who gained their freedom in an
earlier time by the personal efforts of old Matthew Lyon.

The slave owners believed in the necessity of the institution in the East
and would not support any candidate that opposed its expansion into the
West. There were four presidential candidates in 1860, and two of them were
Kentucky born. The Republican Abraham Lincoln was born near Hodgenville and the Southern Democrat John C. Breckinridge was from Lexington.
Stephen A. Douglas, the Northern Democrat, was a Vermont native who had
built his political life in Illinois, and the Constitutional Unionist, John Bell,
was from Tennessee.

In the presidential election, Lyon County favored Breckinridge above the other candidates, giving him 431 votes, a solid advantage over Bell, who finished in second place with 304 votes. Douglas won eleven votes and Abraham Lincoln received none. The statewide tally revealed a slightly different order of finish. Kentucky turned her back on both of her native sons and went instead for Bell, whose philosophy was simplicity itself: the preservation of the Union. That idea appealed to the majority of Kentuckians, who feared that their state would become the battleground between North and South if the Union broke apart. Bell beat the second-place finisher, Breckinridge, by nearly thirteen thousand votes. Douglas finished third, and, once again, Lincoln came in last. However, Lincoln won a plurality of the national vote and became the sixteenth president-elect. Even though Kentucky had rejected him, calm minds in the state realized that Lincoln's election did not mean that all was lost for the conservatives. Certainly not. There were constitutional remedies to Republican excess, as most Kentuckians who followed politics realized. Historian Lowell H. Harrison explains their thinking when he says, "The Republicans would not control either Congress or the courts, and impeachment could be employed if Lincoln exceeded his lawful powers."[1]

The state's secessionist minority rejected this wait-and-see attitude. Kentucky's fire-eaters looked with hope upon the actions of South Carolina and other states of the Deep South which began to secede the month after the election. They believed that when the secession movement reached the upper South, Kentucky would take her place among her sister Southern states. Alabama and Mississippi each sent emissaries to confer with Governor Magoffin and push Kentucky toward the decision to secede. Stephen F. Hale of Alabama and Winfield S. Featherston of Mississippi both met with Magoffin to urge him to convene a convention that would vote for Kentucky to leave the Union. Kentucky's fighting men, along with her farm and mineral resources, would be of immeasurable value to the Confederacy, but even more important was her geographical location. With the secession of Kentucky, the new Southern nation would gain an easily defended northern boundary, the Ohio River. Governor Magoffin refused the overtures of Hale and Featherston. He was an advocate of slavery and believed in its expansion, and as he told the Alabamian, he acknowledged the "intolerable wrongs and menacing dangers" the South faced. He said that Kentucky, too, realized "the importance of arresting the insane crusade so long waged against our institutions," and he asserted that Kentucky would "never submit to wrong and dishonor." Even so, he said, Kentucky would "leave no effort untried to preserve the Union." Governor Magoffin believed that a compromise might still be reached before Kentucky found it necessary to resort to secession. He believed that a regional conference of the states of the upper South might stand as a bloc against

Lincoln, force concessions from the administration, and in that way satisfy the more intransigent voices in Dixie. In addition, Senator John J. Crittenden had introduced a compromise plan that echoed the spirit of Henry Clay and might well save the Union.[2]

The border state conference did not occur, and the Crittenden Compromise stalled in the Senate. On December 27, 1860, Governor Magoffin called the legislature into special session. The time had come to decide the question of disunion, and he requested that the legislature issue a call for a convention to consider secession. The legislature would not agree to his request to assemble a convention and adjourned on February 11, 1861. It reconvened in early April. A week later, Fort Sumter was fired upon, and President Lincoln called for 75,000 volunteers to put down the rebellion.

This was the moment that Hylan B. Lyon decided on his course of action. He was a slave owner and came from a family of slave owners. His U.S. Congressional district, the First, was the most conservative and Southern-leaning of any in the state, and all spring he had heard the tense knots of men who gathered in the Union House Tavern in Eddyville and in the Lyon family's store and mill discussing secession and the dismaying reluctance of the Frankfort government to join her fortunes with the South. As an officer in the U.S. Army, Lieutenant Lyon would have been pressed hard to give his opinion on the situation. He had received a promotion to 1st lieutenant (back-dated to September 27, 1860), while on leave in Eddyville, but his sympathies were with those who were leaving the U.S. Army to offer their services to the Confederacy. He was caught between the proverbial two fires. He hesitated until Fort Sumter was fired upon and Lincoln called for volunteers, an act he and others considered an act of undisguised aggression and a challenge to Southern liberties. Lyon remembered in his autobiographical sketch (and still speaking of himself in the third person), "As he was a secessionist, and in sympathy with the south, he resigned his commission in the United States Army, and aided in organizing a company of infantry for the Confederate Army." The resignation was dated April 30, 1861. As Lyon and his company prepared to march away to the Confederate gathering place, Camp Boone, Tennessee, he must have reflected on the cruel fate that had shattered his life and plans for the future. Gone were his career and the unified country he had served as an officer since 1856, gone was his hope to settle into the tranquil life of a Kentucky farmer, gone was his chance enjoy those priceless and irreplaceable days of early married life with his new wife Laura O'Hara Lyon. They had married on February 12, 1861, in Jefferson County and had only just begun to get acquainted as man and wife before war called the groom away. Furthermore, within four months of their marriage Laura Lyon became pregnant with their first child. He would have to follow the progress of her pregnancy from afar, and it was more than likely that her time would come while he was away on some remote battlefield or distant camp. Hylan B. Lyon's decision to become a soldier of the Confederacy was already a costly one.[3]

Without a doubt, the Kentuckians who were gathering in Tennessee felt encouraged that Governor Magoffin had refused to honor Lincoln's call for volunteers. But, Kentucky "also refused to join the second wave of secession" that swept the upper South and brought the Confederacy to her southern border. On May 16, 1861, the Kentucky House of Representatives voted by a two-to-one margin to maintain a state of armed neutrality. The state senate followed suit, and Magoffin declared on May 20 that Kentucky would take no side in the conflict. Lowell H. Harrison says, "A bewildered observer from abroad might well have concluded that the United States had become three countries: the Union, the Confederacy, and Kentucky." The issue began to become clearer in the special congressional elections of June 20, 1861, when Kentucky voters in nine of the state's ten districts elected Unionists to represent them. The people of the commonwealth had decided: Kentucky would remain loyal to the Union. The one district that stood contrary to the prevailing mood was the 1st, which included Eddyville and Lyon County. Voters in the 1st District elected an ardent secessionist, Henry C. Burnett, to the House of Representatives.[4]

Captain Hylan B. Lyon and his company of Confederates felt right at home at Camp Boone. Exiled Kentuckians had made the camp and named it after their frontier hero. Hundreds of Kentuckians had already gathered there, and more volunteers were coming in daily. Moreover, the camp was commanded by yet another Kentuckian, Colonel William Temple Withers, who held the temporary rank of brigadier general. In a few weeks, when regiments began to form, Lyon's company would be joined to the 3rd Kentucky Infantry, Colonel Lloyd Tilghman of Paducah, commanding. Tilghman, a Marylander by birth, was an 1836 graduate of West Point who resigned from the army shortly after receiving his commission in order to pursue a career as a railroad construction engineer. He was living in Paducah when the war began. Tilghman offered his services to the Confederacy and went across the state line to Camp Boone when Kentucky refused to secede.

A writer calling himself "Kentucky Button" wrote a letter to the Louisville *Courier* (later reprinted in the Memphis *Daily Appeal*) in which he described conditions in the early days of Camp Boone. The letter was dated July 11, 1861, and it said, "Although it is but eight days since the camp was formed, there are already nearly fifteen hundred of us here, all Kentuckians, with daily accessions, in squads of thirty to one hundred and fifty. . . . We are near the State line, about ten miles north of Clarksville, in a magnificent piece of oak woods about a thousand acres. The 'boys' are all in fine health and spirits—with great abundance of good wholesome fare."[5]

"Kentucky Button" continued, "The various companies drill night and morning, each eager to excel in the manual of arms. We hope soon to hear that we are ready for service, and when once pitted against the Republican dogs 'to make them feel southern steel and smell southern powder.'"[6]

There was adequate space to drill at Camp Boone, there was abundant good water and plenty of fuel from the surrounding woods, but there was a shortage of everything the natural world did not provide. William C. Davis writes, "Supply was the most immediate and long-continuing problem, despite the constant smuggling of clothing and equipment across the line from friends in Kentucky. . . . Clothing and food presented less of a problem than medical supplies, but the Kentuckians brought good doctors with them." The surgeon of Tilghman's 3rd Kentucky was Dr. John L. Vertrees of Glasgow. Dr. Vertrees and all the other regimental surgeons soon had as much work as they could handle, for in August, only a month after Camp Boone was begun, measles broke out. Twenty-nine cases of the highly contagious disease were documented in the first week of the epidemic alone.[7]

The citizens of Clarksville soon became aware of the sickness at Camp Boone, and they responded to the call of T. D. Wardlaw, who asked in a letter to the Clarksville *Chronicle* that the ladies of the town send out to Camp Boone "anything they may prepare for the sick." Wardlaw pointed out that it fell to patriotic Southerners to supply the soldiers' medical needs, and he recommended that they contribute: "Tapioca, Arrow Root, well made Crackers, Wine, Soaps and Lint for wounds."[8]

The angels of Clarksville heeded Wardlaw's call for contributions with energy and imagination. In only a few days they organized a concert of vocal and instrumental music for the benefit of the sick at Camp Boone. Performed on August 20, the concert was intended to procure for the infirm "such articles of diet as will aid their convalescence, and which cannot be had in camp." Such civic generosity helped the surgeons provide the best treatment possible in a field hospital, and the measles epidemic was brought under control.[9]

One thing the people of Clarksville and Montgomery County could not supply in the necessary numbers was weapons. The men of the 3rd Kentucky Infantry were armed with flintlocks and smooth bore Belgian muskets. Most of the other arriving men were similarly armed, but late model, military grade weapons were needed for these volunteers and for the hundreds who continued to pour into camp. To Lyon, who had seen the effectiveness of modern small arms in the Coeur d'Alene War, the lack of quality weapons at Camp Boone must have been alarming. Certainly, it was to General Withers, and to him it presented an additional problem. General Withers wrote to Confederate Secretary of War L. P. Walker on July 12, 1861, "Our movements have thoroughly aroused a military spirit in Kentucky. Numerous applications made daily to receive companies composed of best in the State. Shall I receive and have them mustered in? If so, to what extent? I have received, under your instructions, twenty companies, and the other companies are clamorous to be received."[10]

Secretary of War Walker replied that, while he was willing to accept the Kentucky companies, the Confederacy could not arm them. The men continued to arrive in groups large and small. On July 25, General Withers again wrote Walker. He said that "fifty companies from Kentucky have applied to be received into the service of the Confederate States, and at least 10,000 can be enlisted in forty to sixty days." Tennessee Governor Isham Harris urged Secretary Walker to find some way to supply the Kentuckians at Camp Boone with weapons. On August 16, he wrote, "If you can arm the brigade at Camp Boone, under General Withers, I can take care of Middle Tennessee."[11]

The Confederate government was scrambling to make up the deficit in weaponry, and on September 14, 1861, General Albert Sidney Johnston, commander of CSA Department No. 2, was able to report, "There are three regiments of Kentucky infantry and one company of artillery mustered into the Confederate service at Camp Boone. It is expected that their armaments will be completed in a few days. A brigadier-general is needed, and I suggest the appointment of General Buckner of Kentucky."[12]

As Johnston predicted, the arms shortage was solved over time. And, as Johnston recommended, Simon Bolivar Buckner was made a brigadier general and relieved General Withers as commander of the troops at Camp Boone. Buckner was from Hart County, Kentucky. He was a West Point graduate and a veteran of the Mexican War. During the secession crisis in Kentucky, he had been in command of the State Guard. The State Guards' leanings were southern. Buckner insisted that "some of the ablest officers of the Guard are the strongest Union men." Nevertheless, the Unionists on the State Military Board became alarmed enough to order the guardsmen to turn in their arms, and Buckner resigned. He watched through the summer and into the fall to see how events would progress in Kentucky. From a Southerner's point of view, they did not progress in the right direction. The special state legislative election in August 1861, put the Unionists in firm control of the General Assembly. Still, Buckner did not choose sides. The legislature was in session when, on September 3, 1861, the Confederates responded to what they considered an immediate threat from the North by seizing the little town of Hickman, Kentucky. Brigadier General Gideon Pillow, acting under orders from his superior, Major General Leonidas Polk, had violated Kentucky neutrality. The next day, he moved into Columbus. Two days after

Simon Bolivar Buckner, c. 1861.
Library of Congress.

that, on September 6, Brigadier General U. S. Grant led an occupying force across the Ohio River from Illinois and seized Paducah. A week later, on September 11, the General Assembly passed a joint resolution instructing Governor Magoffin to order the Confederate troops to leave Kentucky; not the Federals, just the Confederates, and that was what finally moved Simon Bolivar Buckner to declare for the South. He traveled to Nashville, received his commission, assumed command of the Camp Boone troops, and immediately began planning the advance that would return these exiled volunteers to Kentucky. General Johnston wanted it and General Buckner would carry it out.[13]

On September 16, 1861, while still in Nashville, Buckner ordered that preparations be made for the move north. Camp Boone was on the Memphis Branch of the Louisville & Nashville Railroad, so he anticipated a quick and easy invasion. He wired Colonel Lloyd Tilghman, now commanding the Kentucky brigade, "Sir: You will make the following dispositions for the movement directed by General Johnston. You will replace the telegraph operator at the State line and guard the present operator securely during the day. You will have a small force so disposed as to prevent the escape of the evening train from Louisville. The transportation train will be at Camp Boone, under your orders at 4 PM; you will be in readiness with your command at the

State line by the time of the Louisville train. . . . The troops will be provided with two days' provisions in haversacks and a week's supply in addition." The soldiers at Camp Boone were about to see if their constant drilling had been sufficient.[14]

For one unit, the drilling was almost certainly not sufficient. Captain Lyon had been detached from the infantry to help organize an artillery battery. The work was unusual to the volunteers, far more technical than marching with a musket across the shoulder, and the men had not had their field pieces long enough to become expert in their use before the order came to advance. In his memoir, Lyon said that he equipped the battery. He may have meant that he supplied the men with uniforms and with small items such as pistols and short artillery swords that he bought with funds from his own bank account. He did not provide the cannon. William C. Davis says in *The Orphan Brigade*, "The Confederate Government furnished them with their compliment of field pieces," and an article in the July 1915 issue of *Confederate Veteran* adds more information about the origin of the guns. It said, "For the movement on Bowling Green the company was supplied with the six bronze guns taken from Paducah south and turned over to General [Leonidas] Polk in West Tennessee. The guns having belonged to Kentucky, it was said, were made from Mexican gun metal composing the cannon captured by Kentuckians during the war between that country and the United States."[15]

On the morning of September 18, 1861, five thousand men from Camp Boone moved north toward Bowling Green in two hundred captured L&N RR boxcars pulled by ten captured L&N locomotives. They began arriving in mid-morning. Lyon's artillery did not move at the same time, as is shown by the order Buckner sent Lyon after he had established his new headquarters in Kentucky. It said simply, "Come with your battery to Bowling Green." Lyon's Battery proceeded as ordered. It was formally organized at Bowling Green on September 20, 1861, as the 1st Kentucky Battery, although it continued to be popularly known as Lyon's Battery for as long as he was in command.[16]

The morning the Confederates began arriving at Bowling Green, a young diarist named Josie Underwood was watching from her family home, Mount Air, outside of town. She wrote, "It has come! The Philistines are upon us! Kentucky's neutrality is over!" She could hear the shouting from the L&N depot. Mr. Warner Underwood got his spyglass and trained it on the commotion in time to see the American flag coming down and "a new and strange one run up the pole. . . . Too well we knew what that meant. The Rebels had taken possession of the town." Josie continued, "When I saw that Flag with drooping folds coming slowly down and that other run up quickly to flaunt gaily in its place—I verily believe girl as I am had I been in that crowd I would have shot the man who pulled that Old Flag down."[17]

The very day of their invasion, the Confederates began to spread out to the farms and fields beyond Bowling Green. The following day, September 19, they came to Mount Air and found Mr. Underwood's one-hundred-acre clover pasture to be perfect for drilling. Josie saw General Buckner there. She wrote, "General Buckner, on a beautiful white horse, looks particularly fine, as he is a handsome man and rides superbly, but I can't forget how he has betrayed Kentucky's trust, turning all the State Guard under him over to the Confederacy." Miss Underwood's indignation was just beginning. On September 29, a brigade of Missouri infantry came to the Underwood plantation and made its bivouac there. They stripped Mount Air of its resources, everything from fence rails to milk from the cows in the barn. One morning they came into the kitchen and stole the family's breakfast, and they were rude to the family and the house servants. When a Mississippi unit came to join the Missourians, the damage to the plantation grounds was nearly total. The soldiers chopped down the Underwood's trees and tore down slave quarters to build the field works that they mockingly called "Fort Underwood." The Underwood family was not alone in its distress. Citizens all through the region were suffering the same kinds of losses as Buckner sent detachments out to defend the approaches to the city. They went north up the L&N as far as Lebanon Junction, only a few miles south of Louisville, burning the railroad bridges to prevent a Federal advance, and they occupied small towns all along the line.[18]

Lyon's inclination was toward the artillery. That's where his training was, and he would have been satisfied to remain in command of his battery, had his talents not been needed elsewhere. During the Bowling Green occupation, he was promoted to the rank of lieutenant colonel and transferred to be the second in command of the 8th Kentucky Infantry. Captain Robert Cobb now commanded Lyon's Battery, and it was under the name Cobb's Battery that the artillery unit trained by Lyon won a legendary name in the South.

The 8th Kentucky Infantry had been recruited primarily in Christian County and was formally organized at the fairgrounds outside of Hopkinsville. Its colonel was Henry C. Burnett, the firebrand U.S. Representative from Kentucky's First Congressional District. Burnett had recruited the regiment, but he was not with it much. In November of 1861, in defiance of the Unionist state legislature, the pro-Southern men of Kentucky convened a sovereignty convention behind Confederate lines in Russellville. As one of the leading lights of the secession movement in the Bluegrass State, Burnett attended, and he was elected to be president of the convention. Between November 18 and 20, representatives from sixty-eight of Kentucky's counties passed an ordinance of secession and formed a provisional Confederate government. They named Bowling Green as Kentucky's Confederate capital. George W. Johnson was chosen as Kentucky's Confederate governor, and Henry C. Burnett and two others were chosen as commissioners to travel to Richmond, Virginia, and negotiate Kentucky's recognition as a Confederate state. Provisional Kentucky was subsequently admitted into the Confederacy, and Henry C. Burnett and William E. Simms were elected (by a special canvass of the soldiers in the field) to be Kentucky's senators. The 8th Kentucky Infantry had lost its founding colonel. Lieutenant Colonel Hylan B. Lyon took command of the regiment.

For Buckner's men, the winter of 1861–62 was a time of protecting what they had taken in the autumn. Patrols roamed the banks of the Barren and Green Rivers. Demolition crews destroyed the bridges and locks that would admit a Federal advance, and there were excursions in the direction of Hopkinsville. Here and there, fighting erupted. On December 17, Federal infantry and Confederate cavalry under Colonel B. F. Terry clashed at Rowlett's Station near Munfordville. The Rebels were pushed back, and Terry was killed. A week later, December 28, at Sacramento, Colonel Nathan Bedford Forrest met the Yankees and defeated them, the first victory of his storied career. Such clashes did happen, but they were out of the ordinary. For most of the men in gray, it was a winter of waiting and watching and foraging liberally on the local farmers and country store keepers, who were given a receipt that could be redeemed in Bowling Green for Confederate scrip, which was worthless.

Lyon and the 8th Kentucky Infantry did their share of patrolling, but this way of making war was not enough to keep Lyon's mind from thoughts of home. He wrote his "dear wife" on December 22, from Bowling Green and said, "My yearning to be with you is often so great that I am tempted to abandon the cause in which I have enlisted." Still, though he was personally discouraged, he was confident of the Confederate position. Two weeks later he wrote Mrs. Lyon, "We feel confident we can resist any attack the Federal troops may dare to make," and he said that if the Southerners could get some reinforcements, they might even "feel emboldened to advance." A leave of absence in the second week in January gave Lyon a chance to visit with his wife. The homecoming was by necessity brief, and he was soon back with his regiment in Bowling Green. Events were beginning to move quicker now. The Confederate line in Kentucky was crumbling.[19]

The Rebel line extended from Cumberland Gap in Eastern Kentucky, across Southern Kentucky just north of Bowling Green, to heavily fortified Columbus on the Mississippi River. Two not-quite-complete Confederate forts just below the Kentucky line in northwestern Tennessee helped to protect the western—that is, left—flank. On the Tennessee River was Fort Henry (and its potentially powerful outpost, Fort Heiman, across the river on the Kentucky side), and on the Cumberland River was Fort Donelson. It was a long, wavering line, ominous on paper, but badly undermanned in reality, as the Federals discovered when they tested it.

On January 19, 1862, at Logan's Crossroads in Pulaski County, Kentucky, a Confederate force commanded by Major General George B. Crittenden (but led in the field by Brigadier General Felix Zollicoffer) attacked the Federal division of Brigadier General George H. Thomas. In the fight that became commonly known as the Battle of Mill Springs, the Federals defeated the Confederates and killed Zollicoffer. The Rebels fell back across the Cumberland River into Tennessee. Cumberland Gap was uncovered, and what had been the Confederate right flank was gone. Three weeks later, on February 6, 1862, a Union gunboat fleet commanded by Flag Officer Andrew H. Foote, supported by the land forces under Brigadier General U. S. Grant, attacked and defeated Fort Henry on the Tennessee River. The river was high from the winter rains, the fort was inundated, and Foote was able to steam right up to the walls of the fort, his big naval guns pounding away. Brigadier General Lloyd Tilghman, Lyon's former commander, started as many of the Rebel garrison as possible toward Fort Donelson on the Cumberland and then returned to the flooded fort to direct the defense and to share the fate of those few who stayed to work the guns. The fall of Fort Henry opened shipping on the Tennessee River and partially uncovered the Rebel left. The Confederate defenses at Columbus were now at risk, and so was Bowling Green in the center of the Southerners' line. Department commander Albert Sidney Johnston began making plans to evacuate Kentucky and simultaneously began reinforcing Fort Donelson in order to protect his flank while the retreat was underway. The infantry and artillery were moved down the Memphis Branch of the L&N Railroad to Russellville. As the last of the Confederates left Bowling Green, they burned much of the downtown area, and the Missourians leaving Fort Underwood burned the plantation house at Mount Air.

Buckner and his troops arrived during the first week in February in Russellville, where Brigadier General John B. Floyd was in command. The records do not reveal exactly when the transfer from Buckner occurred, but at least by January 31, 1862, Lieutenant Colonel Lyon and the 8th Kentucky were in General Floyd's division and in Brigadier General Charles Clark's brigade. They were the only Kentuckians in the brigade. The 1st and 3rd Mississippi, the 7th Texas, and the 42nd Tennessee were the other regiments under Clark. On the eve of their first battle, Lyon and his regiment had been assigned to serve under a new commander and among men they did not know as comrades.

The same confusion prevailed at command level. Albert Sidney Johnston was Jefferson Davis's *beau ideal* of a soldier. He is said to have remarked that if Johnston was not a general, the Confederacy did not have one. Yet, Johnston's orders during the reinforcement of Fort Donelson are hard to reconcile with his supposed genius for war. On February 6, 1862, he ordered Brigadier General Bushrod R. Johnson to report to Fort Donelson and take "instant command." Johnson arrived on the night of February 7. On February 9, Brigadier General Gideon Pillow showed up at the fort. General Johnston had ordered him to assume command. Pillow ordered Johnson to take charge of the left wing while Buckner, who had arrived on February 11, took command of the right wing. At daylight on February 13, General John Floyd arrived at Fort Donelson to assume command from General Pillow. Johnston had told Floyd that he had "full authority to make all dispositions of his troops for the defense of Fort Donelson, Clarksville, and the Cumberland." By appointing three commanders at Fort Donelson, each one arguably worse than the one preceding, General Albert Sidney Johnston had created an ineffective mess. In addition, the reinforcements that Johnston ordered forward, though numerous, proved to be a half-measure; they were insufficient to the task of holding back the Yankees that were marching over from Fort Henry and steaming up the Cumberland from Cairo and Paducah.[20]

At Fort Donelson, Lyon's 8th Kentucky remained in the same brigade, but there were some changes. The brigade's strength had been reduced by the absence of the 42nd Tennessee, which had gone off on detached service, and General Clark was no longer commanding. The commander now was Colonel Thomas J. Davidson. Davidson's brigade was assigned to General Bushrod Johnson on the left wing. When the first Federals began to appear from the direction of Fort Henry on February 11, Pillow ordered the construction of rifle pits be commenced. The work was still going on at dusk on the next day when Johnson threw out a work party (behind a line of skirmishers) with the intention of extending the abatis in the center of his line. Brigadier General John A. McClernand's division attacked the party and drove them in.

McClernand's division and that of Brigadier General C. F. Smith had followed U. S. Grant over from Fort Henry that day, and Pillow had allowed them to march unopposed. The only opposition they met at all was a short distance from the Confederate camps when Nathan Bedford Forrest tried to block their approach with his cavalry. Federal infantry came forward and pushed him out of the way. Forrest had the proper instincts, but Pillow was in charge, and he had allowed two Federal divisions to approach to within striking distance and invest his army. Smith took position on the Federal left, facing Buckner, and McClernand lined up his men on the Federal right, facing Generals Pillow and Johnson.

Thus, the Confederate situation was already bleak by the time that General Floyd arrived on the morning of February 13. Buckner could not have been very sorry at the change in command. He had known Gideon Pillow since the time of the Mexican War. He despised him for his machinations against General Winfield Scott and disdained him for his incompetence. Buckner "considered Pillow a fool."[21]

February 13 was a day of indecisive action. The bluecoats tested the graybacks, feeling for weak spots. There was firing in the morning on the CSA right. General Smith sent two brigades toward General Buckner's line. The Federals were repulsed with the loss of one hundred men, and that was that. On Bushrod Johnson's front, an attack was launched against Colonel Adolphus Heiman and the First Brigade. These men had escaped Fort Henry on the day it fell. They were on the extreme right of the left wing. To their immediate right, Buckner's sector began. Heiman's men stood their ground and repulsed two waves of infantry supported by artillery. There was no other attack along General Johnson's line that day, but he wrote that during the attack and until nightfall, the rest of the left wing "was exposed to the fire of sharpshooters and of field artillery." The enemy sharpshooters were a dangerous annoyance. Nathan Bedford Forrest was so nettled by their plinking that he borrowed a rifle from one of his troopers and showed them how it was done when he dropped a Yankee sniper from his tree. Still, the Confederates did suffer some damage. Johnson wrote, "Colonel Lyon's (Eighth Kentucky) regiment, posted in rifle pits, in front of which was planted, at 700 yards, a battery varying from two to four pieces, lost by these and sharpshooters 2 men killed and 10 wounded within six hours." Lyon had little to add in his brief report except for the small correction that the deaths and injuries in his regiment were strictly from artillery fire and to say that "the firing was often terrific."[22]

It may have been during this early phase of the battle that Colonel Henry C. Burnett appeared. Lyon said that, although he offered to step aside so that Burnett could take command, "he would not do so, on the grounds that he had been elected Confederate States Senator, from Kentucky, and because he did not know how to command a regiment." Burnett acknowledged his own limitations and had made the honorable choice. Lyon remained in command of the 8th Kentucky for the rest of the battle. Only his West Point discipline and the urgency of the situation enabled him to focus his attention on the duties at hand, however; his first child had been born only three days before, on February 10. It was a boy, and they named him Hugh S. Lyon.[23]

The night of February 13 there came a cold rain that turned to sleet, followed by several inches of snow. The temperature hovered a few degrees above zero and a stiff wind was blowing. The men were aching from the cold and exhausted from lack of sleep the next morning and in poor condition for fighting. A council of war at Confederate headquarters early that morning had decided that the continuous arrival of enemy reinforcements posed an unacceptable risk to the men at Fort Donelson. A breakout attempt was quickly planned. Pillow would lead the attack. The men were given their orders and were in the process of lining up for battle when an order arrived countermanding the attack. Pillow had decided that the Federals had discovered their plan and he pressured Floyd to call it off. The men went back to their camps and waited to see what would come next. The Union artillery and the sharpshooters persisted, but this was not the day for the land forces to fight. On this day, the Federal navy and the Confederate shore batteries would have their turn.

A little after 2:00 PM, the Confederates in their rifle pits heard the boom of the big naval guns on their right. It was Flag Officer Andrew H. Foote and the navy, who had won the Battle of Fort Henry. If they showed the same skill and had the same luck here, this might be the last day for the fort on the Cumberland. The *Carondelet* had already had a taste of action. She had arrived on February 12, and on February 13, she attacked the water batteries. The fighting had little effect, other than to give the Confederate artillerists some practice at working their guns. It was this day, February 14, when the real fight came, and the Federal gunboats came a-booming. They soon saw that this was not going to be an easy victory like Fort Henry. The Fort Donelson water batteries were on higher ground than the guns at Fort Henry had been, and their plunging fire devastated the gunboats' decks and made them slick with blood. Conversely, the gunboats' fire was doing little damage. Their guns were not properly elevated. The tiered ranks of Rebel guns dismantled the Federal fleet, and Foote was wounded when a 32-pounder shell shattered the pilot house of his flagship, the *St. Louis.*

While the fight was going on, General Pillow took it upon himself to send a frenzied telegram to Tennessee Governor Isham Harris. He said, "The Federal gun-boats are destroying us. For God's sake, send us all the help you can immediately. I don't care for the land force of the enemy; they can't hurt us if you can keep those hell-hounds in check." But once Foote's crippled fleet withdrew, Pillow became his old self again. He sent a wire to General Johnston, "We have just had the fiercest fight on record between our guns and six gunboats, which lasted two hours. We drove them back, damaged two of them badly, and crippled a third very badly. No damage done to our battery and not a man killed."[24]

The news of the Confederate victory on February 14 spread down the line. That night, the freezing Yankees, shivering in their fireless camps and grim with the knowledge that the navy had failed, had to listen to the Rebel celebrations across the way. If they had any comfort at all, it was in the knowledge that they had been reinforced during the day by the arrival of

Brigadier General Lew Wallace's division, fresh from Fort Heiman on the Tennessee River. Wallace took position in line between Smith on his left and McClernand on his right.

That night, the various Rebel commanders held another council of war at headquarters. They knew that Wallace's division had arrived and estimated (incorrectly) that forty thousand Federals now opposed them, not counting Foote's battered flotilla, which was still on the scene and undergoing repairs. General Floyd expressed his view that their only hope was to force back McClernand's division, on Grant's right flank, pour through the resulting gap, and make their way toward Nashville. The plan had been approved in council earlier that day and might have taken place then had not Floyd, at the insistence of Pillow, called off the escape attempt. Now there could be no delay; the critical time had come. Pillow wanted to make the attack, and he wanted to augment General Bushrod Johnson's six brigades with the 2nd Kentucky Infantry from Buckner's wing. After the Federal right was thrown back, Buckner could advance and continue the attack. Buckner would not hear of detaching his 2nd Kentucky, and he did not want to play a secondary role to Pillow, the man he regarded as a fool. He agreed with the overall plan, but he wanted to take part in the opening phase of the battle by attacking McClernand's artillery positions. Silencing the guns would be a critical contribution to Johnson's victory. Pillow agreed, Floyd agreed, and General Johnson (who had been excluded from the discussion) was called in to learn that he would be attacking at dawn. It was now after midnight, the wee hours of February 15, 1862.

Chief Engineer Jeremy Gilmer left the conference feeling that the plan was not fully developed. He said, "The details of preparation for carrying out the plan decided upon, such as the number of rations that should be prepared; whether blankets and knapsacks should be taken or not; what should be the order of the march on retreat for the different commands; who should take the advance, and who should protect the rear, were not arranged to the best of my recollection, in the council of February 14. The decision of the council was in general terms." Worse than the lack of detail in the plan was the outright confusion between the two wing commanders about what would happen after the Northern troops were forced back and the way out was clear. Pillow came away believing that the men would go back to the trenches for their gear; Buckner believed that no one would return once the gate was open, they would charge through and continue into the open country.[25]

Just before the attack was to begin, there was one of those unsettling last-minute changes that always seemed to occur. General Johnson was trying to array his brigades for battle when he noticed that "for some reason Colonel Davidson's brigade did not appear punctually in its place." Johnson went to the Second Brigade headquarters and learned from Davidson's aide that the colonel "was severely indisposed and had only given orders that his command should be in readiness to move." Johnson ordered the brigade to move immediately to its place in line and there ordered Colonel John M. Simonton to take command in place of Davidson. Simonton had been a merchant and politician in Mississippi before the war. He had no particular military experience, but now, for the first time and quite unexpectedly, he was going to command a brigade in a desperate battle.[26]

There was another winter storm blowing that morning. The wind and the accumulating snow made the men miserable, but it is unlikely that they would have felt much better huddled in their thin blankets in camp, and the storm did give the Confederates one advantage; it muffled the sounds of feet marching and horses neighing so that they could move into position without being detected by the Yankees. All was ready by 4:00 AM.

The First Brigade, under Colonel Adolphus Heiman, would not be in the attack. Its position at the juncture of the Left and Right Wings was deemed too important to abandon, and it was decided to have Heiman remain in place to protect Buckner's left flank after the Left Wing advanced. The other brigades stepped off about 6:00 AM. General Johnson said, "At early dawn the head of the column moved, under the orders of General Pillow, who led them, and very soon engaged the enemy with small arms." Colonel William E. Baldwin's Seventh Brigade advanced first and opened fire. It was followed by Colonel Gabriel C. Wharton's Fifth Brigade and Colonel John McCausland's Sixth Brigade, and then Colonel John M. Simonton's Second Brigade moved forward. Lyon had faced enemy fire in the Indian war, and he knew he could take it; the next few minutes would prove whether or not his boys could. Colonel Simonton said, "Owing to the ground and timber we were compelled to march by the flank, and had not moved more than 400 yards when the head of the column was fired upon." After a moment of confusion and missed orders, Simonton "ordered Lieutenant-Colonel Lyon, of the Eighth Kentucky, to file right and move by the flank at double time, which the gallant officer obeyed under a heavy fire of the enemy's musketry. Before they had completed the movement many of his noble men had bravely fallen, but they held their position determinedly." Simonton's other regiments formed around the 8th Kentucky; the 7th Texas and the 1st Mississippi came up on the right and the 3rd Mississippi on the left.[27]

The brigade hunkered there in a small hollow, held down by heavy enemy fire, when the 36th Virginia (of McCausland's brigade) came up on the left. The Virginians caught the enemy in the flank. They recoiled and the brigade advanced. Simonton reported, "I now ordered the entire command to advance and occupy the crest of the hill, which was executed with a coolness and steadiness that would have done honor to soldiers of a hundred battles. That heroic band of less than 1,500 in number marched up the hill, loading and firing as they moved, gaining inch by inch on an enemy at least four times their number." After two hours of battle, the Union right flank under McClernand was collapsing. They were doubling back on themselves and they were running out of ammunition, which "forced regiment after regiment to pull back." Lieutenant Colonel Frank L. Rhoads, commanding the 8th Illinois in Colonel Richard J. Oglesby's brigade, said, "The fire was murderous, as the long list of the dead and wounded sadly shows." And Captain S. L. Marks, who wrote the report for the 18th Illinois, said of the Confederate push, "So rapid was their firing, it was almost impossible to distinguish an interval."[28]

Simonton's brigade fought for another hour, when word reached the colonel that his men had just about exhausted their ammunition. He sent to General Pillow for reinforcements, and then ordered his brigade to charge, "which movements were executed with a spirit and determination that insured success. The enemy's lines gave way." Pillow was jubilant at the apparent success of his battle. At some point he sent another wire to General Johnston, "On the honor of a soldier, the day is ours!"[29]

The Federals fell back a hundred yards and formed a new line behind Captain Adolph Schwartz's four-gun battery. Simonton ordered his men to charge once more, "and soon the enemy was again driven from his position and four pieces of Schwartz's battery [were] in our possession." Simonton's brigade was responsible for the capture of two of the four guns, and this was where Lieutenant Colonel Lyon's regiment suffered the greatest number of casualties. Lieutenant R. B. Ryan, Simonton's aide-de-camp, said, "The greatest loss we sustained was near where the two pieces of artillery were captured, nearly half of Captain [R. C.] Slaughter's company (A), Eighth Kentucky, being cut down in the advance on the position near the top of the hill; in some places it seemed as if a whole rank fell at a time." Nevertheless, the Rebels had the initiative. They continued to advance, and the Northerners fell back over a mile and a half, turning to fire at every ridge top, until, as Simonton recalled, they "disappeared behind the crests of a range of hills about a half a mile in our front. . . . At this point I was ordered to halt my command and await further orders." While they waited, ammunition taken from the dead Yankees' cartridge boxes was distributed among them. They rested in position for about three-quarters of an hour, congratulating themselves on the completion of their assignment—the road to Nashville was in their possession—and making a preliminary tally of the cost. Of the 8th Kentucky's 312 men, twenty-seven had been killed and seventy-two had been wounded. It was the highest casualty rate in the brigade. About noon, as Lyon remembered it, the order that they had been waiting on arrived. Its contents surprised them. They were instructed to return to their entrenchments, the starting point where they had begun this morning's action.[30]

Simon Bolivar Buckner's wing had not been as busy that morning as Pillow's (Johnson's) on the left. Buckner's men came out of their trenches about 9:00 AM to make an attack to take some of the pressure off of the left, but the real attack did not come until later. It was aimed at the left of McClernand's Federal division. The Confederate left wing was still pushing McClernand's right, and now Buckner's artillerists pounded the other end of his line. The 3rd, 18th, and 32nd Tennessee Infantry under Colonel John C. Brown charged forward up a small valley until they engaged with the enemy. Buckner said, "This movement, combined with the brisk fire of three batteries, induced a rapid retreat of the enemy, who abandoned a section of his artillery. At the same time my infantry was thus penetrating the enemy's line of retreat Forrest, with a portion of his cavalry, charged upon their right."[31]

Buckner continued, "About the same time the Second Kentucky, under Colonel [Roger] Hanson, charged in quick time, as if upon parade, through an open field and under a destructive fire, without firing a gun, upon a superior force of the enemy, who broke and fled in all directions. A large portion of the enemy's right dispersed through the woods, and made their way, as was afterwards learned, to Fort Henry." Hanson seemed a little chagrined that the enemy's quick withdrawal had robbed his regiment of its full glory. He later said, "It was not, strictly speaking, a 'charge bayonets,' but it would have been if the enemy had not fled."[32]

A follow up attack forced the Federal line back across the Wynn's Ferry Road. Buckner said, "In this position I awaited the arrival of my artillery and reserves, either to continue the pursuit of the enemy or to defend the position I now held, in order that the army might pass out on the Forge road, which was now completely covered by the position occupied by my division." The gate was open, and Buckner was in place to keep it from closing; all he needed was his field batteries, his reserve troops, and further instructions. "But General Pillow had prevented my artillery from leaving the intrenchments," Buckner said, "and also sent me reiterated orders to return to my intrenchments on the extreme right." Buckner's officers and men were as surprised at the order as he was, and as Johnson's men on the left had been. They had achieved the breakout and had expected to keep going. Brigade commander Colonel William E. Baldwin said that, in anticipation of their escape, "the men were directed to take knapsacks, blankets, and all rations that could be immediately provided."[33]

Only General Pillow seemed to misunderstand the goal of the morning's attacks. Even U. S. Grant over in the Federal lines understood that the

Confederate assaults were a breakout attempt. Grant had been absent from the front all morning. He had not expected any action, so he had ridden over before dawn to consult with Flag Officer Foote, who, because of his wound from the previous day, could not come to Grant. At four or five miles away, Grant had not heard the battle begin and knew nothing of it until white-faced dispatch riders came galloping to Foote's headquarters with the news. Grant hurried back. He began to see the debris and the dead of battle, and he heard men saying that the captured grayback prisoners and the corpses had "knapsacks and haversacks filled with rations." They did not understand what it meant. Grant knew: these were road rations; the Rebel soldiers had expected to fight their way through to freedom and to keep going until they reached Nashville. Yet, now they were retracing their steps back to the field works where they had begun the day. Grant sensed that the Confederate soldiers must be demoralized to be falling back after having won such a victory.[34]

Grant seized the initiative. He sent a note to Foote, explaining his situation and saying, "If all the gunboats that can will immediately make their appearance to the enemy it may secure us a victory." He did not expect them to steam into action, but he did ask for them to "throw a few shells at long range" into the Rebel lines. Then he turned his thoughts to the most effective use of his army. General C. F. Smith, commanding the Federal Second Division, had been relatively idle during the day and the men were fresh. Grant went to the left-wing command post and said to the old veteran, "General Smith, all has failed on our right, you must take Fort Donelson," and Smith said, "I will do it."[35]

Smith's attack came as Buckner's men were just beginning to arrive back at their trenches. Buckner had met General Floyd after receiving Pillow's order to retire. Floyd, who had merely been observing the battle and who had made no contribution to the morning's victory, "seemed surprised at the order" of his second in command, and he appeared to agree with Buckner that they "should avail themselves of the existing opportunity" to get out. Floyd ordered Buckner to halt until he could find Pillow for a consultation. Floyd's most pronounced trait was his extreme malleability. In their conversation, Pillow bent Floyd to his point of view, and in a bit General Buckner was handed an order to continue to his trenches. And it was while the men were arriving there that General Smith's division hit them.[36]

Buckner said, "A division of the enemy under command of General C. F. Smith, assaulted the extreme right of my position, falling upon Hanson's regiment before it had reached its rifle pits. This gallant regiment was necessarily thrown back in confusion upon the position of the Eighteenth Tennessee." Buckner and his officers formed a new line on a hill a few hundred yards back. Other regiments as well as some artillery came up to join them, and from their new position they were able to hold the enemy in check. The Yankees were stubborn, though. The fighting went on for two hours before the fall of night brought the fighting to an end. The Federals settled down in the works they had captured and from which they would launch a new attack next morning.[37]

While General Smith was making gains against the CSA right, Brigadier General Lew Wallace was operating against their left. General Grant had ordered that the morning's lost ground be retaken. McClernand, who had been handled so roughly by Johnson, turned the assignment over to General Wallace. Many of the Confederates were still in the open, seeing to their wounded and collecting the useful plunder of the morning's fight, the arms and equipment, when Wallace's column hit them. They were quick to respond, but they had been caught flatfooted, and they were forced back. The gunboats began lobbing shells in the direction of the fight, as Grant had requested, and by evening the Confederates had lost everything that they had won in the morning. The Federals ended the day actually better off than they had been before the battle started. They had returned to their original lines in General Johnson's front, they had gained ground and made a lodgment on General Buckner's front, and they had ended the day with the momentum on their side.

The Confederate generals conferred that night. General Pillow was still in high spirits. From his standpoint, the day had gone exactly as planned, and he believed that the army could fight its way out in the morning. Buckner's mood was dark. He understood that the army *had* fought its way out at a ruinous expenditure of its human and material resources and was in no condition to repeat the effort in a few hours. He argued that the army was in a desperate situation, and later remembered telling the others that "the troops had been worn down with watching, with labor, with fighting. Many of them were frosted by the intensity of the cold; all of them were suffering and exhausted by their incessant labors. There had been no regular issue of rations for a number of days and scarcely any means of cooking. Their ammunition was nearly expended. We were completely invested by a force fully four times the strength of our own. In their exhausted condition they could not have made a march. An attempt to make a sortie would have been resisted by a superior force of fresh troops, and that attempt would have been the signal for the fall of the water batteries and the presence of the enemy's gunboats sweeping with the fire at close range the positions of our troops, who would thus have been assailed on their front, rear, and right flank at the same instant. The result would have been a virtual massacre of the troops, more disheartening in its effects than a surrender."[38]

Surrender—Buckner had spoken the word. General Floyd seemed to agree with Buckner, as did the army's chief surgeon, and Pillow's jubilant mood turned to gloom. He asked if Buckner could hold out for one more day, long enough to get steamboats up and evacuate at least part of the army. Buckner answered that he could not. The enemy already occupied part of his works and were in position to attack him at dawn with infantry and artillery. His own force was numb with fatigue and would not be able to resist the Yankees. Even so, he said that he would hold his ground for as long as he could if General Johnston had not yet reached Nashville. Keeping Grant off of Johnston's flank during the Rebel retreat from Kentucky was the reason that Fort Donelson had been reinforced in the first place. Floyd replied that Johnston's move south was complete; he was in Nashville. In that case, said Buckner, there was no reason to cause more suffering among men whose defeat was already certain.

During all of this, none of the three generals present seemed to understand exactly what the situation was on the Confederate left, the wing of General Bushrod Johnson (who, as usual, was not included in the council). Johnson was with his men preparing them for what he understood to be the programme for February 16, a renewal of the fight. Colonel Nathan Bedford Forrest, however, was at the council. He had earlier reconnoitered along the left, and he saw that, while the Federals had reoccupied their lost ground and had even extended their line beyond the Southerners' flank, the situation was not hopeless. There was a road along the river. It was inundated in places, but it was open, and the men could escape by that route. The others could see little promise in Forrest's suggestion. The threat of the gunboats was cited once again; they would blast the escaping column and the attempt would fail with a terrific loss of life. Forrest was so disgusted by the defeatist spirit in the room that he left the council. He returned a few minutes later to find that Floyd and Pillow, both fearing capture, had turned the command over to Buckner, and that surrender had been definitely decided upon. Buckner would attend to it and would stay to share the fate of his men. Forrest stomped from the room and rode back to his horse soldiers and said to them, "Boys, those people are talking about surrendering, and I am going to get out of this place before they do or bust hell wide open." A few hundred infantrymen asked to join them, and off they rode. On their way out, they did not meet so much as a single enemy picket and by daylight they were well away in the direction of Nashville.[39]

After daylight on the 16th, Pillow and Floyd escaped Fort Donelson by steamboat. They took some regiments with them, and Colonel Henry C. Burnett of the 8th Kentucky Infantry also found a place on one of the boats. As they fled, Pillow and Floyd might have evacuated a great many of the soldiers, but they were in a hurry and departed with boats half-empty. They did make sure to take their horses. The stranded men on shore, betrayed by their leaders and bound now to become prisoners of war, shook their fists and cursed them as they steamed away. A few who tried to swim to the riverboats drowned.

Only General Buckner was left at headquarters to pen the offer of surrender to General Grant. His note to the Federal commander proposed an armistice while their appointed commissioners met to "agree upon terms of capitulation of the forces and the post under my command." Once the note was on its way to Union lines, Buckner sent word to his field officers that surrender was imminent. Somehow, General Bushrod Johnson was overlooked. He was still acting on Pillow's now outdated orders to be ready to attack at dawn. Johnson remembered, "Between 1 and 2 AM on the 16th, when, having received orders from the commanding general, I drew out the whole of my command with a view to cut our way through the enemy's right and retreat, as proposed on the night previous. The left wing was duly paraded in columns of regiments outside of the left of our intrenchments by 3 AM." He noticed some troops leaving the front and moving toward the Cumberland River landing at Dover, but he had received no fresh instructions and he remained in place, waiting for the order to advance against the enemy. He continued, "After waiting some time for orders, I sent an aide to report my command ready to move, and received a written communication from General Buckner to the effect that the command had devolved upon him, and directing me to await further orders." After waiting a while longer, he went to headquarters and learned that an offer to surrender had been made. No answer had yet arrived. Buckner told Johnson to return to his lines and "communicate with the enemy's pickets and to request that our forces should not be fired upon." Back at his front, Johnson convened a quick council of his brigade commanders to tell them the news, and the word spread down through the levels of command to Lyon and the other regimental officers. All they could do was wait while, at Union and Confederate headquarters, other men decided their fate.[40]

Buckner had believed that he was dealing with a gentleman. He and Grant had been friends at West Point and in the Old Army. When Grant was forced to resign from the army, having ruined his career by drunkenness, it was Buckner who slipped him the travel money to get home. But, General Grant was a thoroughly modern American, and the morning of February 16, 1862, was no time for sentiment; this was business. The gracelessness of Grant's reply offended Buckner. It said, "No terms except unconditional and immediate surrender can be accepted. I propose to move immediately upon your works." Buckner swallowed his anger and answered in the only way he could. He said, "The distribution of the forces under my command incident to an unexpected change of commanders and the overwhelming force under your command compel me, notwithstanding the brilliant success of the

Confederate arms yesterday, to accept the ungenerous and unchivalrous terms which you propose."⁴¹

When Grant came to Confederate headquarters later that morning, he was in a more congenial mood. He and Buckner discussed the battle in professional, not unfriendly terms, and they made jokes at the expense of General Pillow, whom they both disdained. Grant said that if he had captured Pillow he would have released him. "I would rather have him in command of you fellows than as a prisoner," he said. After a while, Buckner and Grant got around to the details of surrender. Buckner estimated that he had from twelve to fifteen thousand men, and Grant offered to distribute Union rations among them. He said that the Rebel officers could keep their side arms and servants; the enlisted men could keep their blankets. The men going north would be supplied with two days' rations. On a personal note, he offered to lend Buckner money, if he needed it, but this Buckner declined.⁴²

In his biographical sketch, Lieutenant Colonel Lyon wrote nothing of the morning of the surrender or of the next couple of days, as the defeated Southerners waited to be transferred by river packet to captivity. Not every soldier at the time of the surrender meekly accepted the word of his superiors that he was to become a prisoner of war. Buckner had asked Grant for permission to send out burial parties. Grant allowed it, and in this way many Confederates made their way to freedom. Pretending to be part of a work crew, they walked out to the battlefield and passed right on through or between the inattentive Yankee pickets. Private Michael Head, a Lyon County, Kentucky, native and a member of Company I, 8th Kentucky Infantry, escaped, and it might have been in just this way. Without question, the most prominent Confederate who escaped after the surrender was General Bushrod Johnson. He had not been included in the councils of war or consulted in the discussion to surrender. He had not even been informed on the battle line, as other officers had been, that a surrender was pending. He owed nothing to the superior officers who had been so discourteous. He had made no promises, had received no parole, and had signed no papers. General Johnson remained at Fort Donelson for as long as he believed he could be of service to his men. Then, satisfied that he had discharged his obligations, he went out one evening for a walk, "and finding no sentinel to obstruct me, I passed on and was soon beyond the Federal encampments."⁴³

Private Head and General Johnson were the exceptions. By the end of the day on February 18, 1862, most of the 11,500 Confederate officers and men of Fort Donelson were aboard river packets, steaming down the Cumberland in the custody of Federal troops.

With trouble across the American map, and before the outcome at Fort Donelson could be predicted with any certainty, General Henry Halleck had pierced through the confusion of war to understand the significance of the contest then occurring on the Cumberland River. On February 16, 1862, he wrote to General George B. McClellan, "Fort Donelson is the turning point of the war, and we must take it at whatever cost." In the end, the victory that Halleck knew the North must have was made possible by a clear-thinking Union commander at the head of gallant troops. Grant had won the day, but not without an unwitting contribution from the highest level of the Confederate command in the West. Ambivalence on the part of Albert Sidney Johnston had set the stage for defeat, and indecision and conflict among the triumvirate of Confederate leaders at Fort Donelson had led to a catastrophic loss. Only the Confederate fighting men and their field commanders were exempt from the blame; they had done everything they had been asked to do and would have done more if their leaders had shown more determination. That they had not was a tragedy for the South and a godsend to the North. Modern scholars have recognized the wisdom of General Halleck's evaluation. Benjamin F. Cooling writes that "the campaign for those twin river forts called Henry and Donelson . . . yielded the key to unlocking the Confederate portion of that fabled region," the Southern Heartland. Cooling goes on to quote Bruce Catton, who said that Fort Donelson "was one of the most decisive engagements of the entire war, and out of it came the slow, inexorable progression that led to Appomattox."[44]

It is safe to say that in the third week of February 1862, a cold and discouraged Lieutenant Colonel Hylan B. Lyon was not busy analyzing either the immediate or historic significance of the Confederate defeat at Fort Donelson. At that moment, his personal concerns outweighed other considerations. He was on his way to an uncertain future in a prison camp in the North.

5
PRISONER

As the steamboat carrying Hylan B. Lyon to prison passed by his hometown of Eddyville on the Cumberland, the lieutenant colonel went to the officer in charge of the prisoners and made what the Northern newspapers called "an impudent demand." He asked that the paddle wheeler stop long enough to allow him to leave his two slaves at his farm. One wonders what was in Lyon's mind. Did he think that they would be more useful to his wife in Lyon County than to himself in prison? Did he believe that his slaves would run away and be lost to him once they were carried, courtesy of the Yankees, to the North? One wonders, too, what the thoughts of the two slaves were when they heard Lyon's request to the Federal officer.[1]

Whatever Lyon's motivation might have been, his request was refused. According to the newspapers, the officer "promptly told him this Government was not made to protect the negroes of rebels." Lyon's temper flared, and he told the insolent Northerner that "they would meet again on even terms," and the officer replied that he was at his service at any time. And there the matter rested.[2]

Lyon and his slaves continued on the crowded, uncomfortable boat to Cairo, Illinois, and there the enlisted men and officers were separated. Lyon and 110 officers proceeded by rail to Indianapolis, thence to Camp Chase, Ohio. From there, the prisoners were escorted to Fort Warren, Massachusetts, by a Major Smith, whom Lyon knew from his days in Washington Territory. The journey from Camp Chase to Fort Warren was not an easy one. Benjamin Cooling says that the prisoners faced hostile crowds in "Buffalo, Rochester, and Albany in New York" on their way to Boston. They arrived at Fort Warren on March 3, 1862. Lyon was miserable in body as well as in spirit as he was turned over for confinement; he was suffering from frostbite.[3]

Fort Warren was a stone-walled, pentagonal structure on Georges Island, about eight miles across the water from the city of Boston. It dated from 1833. Frowning from its walls was a complement of 15-inch and 10-inch Rodman smoothbore guns. In spite of the prison's foreboding appearance, the Southern officers were more fortunate than they perhaps knew in landing there for their confinement. Charles W. Sanders says, "Of all the prisons occupied by Confederate soldiers during the war, only Fort Warren would secure the reputation as a place where conditions were adequate and captives were treated humanely. That reputation was due primarily to the standards and philosophy of command instilled by Colonel [Justin] Dimick."[4]

Colonel Dimick was a Connecticut native and an 1819 graduate of West Point. He had fought in the Second Seminole War and in the Mexican War. He sustained a wound at Chapultepec that won for him a brevet commission. It may have been the debilitating effects of this wound that caused Dimick to be assigned to be the commandant of Fort Warren at the start of the War Between the States. In a letter home, Lyon said of the warden, "Colonel Dimick is, as officers of the regular United States Army generally are, a very clever gentleman and allows us all the privileges that his Government will permit him." Lawrence Sangston, a secessionist member of the Maryland legislature who was also confined at Fort Warren, went even further. He wrote that Colonel Dimick "exhibits every disposition to make us as comfortable as possible; this example necessarily influences the behavior of the subordinate officers and soldiers."[5]

Good intentions notwithstanding, the resources at Fort Warren were pushed to the limit by the arrival of the Fort Donelson prisoners. Sanders explains, "Given the huge numbers of men transferred into the installation at one time, it is not surprising that accommodations were at first inadequate. Prisoners were forced to subsist on short rations. . . . The rooms in which the captives were billeted were small and hopelessly overcrowded, and due to the shortages of furniture, many men were forced to sleep on crude pallets constructed of scraps of lumber and cloth."[6]

Sanders continues, "Dimick worked tirelessly to ameliorate these hardships, and he was largely successful. To relieve the overcrowding, he granted Confederate officers limited freedom to walk about the island. Sympathetic citizens in Boston were permitted to contribute food, clothing, and bedding for the prisoners' welfare, and the captives' health needs were met by competent and attentive medical personnel."[7]

Prisoners also received gifts from home. In February and March of 1862, Lyon received gifts of money from his father-in-law and cousin, for which he thanked them by letter (duly examined by the prison censors), and he would later receive shipments of clothing. He described his situation to his concerned relatives. He told them that he was given freedom to roam the island. He enjoyed watching the coming and going of the sailing vessels, and on one stroll outside the walls of the fort he had been able to see the Bunker Hill Monument. Bunker Hill was a legendary battle and another one where brave rebels had lost. Lyon told his family that he was "Pleasantly situated here, as one can well be under the circumstances." His roommates were General Buckner and Colonels Hanson, Brown, and Baldwin. He sometimes saw other inmates and after a quick survey of the population he said, "I believe Generals Buckner and Tilghman and Colonel Hanson and myself are the only Kentuckians here."[8]

Buckner and Tilghman, as the commanders of Fort Donelson and Fort Henry, respectively, had a somewhat different experience than the other prisoners. On March 6, the Secretary of War ordered Colonel Dimick to see that they were "kept confined in separate apartments and allowed no intercourse with anyone except by his special permission." Dimick had known Buckner in the Mexican War, and he was as considerate as possible within the limits of the order he had been given. He provided Buckner with the best quarters available, rooms in which his own daughter sometimes stayed. The order was subsequently modified, and Buckner and Tilghman were allowed to go out walking, but always separately and always under close guard. Within their cells, they seem to have been allowed all the same freedoms of conversation as the other prisoners enjoyed. Buckner and Lyon spent much of their time reviewing the reports of the Battle of Fort Donelson.[9]

The money they received from home allowed the prisoners to improve their living situation. They contracted with outsiders for their meals and certain amenities. The day after his arrival at Fort Warren, the Marylander Lawrence Sangston met a "sharp Yankee from Boston who offered to furnish two meals a day in good style, for one dollar per day." Sangston and about thirty others accepted his terms. The impoverished at Fort Warren had to be satisfied with the usual ration of fat pork and hardtack. The prisoners could also arrange for the New York and Boston newspapers to be delivered, and Lyon and the Kentuckians sometimes received the Louisville papers from their relatives. Occasionally, the relatives also included in the packages from home bottles of wine or liquor, an unlikely comfort that regulation nevertheless allowed. Those with money at Fort Warren hired the prison's blacks, such as Lyon's slaves and those of other white masters, to clean their rooms. They attended church services on Sunday and when the weather was inclement, cards and backgammon helped the inmates to pass the time.[10]

As relatively pleasant as it all sounds, there were certain things that disturbed Lyon's peace of mind. He was "much grieved" that the men of his own regiment, the 8th Kentucky, were being neglected by their home state while the men of the 2nd Kentucky were being supplied with money and clothes by citizens of the commonwealth. He did not deny the gallantry of the 2nd Kentucky at Fort Donelson but said that the 8th "did as good fighting as any regiment in the fight, as is indicated by the number of killed and wounded if by nothing else."[11]

Lyon also confessed that his spirits were sometimes low because of the separation from his wife and by the thought that he was of little use to the South on account of his imprisonment. The remedy for both was a speedy parole, and it was a constant theme in his letters. "I am greatly consoled in the knowledge that you are thinking of me and that your prayers are for my safe deliverance from the hands of mine enemies and that at an early date," he wrote Mrs. Lyon, knowing all the while that it would take an earthly intervention to set him free. He felt that two members of the Congress in Richmond would be of particular help in accelerating his release. Henry C. Burnett was Lyon's former colonel in the 8th Kentucky and was now at his duties as a Confederate senator, and Willis B. Machen was not only a member of the Confederate House of Representatives, he was also a relative by virtue of his marriage to cousin Margaret Lyon, the daughter of Chittenden Lyon. "If I could communicate with Mr. Machen and H. C. Burnett I think their influence thrown on the side of an early exchange of prisoners would probably bring it about," Lyon said.[12]

His faith in Machen and Burnett's influence was misplaced. Although there had been a few exchanges by the spring of 1862, the governments of the United States and the Confederate States had not arranged a formal exchange system and would not until summer. Machen and Burnett did not have the status to push the matter and could not act beyond the existing state of affairs. Authorization for Lyon's parole and exchange did not come. As the weeks passed, Lyon's hopes began to sink. On April 13, he wrote his wife (who had moved temporarily to Louisville), "I have no hopes of a parole and but little of an exchange." The April 29 death of Colonel Thomas J. Davidson, who had fallen sick at Fort Donelson on the morning of the breakout fight, undoubtedly depressed his mood even more.[13]

By early May, Lyon's optimism about the possibility of release had returned. He witnessed other officers being paroled and still believed that his own freedom could be won by enlisting the help of some influential person in government. Machen and Burnett had not been able to secure his release; now he turned to Senator Lazarus Powell, another Kentuckian, who was serving his first term in the U.S. Senate. Lyon wrote his wife on May 6, "I have to-day written to Senator Powell asking him to endeavor to have me paroled to Richmond to effect my exchange for Lieut. Colonel [George W.] Neff of the 2nd Kentucky Regiment U.S. Volunteers who is now a prisoner at Richmond." Lyon had also written to Neff's relatives in Cincinnati to enlist their help in a plan whose success would be mutually beneficial.[14]

To his disappointment, the Neff scheme failed. The weeks dragged on, and Lyon remained a prisoner at Fort Warren. On July 27, he sent his wife photographs of General Robert E. Lee and General Joseph E. Johnston, "who now rank among the first generals of the world." Once again, Lyon's optimism had rebounded. The newspapers reported progress in the official effort to create a program of prisoner exchange, and Lyon believed that his parole would come soon. He wrote to Laura, "If my hopes are realized in this matter I will inform you by telegraph in time for you to join me at Cairo." From there, she would travel south with him. He urged her to buy new clothing before setting out because of scarcities in the South and because everything was more costly there.[15]

Lyon was right that his parole was imminent. Four days later, July 31, 1862, Lyon, Buckner, Tilghman, and others departed Fort Warren aboard the *Ocean Queen*, bound for Virginia. In a memoir that was sometimes shy of dates, he was very specific in stating that he was exchanged on August 27, 1862, at Aiken's Landing on the James River. He traveled to Richmond, where he met with President Jefferson Davis. The conversation inevitably turned to Kentucky, and Lyon was later able to tell his sister that his host "spoke very affectionately about 'Old Eddyville.'" From Richmond, Lyon made his way west to Mississippi. He wrote his wife from the steamer *Champion* near Vicksburg to inform her of his arrival and to say that he and those of his regiment who had arrived would shortly be going to Jackson, where they would be turned over to Confederate officials. They were free from prison, but they were not free to return to active duty or return to the field until formally notified that their exchange was complete. A backlog of government paperwork sometimes meant that a return to duty took months. Lyon regretted that he and his wife had not been able to meet at Cairo and travel south together. He explained that there had not been time. He said, "If I had been positively informed in regard to the time of our exchange sufficiently early for you to have joined me at Boston or anywhere between Boston and Fortress Monroe I should most certainly have written you to come." But, he urged her now, "Come quickly to your Loving husband." They would have a double reason to celebrate, for Lyon had been promised a promotion to colonel of the 8th Kentucky.[16]

During Lyon's imprisonment, Confederate prospects for victory in the West had darkened. The Rebels had abandoned their stronghold on the Mississippi at Columbus, Kentucky, and they had lost the battle of Island No. 10. Union forces were threatening the middle stretch of the Mississippi River not only from the north, but also from the direction of New Orleans, which had fallen to Flag Officer David G. Farragut in April. The Confederates had lost the Battle of Shiloh that same month, and General Albert Sidney Johnston had died there. The Yankees had won the important railroad town of Corinth, Mississippi, and were approaching Chattanooga. Nashville, Baton Rouge, and Memphis were lost. Military excellence was more important than ever if the South's bad fortune in the West were to be reversed.

The momentum seemed to be on the side of the Federals, but the Confederates were determined to make up their losses by a fall campaign along a broad front. In the West, three columns would advance north. The first prong of the Confederate invasion was Major General Edmund Kirby Smith, who would move out of Knoxville into Kentucky's Bluegrass region to threaten Lexington and perhaps even Cincinnati. At about the same time, General Braxton Bragg would advance from Chattanooga through Middle Tennessee and move into west central Kentucky along the line of the Louisville & Nashville Railroad. It would lead him all the way to the Ohio River. Bragg and Smith would rendezvous in Kentucky. The third prong would be Major General Earl Van Dorn. His Army of West Tennessee would move out of Mississippi, pass through the region that gave the army its name, and emerge in the Jackson Purchase of Kentucky, where the Cumberland, the Tennessee, the Ohio, and the Mississippi rivers all came together. Paducah was there. Furthermore, the Mobile & Ohio Railroad, the overland supply line of U. S. Grant's army, began in the Jackson Purchase. For his invasion, Van Dorn would be joined by the fourteen thousand men of Major General Sterling Price. By these invasions, the Confederacy was going to push its boundary north all the way to the Ohio River, and General Bragg was going to install a Confederate administration in Frankfort. Kentucky was going to become a legitimate part of the Confederacy at last, and Colonel Hylan B. Lyon, by the particulars of military law regarding exchanged prisoners, was going to have to sit it out.

By the time Van Dorn and Price met at Ripley on September 28, the first target had been decided upon by the general commanding. Van Dorn explained, "It was clear to my mind that if a successful attack would be made upon Corinth from the west and northwest, the forces there driven back on the Tennessee and cut off, Bolivar and Jackson [Tennessee] would easily fall, and then, upon the arrival of the exchanged prisoners of war, West Tennessee would soon be in our possession and communication with General Bragg effected through Middle Tennessee. The attack on Corinth was a military necessity." As much as he would have liked to have the exchanged officers and men join him, he could not wait for their exchange to be finalized. He said, "To have waited for the arrival, arming, clothing and organization of the exchanged prisoners would have been to wait for the enemy to strengthen themselves more than we could possibly do."[17]

The Confederates marched on October 2. It would be 22,000 Rebels against fifteen thousand Yankees. They bivouacked ten miles away from the target on the night of October 2 and arrived on the north and northwest outskirts of Corinth on October 3. Their appearance was no surprise. There had been clashes with the bluecoat cavalry during their march, and the Union commander, Major General William S. Rosecrans, had been busy preparing for them.

As they approached the double line of Federal works, General Price moved off to take position on the left of the CSA line, and Major General Mansfield Lovell took position on the right. By 10:00 AM, the men in blue and grey were all arrayed for battle. General Lovell opened the attack, "the beginning of what turned out to be a two-day battle which was one of the most violent of the war."[18]

General Lovell said in his report, "On our right was a strong redoubt, well flanked with infantry and with an abatis of felled timber half a mile in width extending around it in one direction but with no obstruction to the north, in the direction of Price's right." The men moved forward toward what appeared to be an impregnable position. They attacked it on the right and center. After Lovell's division began its attack, Price threw his men forward on the left. General Rosecrans said in his report, "Our troops fought with the most determined courage, firing very low." Perhaps so, but their defense of the outer line was of short duration. By 1:30 PM, the Confederates had carried the works and the Federals were fleeing back to their second line. They turned to fight a mile from Corinth and the Confederates slammed into them. The 3:00 PM fight was one "of unparalleled fierceness," according to Price. For two hours the two armies mauled each other. In the end, the bluecoats broke and fell back and disappeared into their inner line of works. The Confederates bivouacked within easy striking distance, only six hundred yards out.[19]

There had been more of the enemy than they expected; Rosecrans had been reinforced before the Rebels arrived. Still, Van Dorn's men had done a good day's work, and they were confident of their ultimate success. The next morning, October 4, it was Price on the left who launched the attack. His line advanced after an artillery barrage. Lovell stepped off after the sound of musketry reached him. Van Dorn had ordered him to "press forward and attack with vigor." He had barely engaged when he was ordered to send a brigade to Price; the Missourian was having a hard time. In the end, though, it was the boys wearing the Union blue who broke. They fled from their works into the heart of Corinth. Van Dorn said, "A hand-to-hand contest was being enacted in the very yard of General Rosecrans' headquarters and in the streets of the town."[20]

The Confederates had not counted on the strength of the Union forces inside Corinth, especially their artillery. The attackers, successful up to this point, "were greeted by a storm of grape," and they began to retire "under a withering fire." The Federal infantry rallied and chased the Rebels over the battleground of the last two days, and the fight on the CSA left came to an end. Lovell's division did not get into the town. It had been "treated to grape and canister until within 50 yards [and] a murderous fire of musketry, before which they reeled and fell back to the woods." The Confederate attack had failed, as did the counter-attack that followed. The graybacks broke and fell back in disorder, the Yankees in pursuit. It was noon, and the Battle of Corinth was over.[21]

The Confederates camped that night at Chewalla and continued their retreat the next day toward the Hatchie River. A sizeable force of the enemy who tried to check their crossing of the river was repelled "with great slaughter," and yet they persisted. For the next forty miles they pestered the Confederates, who repeatedly had to go into formation to meet the threat. Added to their misery were the unseasonable heat, lack of sleep, physical exhaustion, and short rations. Even so, General Lovell said that "Good order, discipline, and subordination suffered no relaxation under this severe and trying ordeal." They ended their retreat in Holly Springs.[22]

Shelby Foote summarizes Van Dorn's truncated campaign by saying, "What had been intended as a third prong in the South's late-summer earlyfall offensive had snapped off short as soon as it was launched. Including the action on the Hatchie, it had gained the Confederacy nothing except the infliction of just over 3000 casualties on the Federals in North Mississippi, and for this Van Dorn had paid with nearly 5000 of his own." Van Dorn's expedition had been a failure, but it was not the only one. The Confederacy's big gamble in the autumn of 1862 failed all along the line. Edmund Kirby Smith and Braxton Bragg had done somewhat better in the beginning—they had at least gotten into Kentucky—but they had had difficulty coordinating their efforts. They did not effect a juncture until after the Battle of Perryville, at which time they withdrew into Tennessee. Ultimately, their defeat was as complete as Van Dorn's.[23]

A court of inquiry was convened after the Corinth Campaign. It cleared Van Dorn of charges of negligence. He was, however, essentially demoted—given a field command—while his department was assigned to Lieutenant General John C. Pemberton. General Pemberton arrived in Jackson to assume command of the Department of Mississippi and East Louisiana on October 14, 1862.

While Van Dorn had been fighting, General Lloyd Tilghman had sat in Clinton in charge of eight thousand paroled prisoners of war who had theoretically been exchanged but had received no notification. He could not legally lead them to join Van Dorn, though in the aftermath of the battle he was criticized for not doing so. Tilghman's biographer says that it was soon after the defeat at Corinth that the general "received ratification of the exchange and the men could be forwarded." He moved his men by rail to Holly Springs during the second week in October. A few days later, October 16,

1862, in Special Orders No. 53, the men were given their assignments. It said, "The following assignments of exchanged prisoners are made to the divisions of Major-Generals Price and Lovell, and will report immediately. . . . To Major General Lovell . . . Colonel H. B. Lyon's consolidated regiment."[24]

Major General Mansfield Lovell was born in Washington, DC, in 1822. He attended West Point and counted James Longstreet, Earl Van Dorn, John Pope, and Williams S. Rosecrans among his classmates in the Class of '42. War soon called them. In Mexico, Lovell saw action at Monterrey and Chapultepec, and he served on the staff of Mississippi's General John A. Quitman. That seems to have influenced his thinking along secessionist lines. He was in New York when the rebellion began. He traveled south to offer his services to the Confederacy. With his record, it was inevitable that his rise would be quick in the South's new-born army. He became a brigadier general in September 1861 and a major general only one month later. It was while under his command that New Orleans fell, but a court of inquiry attributed that to causes other than his leadership and he was not held responsible. The people who knew him—Joseph E. Johnston, Braxton Bragg, and Judah P. Benjamin, among others—praised him for his intellect, his energy, his almost rash style of courage, and his high sense of morality.

Hylan B. Lyon's eight months as a prisoner of war were over, and now, under this brilliant and brave commander, he was ready to go back to work.

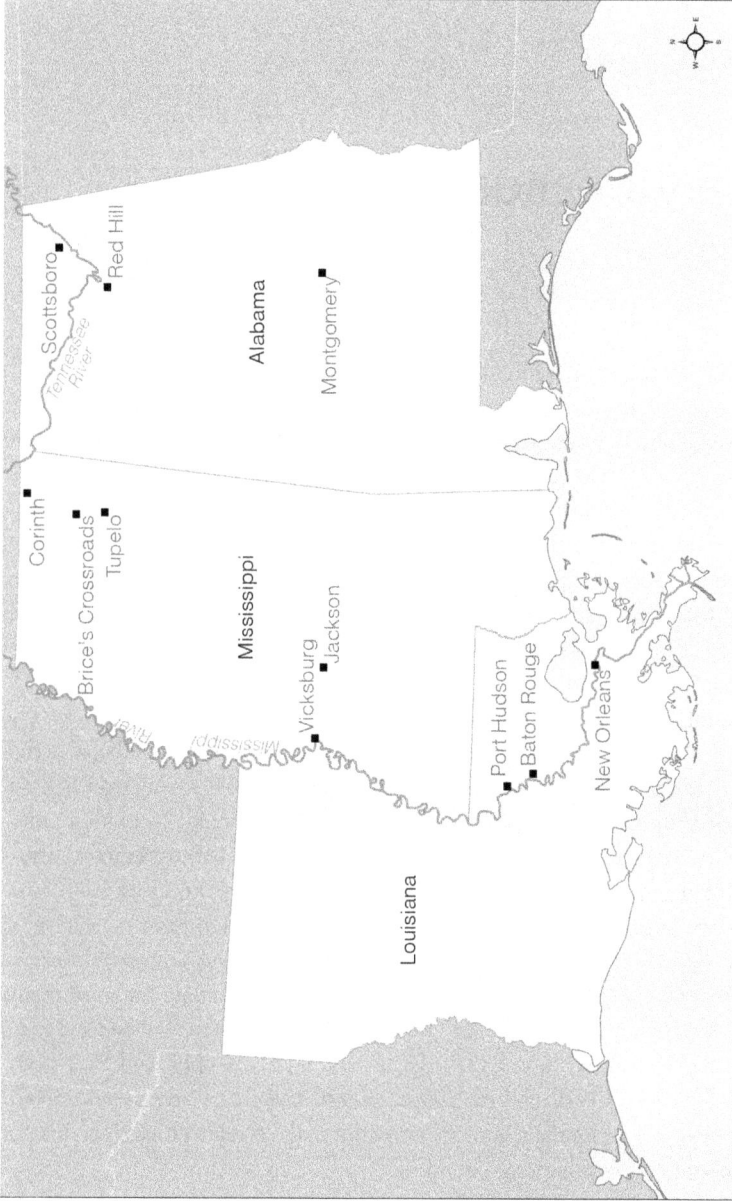

Lyon's Civil War: The Deep South. Map by Sasha Jovanovic.

6

THE VICKSBURG CAMPAIGNS

On October 24, 1862, a foretaste of winter struck the central Mississippi Valley. A storm swept in from the north and dropped an inch of snow as far south as Holly Springs. Major General Ulysses S. Grant took the weather as a warning that he had better move with alacrity if he wanted to squeeze in one more expedition south before the weather forced the armies to go into winter quarters. Grant was the commander of the Department of the Tennessee, and he was eager to have a go at Vicksburg to cap off what had been, for him, a very successful year. He ordered a concentration of troops in and around La Grange, Tennessee. His plan was to advance down the line of the Mississippi Central Railroad and strike the Rebels where he found them.

Grant had the resources and the manpower, and he also had luck. The timing of his Mississippi Central campaign could have hardly been better. The Confederates were in a transitional strait. General Pemberton had superseded Van Dorn as departmental head, but interference from above once again created confusion at command level. The month after Pemberton was appointed commander of the Department of Mississippi and East Louisiana, President Jefferson Davis assigned General Joseph E. Johnston to head what was called the Department of the West. Johnston's headquarters were in Chattanooga, and from there he was expected to coordinate the movements of all Confederate forces in the wide region composed of western North Carolina, Tennessee, North Georgia, Alabama, Mississippi, and East Louisiana. Johnston was Pemberton's superior. However, President Davis ordered Pemberton to ignore the chain of command and "to report directly to him or to Secretary of War James A. Seddon."[1]

President Davis's implied distrust of the supreme commander created a dangerous gap in communications between Pemberton and Johnston, the drawbacks of which were obvious to many observers, if not to Davis. It was an unnecessarily complicated plan imposed on a theatre of war where efficiency, careful planning, and an unambiguous command hierarchy were of

General Pemberton, a post-war portrait.
Library of Congress.

particular importance, both because of the great prize at stake (control of the Mississippi River) and because of the unique challenges of the topography. Historian John Keegan says, "Militarily, the theatre is one of the most complex in which large armies have ever fought, not because geography blocks the correct way forward—indeed rather the opposite, since the great rivers all lead straight south—but because meanders, swamps, and undulation made cross-country communication between separate armies difficult, and usually achievable only by recourse to water transport." Keegan adds that the, "physical geography of the western theatre defied the effort to make organized war." By his interference, President Davis only added to the difficulties.[2]

On November 2, 1862, Grant commenced his campaign. He led five divisions toward Grand Junction, Tennessee. From there, he planned to move along the Mississippi Central toward Holly Springs and Grenada. Grant reached Grand Junction on November 8, and on November 9 he sent a reconnaissance of two divisions and more than one thousand cavalry toward Holly Springs. Grant had selected Holly Springs for his "depot of supplies and munitions of war, all of which at that time came by rail from Columbus, Kentucky, except the few stores collected about La Grange and Grand Junction." He admitted that "This was a long line (increasing in length as we moved south) to maintain in an enemy's country." Military wisdom held that clinging to one's supply line was of paramount importance, and Grant accepted it. The army began arriving to occupy Holly Springs on November 13.[3]

The Confederates had suspected Grant's intentions even before he began his campaign. General Van Dorn, who now commanded Pemberton's cavalry, had been watching, and he reported to his superior as early as October 20, "a number of general officers assembled at Jackson, at General Grant's head-quarters." The next day he reported of the enemy at Corinth, "there are indications of preparations for advance."[4]

Pemberton knew that he suffered a terrible deficiency in numbers. He ordered Van Dorn to resist Grant's advance with his cavalry and immediately began seeking help from General Braxton Bragg at Tullahoma. Bragg could spare no infantry to Pemberton, but he could send him three thousand muskets and some cavalry. He wired Pemberton, "A large cavalry force under Forrest starts to operate in the enemy's rear and create a diversion in your favor." Neither Bragg nor Pemberton could fully anticipate the importance of Forrest's temporary return to West Tennessee.[5]

Grant paused at Holly Springs during the third week in November and continued south on or about November 27. Once again, Van Dorn soon discovered what was happening. He reported to Pemberton on November 29, "Enemy reported advancing rapidly this morning toward our front. No flank movement reported this morning yet. Large reinforcements also reported moving down the river by Memphis." Alarmed by the two-pronged Federal advance, Pemberton ordered the "machinery and ordnance stores at the Briarfield Arsenal, Columbus" to be moved to safety, and he ordered his defensive line to fall back again.[6]

The Confederates abandoned their works on the Tallahatchie River without a fight and made their way in the falling rain toward the Yalobusha River. General Lovell, who was in the rear of the column, had to contend with soft roads that the feet, hooves, and wheels in front of him had made worse. He reported, "The roads are horrible. I cannot get on at all, except by daylight, with trains and artillery." Yankee cavalry and mounted artillery stayed close on their rear, but Van Dorn's horse soldiers kept them off and the retreat continued. On December 4, the Confederates stopped at Coffeeville.[7]

The next afternoon, the Federal cavalry pushed to within a mile of Coffeeville. First to appear was Colonel Albert L. Lee's brigade of Colonel Theophilus L. Dickey's cavalry division. They were skirmishing with the Confederate pickets when General Lovell went out to confront them, taking along six pieces of artillery. This was Colonel Lyon and the 8th Kentucky Infantry's return to war after their enforced eight-month layoff. They were the lone Kentucky regiment in the brigade commanded by Brigadier General William E. Baldwin; the other regiments were the 14th Mississippi, the 23rd Mississippi, and the 26th Mississippi. They took their place on the left of the road when Lovell deployed his infantry. Lovell ordered other regiments to deploy on the right and he also placed four of his guns on a small hill on the right. He set his other two guns on a higher hill three hundred yards behind them. General Tilghman had been attending to official duties in town. By the time he came out to join General Lovell, a "brisk cannonading" had begun. The two officers rode forward to the four-gun battery, but, Tilghman said, "finding that the enemy had obtained the exact range of our guns, I retired with General Lovell to the rear battery." Tilghman took charge of the two Parrott guns there, and under his direction they silenced the Yankees' pieces. Now the infantry and the cavalry came into play. The skirmishers moved slowly forward toward a dense woods that concealed the enemy's exact location. The main line followed one hundred yards behind, with orders "to hold their fire until within 50 yards, to move with caution until the enemy was reached, but then to press them with all their energy."[8]

Tilghman continued, "The line had not advanced 200 yards before the enemy opened on our left a brisk fire. This was answered first by a yell along our whole line, the men moving rapidly and with great enthusiasm until they were within good range, when the Ninth Arkansas, temporarily under the direct command of Col. A. P. Thompson, and the Eighth Kentucky, under Col. H. B. Lyon, opened fire in return." The firing spread from the left down the length of the line as the men pressed forward.[9]

The Federal commander, Colonel Dickey, said, "It was quite evident we had encountered a heavier force than we were able to combat, under the jaded condition of our men and horses. Colonel Lee was ordered to fall back steadily in the center and strong parties were at once sent to the support of our skirmishers on the right and left flanks." Two other brigades were brought forward and "ordered to form successive supporting lines of detachments on each side of the road to cover the retreat of our skirmishers." The Confederates came on, and disorder was beginning to be evident in the Federal retreat. Dickey said, "The moving back of the led horses of the dismounted men and the reversal of wagons and ambulances occasioned considerable confusion."[10]

The battleground was a mixed landscape of woods and flat, open fields. The Yankees used the terrain well. Tilghman said, "On being driven to the edge of a field they mounted and retreated across it, dismounting and sending their horses to the rear. They had all the advantages of position, being covered by the woodland while our men advanced across the open field. At these points the fire of the enemy was terrible, but nothing could stop the onward movement, and our men moved forward without slackening their pace in the least."

The Northerners' Colt's revolving rifles and Sharp's carbines could not stop Tilghman's men. Twice the bluecoats turned at the edge of a woods to make a stand, and each time the Confederates charged across open ground and forced them to flee. "They were not allowed to breathe," said Tilghman. The intensity of the Confederate attack never eased, and some of those on the receiving end began to take it personally. Phineus O. Avery of the 4th Illinois Cavalry said, "I cannot begin to describe the shower of lead that I passed through. Suffice it to say that I took the fire of the whole rebel skirmish line in my front. Every shot was fired at me." Tilghman's Rebels chased the enemy three miles. The 8th Kentucky and the 9th Arkansas endured artillery fire and the heaviest small arms fire they had faced since the start of the fight, and still they drove Dickey's cavalrymen back. The men had been fighting nearly three hours and darkness was falling when Tilghman finally ordered his men to halt.[11]

The day had belonged to the Confederates. Colonel Dickey attributed their victory to a long list of disadvantages his own men could not overcome. He offered the time-honored excuse that his men and horses were jaded, and he blamed the topography of Yalobusha County. "The road was narrow and extremely muddy," he said, "lined nearly all the way on both sides by a dense and almost impenetrable growth of oak trees and underbrush, running over a broken and impractical country, or through river bottoms of a miry character. It was impossible to see the enemy's position or note his strength till we were upon him. It was equally difficult to show a strong front or properly dispose of the wagons and ambulances and the horses of the dismounted men." (Some who survived the battle cited another cause for the Federal defeat; they claimed that Dickey was not on the scene to direct or share in the fight. Lyman B. Pierce of the 2nd Iowa Cavalry said, "No sooner did Col. Dickey see his forces overpowered than he discovered that *his* presence was needed *at the rear.*" Dickey abandoned his brigade commanders and expected them to extricate their men they best they could.)[12]

The Confederates had maneuvered over the same challenging terrain as the Federals, of course, and while they had the benefit of more artillery at the beginning of the contest, the enemy had them outnumbered by a factor of three-to-one and had superior small arms. Why was it, then, that the Rebels were able to gouge the Northern troops out of one sheltered position after another and finally chase them from the field entirely? General Tilghman decided that it was pent-up aggression. His men were recently exchanged prisoners of war, and, as he said, they "seemed to forget everything but the desire showed by all to repay the injuries suffered by them during their long and barbarous imprisonment at the North."[13]

No one showed more initiative than Colonel Hylan B. Lyon. His 8th Kentucky, along with the 9th Arkansas, the 23rd Mississippi, and the 26th Mississippi, had borne "the brunt of battle," and Tilghman said, "I have seldom seen greater good judgment and impetuous gallantry shown by any officers or men." He recommended Colonel Lyon for promotion to brigadier general, though no immediate change in the Kentuckian's rank followed. The fight had cost Tilghman sixty men killed, wounded, and missing; eleven of these had been from Lyon's 8th Kentucky Infantry.[14]

Certain commentators have claimed that it was the Confederate victory at Coffeeville that caused General Grant to suspend his advance on Grenada. This is a misunderstanding of events caused by a coincidence of timing. It is true that Grant did not continue south after the battle, but it was not because one of his cavalry divisions had suffered a setback. Rather, it was because of a telegram that Grant received from General-in-Chief Henry W. Halleck on the very day of Dickey's defeat at Coffeeville. The telegram said, "Destroy the Mobile road, as you propose. It would also be well to disable the others, if possible, to Grenada; but I think you should not attempt to hold the country south of the Tallahatchie." Obviously, it was orders from Washington that caused Grant to halt.[15]

Bored and resentful Yankees sitting idle along the Mississippi Central Railroad were unlikely to behave well; indeed, they had behaved very badly from the very start of their campaign and some later wrote of it. A soldier from Illinois wrote, "Along our march this time there has been more property destroyed than I ever saw before," and another said that between Grand Junction and La Grange, the men of his regiment "burned almost everything on the road, stole lots of niggers, killed a cow and five calves for supper, then camped within the enclosure of La Grange College, also burned all the fence around it for firewood and had one of the most jovial nights I ever experienced." Continuing south, they burned abandoned houses and every cotton gin they passed, foraged with a ravenous spirit, and butchered animals in the presence of the farmer whose protests were muted at the point of a bayonet. Lucius W. Barber of the 15th Illinois Infantry said that his comrades "would rob rich and poor, old age and youth, widows and orphans, weak and helpless alike. I have time and again seen a poor, lonely woman with a house full of little ones, on her knees, begging those wretches not to take the last mouthful from her starving children, and perhaps when they left, she would be houseless and homeless, left with her little ones to starve." Much of the looting that went on was unnecessary, even ridiculous in retrospect. Yankee cavalrymen were seen breaking apart grandfather clocks to get at the little wheels and gears inside, which they used as rowels for their spurs.[16]

General Grant admonished his soldiers for their behavior and ordered them to stop. The order was ignored. One man remembered that, "such orders soon got to be a joke with the men, they in a quiet way giving the

commanding officers to understand that they did not go down South to protect Confederate property." The senseless destruction continued, but a day
of reckoning was near. General Earl Van Dorn, who in the past weeks had
earned his description as "a man of considerable fire," had been appointed to
command the I Corps on December 7, 1862. Soon after, either he or General Pemberton proposed that Grant and his army of arsonists should not
be allowed to rest easy. The Confederates could not marshal enough men to
out-muscle Grant, but Van Dorn could strike him a critical blow by a quick
raid against his huge supply depot at Holly Springs. It would be both a military triumph as well as a moral satisfaction to pay back such an army of van-
dals. Ten days after his appointment, Van Dorn led 3500 men north toward
the Federal supply dump.[17]

Colonel Lyon was part of the column that moved against Holly Springs,
and one must think that it was a graduate course for him in the lightning raid
and the quick withdrawal, lessons that would be of use to him in the future.
Van Dorn began by swinging far to the east to get around Grant's left flank
and then turned west toward his target. He had behind him 2700 men, each
of them supplied, it was said, with "a bottle of turpentine and a box of matches
to enable them the more perfectly to carry out their work of destruction upon
Abolition property." Colonel R. C. Murphy, who was in charge of Holly
Springs, had been warned to expect a raid. Nevertheless, he was unprepared
when the Confederates came riding in on the morning of December 20. Grant
said that Murphy had "made no preparations" to resist Van Dorn, "He did not
even notify his command." The Rebels dashed down on the enemy camp and
set fire to the tents of the sleeping Lincolnites, who left their canvass shelters
with "marvelous speed." The scene was "wild, exciting, tumultuous. Yankees
running, tents burning, torches flaming, Confederates shouting, guns popping,
sabres clanking; Abolitionists begging for mercy, rebels shouting exultingly."
At one swipe, over 1900 Federal officers and men were captured. After such
excitement, the Confederates' capture of the Union supply dump was almost
an anticlimax. Certainly, it was no battle. The immense warehouses down by
the Mississippi Central Railroad were filled with quartermaster and commissary stores; medical supplies and ordnance stores were kept "up town" in the
courthouse and other public buildings and even the livery stable. The raiders
crammed their saddlebags with all that they could carry and torched the rest.
They burned buildings and tore up railroad track, and they destroyed two
locomotives and sixty rail cars. They captured Grant's headquarters with all
his papers and maps, and they burned his "splendid carriage." And they set fire
to the powder magazine. It contained one hundred barrels of gunpowder, and
when it exploded, it shook the whole town and utterly destroyed some nearby
buildings. General Van Dorn scribbled a wire to send to Pemberton before the

telegraph lines were ripped down. The message said, "I surprised the enemy at this place at daylight this morning, burned up all the quartermaster stores, cotton, etc.—an immense amount; burned up many trains, took a great many arms and about 1,500 prisoners. I presume the value of stores would amount to $1,500,000." By sundown their work was done, and Van Dorn's raiders rode out of Holly Springs, well supplied with winter coats and boots and armed with a thousand new revolvers.[18]

Van Dorn "cut our haversack strings," the Northern boys said. It was a quaint way of describing Van Dorn's crowning achievement of his service for the Confederacy. Rabb says, "Van Dorn's army, with limited striking force and little bloodshed, accomplished more to stop Grant's Mississippi adventure in the last two weeks of the year than the combined Confederate army had done in the previous three months."[19]

However, Van Dorn's raid on Holly Springs was not the only blow suffered by Grant's Federals at the end of 1862. Nathan Bedford Forrest had appeared in West Tennessee to operate against the Mobile & Ohio Railroad, Grant's main supply line. Forrest had been released by General Bragg at Tullahoma. He rode west at the head of four regiments and a battery of guns, and it was not long before Grant knew that he was on his way. Grant warned his commanders at Fort Henry, Fort Heiman, Fort Donelson and elsewhere to be ready, but like Van Dorn approaching Holly Springs, Forrest found that he could go where he wanted and do what he liked with little resistance. From Union City to Jackson, Forrest's troopers wrecked stretches of the M&O Railroad (and of the Nashville & Northwestern), burned bridges, and tore down telegraph wires, and Grant suddenly found himself "with no supplies and no supply line, in an area where no living white man would give any assistance to a Yankee army if he could help it." The situation was desperate. Grant moved his headquarters from Oxford to Holly Springs and soon began a slow retrograde movement to the north. All across the front, the Federals had suffered defeat. Simultaneous with Grant's movement south, Sherman had moved on Vicksburg down the east bank of the Mississippi. On December 29, General Stephen D. Lee's Confederates stopped him at Chickasaw Bayou. With setbacks first for Grant and then for Sherman, the first Vicksburg campaign came to an end.[20]

Colonel H. B. Lyon had done his part. For him, personally, 1862 had been a year of ups and downs. The year had begun in defeat and ended in victory. He had been a prisoner of war, and he had won a promotion to full colonel. Now winter had arrived, and there would be a breathing spell until spring, when everyone knew that the Yankees would come back. The Confederates in Mississippi were the guardians of the grand prize, and the Federals would not rest until they had taken it away. The year 1863 would be decisive.

However, the year 1863 is the least well understood of Hylan B. Lyon's wartime career. Lyon's letters from other years are filled with details, but there are no known letters from him dated 1863. His name was hardly ever mentioned in the newspapers and only rarely in the *Official Records*. He had a chronic aversion to official correspondence, so there are few reports or dispatches from him, even though he was the leader of a regiment. It has been suggested that his reports were simply lost; perhaps so, but a survey of his few existing official communiqués reveals an exasperating brevity and lack of detail compared to his rich letters home, and one must conclude that military correspondence had so little appeal for him that he often simply ducked his duty to put pen to paper. In any case, the lack of documents from Lyon's own hand is a regrettable loss to history, for 1863 was one of the most crowded years of his life. The best way to understand Lyon's activities in 1863 is to track the movements of the brigade in which he served.

There was a reorganization in January 1863 that put Colonel Lyon and the 8th Kentucky in a brigade with the 50th Alabama, 14th Mississippi, 20th Mississippi, 23rd Mississippi, and 26th Mississippi. Two batteries were attached to the brigade, and General Tilghman commanded the whole. Major General William W. Loring commanded the division.

Loring ordered his division back to work in February 1863. Winter quarters was of brief duration in the Deep South, and the Federals were already in the field. After the destruction of Holly Springs, they had fallen back toward Memphis, foraging freely in a zone of fifteen miles on either side of the railroad. The rich pickings brought in by the foraging parties was something of a surprise and proved to General Grant that an army could break free from its base and live off the land. That knowledge would be useful later; for now, he turned his attention to opening operations against Vicksburg via the Mississippi River.

Since January, the Army of the Tennessee had been busy, as per General Grant's orders, digging a canal opposite Vicksburg on the Arkansas side. Sherman's defeat in December had shown the impracticality of attacking the Confederates at Vicksburg by way of the Chickasaw Bayou. An inland canal on the west side of the river would allow the Northerners to get their gunboats and troop transports below Vicksburg without exposing them to those ominous shore batteries—if it succeeded.

In February, while work on the west bank canal continued, the Federals commenced a second effort that required less digging and therefore had a greater chance of quick success. They were going to try to force their way south by way of the Yazoo Pass. Yazoo Pass had once provided a way for planters in the interior to get their cotton into the Mississippi, but in the mid-1850s an earthen levee eighteen-feet high and one hundred feet thick had been built across its mouth. The Yankees planned to blow a hole in the levee, pass through into the watery web of bayous and rivers, and proceed south well east of Vicksburg. When they reached firm ground, the troops would disembark and move against the Rebel works from behind. On February 2, 1863, Lieutenant Colonel James H. Wilson and five hundred Federals appeared at the Yazoo Pass levee. The next day, they detonated a mine that breeched the earthen wall, and a cataract of Mississippi River water poured through. By the next day, February 4, the rushing water had scoured a two-hundred-foot wide gap through the levee. Once the water level equalized on each side, the boats would be on their way to Moon Lake, thence to the Coldwater River, thence to the Tallahatchie, thence to the Yazoo, and finally to the dry ridge called Haynes Bluff. If all went well, Vicksburg would soon fall.

The Confederates were alert to what was happening. On February 17, General Pemberton ordered General Loring, Lyon's division commander, to take charge of the defenses. He wanted him to scout the Tallahatchie and the Yazoo Rivers to find a place to erect works and resist the enemy's advance. Loring found the site he was looking for a short distance north of Greenwood, Mississippi, where the Yalobusha and the Tallahatchie join to form the Yazoo. He ordered Major Minor Meriwether to begin work on a fortification, and at the same time he ordered Lieutenant W. A. Gillespie to take groups of slaves (and their overseers) north toward Yazoo Pass to begin chopping down trees to block the channel. Once the work was underway, Loring moved General Tilghman's brigade forward and ordered him to "send without delay a strong regiment of infantry and a field battery to this place."[21]

"This place" was Fort Pemberton, the fortification that Major Meriwether had built. It was described as "a typical Mississippi cotton-bale fortification . . . three to five bales of cotton on top of one another and from four to five bales wide, joined together with sheet iron." The parapets were made of more cotton bales and logs "covered with rawhide so that the enemy shells would bounce off." Inside, Loring had about two thousand men and seven guns, ranging from a single 32-pounder to a complement of 3-inch rifled guns.[22]

After spending some days on preliminary work in the vicinity of the levy, the Federals advanced in earnest on February 26, 1863. The flotilla included two ironclad gunboats, the *Chillicothe* and the *Baron De Kalb*, five tinclads, and twenty-two troop transports. Lieutenant Commander Watson Smith commanded the boats, and Brigadier General Leonard F. Ross commanded the strike force of 4500 men. They began to have trouble when they reached the Coldwater River. Gillespie's slave gangs had dropped in the channel scores of enormous trees, each one weighing many tons. Confederate sharpshooters pestered the Yankee work gangs while they struggled to haul the giant trees out of the water. A lattice of overhanging limbs scraped the tops of the boats and knocked over the smokestacks. Hidden stumps battered the hulls and floating debris and driftwood fouled the paddle wheels. The flotilla crept forward at only two miles per hour. The progress was so slow that some of Ross's soldiers leaped on shore to loot the local plantations. They killed the livestock and raced about catching all the poultry and pigs they could. Officers had to threaten to shoot them to make them stop.

On March 11, the Federals appeared at Fort Pemberton. The Confederates hurriedly swung a raft of gum logs across the channel and sank a derelict side wheeler, the *Star of the West*, behind it. Then they went to their guns. The *Chillicothe* nosed forward at 10:00 AM, and the Rebel artillerists opened up with five of their seven guns. Their gunnery was good, and a battered *Chillicothe* backed away after thirty minutes. She had fired only three rounds. Late that afternoon, the *Chillicothe* steamed forward for a second try. This time she was joined by the *Baron De Kalb*. The fight lasted only seven minutes before the *Chillicothe* was forced to withdraw, and the *Baron De Kalb* soon followed. All they had accomplished was to make the Rebels deplete their ammunition. In a report to Pemberton, Loring urgently requested more, particularly for his 32-pounder, "our main reliance." He also said, "I have ordered a regiment and battery from Tilghman to Chockachuma, on the Yalabusha, and himself to take the balance of his command to Yazoo City as rapidly as possible." Tilghman's brigade's part at Fort Pemberton was over; henceforth they would protect Loring's left flank.[23]

Loring was able to resist all efforts to reduce Fort Pemberton until March 19. That day the Federals began their return to Yazoo Pass, with General Ross grumbling that they had been sent forward ill-prepared for battle; they needed more ammunition of a heavier caliber and better gunboats if they expected to get past the Confederate fort. General Loring sent men to pursue the retreating Federals. In a message to Pemberton the next day, he said, "Enemy in full run, as fast as steam can carry him, and my men after him. This place capable of very strong defense; should be made perfect, and I have given orders to have it so." He felt confident that the Federal defeat at Fort Pemberton represented "a check which will undoubtedly prevent a further invasion of the State of Mississippi by way of the Tallahatchie and Yazoo Rivers."[24]

Loring had underestimated Yankee determination. As the flotilla continued toward the Mississippi on March 21, they encountered a second flotilla coming from the direction of Yazoo Pass. General Grant had ordered Brigadier General Isaac F. Quinby forward to reinforce Ross. Now, Quinby found the first flotilla returning, whipped. He convinced them to turn around and join him in a new effort against Fort Pemberton, citing the "moral effect of the presence of the gunboats" on the Rebels. So, the boats turned about, with several thousand surprised soldiers aboard.[25]

Loring was surprised, too. He had said only two days before that the Federal invaders would not be seen again on the Tallahatchie, yet on the afternoon of March 23, he saw them approaching again. He wired Pemberton, "The enemy in force with their gunboats have again made their appearance, opening fire at 2:15 and immediately ceasing fire."[26]

The afternoon action of March 23 was the height of Quinby's attempt on Fort Pemberton. He saw now for himself what General Ross and Commander Smith had been up against. Between his arrival and April 4, he erected shore batteries and appeared to be making every preparation to attack. Loring was concerned, even as his guns shelled the enemy camps, and he repeatedly asked for heavy guns and more ammunition, for entrenching tools, and even for one hundred rockets. Then, on the evening of April 4, the Union vessels raised steam and disappeared in the Tallahatchie River mist, taking the Union expeditionary force with them. Loring explained the Southern victory, saying, "We waited a short time after their arrival in the hope that they would muster courage to attack us, but it seems that it failed them in the critical moment. We then commenced the offensive by driving away their laboring parties from the works intended for batteries. . . . We commenced shelling on the evening of April 2, and continued through the 3d and 4th." He had also sent reconnaissance parties against both of the Federal flanks. Tilghman's brigade, which included Lyon and the 8th Kentucky, was involved in one such action. With permission of Major General Dabney H. Maury, who had arrived to take charge of the CSA left wing, Tilghman designed an attack against the Union right. Tilghman had a Masonic map which showed the quadrant where Quinby's headquarters was located. From it, he drew a diagram and used it to explain to his artillery and his infantry exactly what he wanted. On the night of April 2, an artillery barrage opened on the target and the infantry stepped forward. The small, successful action had an oversized outcome. Quinby was forced to abandon his farmhouse, and two nights later the bluecoats commenced embarking, "and by daylight they were in rapid retreat up the river." A determined defense and a timely show of aggression had defeated Quinby's attempt to reduce Fort Pemberton.[27]

Grant decided even before the Tallahatchie expeditions failed to send another forward. He later remembered, "I was much exercised for the safety of Ross, not knowing that Quinby had been able to join him. Reinforcements were of no use in a country covered with water, as they would have to remain on board of their transports. Relief had to come from another quarter. So I determined to get into the Yazoo below Fort Pemberton." He gave the mission to General William T. Sherman and Rear Admiral David Dixon Porter. They were to move on Fort Pemberton via Steele's Bayou. The advance commenced on March 14, 1863. Porter had five gunboats and four mortar barges, and Sherman had ten thousand soldiers, well-armed and ready to bring Vicksburg down. Opposing their advance was Brigadier General Winfield S. Featherston, the same Mississippian who had been an envoy to Governor Beriah Magoffin in late 1860 and unsuccessfully lobbied him to lead Kentucky out of the Union. With fewer men and less firepower than the Yankees, Featherston was able to stop and turn the enemy, and on March 27, they were back at their starting place on the Mississippi, having failed as completely as the Smith and Quinby expedition had.[28]

All three of the Yazoo River expeditions had ended in defeat, as had the west bank effort to dig a canal that would allow Federal gunboats and transports to bypass Vicksburg in safety. If Vicksburg was to be taken, the Federals were going to have to run the batteries, get below, and approach from the south. Grant understood this now, and he made his plans known to Porter on March 29. Porter took some convincing. He had stated at the end of the Steele's Bayou Expedition, "There is but one thing now to be down, and that is to start an army of 150,000 men from Memphis, via Grenada, and let them go supplied with everything required to take Vicksburg." The Navy man was advocating an Army solution to the Vicksburg puzzle. In the end, Grant persuaded him, and Porter went to assemble his fleet, which included seven ironclads, one ram, and three empty troop transports. Grant's soldiers would not ride down with the Navy; they were ordered to march south through Louisiana and would meet the boats on the other side at New Carthage.[29]

The flotilla set out at 9:30 PM on April 16. Porter was leading in his flagship, the *Benton*. It was a moonless, windless night. The boats moved in single file, slowly to reduce the noise, and all the portholes were closed. Grant was observing from a steamer upstream, just out of range of Vicksburg's guns. He watched the dark shapes steal by about 10:30, and they reached Vicksburg a little after 11:00. A Rebel picket boat saw them and sounded the alarm. Confederate sentries at De Soto on the Louisiana shore set bonfires and burned an abandoned railroad depot to illuminate the passing boats and the gunners took aim at their slow-moving, perfectly outlined targets. The whole hillside lit up with cannon blasts. Porter thought at first that the city was on fire.

Over the next ninety minutes, the Confederate guns fired over five hundred rounds at the passing fleet. The gunners soon found that the stillness of the wind worked against them. General Stephen D. Lee said, "The firing was generally good, though much interfered with by the smoke of the guns settling in front of the batteries." A second round of firing sounded from the batteries downstream, but the fleet came through, battered but intact, except for one transport that had been sunk. Only minor repairs were needed to put the Federal boats in perfect condition. When a second run—this time transports only—was complete, Grant would be ready to start ferrying men across the river to the Mississippi side.[30]

A disaster had befallen the Confederacy. To capitalize on it and give himself every possible chance of success, Grant authorized an elaborate distraction that would directly affect Lyon and his regiment. On April 17, 1863, Colonel Benjamin H. Grierson led 1700 mounted men south from La Grange, Tennessee. His goal was simple: ride deep into Mississippi and destroy Rebel supply depots and railroad infrastructure all along the way.

Shortly before the Federals ran past the guns at Vicksburg, General Pemberton had reluctantly reduced the size of his force. He was being pressured to reinforce Bragg at Tullahoma, Tennessee. On April 13, Pemberton told General Johnston, "I am collecting troops here, and can send you 4000 at once, if absolutely necessary." Johnston and Bragg thought it was necessary. Accordingly, the brigade of General Tilghman at Canton, and the brigades of General Abraham Buford and General Albert Rust at Port Hudson were ordered to prepare to move. Tilghman's brigade boarded the rail cars at Jackson on April 15. Colonel Lyon and the 8th Kentucky moved with Tilghman's brigade, even though they had been reassigned that very day. When time allowed, they would join a number of other greatly reduced regiments to serve under General Buford. Lyon's men were brigaded with the 54th Alabama, the 27th Alabama, the 35th Alabama, the combined 6th and 16th Alabama battalions, the 35th Arkansas, the 12th Louisiana, the 3rd Kentucky, and the 7th Kentucky. The Kentuckians were excited to be on their way. The rumor had spread that when they reached Tennessee they would be assigned to General John C. Breckinridge and would be going into Kentucky for recruiting duty.[31]

They began their circuitous journey by going first to Meridian on the Southern Railroad and then south to Mobile on the Mobile & Ohio. General Simon Bolivar Buckner commanded in Mobile, and when the trains arrived, he came down to the station to shake hands with the men. It was the first time Lyon had seen Buckner since they were released from Fort Warren, and many of the others had not seen him since Fort Donelson. They had a layover before the boat would come to take them across Mobile Bay to the train waiting on the other side, so the men—the Kentuckians, at least—marched through Mobile to General Buckner's headquarters and went through the manual of arms "just to compliment him." Henry Ewell Hord of the 3rd Kentucky remembered that, when they had finished, Buckner spoke from a balcony and complimented them for "how nobly we had held up the fame of old Kentucky on many battlefields," and he invited the commissioned officers inside for tea. Some of the others went to a local saloon and ordered drinks which they charged to Buckner. Loosened up by the liquor they consumed, the boys did a little looting in the stores and groceries, and when some Alabama cadets who were acting as a police force responded to the disturbance, they were roughly handled and thrown into Mobile Bay. The next day the regiments in transit went down to the wharf to catch the ferry across the bay.

Buckner came to see them off. The boys began to sing "My Old Kentucky Home," and some of them wept at the poignant strains of Stephen Foster's ballad. War had coarsened them, but they lived in a sentimental age and they were moved to tears at the thought of their homes far away.[32]

They continued from Mobile to Montgomery, arriving on April 18. There, they learned that because the Federals had successfully made their run past Vicksburg and were making threatening moves in North Mississippi, General Pemberton had cancelled the troop movement. The men were ordered to return, and, as Hord remembered it, they spent the next few days rushing "up and down the roads of Mississippi, ordered around by telegraph, and saw the Yankees but once." They caught a glimpse of enemy troops at Enterprise, fired one volley at them, and watched them disappear. The 8th Kentucky still traveled with Tilghman, and at the end of their roundtrip they ended up at their familiar camps at Canton.[33]

Lyon and the 8th Kentucky were at Canton with Tilghman on April 24 when an order arrived from Pemberton to "mount the Kentucky regiment." Grierson was on the move, and Pemberton was hard pressed to meet the threat. General Van Dorn and his five thousand cavalrymen had gone to join Bragg in January. Pemberton pleaded with General Johnston and General Buckner to send him reinforcements, and he urged Mississippians everywhere to arm themselves and prepare to defend their state. It was to no avail. Grierson was unimpeded, for the most part, as he blazed a trail through Mississippi. He moved fast and was far to the south before the 8th Kentucky was ever mounted.[34]

General Pemberton, through Tilghman, ordered Lyon's 8th Kentucky Infantry and others down to the Pearl River to prevent the enemy from doubling back. Their assignment proved to be one of fruitless watching and waiting. The Kentuckians were poorly used, but it is unlikely they would have done any better if they had been in active pursuit. No one who tried was able to stop Grierson. On May 2, the Federal raiders rode into Baton Rouge, followed by the large numbers of contrabands who had abandoned their masters to join the passing column, their liberators. Grierson had traveled the length of Mississippi in what many consider the greatest cavalry raid of the war. At Newton Station, Hazelhurst, and Brookhaven, he had destroyed troves of commissary and quartermaster stores, ammunition, tents, and stands of arms, and he had destroyed bridges and miles of railroad track all along the way. He had captured and paroled hundreds of Confederate fighting men and damaged the civilian populations' ability to materially support the war effort by his (perhaps unintentional) liberation of hordes of plantation slaves. He had completely bewildered Pemberton, who had had no idea where Grierson was heading and, in any case, had too few troops on hand to block every possible route.

Pemberton said, "Every effort was made by me to provide cavalry to arrest Grierson's raid." And, still, Grierson got through. The Memphis *Daily Appeal* grudgingly paid him the highest compliment when it editorialized, "The audacity of [Grierson's] detachment equals that of Stuart's raid through Maryland into Pennsylvania, and around McClellan's army, or Van Dorn's achievement at Holly Springs, accomplished by circumventing Grant's grand army. The Yankees are, it must be admitted, imitative when their inventive genius fails them."[35]

General Grant ordered other demonstrations in April to keep Pemberton guessing and off-balanced. Major General Frederick Steele led one feint to Greeneville before returning to Federal lines, and General Sherman led an expedition up the Yazoo. All the while, Generals McClernand and McPherson were leading their corps down the west bank of the Mississippi to Hard Times plantation, where they rendezvoused with Porter and his fleet. Pemberton sent Brigadier General John S. Bowen at Grand Gulf an additional five thousand men to repel the invaders. The reinforcements raised Bowen's total to nine thousand. It was a pitifully weak force to meet Grant's 24,000, but it was all Pemberton could spare with Yankee raiders all over the state and Grierson splitting it in two. Grant had done a masterful job of making Pemberton spread his forces thin to meet multiple points of danger. The situation was dire, yet the Federals were prevented from landing at Grand Gulf on April 29, 1863. General Bowen's shore batteries held them off until Grant decided to try at some undetermined spot lower down. A local black man, who was probably apprehended by a Yankee patrol and brought to headquarters for the very reason that he knew the countryside, advised Grant to try to land at Bruinsburg. Grant followed the man's advice, and the Union troops began to go ashore there on April 30, McClernand's corps first and then McPherson's. They drew three days' rations and moved inland. It was a lovely spring night, and the scent of magnolia blossoms was remarked upon by the soldiers, many of whom were experiencing their first visit to the Southland.

It was Brigadier General Martin Green of Bowen's command who first opposed McClernand's advance. Green was aware that the enemy had come across the river, and though he had no cavalry to confirm the Federals' movements, his tactical sense told him that they would move against Grand Gulf. He prepared through the night to oppose them and got into a minor shooting scrape with McClernand's men before anyone was really ready to bring on an engagement. Nothing came of the encounter. The Northerners continued moving forward, and Green's Confederates fell back to perfect their defenses. Two roads led inland from Bruinsburg, each one on a high, narrow ridge with a deep and jungle-like ravine between them. The Confederates took position on each road. General Bowen had arrived by the time the Federals appeared the next morning, May 1. As the Confederates had guessed, the bluecoats were moving along both roads; what surprised them was the size of the forces approaching.

If Bowen had had the numbers, he could have defeated them in detail at Port Gibson, but he did not. He had one division and two brigades to meet all of McClernand's corps plus half of McPherson's (the other half was still disembarking at Bruinsburg). The three-to-one advantage threw an inexorable weight against Bowen, and by day's end the Federals had pushed Bowen back across Bayou Pierre to his works at Grand Gulf. Bowen burned the bridges as he retreated, knowing all the while that this would buy him only a temporary reprieve.

General William W. Loring and General Lloyd Tilghman showed up that night with two infantry regiments and a battery. Loring placed his infantry and artillery at Grindstone Ford on the Bayou Pierre to block the Yankees and hurried forward to find Bowen. Together, they agreed to evacuate the army. They dispatched a brigade to Grindstone Ford, "it being all important to hold that position." The blocking brigade failed in its mission, as Loring learned a few hours later when he received word that an estimated fourteen U.S. regiments were on the Confederate side of the bayou. He quickly sent a brigade under General Tilghman to resist the Federals and cover the retreat to the Big Black River. Loring said, "This was handsomely done, and we were enabled successfully to cross" the Big Black.[36]

Temporarily safe from a surprise, Loring, Bowen, and Tilghman rested their men at the Big Black. Major General Carter L. Stevenson joined them there with a brigade from his division, raising their strength to about 18,000 men. Major Samuel H. Lockett, Confederate Chief Engineer of Defenses, said in his article for *Battles and Leaders* that Pemberton thought at first that Grant would cross the Big Black and strike north toward Vicksburg. However, he "became convinced that General Grant's intention was to march up the east bank of Big Black River, to strike the railroad at or near Edwards Depot, and thus to cut his communication with Jackson." On May 3, General Stephen D. Lee was left to hold the river crossing, and the army made its strategic redeployment to Edwards Depot, where they would make their stand. Major Lockett looked at the position with an engineer's eye and approved of what he saw. He later remembered, "The position was naturally a strong one, on high ground, with the cultivated valley of Baker's Creek in its front." Here General Pemberton perfected his preparations as he waited to be attacked by Grant, and he ordered the detached regiments of Tilghman's and Buford's brigades—Colonel Lyon's 8th Kentucky and the others—to come by rail and rejoin their comrades.[37]

As it became clear that the Federals were going to threaten Jackson, Pemberton sent a flurry of telegrams to his subordinates: harass the enemy, cut off his wagon trains, send all ordnance and ammunition supplies to Vicksburg. He ordered that all machinery in the threatened city should be sent to Alabama, and he advised Governor Pettus that the state archives and other records should also be sent eastward to safety. Pemberton also sent President Davis a telegram, reviewing what had happened as of May 3 and telling him what steps he had taken. He said that, despite setbacks, "With cavalry in Northern Mississippi and re-enforcements promised, think we will be all right."[38]

In communicating directly with Jefferson Davis, Pemberton was obeying the instructions given to him at the time of his assignment to command the Department of Mississippi and East Louisiana. General Johnston was not yet in Mississippi. He had remained in Chattanooga, making decisions based on insufficient and out of date information, while the situation in the Magnolia State grew steadily worse. Finally, his superiors stepped in. Johnston recalled, "In the evening of May 9th I received, by telegraph, orders to proceed at once to Mississippi and take chief command of the forces there, and to arrange to take with me, for temporary service, or to have follow without delay, three thousand good troops." Even though he protested that he had still not recovered from the wounds he received a year earlier at the Battle of Seven Pines, he agreed to go west by the first train. Three days later, en route, he did, at last, receive a telegram from Pemberton. It was the first message from him in almost two weeks. Dated May 12, the wire said that the enemy appeared to be "moving in heavy force" on his position at Edwards Depot. Pemberton reasserted that he planned to make Edwards Depot *the* battlefield of the campaign.[39]

By the time Johnston received Pemberton's telegram, Grant had all three of his corps with him—Sherman had arrived on May 7—and he was ready to move. He sent McClernand north to threaten Edwards Depot and sent McPherson almost directly east to Raymond. Sherman took his place between them. All three stepped off on May 12. McClernand skirmished with Rebel cavalry at Fourteen Mile Creek, four miles south of Edwards Depot, and pushed them back with the help of a few artillery rounds from Sherman's guns. The Rebels fired the bridge and fell back; the Yankees rebuilt it and followed. By this time, it was growing dark, and the Federals bivouacked for the night.

The fight that McClernand expected and Pemberton wanted at Edwards Depot did not develop. The fighting was elsewhere, at Raymond; at the state capitol, Jackson; at Champion Hill, where General Tilghman was killed by a fragment of artillery shell; and at the Big Black River Bridge. Lyon and his command were not in the thick of the fighting at any of these battles; they were out on the thin edge, performing the important but unglamorous job of picket duty. It was only after the Rebels began their retreat into Vicksburg that Lyon and his regiment were once again part of the main struggle.

The battle at Big Black River Bridge was the last engagement the Confederates fought to hold the Federals back from the works at Vicksburg. They did not fight well at the bridge; after the carnage of Champion Hill, something essential had gone out of Pemberton's fighting men. They were forced from their defenses on the Big Black, and the way to Vicksburg was suddenly wide open. Still, all was not hopeless. As Major Samuel Lockett explained to the discouraged General Pemberton, they had divisions in Vicksburg that had not been at Champion Hill or Big Black River. These fresh units could take the major role in defending the city until their battle-weary brothers had recovered. Furthermore, Vicksburg was strong, and General Johnston was no farther away than Canton, and he would soon be coming with a relief force. What mattered now was reaching the safety of the Vicksburg entrenchments. General Carter L. Stevenson was in charge of the troops retreating from the Big Black, and Colonel H. B. Lyon and the 8th Kentucky Mounted Infantry fell in behind as the rear guard.

The Federals began erecting spans across the Big Black the very day of the Confederate withdrawal, using cotton bales and logs and, as was their custom, the lumber from nearby buildings. If there was any skirmishing at all between Lyon's Kentuckians and the Federal cavalry, it was so insignificant as to escape mention in the reports and memoirs. Pemberton knew that a siege was inevitable and starvation probable, so he issued orders to the men retreating along Haynes Bluff that "all cattle, sheep, and hogs belonging to private parties, and likely to fall into the hands of the enemy, should be driven within our lines." The Rebels requisitioned all the available wagons along the line of retreat and filled them with fresh corn pulled from the stalk. They eventually saw the skyline of Vicksburg, and they began entering just as the sun was setting on May 17. That night, they burned the houses in front of their works to clear their fields of fire.[40]

Pemberton's curving defensive line was eight miles long. General Stevenson was on the right (south). Next to him, in the center, was Major General John H. Forney with two brigades. On the left was Major General M. L. Smith, with three brigades and Lyon's 8th Kentucky. General Bowen's division was held in reserve. The aggregate was 15,500 men. General Johnston had wanted Pemberton to avoid investment at Vicksburg; the men must be saved even if the place fell. He still hoped for a juncture between Pemberton's forces and his own. Pemberton, however, faced the same difficulty as before. Jefferson Davis had been clear in his orders that Vicksburg must be held no matter the cost. Moreover, he had recovered some confidence since the defeat at the Big Black River Bridge, and he believed that he could hold on. He called a council of war after Johnston's communiqué, and he informed Johnston of the result: "I have decided to hold Vicksburg as long as possible, with the firm hope that the Government may yet be able to assist me in keeping this obstruction to the enemy's free navigation of the Mississippi River. I still conceive it to be the most important point in the Confederacy."[41]

In a very short time, the question of whom to obey became academic. Sherman's advance began arriving on the afternoon of May 18, and the entire Federal army was soon deploying outside the city. Sherman was on the right, where he occupied his long-desired goal of the Chickasaw Bluffs. McPherson occupied the center of the Federal line, and McClernand took position on the left. Vicksburg was invested. Not long after taking his place in line, Sherman decided to test General Smith. According to Smith, they "immediately attacked the position with artillery and infantry . . . dark terminated the attack." All that was accomplished by the afternoon attack was to force the pickets and skirmishers back into the main works, which were on a "narrow ridge, and consisted of a line of rifle-trenches, with points prepared for field artillery."[42]

The first real Federal attempt to reduce Vicksburg came the next day, May 19. Grant wanted an early end to the siege, and he saw no reason why he could not have it. He said, "The enemy had been much demoralized by his defeat at Champion's Hill and the Big Black, and I believed he would not make much effort to hold Vicksburg." He ordered an intense artillery barrage to begin at nine o'clock in the morning to be followed by an infantry charge all along the line. The Union batteries barked about 9:30 and continued their clamor until about 2:00 PM. Then the infantry stepped off. McPherson and McClernand faced such difficult terrain that their assaults were slow and uncoordinated; Sherman's was easier as to terrain, but much tougher as to the fighting. He was making a direct attack on General Smith's portion of the works, and a little of Forney's. The first assault failed. The Northerners fell back, regrouped, and tried again. As had been the case at Coffeeville, Lyon and his Kentuckians were back in the fray after an unproductive period on the sidelines, and they fought alongside Smith's brigades with explosive energy. Captain J. J. Kellogg of the 113th Illinois Infantry remembered, "The leaden hail from the enemy was absolutely blinding. The very sticks and chips scattered over the ground were jumping under the hot shower of rebel bullets. As I now recall that experience I can but wonder that any of us survived that charge.[43]

Elements of Sherman's corps managed to get to the ditch in front of the Confederate works, and there they huddled. They had no scaling ladders and could not get over the top. The Rebels fired down on them and lobbed grenades in among them. They tossed the grenades back when there was time, and they fired their muskets the best they could, but to try and withdraw would be suicide, and they could not advance. They began to run out of ammunition. Regimental musicians and even a fourteen-year-old drummer boy made daring trips back to the ammunition train and brought back cartridges. They held on until darkness made it safe to retreat, "leaving five colors on the field, and the ground strewn with the dead and wounded," General Smith reported. Federal artillery and sharpshooters covered their retreat with a heavy fire. Sherman said, "The rebel parapets were strongly manned, and the enemy fought hard and well. My loss was pretty heavy." Grant had expected to take advantage of the demoralized survivors of Champion Hill and Big Black River Bridge. Unfortunately for him, his main attack had come against a sector which was manned by men who either had been in Vicksburg during all that time or, as in the case of Lyon's regiment, had not seen any hard fighting since the Yankees first made landfall at Bruinsburg in April. Major Lockett commented on this, saying that the enemy was "met by troops which had not been in any of the recent disastrous engagements, and were not in the least demoralized." He said, that the bloody repulse of the bluecoats had a good effect among those who had been defeated on May 16 and 17; Smith's small victory "helped to restore the morale of our army."[44]

More than once through the war years, Grant displayed an overeagerness; success created in him a rash confidence, and he would rush into action without his usual deliberate planning. The assault on May 19, 1863, was an example. Shelby Foote describes the basis for Grant's heedless optimism, saying, "In the twenty days since they crossed the Mississippi, they had marched 180 miles to fight and win five battles—Port Gibson, Raymond, Jackson, Champion Hill, Big Black River—occupy a Deep South capital, inflict over 7000 casualties at a cost of less than 4500 of their own, and seize no less than fifty pieces of field artillery, not to mention two dozen larger pieces they found spiked in fortifications they outflanked. In all this time, they had not lost a gun or a stand of colors, and they had never failed to take an assigned objective." Grant's confidence that his army could do the impossible was understandable, but reckless, and the men in the ranks had suffered a stinging repulse. The defeat on May 19 brought Grant's head down out of the clouds, and he spent the next two days planning for the next assault. He erected new artillery emplacements and built supply roads, while keeping the Confederates occupied with cannon fire and musketry. By the morning of May 22, everything was ready.[45]

Colonel Hylan B. Lyon and his Kentuckians were not there to see it. They had found a way out. General McClernand had not extended his line to the Mississippi on the Federal left flank, and on the night of Thursday, May 21, Lyon slipped through the gap and made his escape. His three hundred men were mounted on artillery horses. General Johnston had recommended to Pemberton that these horses be killed; he said, "Can you not get rid of your teams? It would be better to kill them than feed them." Lyon had a different idea, one that would save the valuable horses, and, more importantly, his regiment. Still writing about himself in the third person, Lyon recalled in his memoir, "After repeated applications by its Colonel to Genl Pemberton for some of the fine horses belonging to the Artillery Companies, which would undoubtly [*sic*] starve to death in Vicksburg, and permission to march his regiment out of Vicksburg, the application was granted and permission given. The regiment marched down the Mississippi River and passed between Grant's left flank and his gunboats and escaped without firing a gun." Colonel Lyon and the 8th Kentucky had escaped the Federal investment of Vicksburg. They were on their way to Jackson.[46]

7

THE ARMY OF RELIEF

On their way to Jackson, Colonel Lyon and his Kentuckians captured a "large number of skulks convalescents and sick in the hospitals established by Grant on his march in rear of Vicksburg." They swung around to Raymond and observed the signs of the recent battles that they had not seen, having been on continual picket duty along the Big Black. The roadsides were an endless scene of destruction and despair—and they were nothing compared to Jackson.[1]

The Canton *American Citizen* reported on the behavior of General McPherson's and General Sherman's men during their brief occupation of Jackson. The Northern officers assured the citizens that they would be safe in their persons and property but admitted to them that the soldiers were excited and might prove "hard to control." They assigned a provost guard and posted it around the city, "and for a time matters proceeded quietly enough, under the circumstances. But no sooner had their troops arranged their encampments than the soldiers came pouring in by the hundreds. Then commenced a scene of pillaging and wholesale robbery, the parallel of which has probably not been known, in a city so small as Jackson, since the war commenced. The guards could not prevent it even had they been inclined." The destruction was worse in the south and southwest quarters of the city. There, the Yankees had broken into stores where they found bottles, barrels, and jugs of liquor, and then they began going house to house, demanding something to eat and pilfering whatever they liked. They destroyed furniture and scattered the contents of drawers, bureaus, and desks looking for plunder. Houses were literally "gutted." Even the governor's mansion was looted. When the heads of households requested guards, the request was honored and "to give the devil his due" (the paper said), these homes were spared.[2]

McPherson's corps left Jackson on May 15. Sherman's corps stayed behind to attend to the destruction of government property and property otherwise useful to the Confederacy. Gristmills, foundries, factories, workshops, and warehouses were put to the torch. All stores of foodstuffs were destroyed and all railroad property, of course. When Sherman's troops left the next day, May 16, they burned the Confederate House Hotel and the adjacent properties, and the newspaper office was ransacked and the presses demolished. They took every head of livestock in town, and, said the *American Citizen*, "many negro men and women voluntarily left" with them. The newspaper claimed that many others were forced to leave, but that these soon escaped and came back. The account of the Union occupation concluded, "We could go on and write a week, and then the half could not be told of the destruction and ravaging committed by the Yankees during the two days' sojourn of their army in Jackson." In this, at least, General Grant agreed with his foes. He said that Sherman "did the work most efficiently."[3]

Quite apart from what the civilians experienced was the small-scale military action that continued during the time the enemy occupied the town. Sharpshooters were stationed at likely spots to pick off their opposite numbers on the Confederate side. Samuel C. Jones of the 22nd Iowa was in charge of the sharpshooters on May 16, and, by his account, they had a lively time of it. He said, "The zip zip is as frequent as it is familiar. The boys have a way of locating their enemy by putting their hats on the muzzles of their guns, and pushing them a little out from behind the trees, when zip goes a bullet through them. The smoke of his gun locates the enemy, then it is his turn to take care of himself. Thus we are engaged in killing and maiming. This is war."[4]

A distinguished visitor was there to see the aftermath of the Federal occupation of Jackson. He was Captain Arthur James Lyon Fremantle of the Coldstream Guards who had taken a leave of absence to travel to the Confederacy. He did not represent Queen Victoria; he simply had a professional interest in the war, and his desire to see the South grew out of his admiration for the gallantry of her officers and men. He landed in Matamoros, Mexico, in early April, crossed the Rio Grande into Brownsville, Texas, and began making his way north and east toward Mississippi. He lodged with citizens along the way. He was struck by the poverty of the Mississippi women he found watching over and working their little farms while their men were away at war. "It is impossible to exaggerate the unfortunate condition of the women left behind in these farm houses," he said. "They have scarcely any clothes, and nothing but the coarsest bacon to eat, and are in miserable uncertainty as to the fate of their relations, whom they hardly ever communicate with. Their slaves, however, generally remain true to them."[5]

Though the women were poor, Fremantle was favorably impressed by their gentility. He said of one that she was "well-mannered, and exceedingly well educated; very far superior to a woman of her station in England." Moreover, their ardor for the war was not diminished. They were "red-hot in favor of fighting for their independence to the last." They had "unbounded confidence" in General Joseph E. Johnston. As for Johnston's soldiers, Fremantle became increasingly impressed by their courage and élan. He said, "It appears to me that the Confederates possess certain great qualities as soldiers, such as individual bravery and natural aptitude in the use of firearms, strong, determined patriotism, and boundless confidence in their favorite generals, and in themselves. They are sober of necessity, as there is literally no liquor to be got. They have sufficient good sense to know that a certain amount of discipline is absolutely necessary; and I believe that instances of insubordination are extremely rare."[6]

En route to meet Johnston, Fremantle and his party heard that the Confederates had retreated to Canton and that Jackson had fallen. Reaching the capital, Captain Fremantle observed the destruction the Yankees had wrought, the pillaged houses and the ransacked stores, even the burned Roman Catholic Church, "together with many other buildings which could in no way be identified with the Confederate government. The whole town is a miserable wreck." The population simmered with a desire for vengeance. Fremantle said, "Nothing could exceed the intense hatred and fury with which its excited citizens speak of the outrages they have undergone—of their desire for a bloody revenge, and of their hope that the Black Flag might be raised." He also heard General Pemberton "abused by all."[7]

Finally, on May 20, he reached army headquarters at Canton. In contrast to the excited and passionate citizens in the capital, Fremantle found General Johnston to be "calm, deliberate, and confident." He was "rather below middle height, spare, soldier like, and well set up; his features are good, and he has lately taken to wearing a grayish beard." Fremantle said, "To me he was extremely affable, but certainly possesses the power of keeping people at a distance when he chooses, and his officers evidently stand in great awe of him." Johnston told Fremantle that he would try to relieve Vicksburg "if he could get adequate reinforcements."[8]

Reinforcements were reporting for duty. On May 20, the brigade of General States Rights Gist arrived from General P. G. T. Beauregard in South Carolina. That same day, General William W. Loring brought in his division. They had become separated from General Pemberton after Champion Hill and did not follow him into Vicksburg. On May 21, Brigadier Generals Matthew D. Ector and Evander McNair brought in their men. General Braxton Bragg in Tennessee had sent them west. On May 23, Brigadier General Samuel B. Maxey's brigade came from Major General Franklin Gardner, who was at Port Hudson. And on or about June 1, Colonel Hylan B. Lyon announced to General Johnston that he and the 8th Kentucky Mounted Infantry had come out from Vicksburg and were at Raymond. Lyon reported that they had had a close encounter with one of the cavalry patrols of Brigadier General Peter Osterhaus, who was with his division at Big Black River. Osterhaus informed his superiors of the encounter on May 30. He said, "Patrol No. 1 went on the road where the rebels were seen in the afternoon, leading from our Big Black River hospital (Smith's Plantation), into the Raymond road. On the arrival at the point in question, the enemy had changed his position and had moved in a northern direction. They were about 300 strong, under a Colonel or Major Lyon, and all of the Eighth Kentucky. The regiment . . . is now on a patrolling and cotton-burning tour." Osterhaus was frustrated that Lyon's Rebels would not stand and fight on that day, but they would meet again.[9]

On June 2, Lyon received a new assignment. By Special Orders No. 93, he was "assigned to the command of all cavalry force in the direction of Clinton. . . . Colonel Lyon will establish his headquarters as near Big Black as possible, and send his scouting parties as far in advance as he can, and will give every protection in his power to the people of that region by checking and preventing marauding incursions by the enemy." Lyon's immediate superior would be Major General John C. Breckinridge, his fellow Kentuckian.[10]

General Breckinridge had arrived by rail on June 1, having been ordered west by Braxton Bragg. Breckinridge brought with him 5200 men, the brigades of Daniel W. Adams, Ben Hardin Helm, and William Preston (the last commanded at this time by Marcellus A. Stovall). With them was Robert Cobb's battery of artillery, the very artillery unit that Lyon had organized back in 1861. Any reunion that Lyon and his regiment may have had with their old friends from Camp Boone and Bowling Green was necessarily a brief one. General Johnston assigned Breckinridge the command of Jackson, and he went to work at once, "sending out reconnaissances in force toward the Federals near the Big Black River. He impressed local slaves to act as hospital stewards and called on Governor John J. Pettus for an additional two hundred Negroes to work on Jackson's defenses." Breckinridge's biographer, William C. Davis, adds, "With the fall of Vicksburg imminent, he worked feverishly to put Jackson in shape for a defense, as well as to serve as a base for an attack on Grant."[11]

In their constant patrols for General Breckinridge along the Big Black, Lyon and his men again faced the troops of Brigadier General Peter Osterhaus. Osterhaus's men were rebuilding the burned railroad bridge on the Big Black, guarding the hospitals around Champion Hill, and keeping a watch on Johnston to prevent him from making a surprise march behind General Grant at Vicksburg. Lyon's troopers and Osterhaus's frequently clashed. "Yesterday night," Osterhaus reported on June 6, "my pickets beyond the river, on the Edwards Station road, were attacked by some rebel force. There was quite lively firing for some time, and the commander of my picket considered it prudent to fall back on the infantry picket at bayou bridge. . . . The enemy, which I found out since was the Eighth Kentucky Mounted Infantry, did not follow up." This was the kind of slashing, hit fast and back out faster kind of action that Lyon seemed to enjoy. The next day, informants told Osterhaus that the 20th and 22nd Mississippi Mounted Infantry had joined the 8th Kentucky, and he asked for more cavalry to meet Lyon's ersatz brigade. In the meantime, Lyon did not let up. Before more mounted forces could arrive to aid Osterhaus, Lyon's horsemen attacked the harried general's outposts again.[12]

Lyon's men had faster horses than the Federals, as Osterhaus pointed out in his account of the skirmish that occurred on the morning of June 7. The 6th Missouri Cavalry (U.S.) had come away with two prisoners of the 20th Mississippi Mounted Infantry; Major Samuel Montgomery explained to Osterhaus that "he could not secure more, these fellows being better mounted than expected." That afternoon, Montgomery thought he had all three of Lyon's regiments trapped. He caught up with them near Hall's Ferry and charged. A four-mile chase resulted before the Rebels split into smaller bands and got away. They were "better mounted than anticipated," Osterhaus reported. The fast and fluid Confederates continued to hover near Osterhaus's headquarters, shouting taunts that they were just the vanguard of a larger force, and forming in battle line and firing into the Union pickets before fading away.[13]

There were more peaceful interactions occasionally. Lyon sent Osterhaus a note through the lines on June 8 that furthered a humanitarian aim. "Your ambulances under flag of truce will be permitted to move your sick and wounded from Champion Hill Hospital and the hospitals in its vicinity. I will be glad to have your ambulance train move the Confederate wounded from the hospitals near the Big Black Bridge." He added, "I hope for the honor of your Government you will not permit violations of your flag of truce."[14]

The next day, it was back to the more familiar work of war when the 8th Kentucky attacked Osterhaus's pickets on the Edwards Station Road. They left behind a man, either by capture or intentionally to spread misinformation among the enemy that "General Johnston will soon attack Snyder's Bluff and Breckinridge Big Black Bridge." Osterhaus was getting his fill of Lyon and took to gossiping about him in his reports to Grant's headquarters. "By the way," he said in a communiqué dated June 10, 1863, "I have to state that this Colonel Lyon is described as overbearing, and toward our wounded at Champion's Hill a very rude character."[15]

Osterhaus did not know that he was soon to be given a break from Lyon's constant aggression. On June 11, by Special Orders No. 101, Colonel Lyon was "temporarily relieved from his present duty, and will immediately proceed to the southwestern part of this department, in the vicinity of Port Hudson, and assume command of all troops there." His specific assignment was to "use every exertion to interrupt the progress of the siege of Port Hudson, and to harass the enemy by intercepting his supplies, cutting off his communications, attacking his detachments, or in any manner you may deem practicable. . . . General Johnston has selected you for this very important duty because of his confidence in your skill and judgment, and has no doubt that it will be well performed." In his memoir, Lyon remembered what Johnston did not include in the written orders. Johnston told Lyon that he was "to cut his way to Port Hudson and show General [Franklin] Gardner how to cut his way out."[16]

Johnston had wanted Gardner to "cut his way out" of Port Hudson since before the beginning of the investment. Gardner delayed until he found himself completely besieged. General Nathaniel Banks had fourteen thousand men to Gardner's seven thousand, and while Gardner did repulse an attack on May 27, the outlook remained grim. Gardner pleaded for reinforcements. Johnston "repeated my order to him to evacuate the place, informed him that he could not be reinforced, and told him to march toward Jackson." Pemberton, too, had been urging Gardner to escape. He wrote to him from Vicksburg on May 4, "You must come and bring with you 5000 cavalry." However, Gardner was under the same orders as Pemberton; namely, that he must defend his post at all costs, and he would not evacuate Port Hudson. He delayed until he had no other choice except to hold on.[17]

General Johnston wanted Gardner out, and he dispatched Colonel Lyon to lead the escape. Lyon arrived on the outskirts of Port Hudson in mid-June. He found that his opponent was Benjamin Grierson. He must have longed for a larger force with which to strike the Yankee cavalryman who had led everyone on such a frustrating chase back in April and May, but he discovered that he had too few men available to be able to hit Grierson very hard. Certainly, he could not rescue General Gardner as Johnston wanted. All Lyon could hope to do was harass the Federal trains, and his chance came about a week after his arrival when he attacked a wagon escort of Grierson's men and captured seven wagons and fifty prisoners before "putting the remainder to flight." Such small actions did nothing to lift the siege. Subsequent attacks on the enemy's wagon trains were of so little importance that they were not mentioned in the Union reports, and Lyon, as was typical, submitted no report of his own. His only reference to it was in his memoirs, when he said that "after capturing a large number of wagons and their teams, [he] was returned to his command on Big Black River."[18]

He was back on the Big Black by late June, and his brigade was increased to 2500 men. He now commanded his own 8th Kentucky, plus the 3rd, 16th, 20th, and 22nd Mississippi. As before, General Osterhaus was flummoxed by his inability to limit the free movements of Lyon's horse soldiers. He said, "They are of no desperate description, but they make their appearance at almost any point from Bridgeport Ferry to Baldwin's Ferry, and are busily engaged, besides so watching our movements, in collecting negroes and articles of subsistence."[19]

Johnston now had over 31,000 effectives in and around Jackson. He had promised Pemberton that he would march to his relief as soon as General Breckinridge's division joined him, yet, a month later, only Lyon's brigade of mounted infantry showed any aggressiveness at all. The "Army of Relief" had not moved a mile. Johnston found that he had a serious deficit in wagons and explained that he must delay any advance until that situation improved. Richmond was urging him to move. Johnston resisted the suggestion. He protested, "The odds against me are much greater than those you express," and he added the startling statement, "I consider saving Vicksburg hopeless." Secretary of War Seddon replied, "Your telegram grieves and alarms me. Vicksburg must not be lost without a desperate struggle. The interest and honor of the Confederacy forbid it." He told Johnston that he must act to save Vicksburg. Johnston was adamant that the odds he faced were impossibly long. "I think you do not appreciate the difficulties in the course you direct, not the probabilities or consequences of failure," he said. Seddon was equally insistent and told him that the eyes of the Confederacy were on him, and that "it were better to fail nobly doing than, through prudence even, to be inactive. . . . I rely on you for all possible [efforts] to save Vicksburg."[20]

Richmond was not demoralized, and the defenders of Vicksburg still had hope. They held fast to the belief that they could emerge victorious. "We expected relief from General Johnston, in which event we hoped to destroy our adversaries," one soldier said; but Johnston was a commander who did not like to attack unless conditions were ideal, and he could see nothing but difficulties. His bleak outlook was further depressed by the misinformation being supplied to him by a trusted informant, Charles S. Bell, who was, in reality, a Union spy. Bell convinced Johnston that Grant had 85,000 men outside of Vicksburg, a daunting number that was too high by twenty thousand. Johnston stalled Richmond as long as he could while he, feeling sadly misunderstood and unappreciated, struggled bravely to improve his chances. Finally, on June 28, Johnston decided that he could delay no longer. He said, "The supplies and field transportation having been procured, the equipment of the artillery completed, and a serviceable floating bridge finished (the first construction proved a failure), the army was ordered to march next morning toward the Big Black River." The departure date of June 29 was overly optimistic; the army did not begin its march until July 1.[21]

By the time Johnston finally moved to the relief of Vicksburg, Pemberton's men were nearing the end of their endurance. They had been on quarter rations for days. The side items on the menu were half-ripe blackberries, cane shoots, and bread made of ground peas; the main course was mule meat and rats. They were weakened by their poor diet and worn down by constant duty on the firing line. Major Samuel H. Lockett said that "no man within the lines had been off duty more than a small part of each day; and in response to inquiries of the lieutenant-general commanding, every general officer and colonel had reported his men as physically exhausted and unfit for any duty but simply standing in the trenches and firing." Their barricades were battered to pieces, their ammunition was low, and many of their artillery pieces had been dismounted. To have any chance of saving Vicksburg, the Army of Relief would have to make a rapid march. Johnston would have to drive his men. Instead, he called a halt at the Big Black River.[22]

For more than two days they reconnoitered. On July 3, Johnston wrote to Pemberton that he expected to attack Grant on the 7th. When he did, Pemberton must attack from the other direction and try to break out. Johnston repeated his overworked platitude, "If Vicksburg cannot be saved, the garrison must." However, by the time his reconnaissance ended, Johnston was showing renewed signs of the hesitancy that had afflicted him since the siege began. He wrote, "Reconnaissances to which the 2d, 3d, and 4th of July were devoted, convinced me that no attack upon the Federal position, north of the railroad, was practicable. They confirmed the previous reports of our scouts, that the besieging army was covered by a line of fieldworks, extending from the railroad-bridge of the Yazoo; that the roads leading to this line had all been obstructed with felled trees, and that strong bodies of Federal infantry and cavalry observed and guarded the river."[23]

On the morning of July 4, the Confederates on the bank of the Big Black noticed for the first time since mid-May that the guns in the direction of Vicksburg were silent. When and how their suspicion that Vicksburg had fallen was confirmed varies from account to account. It may be that each is true. An army is a large organization, and different things happen at different times to different parts of it. William C. Davis says that a Union prisoner confirmed Pemberton's surrender late on the evening of July 4, and Johnston seemed to confirm this in his *Narrative*. The men and officers did not learn of the surrender until the next morning, July 5. Lyon wrote, "The 8th Kentucky Regiment was the advance of one of the Divisions, and was crossing Big Black River when an order to retreat was given, as Vicksburg had surrendered the day before (the 4th of July)."[24]

Now Johnston had a new problem. The Federals were free to turn on him, and he was in the open, twenty-five miles from the works that General Breckinridge had been preparing so diligently. Johnston's counter-march was made with uncharacteristic speed. The weather was hot, and the roads were deep with dust. The men suffered from thirst. Water was scarce, and Johnston purposely ruined what water there was in order to hinder the march of the army that he knew would be coming up behind him. He ordered his men to leave the carcasses of farm animals in ponds and cisterns along the road. General Loring lingered behind, waiting for the enemy to appear. He fought General Osterhaus in a three-hour delaying action on July 6. The Southerners suffered heavy casualties, fell back, and the Federals came on. Even the Almighty seemed to have turned his face from the Confederates, for after weeks of dry heat and clear skies, the clouds gathered, and a drenching rain began to fall on the night of July 7. The whole countryside was dappled with pools of fresh water and the bluecoats drank their fill. Of course, the rain presented the Federals with a different hindrance—mud—but these were men hardened to discomfort, and they marched on through the muck with high spirits. They believed that their capture of Vicksburg would soon bring the war to an end; there was just this one last detail to attend to.

The citizens of Jackson knew they were coming. They had suffered through one visitation of the Yankees, and they heard now from their country neighbors that the approaching Union troops were "burning every dwelling they pass." Even if by some miracle Johnston were able to hold them back, the capital was sure to be shelled. The people prepared to flee. A reporter for the *Lancaster* (SC) *Ledger* filed a report from Jackson on July 8 that said, "Everything is in the wildest state of excitement here, the citizens are flying in every direction. The streets are filled with stock, negroes, families, ox carts and every species of conveyance." Some made good their escape; many others were too late.[25]

Their defenders, the Confederate cavalry, were pushed steadily back. On July 9, they were skirmishing only three miles out of the city, and by July 10, nine U.S. divisions were on the outskirts of Jackson. There was heavy skirmishing and artillery fire through the day, and on July 11, the Federals attacked. Johnston was still positioning his troops. General Abraham Buford's brigade of Loring's division was northwest of the city, on the extreme right of Johnston's defensive line, on the Pearl River. From right to left, they were ordered to fall in: 12th Louisiana, 3rd Kentucky, 7th Kentucky, and 8th Kentucky. The 8th Kentucky was working on a line of breastworks when the enemy appeared. A veteran of the regiment later remembered that Colonel Lyon called in his skirmishers and ordered his men to lie down. When the enemy approached, he gave the order, "Rise up—forward—commence firing." The veteran said that the fight that followed was "hot and furious, the enemy in many instances falling within ten or fifteen paces of our line. This sort of work could not last long; but no sign of giving way was manifested along the line of the 8th, watched over and guided as it was by Colonel Lyon."

Buford rushed the other regiments of his brigade to where the 8th Kentucky was fighting, and the Yankees recoiled. In this test of Confederate strength, the 8th Kentucky, on whom the attack fell most heavily, suffered a loss of one-third of its numbers killed and wounded.[26]

The Kentuckians went back to work fortifying their position, where they "had the fun of receiving Sherman's artillery fire without the privilege of re-plying to it." Little wonder that they welcomed the civilian "walking saloons," who appeared in camp and wandered through, selling whiskey at a dollar a swig. That afternoon, the enemy made a demonstration on the Confederate left center, which had no better success than the morning attempt, but which did cost Johnston another 140 men. When the Federals fell back, the Con-federates sent out parties to burn the houses that the enemy had turned into sharpshooters' nests.[27]

On the morning of July 12, the enemy opened an artillery barrage on the Confederate left. They charged the position of Cobb's Battery and "were re-pulsed with heavy loss." The Southerners captured three hundred prisoners and three strands of colors, and the rumor spread that General Osterhaus had been killed. The Rebels grasped at any chance to feel elated, for the overall signs were ominous: the Yankees were still arriving, and they were extending their line to the right. With the enemy's numbers growing by the hour and their lines forever growing beyond the Confederate flanks, even the greenest recruit in the Confederate trenches could foresee what the outcome would be.[28]

In the midst of all this national drama, small personal dramas were also being played out. On July 13, General Pemberton and his staff arrived in Jackson, fresh from Vicksburg. By the terms of his parole, Pemberton was to report to General Johnston. This he did, and it led to an uncomfortable scene. Johnston saw Pemberton approaching and he rushed forward to greet him. He said, "Well, Jack, old boy, I am certainly glad to see you," and he offered his hand. In reply, Pemberton snapped to attention, gave a salute, and said, "General Johnston, according to the terms of parole prescribed by General Grant, I was directed to report to you." Shelby Foote says, "The two men stood for a moment in silence as Johnston lowered his unclasped hand. Then Pemberton saluted once more, punctiliously formal, and turned away." This was the last meeting between Pemberton, "the general who tried and failed," and Johnston, "the general who failed to try."[29]

The Federals continued to lengthen their lines until the Confederate works were surrounded on the north, south, and west, and they kept up an almost continual fire. The Rebels were being pounded to pieces and so was the city behind them. On July 15, Union artillery fire destroyed an entire block of Jack-son, and a shell went through Johnston's headquarters. The enemy was ob-served "planting siege guns on their redoubts." Artillery was the key to victory for Sherman. On the day of the heaviest artillery fire yet, July 15, Loring's and W. H. T. Walker's divisions repulsed an infantry attack, but nothing stopped the U.S. shells from falling. The next night, July 16, 1863, the Confederates began withdrawing from Jackson. They crossed the Pearl River on pontoon bridges and moved east, taking with them the sick and wounded and every moveable piece of government property. Johnston was masterful in the art of retreat and throughout the war his habit was to leave behind nothing useful for the enemy. They traveled for two days in the direction of Meridian before halting at the Deer River.[30]

General William T. Sherman wrote his brother, "I let the enemy move, pursuing him only to ensure a good Start. I have sent North and destroyed Railroads locomotives cars etc at Canton, and a large Bridge 12 miles beyond, and I have cavalry doing destruction 60 miles south to Brookham, and four thousand men are working to destroy Railroads here." Jackson itself received the full effects of Sherman's destructive genius. He blandly said, "Jackson will never again be a point where our enemy can assemble and threaten us on the River." Sherman's words, while accurate, lacked his usual flair for description. In this instance, it was the new name bestowed on Jackson by Sherman's men that unveiled the true condition of the city when their visit was done. To them, Jackson had become Chimneyville.[31]

On July 23, 1863, Sherman pulled his men back to the Big Black River where they camped and awaited their hard-earned furloughs. Grant said, "I wrote to Sherman: 'Impress upon the men the importance of going through the State in an orderly manner, abstaining from taking anything not absolutely necessary for their subsistence while traveling. They should try to create as favorable an impression as possible upon the people.'" Sherman ignored the order and made no effort to restrain his men. In a July 28 letter to his brother-in-law, Sherman said, "Our men are now all Expert thieves, sparing nothing not even the clothes of women children & Negros. Nothing is left between Vicksburg & Jackson so I can have peace here." The Confederate soldiers in the field knew that their families were suffering and would suffer more before they could return to them. Colonel Hylan B. Lyon was not spared the pain of personal tragedy. On July 23, back in Eddyville, his first born child, Hugh S. Lyon, died at the age of seventeen months.[32]

8

THE WAR CHILD AND THE WIZARD

After the fall of Jackson, Colonel Lyon received the order to report to General Braxton Bragg in Chattanooga, and the evidence is that he took his grieving wife with him. In November 1863, Laura O'Hara Lyon became pregnant with their second child.

Lyon had undoubtedly heard about Bragg from General Breckinridge or Captain Robert Cobb, and it is unlikely that the assignment pleased him. General Bragg had a reputation for hating Kentuckians since the fall of 1862. During the Kentucky invasion that culminated in the Battle of Perryville (October 8, 1862), Bragg had beseeched the boys of the Bluegrass State to hasten to his army and take the opportunity to liberate their state from the grip of the Northern tyrants. They did not respond to his call. They did not take up the rifles he had brought for their use, and Bragg returned to Tennessee, defeated, blaming them for the failure of his campaign. Bragg continued to brood through the fall and winter on the Kentuckians' rejection of the chance he had offered them, and he punished them for it when he sent their sons and brothers in the 1st Kentucky Brigade on a suicidal charge at Stones River on January 2, 1863. It was at the end of that slaughter that their distraught division commander, John C. Breckinridge, gave the men their enduring name, the Orphan Brigade.

Things were relatively quiet for several months after the terrible fight at Murfreesboro, but in the summer of 1863, Bragg let himself be maneuvered out of Middle Tennessee by General William S. Rosecrans and the Army of the Cumberland. He struck back at the Battle of Chickamauga (September 19–20, 1863), where he handed the Cumberlanders their worst defeat of the war. He followed them back to Chattanooga, but he ignored the advice of Nathan Bedford Forrest and others to attack the Yankees and finish the job. He decided instead to put Chattanooga under siege and starve Rosecrans's army into surrender. Simultaneously, he had to keep an eye on General Ambrose Burnside at Knoxville and take measures to keep him from advancing to

Rosecrans's aid. He sent the corps of General James Longstreet, who had come to him on loan from the Army of Northern Virginia, to keep Burnside at bay. With Longstreet was Major General Joseph Wheeler and his cavalry.

In Chattanooga, Bragg had lost the momentum. He was stalled, and he had no work for Colonel Lyon when he reported to headquarters on November 10, 1863. Bragg sent him on to General Wheeler. The note of introduction said that Lyon "applies for cavalry and I send him to you; but not for a command until you try him. Employ him on staff duty, giving him small commands occasionally to try him until you can discover his calibre and then decide for yourself."[1]

When Lyon arrived at Wheeler's headquarters two or three days later, he found a situation entirely different than that at Chattanooga. Longstreet's army was in motion, pressing Burnside's men back toward their works in Knoxville, and it did not take long for General Wheeler to find an assignment for Lyon. On November 19, he ordered the Kentuckian to "proceed to Kingston, Tenn., and take command of the cavalry at that point, reporting at least four times a day to General Longstreet."[2]

At Kingston, Lyon commanded two regiments of cavalry, an aggregate of 320 men. In front of him, he found two mounted Federal regiments (he was not sure if they were cavalry or mounted infantry), and two field pieces.

General Wheeler, c. 1863.
Library of Congress.

He sent his first dispatch to General Longstreet at 8:00 PM, November 20. He indicated right away that, despite Wheeler's order, he would not be sending dispatches four times a day. "I suppose it will not be necessary to report any more often than I have something of importance to report," he said. On this occasion, he did. He described what he had before him and asked, "Is it your desire that I should attack and attempt to drive these Federals beyond Clinch River?" Lyon had been in East Tennessee less than two weeks and was already champing at the bit. Longstreet directed his reply to General Wheeler. He repeated Lyon's description of the Union forces in Kingston and said, "It appears to me that you could capture this party by throwing a brigade in rear of it at Clinton, and increasing Colonel Lyon's force by one other regiment and a battery. . . . To execute, he should attack at Kingston after the other force has had time to get in rear of it." He gave Wheeler the option of sending a force forward or leading it himself but urged him in any case to move quickly so that he could return in time to join the main action against Burnside.[3]

Wheeler decided to lead the party in person. He and his men marched over narrow and neglected mountain roads, and they arrived worn out on November 24. They found the Federals were in position, prepared to meet them. Wheeler sent skirmishers forward. When they could discover no weak spot in the Federal line, Wheeler ordered his men to withdraw. The enemy did not follow. The action that was precipitated by Lyon's dispatch to General Longstreet came to an end and with it the Kentuckian's one and only chance to prove "his calibre" in the East Tennessee Campaign, for as the retreat ended, General Wheeler received orders to report with his staff to General Bragg in Chattanooga, and Colonel Lyon went with him.

They did not find Bragg in Chattanooga. On November 24, Bragg had been defeated in a preliminary action on the slopes of Lookout Mountain, and on November 25, his main line had been shattered on Missionary Ridge. The Army of Tennessee had fled in panic, abandoning their field pieces and flinging away their muskets and knapsacks as they raced down the back of the ridge. Wheeler and company found them en route to Dalton, Georgia, and helped cover the retreat. Colonel Lyon took command of the artillery at the request of Colonel James H. Hollenquist, an old acquaintance from the West Point days who now served as Bragg's chief of artillery. Lyon said that "although it was seriously apprehended that by a Federal charge the artillery could be easily captured, the artillery was so handled as to avoid any charge made, and reached Dalton in good condition." If he expected to see the four guns of Cobb's battery once they were safe in Dalton, he was disappointed. They had been lost with the other thirty-seven field pieces that were abandoned during Bragg's retreat. When Lyon went to report his safe arrival to General Bragg, he found the commanding general completely unstrung, too demoralized to receive him. He made the report instead to Bragg's adjutant general, Colonel George W. Brent. On December 1, 1863, Bragg was relieved of command of the Army of Tennessee by his own request, and on December 27, his successor arrived. One can only speculate what Lyon thought when he saw that the new commander was the man whose department he had left just weeks earlier, General Joseph E. Johnston.[4]

Johnston ordered a review of the troops at Dalton, and what he saw did not encourage him. The Army of Tennessee was ragged and painfully reduced in strength, only about 36,000 men, and Johnston watched as this army of scarecrows "fell into ranks from the tentless camps, 6000 without arms, thrown away in the recent rout, many yet with bare feet, few with blankets. The horses that guided the guns and caissons down the hill were too poor to bring them back." Nevertheless, despite the wretched condition of the men, President Davis was urging Johnston to go on the offensive and reclaim Middle Tennessee. Johnston's response was typical of what made the president despise him and his soldiers worship him. He did not advance to battle in Middle Tennessee. Instead, he devoted his time to outfitting his men with new uniforms, arms, good tents, blankets, and plenty of rations, and building up his army with recruits.[5]

Not that the soldiers were left idle. Johnston's other typical characteristic was his constant urge to fall back, and that was in his mind even in his first weeks in Dalton. He ordered the roads back to Resaca, fifteen miles south, to be rebuilt or repaired. At the same time, he ordered Wheeler's cavalry to keep watch on the Yankees to the north. Wheeler's patrols engaged "in almost continual conflicts with the advanced posts of the enemy, capturing prisoners, horses, arms, etc., almost daily." Lyon seems to have seen little of these attacks on wagon trains and attacks on Union outposts. By December, he was acting as Wheeler's chief of staff and was more involved in managing the volume of correspondence and the myriad of office details than in crossing blades with the Federals. Wheeler needed an efficient chief of staff, for, as one biographer says, he was a "notoriously poor administrator and record-keeper." With Johnston's approval and Lyon's help, Wheeler established schools "whose mission was to ensure that officers and men alike 'would be properly instructed in cavalry tactics.'" The number of recruits coming in made the training doubly important. Colonel Lyon spent some time on recruiting duty in Alabama, and it speaks well of his skills in drawing volunteers from the ever-dwindling pool of Southern manpower that Wheeler had approximately nine thousand effectives by the commencement of the 1864 spring campaign. Lyon was not on hand to see how well his enlistees fought when General Sherman moved south in May, the beginning of the Atlanta Campaign. He had been ordered to rejoin his regiment in Mississippi. His brigade commander would be Brigadier General Abraham Buford, and his division commander would be Major General Nathan Bedford Forrest.[6]

General Wheeler was "Fighting Joe," the Confederate "War Child," and his reputation as a cavalry leader was well earned. But no one—not Wheeler, not John Hunt Morgan, not J. E. B. Stuart nor Fitzhugh Lee—was the match of Nathan Bedford Forrest for raw courage and aggressiveness. Hodding Carter said that "Forrest, in peacetime an almost illiterate Memphis slave trader, was a daring cavalryman, a brilliant strategist, and a killer." At the beginning of the war, Forrest was a self-made millionaire and a Memphis city alderman. However, he was no gentleman. He had grown up in the lowest rung of Southern society, a world of prickly honor and sudden blood-letting, where, as Brian Steel Wills says, "he learned to use any means at his disposal to disarm and defeat his foes. Exacerbated by a quick temper and an assertive personality, this intimidating element became a decisive part of Forrest's personal arsenal. He learned that he could obtain desired results in this manner, often without fighting, simply by overwhelming an opponent or potential opponent with his reputation." Of course, he earned that reputation by swift movement, unpredictable tactics, and a bold, even reckless appetite for violence. At times he would hit suddenly, fight with bared fang intensity, and

General Forrest, c. 1863.
Library of Congress.

disappear as quickly as he had appeared; at other times he would stand toe to toe with the enemy and slug it out. Utterly untrained except by experience, his reading of battle conditions was so intuitive, his ability to improvise on the spot such a rare quality, that his various war names evoked the supernatural. Forrest was the "wizard," he was the "devil."[7]

Forrest's approach to fighting was grounded in brutal reality, however. He never turned his back on the harsh lessons of his youth. Some held Forrest's hardscrabble background and low-class livelihood against him and disapproved his rough-handed style of leadership. Some refused to serve with him. One young squire cited his lack of gentility and his civilian life as "a negro trader, gambler." While conceding that Forrest "may be and no doubt it the best Cav officer in the West," he nevertheless objected "to a tyrannical, hot headed vulgarians' commanding me." Forrest was a man with the bark still on, and he never acquired the polish that would satisfy those who disdained him, but his detractors did not include Hylan B. Lyon. The early Forrest biographer John Allen Wyeth said that Lyon was "one of Forrest's most devoted followers," adding that Lyon, too, was a "stubborn fighter."[8]

Lyon had first seen Forrest in action at Fort Donelson. He fought at Shiloh while Lyon was a prisoner in Fort Warren, Massachusetts; fought in Middle Tennessee and the first part of the Perryville Campaign; returned to West Tennessee to wreck the Federals' railroad supply line during Grant's first Vicksburg Campaign; fought at Chickamauga; and was at the siege of Chattanooga until he argued with Bragg over the re-assignment of his cavalry. The climactic confrontation between Forrest and Bragg at army headquarters revealed much about how Forrest chaffed under the command of another. He reviewed his mistreatment under Bragg's hand going back to 1862 and ended by saying, "I have stood your meanness as long as I intend to. You have played the part of a damned scoundrel, and are a coward, and if you were any part of a man I would slap your jaws and force you to resent it. You may as well not issue any orders to me, for I will not obey them, and I will hold you personally responsible for any further indignities you endeavor to inflict upon me. You have threatened to arrest me for not obeying your orders promptly. I dare you to do it, and I say to you that if you ever again try to interfere with me or cross my path it will be at the peril of your life." Shortly after, President Davis authorized Forrest to leave Bragg and return to Mississippi, where he would have an independent command. Called by the rather imprecise title of Forrest's Cavalry Department, it embraced the cavalry of West Tennessee and North Mississippi.[9]

Forrest built his command as quickly as he could add recruits to the regiments the government assigned to him. He soon became such a nuisance to General William T. Sherman that the Ohioan wrote to his wife, "It is exceedingly difficult to deal with these Mounted Devils and I am sure all we can do is to make the Country feel that the People must pay for all these wandering Arabs."[10]

At the time Colonel Hylan B. Lyon arrived to join them in late May, Forrest and his men were flush with victory. They had just made two notable raids on Paducah, Kentucky, and an equally successful but far more controversial attack on Fort Pillow, Tennessee. Already, the fight at Fort Pillow was being called a massacre, but Forrest's cavalry were unconcerned by what they considered Yankee propaganda. They were at or near full strength and no one could catch them, and no one could defeat them. Colonel Lyon was assigned to command the Kentucky Brigade in General Buford's division.

Buford was a Kentuckian and a cousin of General John Buford, the Federal cavalryman of Gettysburg fame, and of General Napoleon Buford (John's brother), who had served under U. S. Grant and John Pope in the river campaigns of the West. Abraham Buford was a graduate of Centre College in Danville, Kentucky, and of West Point, class of 1841. He was a veteran of the Mexican War, and he remained in the service until the mid-1850s, when he resigned his commission in order to return to Kentucky. Life on his horse and cattle farm, Bosque Bonita, suited him perfectly. His devotion to the pastoral life kept Buford out of the first year and a half of the war between North and South. He did not join the Confederates until Bragg's invasion of the state in the fall of 1862. At that time, he raised the 3rd, 5th, and 6th Kentucky Cavalry and helped to cover Bragg's withdrawal from the state. Afterward, Buford was formally appointed brigadier general. He traveled west in January 1863 to take part in the Vicksburg Campaign and served under General William W. Loring until he joined Forrest in March 1864. Some found him to be pleasant company and the epitome of Kentucky hospitality. Lieutenant Mercer Otey of Forrest's staff, in his reminiscence of the war years, wrote, "We enjoyed a visit when Gen. Buford dropped by at our headquarters, for he was a genial, jovial companion, full of war reminiscences, and generally his chief commissary kept a supply of good Nelson County Bourbon, which he always sat before us when we returned the General's visit." There was another, less cheerful view of him. Marshall D. Krolick says in *Kentuckians in Gray* that Buford was "an extremely large man for the times, weighing well over three hundred pounds and standing over six feet tall. His character matched his size, as he was aggressive, domineering, and very much a martinet."[11]

In the spring of 1864, Colonel Lyon hardly knew Buford. Buford had first commanded Lyon and the 8th Kentucky Infantry in April 1863, just before the start of Grierson's Raid. Much of the time since then, however, Lyon had been on detached service and had had no real opportunity to form an opinion of the man, certainly not as a division commander. In the months ahead, Lyon would come to know Buford well. By the time their association was over, Lyon would not think as highly of Buford as Lieutenant Mercer Otey did.

During the first week of May 1864, General William T. Sherman began his Atlanta Campaign. His supply line stretched back to Nashville, and it was essential that he protect it. He remembered how General Don Carlos Buell's North Alabama Campaign had been defeated in the summer of 1862, not by direct attack but by Confederate raiders who, at very little risk to themselves, hit the railroads that kept Buell's men fed, clothed, and armed. Sherman was especially concerned about Nathan Bedford Forrest, who he expected to move into Middle Tennessee. Sherman wanted General Samuel D. Sturgis to lead an expedition against Forrest; a serious enough threat coming out of Memphis would keep the Wizard occupied, and Sherman could proceed through Georgia with one less worry.

Sherman had foreseen with perfect clarity what the Confederates were planning. General Joseph E. Johnston wanted to hamper Sherman's advance toward Atlanta by destroying his railroad lifeline. He turned to General Stephen D. Lee, Pemberton's successor in command of what was now called the Department of Alabama, Mississippi, and East Louisiana, and Lee turned to Forrest. On June 1, 1864, Forrest left Tupelo at the head of two thousand horsemen plus a six-gun battery of artillery. Their destination was Middle Tennessee, and their target was the Nashville & Chattanooga Railroad.

Three days out, just as he was about to cross the Tennessee River, a courier caught up with Forrest. He handed Forrest an order from General Lee. He was to return at once. General Sturgis had left Memphis and was moving toward Tupelo. Sturgis's column was eight miles long. He had 4800 hundred foot soldiers, 3300 hundred cavalrymen, four hundred artillerymen with twenty-two cannon, and 250 wagons behind him. General Benjamin Grierson commanded the cavalry, and Colonel William L. McMillen commanded the infantry. McMillen's foot soldiers might have been hated even more than Grierson's infamous cavalry, for they included two regiments of United States Colored Troops and one section of U.S. Colored Light Artillery. On its face, Sturgis's mission was the same as Forrest's, to destroy one of his enemy's lifelines—in this case the Mobile & Ohio Railroad—but an encounter with Forrest was the real intent. Sturgis would keep Forrest in Mississippi, and if he could defeat him, the threat could be eliminated permanently.

Forrest obeyed Lee's order and returned. By June 5, he was back in the vicinity of Tupelo, in position along the Mobile & Ohio Railroad. He had won the race against the Federals, whose massive column had been slowed by soft roads and streams swollen by recent heavy rains. Conditions were so bad that Sturgis had wanted to turn back. It was Colonel McMillen who insisted that they go on. Sturgis reluctantly agreed to continue.

By June 9, Forrest knew where Sturgis was going. The Yankees were marching east along the Ripley-Guntown Road, and Forrest decided to meet them at or near the place where the Pontotoc-Baldwyn Road crossed it, a rustic intersection called Brice's Crossroads. At a council of war that night, Forrest explained the situation to his subordinates. General Buford advised, "Fight 'em, and fight damned quick." Forrest agreed. Orders went out that night for the men to be ready to march before daylight. The Confederates moved west on the Baldwyn Road, with Forrest and his one-hundred-man escort and Lyon's Kentucky Brigade leading the way.[12]

It rained again that night, but on the morning of June 10, the sky was clear, and the sun was broiling hot. More than sixty years later, Captain James Dinkins of Forrest's staff still remembered how the steam rose from the damp roads, making the march "almost unbearable for the men and horses." Forrest sent Lieutenant Robert J. Black and a detachment of the 7th Tennessee Cavalry scouting ahead. Near the crossroads, they bumped into the advance of Grierson's bluecoats and began skirmishing with them. Forrest ordered Colonel Lyon to hurry forward with his eight hundred men and for Bell, who was coming up behind, "to move up fast and fetch all he's got." Buford was ordered to come up as well with the rest of his division and, en route, to send a flanking party to the right.[13]

The fight built slowly. About two miles from the crossroads, a company of the 7th Kentucky Mounted Infantry went forward under Captain C. L. Randle and made contact with the Federals, and Forrest personally ordered Captain Henry A. Tyler to lead two companies of the 12th Kentucky Cavalry forward and see if he could determine exactly how many of the enemy they were up against. They found Colonel George C. Waring's brigade waiting for them. Two companies could not contend with a brigade, and the Confederates fell back under fire. Captain Tyler admitted, "I withdrew perhaps a little faster than I advanced." Forrest now ordered Lyon's entire brigade to form for battle. The Number Fours led the horses to the rear while the rest of the men spread out on either side of the Baldwyn Road. The 3rd Kentucky moved to Randle's support, the 7th Kentucky advanced on the right of the road, the 12th Kentucky on the left, and the 8th Kentucky was held in reserve. They struggled through the cedar scrub, but Henry George said that Colonel Lyon forced the enemy back "and formed his men on the summit of a ridge from which the Federals had been driven." They came under fire, and Lyon ordered his men to pile up logs and fence rails for a barricade. Forrest instructed them to hold their position and not try to advance farther until his other brigades arrived.[14]

When Colonel Edmund W. Rucker's Sixth Brigade came up, Forrest posted it on Lyon's left (south). Two regiments, the 18th Mississippi Cavalry and the 7th Tennessee Cavalry, dismounted and took their place on the firing line, while the 8th Mississippi Cavalry remained in the saddle; they rode over to the extreme left to guard against a flanking movement by Colonel Edward F. Winslow's horse brigade. Colonel William A. Johnson's all-Alabama brigade came up next and was placed on Lyon's right (north), which also put it on the right of the Baldwyn Road.

Now Forrest was ready to advance. He ordered his three-brigade front forward. Johnson and Lyon faced Colonel George E. Waring's brigade. The 7th Indiana Cavalry and the 4th Missouri Cavalry were on the firing line. A third regiment, the 2nd New Jersey, was in reserve and the 3rd and 9th Illinois were posted in front as skirmishers. The 4th Missourians had their battery posted close to the road where it was in position to play most heavily against Lyon's portion of the line. These Federals had been ordered to stand their ground to the last, and this they intended to do. Stewart L. Bennett says, "The skirmish line came to life with heavy fire as the Confederates attacked along the lines of Lyon and Johnson." The Confederates were cheering as they advanced. The men on the Yankees' main line had not been firing, but as soon as the Confederates were within range they delivered such a powerful blast of musketry and artillery fire that the Rebels were forced back to the hill where they had started. They dressed their lines and charged again into a storm of lead and iron. They suffered badly from enemy artillery fire and had to fall back once more. They formed up and charged again. This time, Lyon's men crashed into the Federal battle line. The defenders emptied their seven-shot Spencers at point blank range and then used them as clubs. Rucker's men were firing obliquely into the enemy's right flank, and Lyon's men continued to push them hard from the front, and the Yankee line gave. They fell back, taking their heavy guns with them. The Confederates pursued, and the bluecoats resorted to their Colt revolvers. Their rapid fire slowed down Lyon's men, but the pressure from Rucker's brigade against the Union right was relentless and the Federals were slowly pushed back to the crossroads. They kept fighting at close range the whole way until they formed a tight semi-circle around the tiny cluster of buildings where the roads crossed.[15]

Brice's Crossroads was a clearing of fifty acres or so in which there were a church and cemetery, a store, the two-story home of the William Brice family, and a few dependencies. Seen on the map, the crossroads looked like an elongated capital letter "X" lying on its side so that it resembled a St. Andrews Cross. Heavily traveled though it was, this rural intersection had never seen anything like the hundreds of U.S. cavalrymen that had proudly passed by in the morning and who had now returned. They were shaky and sweaty, leaning wearily against their horses or sprawling bloodied and exhausted on the lawn. They crowded around, grimy from black powder, gasping in the smoky heat. The Confederates who circled them in a half arc a few hundred yards out were in no better condition. Southerners and Northerners alike were suffering from the effects of the Mississippi sun, and the chance to rest for a few minutes was welcome.

It was just after noon, and Forrest had defeated Grierson, but that was just the first part of the Confederate commander's plan. He knew that the Federal infantry would hurry forward when the cavalry engaged, and that was exactly what he wanted. Forrest had told Rucker, "As soon as the fight opens they will send back to have the infantry hurried up. It is going to be as hot as hell, and coming on a run for five or six miles over such roads, their infantry will be so tired out we will ride right over them." Phase One of Forrest's plan had ended in success, and Phase Two was about to commence.[16]

At 1:00 PM, Colonel Bell and his brigade appeared, along with the artillery batteries of Captain John W. Morton and Captain T. W. Rice. General Buford was with them. Forrest said, "On the arrival of the batteries I directed General Buford to move them in position and open fire, in order to develop the position of the enemy's batteries and his lines." Only two Federal guns responded, and Forrest ordered Lyon and Johnson to ease forward and threaten the enemy. Forrest left Buford in command of the center and right, while he rode over to direct the action on the left flank, where Bell's brigade had joined Rucker. This is where Forrest intended to launch his attack. The left advanced through heavy timber to within thirty yards of the Yankees and opened fire. "In a few seconds the engagement became general, and on the left with great fury," said Forrest. "I sent a staff officer to General Buford to move Lyon's and Johnson's brigades forward and press the enemy on the right."[17]

Waring's men began to show signs of collapsing under the weight of Lyon's and Johnson's assault, and it was just as they began to fall back that General Sturgis made his first appearance on the battlefield. He had been traveling with Colonel McMillen and the infantry column. Sturgis found Grierson, who apprised him of his men's dwindling supply of cartridges and of the immediate need for infantry support. Confederate shells began to fall on the crossroads. Word came from Colonel Winslow on the Union right that he must have reinforcements, but the infantry was still some minutes away, and Waring was in retreat. When all seemed hopeless, the first of the Federal infantry appeared. As they piled in, Grierson appealed to Sturgis for "authority to withdraw the entire cavalry, as it was exhausted and well-nigh out of ammunition." Sturgis authorized Grierson's withdrawal "as soon as sufficient infantry was in position to permit it"[18]

Colonel McMillen's bluecoat infantry brigades had been coming up slowly. Tishomingo Creek slowed them down. Normally, the creek was a sluggish, yellow nuisance, but recent rains had raised it to a dangerous level, and there was only one rickety, ten-foot wide pole bridge across it. Worse than the bottleneck at Tishomingo Creek was the heat. The temperature is said to have been 107°Farenheit. One soldier compared the glaring sun to a blast furnace, and the head surgeon recalled seeing "scores and hundreds" of men "falling out by the way, utterly powerless to move forward." They collapsed and could not move. Men were actually shedding tears, crying from the agony. Nevertheless, the repeated summons from Grierson and then Sturgis caused McMillen to order Colonel George B. Hoge and the Second Brigade to move forward without further delay. Hoge prodded the men forward. They moved as quickly as they were able, up the rising road to the top of the bluff where the cavalrymen had been fighting for hours. Colonel Alexander Wilkins's First Brigade was behind them, and Colonel Edward Bouton's Third Brigade (United States Colored Troops) remained behind to guard the wagon train.[19]

Colonel McMillen rode ahead with his staff and was at the crossroads before the Second Brigade began to arrive. Confederate shells were falling all around. McMillen later described the scene, saying that "the cavalry were falling back rapidly in disorder and the roads at Brice's house were filled with retreating cavalry, led horses, ambulances, wagons, and artillery, the whole presenting a scene of confusion and demoralization anything but cheering to troops just arriving." About half past one o'clock, the Second Brigade appeared. They relieved Waring on the left of the Federal line. The First Brigade arrived a few minutes later and took the place of Winslow on the right.[20]

This was a critical moment. The Federal infantrymen who were forming in their front were equal in number to Forrest's four brigades, and, though they were spent from the heat and the pace of their march, they had not been in battle and did not carry the burden of having been defeated like the cavalrymen, and they had plenty of ammunition. It was coming down to who was tougher. Forrest's men might have wilted at the sight of relatively fresh troops arriving; the Yankees infantry had been marching in the heat, but the Confederate cavalry had been *fighting* in the heat, and it would have been understandable if they had lost heart at the thought of the new and difficult task before them. And, in fact, some did.

A short time after the afternoon fight began, a crisis developed on the Rebel left. Edwin C. Bearss says that the contest between Bell's all Tennessee brigade and Colonel Wilkin's Union First Brigade "was close and vicious, visibility limited. In the blackjack, the dismounted Confederates in the three Tennessee regiments employed their Colt navy revolvers. They had extra loaded and capped cylinders in their pockets." They had had success, at first. They pushed the flank of the First Brigade back, and then Wilkin threw in his reserve. Seeing this, the 8th Mississippi of Rucker's brigade broke and ran. Since morning, the 8th had been on the extreme left of the Confederate line for the purpose of guarding the flank. Now they abandoned the flank, uncovering Bell's left, the 19th Tennessee, by their retreat. The Tennessee regiment followed the Mississippians' example and fled. Unless the panic was checked, the whole flank was in danger of collapsing. Forrest, in his shirt sleeves and with pistol in hand, led his escort to the crumbling end of his battle line. They delivered a withering fire into the Federals and stopped their counter-attack. Calamity on the left was averted. Forrest now spurred his horse toward the other end of the line to discover why he was not hearing more noise from Buford's sector. Forrest said that he feared his order to Buford had "miscarried." He found that Lyon and Johnson were not advancing as he wished and that only two of Captain Morton's eight guns were firing. Forrest ordered Morton to move all of his pieces closer to the action, load them with double canister, and go to work, and he ordered Buford to get the right flank moving. Now, at last, the whole of Forrest's cavalry was in action. The Yankee infantry was proving to be difficult to push back, however. At times the lines were only thirty paces apart. For two hours the battle raged along lines that were mostly stationary. Then, the bluecoats began to waver.[21]

George said, "The Third, Eighth, and Twelfth Kentucky moved directly down on the concentrated Federal batteries around Brice's house, while the Seventh Kentucky, which was on Forrest's extreme right, bore to the right of the cross-roads, crushed the Federal's left wing, and intercepted the Ripley road, on which they were attempting to fall back."[22]

Pressed back they might be, but the Northerners were fighting stubbornly and with no sign of panic until a new and unexpected threat appeared from the woods on their left rear. In the morning, as he approached the crossroads, Buford had detached a regiment to march by an obscure country lane to try to get behind the enemy. Forrest had ordered it. Buford selected Colonel Clark R. Barteau and the 2nd Tennessee Cavalry for the mission and sent them off. Now, hours later, Barteau and his men appeared just where they could do the most good. Barteau arrayed his men in a long single line to create the illusion of a heavier force. He said, "I deployed the regiment into a line nearly as long as that of the line of battle and at once began an attack by scattering shots." The Federals were caught by surprise; they had been concentrating on the fight in the front and had not expected a flank attack. To continue the valuable ruse that he commanded a much larger force than his single regiment, Barteau "instructed my bugler to gallop along the whole line and at various points to sound the charge." It was a deception as old as Joshua and it worked.[23]

Barteau was able to advance his thin gray line to where he would cut the bluecoats off from the Tishomingo Creek bridge. The sound of musketry behind them alarmed the Yankees at the crossroads and encouraged the Rebels.

Forrest said that Barteau's attack "created confusion and dismay to the ene-my's wagon train and the guard attending it . . . and the enemy now in front made a last attempt to hold the crossroads; but the steady advance of my men and the concentrated, well directed, and rapid fire from my batteries upon that point threw them back, and the retreat or rout began." Wills says, "The Confederates surged forward, and Lyon's men achieved a breakthrough that caused the Federal regiments to retreat."[24]

The Federal lines around the Brice house had been pounded into a hard, formless knot. There was no cover and no room to maneuver. From the sounds coming from the rear, their only escape route was being threatened, and, as Forrest said, the rout began. As the Federals ran for their lives and the Confederates streamed by the Brice house in pursuit, the daughter of the family came outside and waved her handkerchief in celebration. The cross-roads was won. Phase Two of the battle was over, and the third and final phase was beginning.

The Union troops streamed from the crossroads, down the bluff toward the Tishomingo Creek bridge. Sturgis said, "Order soon gave way to confu-sion and confusion to panic. . . . Everywhere the army drifted toward the rear, and was soon altogether beyond control." Bearss adds, "Wagons and artillery as they sought to cross the bottom sank axle deep into the mud and became inextricable. No power could check the panic-stricken mass as it swept to-ward the rear." They found the narrow bridge blocked. Sections of the wagon train had foolishly come too close to the fighting and in their attempt to re-cross the bridge, a wagon overturned. A deadly bottleneck resulted. Forrest's artillery chief, Captain John W. Morton, said, "Infantry, cavalry, and wagon trains became entangled in a hopeless coil. Upon this mass, Captain Morton brought to bear Morton's and Rice's Batteries with fearful carnage. Panicked bluecoats jumped down the high banks to avoid the bridge and take their chances wading across. Men on the bridge cut the draft animals' traces and rode over everything in their way to escape." More than one hundred were killed or wounded trying to get over or around the bridge. The Yankees who made it to the far bank continued across the bottom toward the ridge on the other side.[25]

The Rebels were after them. They had cleared the bridge of its obstruc-tions. The wagon, dead horses, and dead men were heaved into the creek, and the Southern artillery crossed along with some of the cavalry. Others forded above and below the bridge. Forrest and one group forded about a quarter mile below. They passed through a junk yard of abandoned knapsacks, hav-ersacks, guns and burning wagons. Before attaining the top of the ridge, the Confederates encountered the black soldiers of the Third Brigade on the west side of the creek. They may have seen two companies of the 55th United

States Colored Infantry even before they came to the bridge (some sources say that the black foot soldiers of the 55th reached the east bank of the creek before the traffic jam at the bridge occurred), but if they did not see them there, they certainly did once they crossed. Seven companies of the 55th were waiting in battle formation to cover the Federal retreat. They wore cloth badges on their uniforms that read, "Remember Fort Pillow." They opened their line to let the fleeing soldiers from the fight on the ridge pass through and then closed up again and fired a volley into the Confederates that "seemed to hold in check his right and center." The Confederates were not checked for long. D. B. Castleberry of the 3rd Kentucky Infantry said, "The sight of those Negroes we had to meet so enraged us that nothing could stop us." And W. D. Brown of the 8th Kentucky said, "We were in no mood to accept negro supremacy." The Confederates formed ranks and fired. Captain C. P. Bailey, who commanded a company in the 55th U.S. Colored Infantry said they received a "galling fire from the enemy. Our men were cut down like grass before the scythe."[26]

The Confederates pursued the retreating 55th a half mile, to where the Third Brigade commander, Colonel Ed Bouton, had formed a new battle line consisting of the 59th U.S. Colored Infantry, two guns of Battery F, 2nd U.S. Colored Light Artillery, and about 1500 white infantrymen of Wilkin's brigade. They were near the home of Dr. Enoch Agnew. Bouton's guns were firing over the heads of the retreating 55th, and still the Confederates came on. Colonel McMillen, the division commander, was on the scene and Bouton explained his deployment to him. McMillen approved. He said, "That's right. If you can hold this position until I can go to the rear and form on the next ridge, you can save this entire command. It all depends on you now." A skirmish line of the 8th Kentucky was coming up the Ripley Road with the rest of the brigade behind them. The battle was joined, and Bearss says that "Morton's artillery boomed and Forrest's 'critter cavalry' stormed forward. Savage hand to hand fighting ensued, particularly between black and white soldiers." As so often happened, the soldiers soon lost sight of the battle at large and became aware only of their individual combat. One of the Rebels later said, "I could see the Yankee skirmishers dodging from one tree to another for shelter. I went through a yard by a little log house to my left, and crossed the fence into the woods, . . . A Yankee crept up obliquely to my right just across the public road, taking advantage of a stump for shelter, and as he put his gun over the stump . . . Capt. Jameson saw him and hollered to me, 'Look out!' at the same time firing his pistol at Mr. Yankee, who quickly took shelter behind a friendly tree just in time to save his scalp."[27]

It soon appeared that the Federal line was about to be flanked on the right. Colonel Bouton ordered his guns to retire. Sturgis had gone to the rear,

completely unnerved. (That night, when urged by Bouton to bring some order into the retreat, Sturgis would cry, "For God's sake, if Mr. Forrest will let
me alone I will let him alone. You have done all you could and more than we
expected of you, and now all you can do is to save yourselves.") So, Bouton
was on his own. The fight lasted just a little longer. Lyon's Kentuckians hit
the Federal line "with loud cheers [and] hurled them back with so stormful
an onset, that the Federal array dissolved before it . . . and their defeat was
consummate." Organized resistance collapsed. The Federals fled up the Ripley Road. The retreating black soldiers tore off the "Remember Fort Pillow"
badges and threw them away. Even so, one Federal later said that the Confederates showed them no mercy. He said that they, "flushed with success,
committed all sorts of cruelties upon the fugitives they could capture. Negro
soldiers were shot down by squads, after they had surrendered, and white
soldiers did not fare much better."[28]

George said, "The Federals left strewn along the road about twenty pieces
of artillery and the same number of caissons, over two hundred wagons
loaded with supplies and about twenty-five ambulance wagons. All evidence
of the worst routed army of the war was plainly visible." The sun was setting,
and the Battle of Brice's Crossroads was over.[29]

Forrest ordered some of the men to follow the retreating enemy and the
rest "to halt, feed, and rest." The Confederates began breaking into the wagons and gorging themselves on U.S. grub. There was plenty for all; the wagons had been loaded with 150,000 rations. Kentucky Brigade historian Henry
George was a private in the 7th Kentucky Mounted Infantry at the time of
the battle. He looked back on Brice's Crossroads in later years and called it
"Forrest's most signal victory, and, taking everything into consideration, it was
one of the most brilliant victories of the war." The same judgment ran from
the lowly private to the department commander, General Stephen D. Lee, who
called it "one of the most signal victories of the war."[30]

The Kentuckians had displayed valor throughout the difficult day, none
more than those in Lyon's old 8th Kentucky. W. D. Brown said, "The Eighth
Kentucky ought to be crowned with imperishable honors for running through
the enemy's lines and pushing them with such vigor. Gen. [sic] Lyon was to be
found on the front line all that day."[31]

Lyon's performance was widely praised. Young wrote, "To him belongs
the credit of having opened the greatest of all cavalry battles, and to have
done more than any one Confederate officer, other than Forrest, to win the
crushing defeat of the Union forces on that historic field."[32]

For Colonel Lyon, the day had been personally satisfying and profession-
ally promising. He had been disappointed when the expedition into Middle
Tennessee was recalled. He believed that he would be able to wangle a side trip

into Western Kentucky for a quick visit with his wife, who was eight months pregnant with their second child. The plan fell through, but the consequence of the return to Mississippi was the Battle of Brice's Crossroads, which he called in a letter home, "The only complete victory in which I have participated since the beginning of the war." He continued, "My command fought very gallantly and its conduct will probably give [me] a promotion. If President Davis refuses to give me a promotion now after having been recommended by Forrest, Buford, Lee and Wheeler I shall regard him as personally unfriendly to me and I shall despair of being promoted." As for his commanding general, he told his wife, "I find him a very gallant man, with much more discretion than I had expected and very kind hearted . . . he was with me frequently during our fighting on the 10th." At one point, Forrest had even patted him on the back and congratulated him.[33]

Having worked so hard during the day, at least part of the Kentucky Brigade was excused from joining in the pursuit, which began at 1:00 AM on June 11. Instead, they were "detailed to take charge of the battlefield, prisoners, plunder, etc." Their comrades chased the Northerners through Ripley, skirmishing lightly along the way and capturing even more vehicles and ordnance stores to add to the total. Beyond Ripley, the Confederates divided and chased the Yankees in two columns. Buford led one group down the main road while Forrest took the other by a more roundabout route to get ahead of the enemy. The plan was to cut them off at Salem. It failed only because Forrest's group was delayed by a mishap. The exhausted general tumbled from the saddle and was knocked unconscious. His men stopped and waited for Forrest to recover while Buford and the other column pushed on along the other road. The Federals passed through Salem before Forrest could get into position. From Salem, Rucker and Johnson doubled back to pick up Union stragglers and jettisoned property, while Buford continued the chase with some of Lyon's brigade and a single regiment of Bell's brigade, the 20th Tennessee Cavalry. At Davis' Mill, Forrest called off the chase. Uncle Sam's demoralized lads continued to run as if the Rebels were nipping at their heels, all the way to Memphis.[34]

Jordan and Pryor said, "It has been thought and asserted by many that [Forrest's] successes were largely due to uncommon good fortune, coupled with audacity; but it must be apparent that this brilliant victory was won by his prompt comprehension of the situation on the morning of the 10th [of] June." They add, "Forrest brought his entire strength into the situation, and kept no reserves unemployed. . . . Victory is surest won on such occasions when every man is launched and every gun employed, as strenuously and swiftly as possible." Bennett Young said that Forrest's victory "stands pre-eminent . . . it has no counterpart in any engagement fought entirely on one side by cavalry."[35]

Certainly, Forrest had won at Brice's Crossroads a complete victory over a superior foe. He had lost 492 killed and wounded, and some of his brigades had suffered particularly high losses (Lyon had suffered approximately twenty percent casualties), but in the final tally Forrest inflicted on Sturgis over 2200 killed, wounded, and missing. He had captured 176 wagons and their contents, nearly two hundred horses and mules, sixteen field pieces, and quantities of small arms.

And yet, despite his resounding defeat at the hands of the Rebels, General Sturgis had emerged successful in the larger sense. His short campaign had kept Forrest off of Sherman's supply line, and the three armies under his command were approaching Atlanta.

9
THE FEDERALS TAKE THEIR TURN

The morning after the Battle of Brice's Crossroads, Reverend Samuel A. Agnew, the son of property owner Dr. Enoch Agnew, returned to the family home, where the bluecoats had made their last stand. The Agnews were relatively prosperous at the beginning of the war. They owned a few slaves, and they owned personal property and real estate evaluated at a bit over $85,000. Their life was ordered and tranquil, and then, on June 10, 1864, the armies came. Reverend Agnew was grateful that none of his family had been killed, but said, "Our once pleasant home was a wreck . . . the Yankees had taken every grain of corn and every ounce of meat, leaving us with nothing to eat. The family had not eaten anything since the previous morning, and the house had been plundered. Everything was turned upside down, and much was missing. Dead and wounded were lying in the house, upstairs and downstairs. Bullets had penetrated the walls in various places." As the hours turned into days, the stench of the battlefield grew nearly unbearable. Agnew took disapproving notice of the shallowness of the graves the Union prisoners dug. And soldiers were still everywhere. Sad caravans of prisoners were herded past the Agnew house. On June 13, Agnew observed a line of eight hundred enemy prisoners passing by, the black soldiers in the rear. The blacks at the back of the column were the survivors, luckier than their fellows, it seemed, but some soon found that their good luck was only a reprieve. Agnew implied that the killing of USCT prisoners continued after the battle. He said that "most of the Negroes were shot, our men being so much incensed that they shoot them wherever they see them. It is certain that a great many Negroes have been killed." Soldiers remained in the area for days, and the behavior of the Confederates was, at times, as larcenous as that of the Federals had been. When a squad of graybacks came to the Agnew farm claiming to be authorized to search the estate for stolen property, one of them confiscated some tobacco and a mirror from one of the slave cabins.[1]

Dr. Enoch Agnew went to Guntown to speak to General Forrest about settlement for damages to civilian property during the battle. It was not just the Agnew home; the Brice house and the church had been chewed up badly by small arms fire, and each was filled with the sick and wounded of both armies. When he arrived, Dr. Agnew found that Forrest had gone to Tupelo. He had to be satisfied with an interview with General Buford, who promised to send a commission to look into the matter. Before said commission ever came to evaluate the claims, Forrest's cavalry moved on to Baldwyn.

Now that the battle was over, the officers and men were taking stock of what had happened, and how all had behaved. Some came up lacking, and the recriminations were fierce. Colonel Lyon wrote his wife from Baldwyn on June 19, 1864. He complained of the continuing heat wave, and of his division commander, saying, "I suffer physically, and I will suffer mentally, until I am relieved from the command of the dog Buford. All Kentuckians yet feel disgraced by having to serve under so great a Brute and coward. In the fight of the 10th at Tishomingo Creek I have been able to find but one man who saw him under fire and yet the dog claims the entire credit for the success. I have had no new outbreak with him and probably will not as I regard him beneath contempt." Lyon's attitude toward his commander might have been, in part, the result of what does seem to have been a below average performance by Buford during the Battle of Brice's Crossroads. As has been seen, Buford was so tardy in carrying out his instructions at one point that Forrest feared his order had "miscarried." He rode over to Buford's wing to investigate matters for himself and had to repeat his order to engage. Even so, in his report of the battle, Forrest (a man not known for his willingness to forgive incompetence) thanked Buford for his energy and prompt obedience of orders. Buford's conduct in the battle does not seem to have been enough, by itself, to deserve such ire on Lyon's part. Lyon specifically mentioned Buford's performance and called it cowardice, but he also called Buford a brute and said that there had been no *new* outbreak, which suggests that his disdain for Buford predated the events of that single day, June 10, and that the two Kentuckians had clashed. It must be that Lyon had seen the martinet side of Buford too many times in the months since he first joined the organization. He had obviously come to hold "the dog Buford" in low esteem. The depth of Lyon's scorn might have surprised Buford, had he known. Certainly, Buford did not seem to return Lyon's disapproval. Lyon admitted in his letter home that Buford had told him that he had wired Senator H. C. Burnett to have him promoted to brigadier general. Forrest had gone even further; he had telegraphed President Davis to have Lyon immediately promoted. "Forrest compliments both my Brigade and myself very highly," Lyon said.[2]

Buford's and Forrest's recommendations, and, it is believed, the promised one from General Joe Wheeler, turned the trick. Just days later, Lyon was promoted to brigadier general, but with the promotion came an unsettling order from Richmond. As Lyon later recalled it, he was directed "to proceed to Western Virginia—and assume command of Morgan's Cavalry, as Genl Morgan had been murdered a short time before." Lyon told his wife that when he reported this addendum to his promotion to Forrest, the general pitched a small fit. He said, "You shall not go. I will immediately telegraph the War Department at Richmond, Va. and ask that this order be rescinded and that you be ordered to remain with my corps." The Wizard's demands carried weight in Richmond, and Lyon was allowed to remain with Forrest.[3]

Anyway, it was no time for Forrest to be giving up one of his most talented brigade commanders. A new expedition was shaping up in Memphis for the same purpose as Sturgis's: to keep Forrest away from Sherman's supply line in Tennessee. Five days after the Battle of Brice's Crossroads, Sherman showed his determination to deal with the threat posed by Forrest when he wrote to Secretary of War Stanton. He called Forrest "the very devil," and said that he was going to send out another force right away "to go out and follow Forrest to the death, if it costs 10,000 lives and breaks the Treasury." The commander of the new expedition was to be Major General Andrew Jackson Smith. Sturgis was out.[4]

General Sturgis's career was left in ruins after the Battle of Brice's Crossroads. Many of the soldiers who were there pointed the finger directly at him for the defeat. William S. Butler of the 120th Illinois Infantry was still angry about it nearly twenty years later. He wrote a letter that echoed the sentiments of many when it appeared in the Toledo *Blade*, "Every man that was there knows that Sturgis is a cowardly, whiskey-bloated imbecile, unfit to command a team of six respectable mules, much less an army of 10,000 or 12,000 men."[5]

The charge of drunkenness was widely leveled against Sturgis, although in this, at least, he had his defenders. Colonel E. M. Lowe, who commanded the 55th U.S. Colored Infantry, saw the general late in the battle, and he denied that Sturgis was drunk. Lowe blamed the defeat on Grierson, who brought on the battle too soon. Lowe said, "General Grierson thought he could defeat Forrest without any help, and by doing so add another star to his straps, but he caught a Tartar."[6]

Forrest the Tarter even weighed in on the accusation that his opponent of June 10 was drunk. He said it was merely the "force of surprise" that had defeated Sturgis. Forrest's explanation of what had happened is a fair summary of his philosophy of war. He said, "Sturgis knew that [Stephen D.] Lee and I were separated and thought that, according to book and rule, I would not dare try a forced march and battle on a scorching hot day with a mere handful of men. In any fight, it's the first blow that counts; and if you can keep it up hot enough, you can whip 'em as fast as they can come up." He had put this principle into effect in his first battle orders to Lyon that morning. Lyon told

Captain John W. Morton that Forrest had said, "Charge and give 'em hell, and when they fall back keep on charging and giving 'em hell, and I'll soon be there with you and bring Morton's Bull Pups."[7]

In a June 14 letter to headquarters, District of West Tennessee, General Sturgis said, "In view of the fact that my campaign has ended disastrously and will be severely and perhaps unjustly criticized and misrepresented, I would respectfully request that I be relieved from further active duty (for the present) and that an investigation of the cause and failure be made as early as possible." A court of inquiry convened in Memphis on June 27. It concluded its investigation on July 30 and submitted its report, but its recommendations were not made public. Cowden summed it up bitterly, saying that General Sturgis "was not dealt with further, as a volunteer officer would doubtless have been; but the finding of the court was suppressed, and he was permitted (or ordered) to retire to Covington, Ky., on 'waiting orders,' to continue to draw pay and live in idleness and ease." And so it was that General A. J. Smith was assigned to lead the new expedition against Forrest.[8]

General Smith set out from Memphis beginning on June 22, 1864, with two divisions of infantry, including a brigade of United States Colored Troops under Colonel Edward Bouton. The infantry moved by rail, the artillery by road to Moscow. Beyond there, the railroad was out of commission, and they proceeded on foot through the heat and dust to the staging area at La Grange. They left there on July 5. As they moved east, they foraged freely. W. H. Tucker of the 14th Wisconsin Infantry boasted that the Wisconsin boys "never passed through a country without becoming familiar with every sweet potato patch, every chicken roost, and every smoke house for miles around." Including Grierson's horse soldiers, the column numbered more than fourteen thousand men, and it included thirty field pieces.[9]

Sherman wanted Smith to destroy the country as he marched, so the Federals burned Ripley on July 8, and "passed on across the Tallachatchie and through New Albany, trailed by a swath of desolation ten miles wide." They plundered and destroyed at their pleasure, and they burned the domicile of every family that had shown discourtesy or worse to the Yankees retreating from Brice's Crossroads. But they did not march unopposed. Buford's division had been sent out to delay Smith's advance. Henry Ewell Hord said that Smith "could not water his horses without taking his army to the creek with him, and he camped every night in line of battle, with heavy skirmish lines thrown around him." It was ultimately pointless; a single division could not stop Smith. Despite the constant harassment, the bluecoats passed on to Pontotoc, and there they stopped to rest. On July 12, they eased a short distance out the road to Houston, but they were turned back by a detachment of Colonel Robert McCulloch's brigade. Another probe "was promptly met by General Lyon's brigade and easily driven back." Lyon's horse soldiers had taken position behind a breastwork of logs and fence rails when a regiment of Illinois cavalry came charging up the Okolona Stage Road. The Kentuckians let them get close before they opened fire. The enemy turned back the way they had come and left thirty of their men dead.[10]

Such skirmishes were the agenda for the moment. Department commander General Stephen D. Lee had sent orders for Forrest not to bring on a fight until he arrived. He soon did, bringing with him two thousand additional troops. The reinforcements raised Forrest's aggregate to nine thousand men, so many that he did not have mounts for them. He turned the unmounted troopers into an infantry division and, on the night of July 12, assigned General Lyon to command them. One must think Lyon obeyed the order with some reluctance. Winning victories in the face of great hardships forges a strong bond between men, and Lyon had led his men successfully. Now, his brigade of fighting Kentuckians was taken away from him and he was given this unformed mass of slow-moving infantry to lead instead. With little time to train, they could not do effective work. Lyon must have realized that commanding these 2100 foot soldiers would consign him to a secondary role in the battle that was coming.

Lee had arrived in Okolona in somewhat of a dither. Mobile was under threat from a Federal force from New Orleans, and he was eager to be done with General Smith quickly so that he could return south and turn his attention to the defense of the important coastal city. It looked at first as if he could go back to Mobile sooner than later. The Federal pause at Pontotoc convinced Forrest that Smith intended to return to Memphis. Then, on the morning of July 13, the Rebel scouts discovered that the enemy camps were empty. The bluecoats were marching toward Tupelo. Lee and Forrest reacted quickly to the news. Forrest took Colonel Hinchie P. Mabry's brigade, augmented by a battalion led by Lieutenant Colonel James M. Crews and four guns, to attack the Union rear guard while Lee took the divisions of General Buford and General James Chalmers to strike the enemy's flank. Thomas E. Parson says that "Lyon was ordered to follow on foot as best he could," a difficult task for "men who were unaccustomed to walking, particularly in their clumsy cavalry boots." The Rebels moved along roads to the south of and parallel to the Yankees' line of march. As opportunity presented, they could turn north on the connecting country lanes and strike the enemy's right flank.[11]

Late on the morning of July 13, 1864, a few miles from Tupelo, Forrest struck the rear of the Federal column, the 7th Kansas Cavalry and the 61st U.S. Colored Infantry. He put such pressure on them that they had to call for support from the men ahead. Three regiments fell back to reinforce them. Their arrival strengthened the tail of the enemy column so that Forrest could not overwhelm it. Still, he did not cut off the effort. The running skirmish, really more of a marching skirmish, continued into the afternoon. Forrest said that he finally stopped because he was not hearing a flank attack from his front and "was fearful that he [the enemy] was driven too rapidly." That is to say, he feared that the Federals had moved so fast that the Confederates ahead had not had time to set their traps.[12]

He need not have doubted General Lee. His men were taking position a few miles up the road near a tiny crossroads called Bertram's Shop. They had missed the head of the column, but they were poised to attack the enemy's wagons, which Rucker's brigade (now of Chalmers's division) did at 2:00 PM. The surprise was complete and they were able to break the column. Tucker of the 14th Wisconsin said, "We were penned in, rebs to the front, rebs on the right, and in the rear and heavy timber on the left, nothing now but fight and fight it was." The Union infantry quickly turned the situation around. Regiments from the front as well as from the rear, where the threat from Forrest was at a temporary end, filed in on each side of the Rebels "and the field quickly became a trap for the Confederates." They began to withdraw "with heavy casualties and most of them were left behind on the field."[13]

The Yankees burned the wagons and caissons that were too badly damaged to roll and continued in the direction of Tupelo. Some of Grierson's cavalry had already arrived there and were busy destroying the tracks of the Mobile & Ohio Railroad.

Buford was waiting for the Federals further up the road near Camargo Crossroads. He had with him Colonel Tyree Bell's brigade and Crossland's (formerly Lyon's) Kentucky Brigade. Bell's men hit the enemy flank about five o'clock, but an error had been made that doomed their effort. The attacking force was Colonel C. R. Barteau's 2nd Tennessee Cavalry, and it had begun the fight before either the rest of Bell's brigade or the Kentuckians were ready. It was a critical mistake. Parson says, "Instead of an attack by two brigades, the success of the charge hung on the pluck of a single regiment."[14]

Lieutenant Joseph R. Reed of the 2nd Iowa Light Artillery began firing canister rounds toward the attackers and Yankee infantry was piling in. The action lasted only fifteen minutes before the Confederates—most of them never having been engaged—began to withdraw. Now the Federals took their turn. Their counterattack jammed two regiments of quickly retreating Rebels, the 2nd Tennessee and the 15th Tennessee, back into the rest of Bell's brigade, which had been hurrying to the sound of the guns. The narrow road became a hell of confusion and fear as the units tried to untangle themselves under a storm of U.S. lead. Captain John W. Morton's artillery saved them. The guns held the enemy troops back until the Tennesseans could remount and ride back to Buford's defensive line, the Kentucky Brigade. The Confederates waited for an attack that did not come. The blue column passed on.

The last attempt to stop General A. J. Smith had failed. The Federals continued east, with the Rebels nipping ineffectually at their heels, to Harrisburg, a deserted village two miles short of Tupelo. There, Smith called a halt. His men threw up their works along a low ridge between two creeks with wide expanses of open ground to the west, the direction from which Forrest and Lee would have to attack.

On the night of July 13, Forrest personally reconnoitered the enemy position, actually passing through the Union pickets, who fired on the general and his party when they realized that the riders were Confederates. Forrest seems to have come away impressed by the strength and disposition of Smith's forces, and in a war conference with General Lee that night he suggested that there was no need to attack the Northerners in their works. He said that the enemy would have to come out soon and when he did, "I will be on all sides of him, attacking day and night. He shall not cook a meal or have a night's sleep, and I will wear his army to a frazzle before he gets out of the country." The trouble was, Lee did not have the luxury of time; Mobile was threatened and he must get back. Lee rejected Forrest's suggestion and ordered an attack for the next morning. Forrest "was either won over or resigned to Lee's plan to fight," and yet he was uncomfortable with the decision. Forrest was in a peculiar mood. Maybe it was simply that he was worn down. He was suffering a massive outbreak of boils. They were relentlessly painful, and the heat was nearly as bad as it had been at Tishomingo Creek. Between his physical pain and the terrible heat, Forrest was drained. Brian Wills agrees that "some of Forrest's enormous reservoir of energy seemed to be gone." An equally plausible explanation for Forrest's ennui was the fact that a superior officer was forcing him to obey a decision about which he had misgivings, the decision to attack a foe who was dug in and held two-to-one odds. He had never been a cheerful subordinate and rarely a compliant one. Whatever the explanation, Forrest made an unusual demand of Lee. He insisted that Lee assume field command in the next morning's attack. He, Forrest, would relinquish control and command the right wing only.[15]

Lee resisted the suggestion. He pointed out that the majority of the men were Forrest's own. They knew him, had fought with him at Brice's Crossroads, and would have more confidence in his leadership when the battle came. Forrest refused, arguing that Lee was the senior officer and should assume responsibility. Lee finally agreed, and they planned the battle. Brigadier General Philip D. Roddey's division would be on the right, and General Buford's would be on the left. In Buford's wing, the deployment would be thus: Colonel Crossland's Kentucky Brigade would be on the right, next to and touching Roddey's division; then would come Colonel Mabry's brigade; and then Colonel Bell's. Bell would be the extreme left of Buford's division and of the Confederate line. General James Chalmers's division and General H. B. Lyon's infantry would be held in reserve.

When they met the next morning, July 14, 1864, Lee and Forrest synchronized their watches, agreed on a start time, and supposedly agreed that a single cannon shot would be the signal to step off. However, Forrest's trusted artillery chief, Captain Morton, said in his memoirs that he "was never directed by General Lee, to whom he reported and from whom he was receiving orders, to fire a signal gun for opening the fight. He received no intimation of such an order from General Lee or anyone else." Morton shared Forrest's unhappy mood that morning. He had recommended to Lee that he "be allowed to concentrate all of the artillery on the left center and make a breach in the Federal lines, creating confusion in their ranks, which would give the Confederate cavalry easy work." Lee disagreed. He ordered Morton to scatter his artillery, with one battery going to Roddey, one to Crossland's brigade, another to Bell's, and two others to be in the reserve with Lyon.[16]

An artillery duel had been going on for thirty minutes when the Confederates moved into position in the trees, the sun at their front, the morning already hot. Suddenly, the Kentucky Brigade gave a cheer and leaped forward at the double quick, led by Colonel William W. Faulkner's 12th Kentucky Cavalry. The brigades to their right and left were stunned. They had heard no identifiable signal in the midst of all that cannon fire. George says that the mistake was Faulkner's. He says, "Colonel Faulkner, the gallant commander of the Twelfth, ordered his bugler to sound the charge. Whether it was that bugle or a general impulse, the whole brigade started forward in their charge to death to so many." The Kentuckians moved across the half-mile of open ground in front of the Union lines completely unsupported. The enemy's artillery began to play upon them, but they kept on. They drove in the bluecoat skirmishers and pressed forward under heavy fire. Henry Ewell Hord said, "The Yankees were concentrating their fire from twenty-four guns and a heavy line of infantry behind breastworks. It was awful. The two end batteries could enfilade our entire line." Colonel Faulkner was struck by two bullets and went down, badly wounded, at almost the same instant his horse was killed by an artillery round. The men went on.[17]

They did not see in front of them the brigade of Colonel Charles D. Murray who had come forward from the Federal works and lain down in the tall weeds. Suddenly, Murray's men stood up and fired into the faces of Faulkner's Kentuckians. Parson says, "The resulting volley was devastating and when the smoke cleared hardly a Confederate was still on his feet." Twenty yards from the Union works was the 12th Kentucky's high-water mark.[18]

Other regiments fared a little better. Buford reported that, in spite of the "galling fire of musketry and artillery," some of his Kentucky regiments made it to the Federal intrenchments. Hord says that they reached the breastworks and "fired across with our guns almost touching the enemy's." The bluecoats swarmed over the top of their works and the fighting was hand to hand, "clubbed guns against bayonets." Colonel Crossland "rushed into the fighting like a wild man, and yelling, 'Die in your tracks; don't give an inch!' but . . . they crowded us back step by step."[19]

Colonel Crossland said, "The ranks were decimated; they were literally mowed down. Some of my best officers were either killed or wounded." The Kentucky Brigade had to fall back. The survivors of the suicidal charge went stumbling down the slope to the trees where they had begun. The enemy continued firing into their backs as they retreated into the shadows. Their part of the battle was done. Crossland said afterward, "The action on the 14th was the most severe and destructive ever encountered by the troops of this brigade, who are veterans in the service. Their loss was unprecedented."[20]

Buford had seen the slaughter of his Kentucky Brigade and sent his other two brigades, Bell's and Mabry's, into the fight to try to relieve some of the pressure. They moved across the open field toward General Joseph A. Mower's First Division. Parson says, "Three [Union] brigades were in a line barely 400 yards in length. Within that short distance the line had three distinct 90-degree angles, which created several fields of converging crossfire. It was a far more dangerous position than Crossland had faced." Still, they advanced bravely. Buford said, "Mabry's and Bell's brigades advanced to within close musket-range and engaged the enemy. Approaching gradually they poured a very destructive fire upon his line." But, those converging fields of fire proved to be too formidable, and they had to fall back. Buford said that "after penetrating some fifty steps, they retired to the cover of the timber."[21]

Once again, too late to be of any use, a supporting force was thrown forward. After three hours of fighting had passed, General Chalmers, whose division had been held in reserve, came forward to relieve Buford. All morning long, General Lee had seen his battle plan foiled as well as the failure of the successive improvisations that had replaced it, and it was not over. Lee ordered Chalmers to the attack, but General Forrest stopped him and ordered him to lead his men to the support of General Roddey, who was not engaged at all. Chalmers obeyed Forrest's order. Lee stepped in to exert his authority once he realized what had happened. He ordered Colonel Edmund W. Rucker's brigade to attack. One wonders what Lee thought a single brigade could accomplish against two entrenched Federal divisions well supported by artillery. Rucker's men had to cross a field on which hundreds of their dead and wounded comrades lay. They were taking artillery fire, and before the third charge of the day was called off, one-third of them were dead.

Now, the Federals took their turn. General Mower ordered his men forward in a counterattack. They forced three CSA batteries to retire and followed them to a position just short of the woods where the Confederate cavalry waited. They stood in the open for an hour, hoping the Rebels would come out to meet them, but Lee was done. When it became clear that their challenge would not be accepted, Mower recalled his men to their ridge top works.

The Battle of Tupelo was over. The Confederates had suffered over 1300 casualties (Crossland's Kentucky Brigade had lost forty-five percent of its strength), while the Yankees had lost only about 650. None of the Confederate dead were from Lyon's infantry division. If Grierson's cavalry, much of which was still on the line of the Mobile & Ohio Railroad in Tupelo, had come out to strike the Confederates from the rear, Lyon's infantry might have found themselves in a scrap. As it was, they had not done any fighting at all, had never fired a shot except for the guns of Captain James C. Thrall's 3rd Arkansas Light Artillery, which was ordered forward late in the day to help cover the final retreat. The others had spent the day digging trenches and erecting breastworks on the farm of a widow woman named Sample.

George said, "I have very high regard for General Stephen D. Lee, and know that he rendered brilliant services to the Confederacy, and I know General Forrest was one of the greatest geniuses developed during our war; but the fact still remains—there was a blunder made at Harrisburg, Miss." In fact, he identified four blunders. They were: fighting the Federals while they were behind breastworks on ground of their own choosing; charging the broad front of the enemy instead of the narrow flank (as Buford had advised); uncoordinated attacks; and the failure to order the reserve into the fight. Such bungling led to a humiliating defeat and no one wanted to accept responsibility for it. G. J. Puryear said in an article that appeared in *Confederate Veteran* that Tupelo was called "No Man's Battle" because, from General Lee down, "all the generals in the engagement . . . disclaimed responsibility for the charge by the Confederates that opened the battle, laying it all on Colonel Faulkner's bugler who blew the charge." General Lee did not even submit a complete after-action report of the battle; his only account of what had happened consisted of one paragraph, dated July 14 and sent to headquarters from the field.[22]

That night the Kentuckians shifted to the right to a camp on the Tupelo-Verona Road with orders to "guard against any advance the enemy might make on the former place." As they moved, they heard the sounds of firing on their front. Forrest was leading Colonel Rucker's brigade on a night reconnaissance against the Union left. Forrest said, "By meandering through the woods I approached very near his camp before he discovered my presence. I ordered my men to open fire upon him, when the first line fell back to the main body and opened upon me one of the heaviest fires I have heard during the war. . . . There was unceasing roar of small-arms, and his whole line was lighted up by a continuous stream of fire." All that prevented a serious loss of life on the Confederate side was that the darkness hampered the Federals' aim. They fired too high to do much damage. Still, their demonstration of strength brought an end to any further attack on that flank.[23]

Forrest returned to headquarters, where General Lee called a midnight council of war. Parson says, "Forrest arrived from his aborted attack in a foul mood," and he edged very close to insubordination when Lee asked his assembled officers what ideas they could offer for the next day. Forrest said, "I've got ideas, and I'll tell you one thing, General Lee. If I knew as much about West Point tactics as you, the Yankees would whip hell out of me every day. I've got five hundred empty saddles and nothing to show for them." The Southern yeoman's traditional contempt for the highly educated revealed itself in Forrest. He blamed the West Pointer Lee and lightly mocked his professional training while he refused to acknowledge his own mistakes that had contributed to the day's defeat.[24]

Whatever action the unhappy group decided upon before the council adjourned, it could not have taken into account the situation they faced the next morning. General Smith's brigades were withdrawing. They were low on ammunition and down to one day's ration per man. That was one factor that influenced Smith's decision to return to Memphis. The other was that he had defeated Lee and Forrest, had kept Forrest from striking Sherman's supply line in Tennessee, and Grierson's cavalry had destroyed the M&O Railroad in Tupelo. His mission was accomplished, in his view; he could do no more at present, and now he must save his army. The Federals began to move out on the morning of July 15, and so, says Shelby Foote, "There followed the curious spectacle of a superior force retreating from a field on which it had inflicted nearly twice as many casualties as it suffered and being harassed on the march by a loser reduced to less than half the strength of the victor it was pursuing." Smith's withdrawal gave Lee a reason to claim that the Battle of Tupelo was a draw; after all, it was not the Confederates who left the field. For his part, Smith began the return march to Memphis satisfied in the knowledge that he had done something very few had done—he had beaten Forrest.[25]

He soon had reason to fear that he may not have beaten Forrest for good, however. The Confederates began a vigorous pursuit. Lee ordered Forrest to lead it, and Forrest ordered Crossland's and Bell's brigades under Buford to spearhead the chase (Henry Hord said, "Gen. Forrest always favored the Tennesseans, but when he wanted Bell to get down to his level best, he would say, 'Watch those damn Kentuckians and stay with them.'"). Part of Chalmers's division followed, and, once again, Roddey drew the lightest duty of all. His division remained behind to guard Tupelo.[26]

The Confederates snapped at the Federal rear guard, Grierson's cavalry, through the morning and most of the afternoon. About 4:00 PM, and only five miles from Tupelo, they discovered that the enemy had stopped at Old Town Creek. Buford placed Captain Thomas Rice's battery and advanced with Bell's and Crossland's dismounted brigades on the right and left of the road, respectively. Crossland's men picked their way forward through a thick woods and heavy underbrush, "not more than seven hundred men [to contend] against four thousand of the enemy," said Henry George. The Confederates did well, at first, though the enemy's fire was heavy. Buford said, "I drove the enemy's rear before me to the creek bottom, with considerable loss. Rice's battery did good execution." Then, the Federal rear guard was reinforced with two brigades of infantry, and the fight settled down into a thirty-minute contest in which the Northerners began to gain the advantage by attrition on the other side. Colonel Crossland was badly wounded in the fighting, and command of the Kentucky Brigade devolved on Lieutenant Colonel A. R. Shacklett. Many regimental officers went down. Forrest arrived to find Buford stalled, and he began to direct the battle himself. Then, he took a wound, "a painful wound which incapacitated me from further service," he said. Forrest had been hit in the right foot by a rifle ball. Chalmers had arrived by this time and he assumed command. A field dressing was applied to Forrest's wound, and he remounted to oversee the retreat of the Rebels.[27]

After Old Town Creek, the Kentuckians were judged to have "suffered so heavily," that they were excused. They returned to the rear and helped to bury the dead. They were not badly missed, for there were no more engagements. The Rebels continued to follow the Yankees as far as the Tallahatchie River, where they brought their observation to an end. General A. J. Smith's brief campaign was over. Edwin C. Bearss says, "Although Smith failed to destroy Forrest's corps at Tupelo on July 14, he did break its combat effectiveness. Forrest would rally his horsemen for more daring raids, but never again would they be able to fight and defeat infantry."[28]

Perhaps Forrest brooded on how his fortunes had gone to smash as he returned to Tupelo. His wound forced him to travel for the next few weeks in a buggy, his bandaged foot elevated, a galling state of affairs for The Wizard of the Saddle. He was at a low point in both mind and body. A colleague described him at this time as "sick-looking, thin as a rail, cheekbones that stuck out like they were trying to come through the skin, skin so yellow it looked greenish, eyes blazing."[29]

Many were recovering from wounds. All were coping with the disappointment of their worst defeat of the war, but for General Lyon there was a personal bright spot. As the Tupelo Campaign ended, he became a father for the second time. On July 23, 1864, one year to the day after their first-born died, Laura O'Hara Lyon brought forth a son they named Hylan F. Lyon.

10
FORREST RESURGENT

General William T. Sherman was not satisfied with the outcome of A. J. Smith's Tupelo Campaign. Note the language of Sherman's communiqué to Secretary of War Stanton on June 15; he expected Smith to "follow Forrest to the death." This was not figurative language on Sherman's part. He wanted Forrest permanently neutralized as a threat, and in this Smith had failed. So, shortly after Smith's return to Memphis, Sherman ordered him to lead another expedition into North Mississippi. In early August, Smith ventured out with eighteen thousand men. Forrest had a mere five thousand with which to meet him, but at least they were *his* men to command this time. General Stephen D. Lee was no longer the department commander. He had been reassigned to the Army of Tennessee. As of July 26, the new commander of the Department of Alabama, Mississippi, and East Louisiana was Major General Dabney H. Maury, a Virginian who had spent almost his entire career as a Confederate in Mississippi. Maury promised his cantankerous subordinate, Forrest, that he would follow a policy of non-interference.

When Smith marched east from Memphis, Forrest sent General Chalmers's division forward to the Mississippi Central Railroad to block him. Chalmers was outnumbered and could have used the help of Buford, who was with Forrest in Pontotoc. However, Forrest decided not to deplete his own strength by sending Buford away. He wired Chalmers, "I don't wish to throw any more force on your front. You will assume command of [Colonel Hinchie P.] Mabry's brigade and fall back in front of the enemy, contesting all the ground, while I will operate on his flank and rear." Chalmers retarded the enemy's advance as best he could with his inferior forces until he was flanked at Abbeville. He began retreating in the direction of Oxford. Forrest told Chalmers, "Contest every inch of ground." This Chalmers vowed to do, but he was forced back into Oxford, nevertheless.[1]

The Confederate stand at Oxford was very brief. On August 9, Brigadier General Edward Hatch's Federal cavalry appeared. When the bluecoats charged, the Rebels withdrew. Wills says that Chalmers left Oxford "so rap-idly that he abandoned several artillery caissons" and some other equipment that the Rebels could scarcely afford to lose. The Federals had no use for Oxford or its inhabitants. They spent the next twenty-four hours "robbing and plundering indiscriminately men, women, children, and negroes." On August 10, they left the traumatized citizens of Oxford behind and they rode back toward Abbeville. General Forrest rode in, and Oxford was Confederate once more.[2]

Forrest had realized even before this unproductive back-and-forth that he was going to have to adopt a new strategy. Outnumbered as badly he was, he could not defeat Smith, but he could defeat Smith's aims. The plan he hit upon was audacious. He would leave Chalmers and Buford behind to enter-tain Smith and simultaneously would send a handful of men to cut Smith's supply line by destroying the M&C Railroad behind him. Smith's thrust into Mississippi would be stalled while he was dealing with these threats in his front and rear, and meanwhile Forrest would lead a column of two to three thousand men plus Morton's artillery into Memphis itself.

Captain Henry A. Tyler of Co. A, 12th Kentucky Cavalry commanded the railroad destroying party. He led 125 selected men to General Smith's rear, where, Tyler said, they "burned a sixteen-span trestle four miles south of Holly Springs [and] some four or five small trestles." At 3:00 AM on August 21, Forrest reached Memphis. He sent detachments scattering to destroy en-emy transportation and to capture Union Generals Stephen A. Hurlbut and Cadwallader C. Washburn. They did not bag the generals, but they did fight numerous skirmishes in the city, seize six hundred prisoners, and collect a large number of horses before they rode out again at 9:00 AM.[3]

Forrest's six hours of terror in Memphis caused a scramble of Federal forces across the region. General Smith had reoccupied Oxford on August 21, the same day of Forrest's strike, but at mid-morning the next day he received the first of several telegrams from General Washburn describing what had happened in Memphis and ordering him to mount a pursuit at once. Wash-burn said that Forrest and his men "must be cut off and caught. Move rapidly and spare not horse flesh. Their horses must be jaded and they can be caught." As the Federals left Oxford, they applied the torch. Post commander Captain Charles T. Biser reported that they burned "34 stores and business houses, court-house, Masonic Hall, 2 fine large hotels, besides carpenter, blacksmith, and other shops; also 5 fine dwelling houses." He added, "General Smith in person superintended the burning. He refused to allow the citizens to remove anything of value from their burning dwellings."[4]

Smith sent one cavalry division to try to intercept Forrest at New Albany, and he himself went there via Abbeville. He wired Washburn that an effective pursuit of the Confederates was going to be difficult. The river was high "and our bridge broke down. There is no forage between here and Oxford, and I have to send on the north side of the river for it. Recent rains in this region have made the roads almost impassable." His many difficulties gave him cover for his failure to catch Forrest. He returned to Memphis in a few days, his campaign forced to an early end.[5]

The scare that Forrest had thrown into the Union leaders had ended Smith's expedition, but it had also delayed for another month his own plan to raid Middle Tennessee and for that Sherman was grateful. He wrote to General Washburn, "If you get a chance send word to Forrest I admire his dash but not his judgment. The oftener he runs his head against Memphis the better." Sherman was in a noticeably more relaxed mood. He had crossed the Chattahoochee River north of Atlanta in early July. General Joseph E. Johnston had continually retreated before him, digging in, falling back, digging in, falling back, fighting occasionally, but never making a determined stand except at Kennesaw Mountain, after which he fell back once more. When he failed to give battle at the Chattahoochee, President Davis relieved Johnston of command of the Army of Tennessee. Lieutenant General John Bell Hood succeeded him. Hood was cut from different cloth than Johnston. He repeatedly assailed Sherman's lines and was defeated with terrific loss each time. Sherman was soon at the gates of Atlanta facing a greatly reduced enemy, and the successful conclusion of his brilliant campaign was only a matter of time. Forrest did not worry him so much now.[6]

In fact, Sherman had less reason to worry than ever before. It appeared that Forrest was going to be occupied in another region for the foreseeable future. On August 24, General Maury wrote Forrest, "You have again saved Mississippi. Come and help Mobile. . . . The attack on the city will be made at once I expect. Will the retreat of the enemy from North Mississippi enable you to come with any of your forces? We are very weak."[7]

Forrest and his staff moved toward Mobile ahead of the men. There was no need to be concerned about leaving them to their own devices for a while. The Federals were subdued, and his two division commanders were experienced, as were the brigade commanders who served under them. General James Chalmers was in overall command, temporarily, and continued at the head of his own division, which consisted of the brigades of Colonel Robert McCulloch and Colonel Edmund W. Rucker. Chalmers and his division were posted in Water Valley. General Abraham Buford's division consisted of the brigade of Colonel Tyree Bell and that of Brigadier General Hylan B. Lyon. The experiment of having Lyon command an infantry division was ended. He was now back at the head of his Kentuckians. Buford's division was posted in Oxford.

Forrest's official trip to Mobile ended short. En route to the city on the Gulf, Forrest learned that General Maury had been succeeded by Lieutenant General Richard Taylor, who waited for him in Meridian. Taylor, the son of General and President Zachary Taylor, was born on the family plantation near Louisville, Kentucky. He was a Yale graduate, which would not have impressed Forrest—more likely, it would have been a deficit in his view—but Taylor had also proven himself to be a fighter. At the beginning of the war, he had left his Louisiana sugar plantation to lead the 9th Louisiana Infantry. The regiment was sent to the Eastern Theater and arrived there just after the Battle of First Manassas. Taylor and his men were assigned to General Thomas J. "Stonewall" Jackson, whose rigid Presbyterian principles were slightly offended by the Louisianans' *joie de vivre*. Taylor's men fought under Jackson during the Valley Campaign and the Seven Days Before Richmond, after which Taylor, now a major general, returned to the West to command the District of West Louisiana. Under his leadership, the Confederates turned back General Nathaniel Banks's Red River Campaign. He was promoted to Lieutenant General and succeeded General Maury as head of the Department of Alabama, Mississippi, and East Louisiana in August 1864. Forrest paid a call on the new department commander at his Meridian headquarters on September 5. Until that day, Taylor and Forrest had never met, and the cavalryman seems to have been wary. He saw before him a man five years younger than himself, urbane, serious, a straightforward man with plenty of battle field experience of his own. Taylor saw in Forrest "a tall, stalwart man, with grayish hair, mild countenance, and slow and homely of speech."[8]

Taylor said, "In a few words he was informed that I considered Mobile safe for the present, and that all our energies must be directed to the relief of Hood's army, then west of Atlanta. The only way to accomplish this was to worry Sherman's communications north of the Tennessee river, and he must move his cavalry in that direction at the earliest moment." Taylor was proposing that Forrest carry out the very mission that he had been eager to launch since early June.[9]

Taylor was surprised that Forrest seemed filled with doubts. He asked "how was he to get over the Tennessee; how was he to get back if pressed by the enemy; how was he to be supplied; what should be his line of retreat in certain contingencies; what was he to do with prisoners of war if any were taken, etc." Was this worried man the famous Wizard of the Saddle? Taylor said, "I began to think he had no stomach for the work."[10]

Forrest spent some time weighing the difficulties and their possible influence on his chances of success. Finally, he asked to see L. J. Fleming, Taylor's railway superintendent. Fleming described the repairs that had been made on the railroads as far as the Tennessee state line, and assured Forrest of their current excellent condition. As Fleming talked, Forrest was transformed.

Taylor said his "whole manner now changed. In a dozen sharp sentences he told his wants, and said he would leave a staff officer to bring up his supplies, asked for an engine to take him back north twenty miles to meet his troops, informed me he would march with the dawn, and hoped to give an account of himself in Tennessee.[11]

Forrest's preparations proceeded at a rapid pace. The men checked their arms and horse equipage, and the quartermaster distributed ten days' rations. Each man carried forty rounds of ammunition, one blanket, and one change of clothing. Buford's entire division, the brigades of Lyon and Bell, was chosen to go, as well as the brigade of Colonel David C. Kelley. George said, "They understood their leader and had implicit confidence in him, and he knew his men and knew he could rely on their doing their duty under any conditions." They were "as reliable troops as there were in the Confederate army." On September 21, 1864, the Rebels crossed the Tennessee River. The artillery and the ordnance and supply trains were ferried across at Newport, and the cavalry forded at Colbert's Shoals. They rendezvoused near Florence, Alabama, where, the next morning they were joined by Colonel William A. Johnson and one thousand men of General Philip D. Roddey's command. With the addition of Johnson's men, the column reached its peak strength of approximately 4500. About four hundred of these men were without horses, but Forrest expected to find mounts for them among the enemy.[12]

The Federals had by this point in the war erected a thorough system of log stockades and blockhouses to protect bridges, trestles, and other points deemed important along the railroads. While some of the blockhouses were octagonal in shape, the cost and more sophisticated construction of that design meant that a simpler plan—the rectangle—was most often used. A ditch several feet wide backed by a slanted slope of earth surrounded them at the base, and, for protection from plunging fire, "the roof of the block-house was made of a layer of logs laid side by side and covered with earth. On top of all was a roof of shingles (when they could be procured), or of boards and battens." So that the garrisons could live inside, each of the blockhouses was equipped "with ventilators, cellars, water-tanks, and bunks." This was the kind of substantial obstacle Forrest's cavalry faced each time they attacked a target on this raid, and the manpower was equally daunting. The North detailed enormous numbers of men to garrison these defenses; late in the war the infantry guard usually consisted of a white officer in charge of United States Colored Troops. John E. Clark, Jr., says that upwards of 112,000 Federal soldiers, "as much as 30 percent of the Union's manpower advantage," were assigned to guard duty along the railroads.[13]

The works at Athens, Alabama, were particularly strong, two blockhouses and a stockade. General Lyon described them as "almost impregnable." They were manned by about five thousand men drawn from the 106th, 110th, and

111th United States Colored Infantry, and a detachment of the 3rd Tennessee Cavalry, all under the command of Colonel Wallace Campbell. When Forrest approached on the evening of September 23, Colonel Campbell's pickets fell back into their fort. The Confederates chased them a short distance but stopped when they began taking fire from the artillery inside the works. They retired to a safe distance. A locomotive whistle was heard on the Nashville & Decatur Railroad nearby. Forrest sent Colonel C. R. Barteau's 2nd Tennessee Cavalry and his own escort to break the railroad north of town and to cut the telegraph wires. This they accomplished, along with the capture of one hundred horses, which, ironically, were being sent to a place where they would be safe from the Rebels. While Barteau and his detachment went about their work, Forrest deployed his brigades. Lyon's brigade was sent to the west, Bell's to the East, and Kelley's to the southeast. Morton placed his artillery batteries so as to command the fort. Their arrangements made, the Confederates settled down to an uncomfortable night in the rain.[14]

Henry George remembered that a little before 7:00 AM on September 24, Forrest informed the men that momentarily "they were expected to move forward and take the fort. General Lyon, cool and deliberate, as he uniformly was under trying circumstances, passed along the line making his arrangements for the charge, informing the troops what was expected of them, and admonishing them to have their guns and ammunition in readiness for quick and effective work." Looking at the enemy works, the men knew that they might well be seeing their last dawn. George said of his comrades, "Never did they appear more serious than on that occasion."[15]

The advance began at seven o'clock. Morton's artillery opened fire and Lyon's and Bell's brigades moved forward, while Kelley's remained in place to confront the reinforcements that were reportedly coming from Decatur. The attack was underway when Forrest ordered a halt. He said, "Knowing it would cost heavily to storm and capture the enemy's works, and wishing to prevent the effusion of blood that I knew would follow a successful assault, I determined to see if anything would be accomplished by negotiations." He sent in a demand for Colonel Campbell to surrender. When Campbell refused, Forrest requested an interview "at any place he [Campbell] might designate outside of the fort." Campbell agreed to this, and Forrest escorted him on an inspection, from a distance, of his disposition and strength.[16]

Campbell did not realize that Forrest was shifting his forces around to create the illusion that his 4500 men were a multitude. The Yankee colonel came away convinced that Forrest had ten thousand men ready to assail his works. He was also convinced by now that none of the reinforcements he had requested from Decatur the day before would arrive in time. He decided to surrender. He returned to his garrison and said, "The jig is up; pull down the flag." Campbell had surrendered without a fight what Captain Morton considered "the best fortification on the line of the Nashville and Decatur Railroad." A writer in the Nashville *Daily Union* agreed that Campbell had shown a disgraceful lack of resolve. He said, "The surrender of Athens, Ala., is considered among the most shameful acts of the war."[17]

Colonel Campbell had given up on the relief force from Decatur, but one had been dispatched. Kelley's brigade had met the reinforcements while the truce was in effect at the fort, blocked them and surrounded them, and soon they, too, surrendered. Guarded by the graybacks, they "marched up just in time to see Campbell's garrison march out of the fort and stack their arms." The Federals in the second blockhouse refused to come out until Captain Morton sent in a couple of artillery rounds and persuaded them that, in Campbell's words, the jig was indeed up.[18]

Now the acts of destruction and property seizure began. Forrest said, "Everything of value being removed, the block-houses were burned and such parts of the fort as could be consumed by fire. Two locomotives and 2 trains of cars were also burned. . . . Two pieces of artillery, a large amount of small arms, 38 wagons, 2 ambulances, 300 horses, and a considerable amount of ordnance, quartermaster's, and commissary stores were captured." As the column rode off in the direction of Pulaski, the surplus captured property and the prisoners were escorted behind the lines, far behind the lines in the case of the United States Colored troopers. The blacks were sent to work on the fortifications at Mobile, Alabama. It is notable that they were not murdered or apparently even mistreated, which suggests that Forrest *could* exert control over his men in such situations, something he had not done during the massacre of black soldiers at Fort Pillow or during the aftermath of Brice's Crossroads.[19]

Four miles north of Athens, Forrest paused to destroy another blockhouse and trestle, and continued a short four miles beyond before he stopped for the night. The next morning, September 25, he moved on to Sulphur Branch trestle where, as at Athens, two blockhouses and a fort stood guard over a long trestle. A thousand men watched from inside the works while Forrest placed his cannon. Soon Morton's guns began to speak, and under the cover of their fire the cavalry crept toward the walls. The defenders of the Sulphur Branch works were more determined than those at Athens had been, and Forrest was growing frustrated. After two hours of artillery fire, Forrest called a truce and sent in a demand for surrender. He said to General Lyon, "I have sounded a parley, and intend demanding the surrender of this fort and if it does not surrender, and I am compelled to take it by assault, I will kill every man in it." Lyon supported his decision, but an assault proved to be unnecessary. The acting commanding officer, Colonel J. B. Minnis, surrendered. Forrest had lost thirty men wounded and one killed. It had been much worse for the Yankees.

Jordan and Pryor said, "The interior of the work presented a sanguinary, sickening spectacle . . . all the buildings within the parapets had either been razed or burned to the ground. Eight hundred rounds of ammunition had been expended by the Confederate artillery in this affair, and at least two hundred Federal officers and men lay slain within the narrow area." One of the dead was the commander, Colonel William H. Lathrop.[20]

As the garrison was surrendering, a relief party of eight hundred men from Elk River appeared and opened fire on the Confederates. After twenty minutes, they withdrew, and Buford was ordered to follow them with Lyon's brigade. Meanwhile, the others collected plunder and set fire to the works. They found "700 stands of small-arms, 2 pieces of artillery, 3 ambulances, 16 wagons, 300 cavalry horses and equipments, medical, quartermaster's, and commissary stores." It was an embarrassment of riches, but what they needed the most they did not find. There was a disappointing lack of artillery ammunition among the U.S. stores. In his barrage of eight hundred rounds, Morton had used up most of his supply of shells, and he had hoped to replenish it by capture. That failing, he decided to send four of his guns back south, along with the prisoners and loot from Sulphur Branch. Brian Wills points out that Forrest was growing weaker with each victory. He says, "Every time he sent prisoners and equipment back to the Tennessee River, he had to send his own men to guard them. Ironically, success was draining his manpower."[21]

At the very time that he was growing weaker, Forrest faced another problem that was a consequence of his success. The Federals, realizing the threat that they faced, were mobilizing against the Confederate raiders in ever greater numbers. Of course, sheer numbers would not suffice to drive Forrest away. There had to be men who would stand and fight. That is not what Buford and Lyon found at Elk River, where they had been sent from Sulphur Branch. They discovered that the white officers and black soldiers at Elk River had abandoned their works. Their cowardly withdrawal made the Confederates' work easy. The raiders burned the empty blockhouses and the long railroad bridge and moved eight miles farther up the railroad toward the railroad bridge at Richland Creek. En route, they destroyed another deserted blockhouse and ten thousand cords of firewood that was stacked beside the railroad for the use of the locomotives. As the fires burned behind them, they moved on to their juncture with Forrest at Brown's plantation, where there was a U.S. government stockade. Forrest said, "At this place I found about 2000 negroes, consisting mostly of old men, women, and children, besides a large amount of commissary stores and medical supplies." The blacks were evidently a contraband camp, and Forrest deplored what he found. He said, "The negroes were all ragged and dirty, and many seemed in absolute want. I ordered them to remove their clothing and bed clothes from the miserable huts in which they lived and then burnt up this den of wretchedness." He did not report that he tried in any way to relieve their "absolute want," but he did issue his reunited command "several days' rations [and] as much sugar and coffee as they needed" from the government stores.[22]

At Richland Creek, they found a single blockhouse guarding a long railroad bridge. Though their installation was small compared to others along the line, the garrison of fifty officers and men at Richland Creek showed more fight than any the raiders had met since Sulphur Branch. They initially fell back at Forrest's approach, and then they stopped, turned and "made a furious assault upon my troops." Forrest and his staff made a wide loop around them and surprised them from behind. Surrounded, they agreed to his demand for surrender, and another blockhouse and bridge went up in flames.[23]

The Federals officers whose job it was to stop Forrest decided that Pulaski was the place they would make their stand. On September 25, Major General Lovell Harrison Rousseau, commanding the District of Tennessee, informed General George H. Thomas, head of the Army of the Cumberland, "General [John T.] Croxton left Franklin with a brigade of cavalry at daylight this morning. I have sent by train to Pulaski 1300 cavalry and a battery, and will follow in an hour with all the other force that can be spared from here." In addition to the men from Nashville and Franklin, two train loads of troops from Chattanooga were on their way to Pulaski. Brigadier General John C. Starkweather's entire force at Pulaski previously numbered a meager twenty-three officers and 519 men. The reinforcements that began arriving at mid-day on September 26 raised his aggregate to six thousand.[24]

The Confederates appeared outside of Pulaski on September 27. There had been skirmishing as they came up the road from Richland Creek, and the closer they came to Pulaski the more determined Federal resistance became. When Forrest's advance was forced back, he ordered Buford's division to hurry forward and ordered his escort to deploy on Buford's right. Forrest said, "The resistance of the enemy was most obstinate. He contested every inch of ground and grew more stubborn the nearer we approached town, but my troops drove them steadily back." Three miles from town, the Yankees refused to be driven farther. Kelley was on the left, Johnson in the center, and Buford on the right. "The engagement was becoming a general one," Forrest said. The fire from Morton's battery disrupted a flanking movement around Forrest's left, and the bluecoats continued their retrograde movement. One, who called himself "Telegraph," said in a letter to the Nashville *Daily Union*, "We re-established our line on the hill south of the village and awaited the approach of 'Mr. Forrest' and his Southern chivalry, who were not long in making their appearance." Forrest indicated in his report that there was no interval in the fighting, as "Telegraph" seemed to suggest. Forrest said that from the end of the Yankee stand three miles outside of town, the enemy "was closely followed up and driven into town and into his fortifications. My command reached Pulaski about 1 o'clock." Forrest's men had kept the pressure on. His skirmishers edged up to within forty yards of the Union fortifications, but there they stalled. The contest had been going on for seven hours and everyone was ready for a breather. During the lull, while his skirmishers kept the defenders down and a work crew destroyed railroad and telegraph wire north of town, Forrest made a reconnaissance. What he saw was discouraging—a complex of redoubts linked with rifle pits, faced with a line of abatis and studded with cannon.[25]

Not liking his chances against such powerful fortifications, Forrest "determined to make no further assault." He went back to his officers about nightfall and told them to prepare to withdraw. While the skirmishers peppered the Federals with sporadic fire, the men built campfires along the line and slipped away, beginning about 10:00 PM. A rainstorm helped muffle the sounds of their withdrawal, and the enemy inside Pulaski had no idea that Forrest was leaving.[26]

Neither did General Lyon. His Kentucky Brigade was on the extreme flank and did not get the word of the withdrawal. After several hours of relative inactivity, Lyon decided "to go to Genl Forrests Head Quarters and ascertain what further move he contemplated, and when he reached Head Quarters he found General Abraham Buford in command, and to Lyon's question 'Where is Genl Forrest' Buford answered, 'He's gone and By God I am going too, and you must withdraw the troops.'" Lyon was presumably the last to leave Pulaski that night, and he did so without the loss of a man.[27]

General Rousseau had been in Pulaski during the fight and the brief siege that followed. He reported to General Thomas on the morning of September 28, "The enemy withdrew from this place last night going south. The wires are cut and almost sixty yards of the track on one side burnt." He was under no illusions that the raid was over; in fact, he anticipated Forrest's next target—Tullahoma—and he began shifting troops to block him. "Forrest may go up on south side of the Elk River to Tullahoma," Rousseau said. "Have ordered a force to follow and ascertain his intention. . . . To resist him successfully we must have more cavalry." The need for more cavalry was a theme Rousseau continued to strike over the following days. He said, "Forrest is here to stay unless driven back and routed by a superior cavalry force. Infantry can cause him to change camp but cannot drive him out of the State. . . . [This] is more than a raid; I regard it as a formidable invasion, the object of which is to destroy our lines, and he will surely do it unless met by a large cavalry force and killed, captured, or routed."[28]

At Pulaski, Forrest had had a mere taste of the forces that were massing against him. He understood the need for speed, but the same rain that covered the sound of his retreat also made the roads soft and hindered his march, and the raiders made only six or seven miles before stopping for the night. The next morning (the same morning the Federals discovered that they had disappeared), they proceeded toward Fayetteville. Forrest sent two detachments ahead, one from his escort and one from the 12th Kentucky Cavalry, to destroy the telegraph wires north and south of the town. The main column slogged along to within four miles of Fayetteville and camped. The next morning, September 29, they continued toward the Nashville & Chattanooga Railroad at Tullahoma, just as General Rousseau had guessed they would. En route, Forrest learned from his scouts "that the enemy was in strong force at Tullahoma, and at all vulnerable points on the railroad in that direction. Re-enforcements from Atlanta, Chattanooga, and other points were being hurried forward. There were not less than 15,000 troops sent forward to intercept my movements." He took stock of his own strength: low on artillery ammunition and down to half the number of guns he needed and with fewer men than he had started, considering casualties and the guards sent back to Alabama with the captured prisoners and property. He said, "Under these circumstances I deemed it hazardous and unwise to move upon the enemy, who was prepared to meet me with overwhelming numbers."[29]

The time had come to return south. To spread the destruction over as wide an area as possible, Forrest divided his command. General Buford was ordered to take the artillery and part of his division, as well as portions of Colonel William A. Johnson's and Colonel David C. Kelley's brigades, toward Huntsville, Alabama. He was to capture Huntsville if he could—an unlikely outcome with only 1500 men behind him—and demolish as much of the Memphis & Charleston Railroad as possible between Huntsville and Decatur. Forrest would keep parts of Lyon's and Bell's brigades, the 7th Tennessee, and the battalion that was known (confusingly) as Forrest's Old Regiment and go west for another strike against the Nashville & Decatur Railroad. If the condition of his horses would permit it, he would go all the way to the vast Federal supply depot of Johnsonville before returning to Mississippi. The two columns set out on the evening of September 29.

Forrest bivouacked on the Duck River north of Lewisburg on the night of the 30th and arrived at Spring Hill at mid-day on October 1. He immediately seized the telegraph office, where he found some dispatches detailing the location of the Federal patrols that were chasing him. Forrest took a page from the late John Hunt Morgan's book and sent a flurry of misleading wires from the Spring Hill office, hoping to send his pursuers in wrong directions. Before leaving town, he captured some U.S. government horses and wagons, and destroyed the nearby trestles. Columbia was the next stop on his itinerary.

Though his strength was reduced by half and he had no artillery, before the end of the day Forrest accomplished an impressive amount of destruction.

He destroyed piles of cordwood intended for railway fuel, four blockhouses, three railroad bridges, and a sawmill; captured twenty head of cattle; and accepted the surrender of 120 Yankees. The Confederates marched until ten o'clock that night, moving "by the light of the burning ruins, which illuminated the country for miles."[30]

General Forrest's troubles were mounting, however. His scouts reported that Buford had been unable to capture Huntsville and had made poor work of his assigned railroad demolition. Major General James B. Steedman was approaching with a column of 8000 infantry, General Rousseau was leading a mixed column of infantry and cavalry, and a third column of cavalry was heading his way from Tullahoma. Johnsonville would have to wait until another time. Forrest needed to move south quickly to evade these fifteen thousand Federals and to make a juncture with Buford.

The morning of October 2, Forrest drove in the Union pickets at Columbia and sent Bell's and Lyon's men to envelop the town. He said, "The reasons that prevented my storming and capturing Pulaski now existed with redoubled force, for I had not a single piece of artillery, and only half the troops I had with me at Pulaski." He characterized the action at Columbia as a reconnaissance in force "to take observations for future operations." Lacking the strength to reduce the substantial works in front of him, he had to content himself with burning a few trestles and gathering some supplies before he pressed on toward Lawrenceburg. Speed was the object now. The raiders passed through Lawrenceburg, and, on the fifth of October, they reached Florence on the Tennessee River. The river was a mile wide at this point and high from recent rains. George said, "The river was found to be much swollen, so much so that it was out of the question to attempt to ford it." Crossing was going to take some time, and the Yankees were bearing down. He sent the 2nd, 16th, and part of the 7th Tennessee back to the state line to fend off Generals Steedman and Rousseau, and he sent the 4th Alabama on a wide loop to hit the Federal rear. Meanwhile, the rest of the men began to cross. It was going to take time. They had only three rickety flatboats. The horses had to swim while the men paddled with all their strength against the current and the chop.[31]

The Federals appeared at Florence the next day, October 6. Forrest said, "The enemy were pressing upon my rear, which was greatly endangered. At this critical juncture I ordered all troops on the north side of the river, with the exception of one regiment, to mount their horses and swim them across a slough about seventy yards wide to a large island, which would afford them ample protection and from which they could ferry over at leisure." The regiment that was left on the north bank as a rearguard was the 16th Tennessee Cavalry under Colonel Andrew N. Wilson. Wilson's obstinacy allowed every other man to reach the island, but for two who drowned. Forrest said that Wilson was "entitled to the commendation of his Government and the lasting gratitude for the faithful [manner] in which he performed this important and hazardous trust." Amazingly, Wilson suffered only six casualties, and, after everyone else was across, he swam his regiment over and rejoined the column.[32]

The Confederates had escaped the Federal trap, and by October 6 they were back at their starting point. Forrest said, "During the expedition I captured 86 commissioned officers, 67 Government employés, 1274 non-commissioned officers and privates, 933 negroes, besides killing and wounding in the various engagements about 1000 more, making an aggregate of 3360, being an average of one to each man I had in the engagements. In addition to these I captured about 800 horses, 7 pieces of artillery, 2000 stand of small-arms, several hundred saddles, 50 wagons and ambulances, with a large amount of medical, commissary, and quartermaster's stores. . . . The greatest damage, however, done to the enemy was in the complete destruction of the railroad from Decatur to Spring Hill." In addition, he had destroyed eleven blockhouses, which is considered to have been "the most serious destruction of block-houses" by any Confederate cavalry leader in the war. And he had lost only forty-seven killed and 293 wounded.[33]

The men had impressed themselves by what they had done in their two-week adventure in Tennessee. Henry Ewell Hord said, "The Yankees had time to collect a considerable force to go after us. We were burdened with prisoners, mules, and horses, with Yankees in front of us and behind us. Old Forrest cleared the road in front, and Buford stood them off at our rear. Sometimes we had to fight all day and then ride all night, but we crossed in spite of gunboats or Yankees and never lost a prisoner."[34]

Forrest's Middle Tennessee Raid was colorful and daring, and no one could deny the skill with which it was conducted. But, of what importance was it, really? In the final analysis, not much; a fact that at least some of the men later admitted. Henry George of the 7th Kentucky Mounted Infantry, writing in 1911, said that if the raid "had been eight or ten months sooner it no doubt would have changed materially Sherman's campaign about Atlanta. While the campaign was brilliant beyond cavil, and a success from start to finish, yet it had been postponed too long to accomplish the purpose for which it was originally intended." The passage of a half century did not alter that evaluation. The Mississippian Shelby Foote, an admirer of Forrest, agrees with George, except that he considers the gap between the time of the raid and the time when it might have foiled Sherman to be even shorter than "eight or ten months." Foote says, "If the raid had been made a month or six weeks earlier, while the Federals were fighting outside Atlanta, opposed by an aggressive foe and with both overworked railroads [the Nashville & Decatur and the Nashville & Chattanooga] barely able to meet their daily subsistence needs, the result might have been different." That is what *might* have been. As it *was*, General Sherman scarcely took notice of the raid, and the thousands of Federal soldiers who were detached from other duties to chase Forrest were barely missed.[35]

That wider view of the raid came into focus only later. In October 1864, the men were proud of what they had accomplished, and Forrest was proud of them. He was generous with his praise in his official report. Of Buford and Lyon he said, "General Buford's division fully sustained that reputation it has so nobly won. General Lyon and Colonel Bell added new laurels to the chaplet which their valor and patriotism has already won."[36]

11

JOHNSONVILLE

Forrest's mention of "General Lyon and Colonel Bell" in his report revealed an unseemly situation. As a brigadier general, Lyon outranked everyone in Forrest's cavalry except for Forrest himself and Buford, who was superior only in seniority. Considering his rank, his military experience, and his talents, it was a misappropriation of resources for Lyon to continue as a brigade commander. It was inevitable that he would eventually be reassigned. In fact, the new assignment came during the raid, on September 26, 1864, while the raiders were at Richland Creek. Special Orders No. 228 said, "Brig. Gen. H. B. Lyon, Provisional Army, C.S., is assigned to the command of the department lately created in the State of Kentucky, and will report accordingly." The department "lately created" was the Military Department of Western Kentucky, and it was only three weeks old. Created by Special Orders No. 211 on September 6, it was described thus: "Commencing at the mouth of Salt River, Ky., and extending through Elizabethtown, Glasgow, and Tompkinsville, Ky., to Carthage, Tenn., thence along the Cumberland River to Nashville; thence with the line of the Northwestern railroad to the Tennessee River; thence west to Hickman, Ky., thence along the Mississippi River to the mouth of the Ohio River; thence along the Ohio River to the beginning of the line." Headquarters were in Paris, Tennessee. The first commander of the department was Brigadier General Adam R. Johnson, but Johnson was blinded in a skirmish with the Federals near Grubb's Crossroads, Kentucky, on August 21, 1864, even before the department's boundaries were officially delineated. When the government in Richmond learned of Johnson's irreversible disability, they assigned General Lyon to command.[1]

Lyon's assignment met with the approval of the officers with whom he would serve. It was one of his brigade commanders, Colonel James Q. Chenoweth, who said, "I had long known General Lyon and had previously served under him and for him personally entertained a great admiration. He was under all circumstances as cool and self-contained as Adam Johnson and considered by army men in the Confederacy amongst the bravest of the brave."[2]

The timing of events shows that sometime soon after the perilous crossing of the Tennessee River, Lyon left Forrest and traveled directly to his department headquarters at Paris. Forrest reached his starting point at Cherokee Station on October 6; Lyon launched a raid from Paris on October 7. He had a number of reasons for his expedition. He wanted to collect conscripts, horses, and cattle, he wanted to see the condition of his department, and—most important to him on a personal level—he wanted to see his wife and new son. Lyon and about 350 men set out from Paris, captured the steamboat *Chambers* at Clarksville and used it to cross the Cumberland River, and passed into Kentucky. At Hopkinsville, they briefly fought with Captain Samuel Jarrett and Co. K, 48th Kentucky Mounted Infantry. Jarrett was well dug in and refused both of Lyon's surrender demands. After a few hours, Lyon broke off the attack and made for Eddyville, taking with him a few prisoners, sixty horses, and an ambulance.

The Confederates arrived at Eddyville on October 13. Word had spread of the raid; the Washington newspapers were saying that Lyon had between two and three thousand men with him. The Louisville *Daily Journal* was closer to the facts when it reported the number of raiders to be five hundred men. Lyon found his hometown occupied by another company of the 48th Kentucky Mounted Infantry, along with eight recruiting officers of the 13th U.S. Colored Heavy Artillery, and the twenty-seven men they had recruited. The Yankees surrendered after a short fight, claiming a shortage of ammunition. Colonel John D. Abey, 13th United States Colored Heavy Artillery, who was at that time on his way from Louisville to assume command of the post of Eddyville, later reported that the prisoners were escorted out of town. Abey's report is vague as to time, so it is impossible to know how much time passed between the surrender and the removal of the prisoners out of Eddyville, and how much time passed between that and the arrival of the U.S. gunboat *Silver Lake, No. 2.* It was certainly more than hours; it may have been a number of days. Whatever the interval may be, the *Silver Lake* came to secure the release of the officers among Lyon's prisoners. The boat shelled the town, then a party of sailors came ashore and kidnapped General Lyon's wife. They held Mrs. Lyon as a hostage and let it be known she could be ransomed only by the release of the Federal officers in Lyon's custody. Abey said, "Word having been sent out to the general of this fact, he at once paroled the officers, but carried off the colored recruits." Mrs. Lyon was released once the officers were set free. One wonders what became of the black men who remained in General Lyon's custody. The record is silent, which is a clue in itself. If there had been a massacre or an atrocity of any sort, the newspapers and the Northern authorities would certainly have made it widely known. Probably the black prisoners were placed under guard and taken south, where they were returned to their slave masters or used as laborers on Confederate fortifications.[3]

During his all-too-short visit home, Lyon spread misinformation, intimating that an attack on Paducah was soon coming and that Nathan Bedford Forrest was coming to make Eddyville his headquarters. Colonel Abey promised his superiors that he would defend Eddyville "to the last extremity." He added "To enable me to accomplish this I should ask [for] about 400 men, colored troops, and one half battery of artillery. I believe I could, in about ten working days, so intrench the position as to render abortive an attack of far superior forces."[4]

Abey's plans were made with an eye toward the future. For the time being, Lyon remained in control of Eddyville, and that is where Colonel James Q. Chenoweth came to join him, bringing an additional one hundred men. Chenoweth reported that, en route, his party had come up behind a large group of black infantry returning from a foraging expedition. They charged into the rear of the USCT column and "drove them about a mile strewing the road with their dead." They chased the blacks to a farm, which was, to Chenoweth's "amazement," occupied by enemy troops. He said that "a deadly fire was poured out" from the farm house and the tobacco barns. The blacks rallied and added their fire to that of the unseen defenders. Two Rebels were killed and twelve wounded before Chenoweth could extract his men from the trap. They burned the supply wagons they had captured and proceeded to Eddyville, where they met with General Lyon.[5]

They camped together for a day before starting back, by separate routes, to Tennessee. Lyon's column began by swinging north to Smithland before turning east and then south on a line that took them into Logan County. Along the way they picked up the guerrilla band of Colonel Lee A. Sypert, whom the Louisville *Daily Journal* called "the rebel commander of that section of the country." Sypert had business in Logan County. He wanted to pay a visit to the Unionist leader Urban E. Kennedy. In a long letter to the *Daily Journal*, Kennedy explained what happened. He said:

> On the 20th of October, about sunrise, while putting on my clothes, I was informed by my family that the rebels were coming. I looked out, and the advance was then in my lots and stables taking my horses. I looked further up the lane and saw, as I thought, 1000 more, but in fact only about 300, with the Confederate flag flaunting in the breeze. They made no particular demonstration of hostility. Some asked for something

to eat. After the main column had nearly passed on, an officer rode to my steps and called for me to appear at the head of the column. I was quite sick and feeble, not having been out of the house or yard for more than two weeks. I told the officer I could not go. . . . He said I must go, dead or alive. . . . He told me that Col. Sypert had some demands on me, and I must go to where they would stop for breakfast. Off we went, and at the end of four miles they halted, and Gen. Lyon alighted and came to my buggy; then called Col. Sypert, with whom I had been acquainted in former days. [Sypert said], "You, Mr. Kennedy, was a member of the Kentucky legislature in 1861–62 and part of '63, and voted for all those obnoxious laws passed by that body."[6]

Mr. Kennedy admitted that he was the man and said that Sypert had described his legislative record truly. He showed a great deal of pluck by adding that he would do the same things again if the circumstances were the same. His captive's identity being verified, Sypert named his demands. Kennedy continued:

He [Sypert] then said he had a friend in prison in Louisville for whom I must stand as a hostage, and that he would parole me to use my influence to have his friend, B. P. Wallace of Webster County [a guerrilla] to report to Paris, Tenn. If unsuccessful, I was to report there myself in 20 days. . . . I must here say that Gen. Lyon treated me very kindly and made some modest remonstrances against Sypert's course, but finally agreed to take my parole. . . . So I was released but badly whipped and returned home. My particular friend, Col. B. H. Bristow, was then in Louisville, to whom I appealed for assistance. He went to work for my relief and finally B. P. Wallace was released.[7]

The Federals had taken general's wife hostage, and now General Lyon's men had captured Mr. Kennedy. It seems that seizing civilians toward the attainment of a military goal was the fashion for both blue and gray in Kentucky that fall. Lyon swung east from Logan County and made his next appearance at Woodburn, below Bowling Green, on the evening of October 21. His men threw a southbound freight train off the Louisville & Nashville tracks and dashed out of the dark to capture the train. When a second locomotive, that of a construction crew, rolled onto the scene, they captured it, too. The two crews were taken prisoner. The newspaper reports of the incident did not mention any robbing, but considering the poverty of Lyon's department, it is hard to believe that none occurred. The two trains were burned with all their freight, and the railroad was closed for a while between Bowling Green and Franklin.

General Lyon was returning to Tennessee with several hundred horses and more than one hundred recruits. He had to weave his way through enemy patrols and travel fast, and it was inevitable that small groups of men would be cut off and left to make their way back to Paris the best way they could. Some who were shaken loose from their regiments did not seem to make too strenuous an effort to rejoin their general. They were representative of the increasing number of Confederates who were giving up the cause as lost and taking every chance to excuse themselves from any further participation. Private J. M. Stevens and two of his comrades were among those who were left behind during Lyon's October raid. They became separated early in the raid. Every place they tried to cross the Cumberland River was guarded, so they gave up trying. They found their way to the little town of Saratoga and went to a saloon. The bartender was anxious to get the three Rebel stragglers out of his establishment, so he told them about a Yankee supply train that had passed by on the way to Eddyville. They filled their canteens with whiskey and left. After a little more drinking, they decided to ambush the wagons. They rode ahead through the woods and fields to find a good spot for their attack. When the wagons approached, they fired, wounding two of the guards and killing another. Then they fled. The ambush had been ill-considered; three men could not take on a full complement of wagon guards. The country was soon crawling with patrols seeking them, and the three decided that there was no escape. They sent word to the Union headquarters in Princeton to ask what terms they could expect if they surrendered. The answer came back that they would be paroled. On the strength of this assurance they went in, but in Princeton they were accused of being guerrillas and taken into custody. They were placed under the guard of some black soldiers. Stevens said they decided to "knock down these guards and make our escape." The other two got away, but Stevens could not break free. He was subdued and then confined.[8]

The next day, a detail of twelve Federals showed up and took Stevens into the woods to execute him. They stripped him of almost everything, even his hat and shoes, and the captain in charge of the firing squad asked him if he wanted a blindfold. He said no, all he wanted was to pray. He said that, as he knelt, "something whispered to me: 'Jump the fence.'" This he did. He fell just as the guards fired and their shots went too high. Stevens leaped up and dashed into the timber. The Yankees followed and searched for him. It was lucky that they did not look up, for he had scrambled up a tall cedar tree.

Finally, they fired a volley just beneath his perch, dug a grave in which they laid a cedar limb to rest, and returned to their post. Nearly naked, Stevens made his way to his father's house, fourteen miles away. He later heard that the bluecoats had reported that they had executed him, as ordered. For Stevens, the war was over, except for an epilogue. He was later discovered, presumably at his father's house and by some soldiers who did not recognize him, and was again taken into custody. He was paroled from Fort Donelson on May 12, 1865.[9]

Short a few stragglers, but with more than enough recruits to make up the loss, Lyon crossed the state line and was back in his Paris, Tennessee, headquarters by the last week in October. Young Nannie Haskins wrote in her diary about how some of her friends had seen General Lyon and his men when they passed through Clarksville. She admired the splendid looking men who, in her view, were defending the homeland against a tyrannical foe. She wrote, "Oh, how I envy them." Lyon's time at his headquarters was brief. He did not do much more than pause there for a change of clothes before he was off again. Federal scouts reported that he crossed the Nashville & Northwestern Railroad with six hundred men on October 24. They were going south to join General Forrest on another raid, this one against the great U.S. supply depot at Johnsonville.[10]

Johnsonville was on the east bank of the Tennessee River about eighty miles from Nashville. It was connected to the Tennessee capital by the Nashville & Northwestern Railroad, which had been built to guarantee an uninterrupted flow of supplies in case the Louisville & Nashville Railroad was broken and the Cumberland River low, both of which had happened too often for comfort. Johnsonville's importance to the Union effort in the West was indicated by the size of its garrison, described as: the "Forty-third Wisconsin Volunteers . . . detachments of the Twelfth, Thirteenth, and One hundredth U.S. Colored Infantry . . . [a] detachment of the Eleventh Tennessee Cavarly . . . [the] First Kansas Battery . . . Company A, Second U.S. Colored Artillery," and eight hundred armed employees of the Quartermaster Corps. The aggregate was more than 1500 infantry- and artillerymen to guard the monstrous complex of warehouses and rail facilities that sat hunched on the river bank in a raw setting of tree stumps, mud, and the haze of a thousand campfires. The land forces were under the overall command of Colonel C. R. Thompson, 12th U.S. Colored Infantry. Lieutenant Commander Edward M. King was in charge of the three gunboats that were moored in the river: the *Key West*, the *Elfin*, and the *Tawah*.[11]

Forrest had hoped to hit the Johnsonville supply depot at the end of his Middle Tennessee Raid. He was foiled when Rousseau's and Steedman's pursuit columns converged on him too quickly and forced an early end to his

The Federal supply depot at Johnsonville, Tennessee, 1864. Library of Congress.

expedition. Now he was ready. The Wizard was in Jackson with Colonel Edmund W. Rucker's brigade, which, when joined by five hundred men under General James Chalmers, constituted a division with Chalmers in command. Forrest ordered Colonel Tyree H. Bell to move with his brigade to Lavinia and General Abraham Buford to move with the Kentucky Brigade to Lexington. Lyon either joined Buford and the Kentuckians at Lexington or when they passed through Paris on the way to Fort Heiman, Kentucky. Fort Heiman was opposite Fort Henry on the Tennessee River. The raid on Johnsonville was going to commence with blockading that river. That was Lyon's and Bell's assignment. Lyon was placed in charge of Fort Heiman with the Kentucky Brigade and a masked battery of two 20-pounder Parrott guns. At the same time, Bell was posted upstream at Paris Landing with his brigade and another section of artillery. The distance between them was five miles, and they represented the ends of a deadly hot box about which the Federals knew nothing until the morning of October 29, 1864, when the gunboat *Mazeppa* steamed upstream past Fort Heiman and directly into the trap. Three rounds of artillery fire were all it took to persuade the pilot to scuttle his boat. When a round clipped her steam pipe and disabled her, the man at the wheel steered her into the opposite bank, and the crew scattered into the trees. The

Confederates did not have so much as a canoe with them. How to get to the enemy vessel on the far side of the Tennessee River presented an aggravating problem. Finally, Captain Frank P. Gracey swam the river to the *Mazeppa*. In later years, a minor tempest developed over who the swimmer had been, but General Lyon confirmed that it was Captain Gracey in a 1902 letter to Gracey's son. The letter was later reprinted in *Confederate Veteran*. Lyon said to Julian F. Gracey, "I recollect that your father swam the Tennessee River, took possession of the steamer *Mazeppa*, which had been disabled by our artillery and landed against the eastern shore of the Tennessee River in order that her crew might escape from our forces, then on the west bank of the river, and he used one of the *Mazeppa*'s yawls in sending to us one end of a rope, the other end of which was tied to the boat, and we used this rope in pulling the *Mazeppa* to our (west) bank of the river."[12]

It was a good first capture. The boat itself was valued at $40,000, and the cargo was estimated to be worth $200,000. Henry George remembered that the *Mazeppa* was "loaded with army blankets, shoes and other valuable things of which the Confederates were so badly in need." An article in the Chicago *Tribune* was more specific about her cargo. The *Tribune* said that the *Mazeppa* carried one thousand barrels of flour, eighty cook stoves, fifty-nine bales of hay, three hundred boxes of brogans, three hundred boxes filled with coats, one thousand sacks of grain, an unspecified number of bales of blankets and boxes of hardtack, and "several bales of Government goods." One item that particularly delighted General Buford was the French brandy on board. Buford and some others re-crossed the river in the yawl that brought the rope, and it was once on board the *Mazeppa* that he discovered the liquor. Captain John W. Morton wrote, "As the boat was being pulled across, General Buford, who was on the hurricane deck, raised the jug to his lips. The men on the bank chaffingly called to him not to take it all, and the General replied, 'Plenty of meat, boys, plenty of hard-tack, shoes, and clothes for all the boys, but just enough whiskey for the General.'"[13]

The cargo of the *Mazeppa* was unloaded, and, late in the afternoon, the boat was burned. As the work went on, a small flotilla of the enemy's gunboats came steaming downstream. Bell's gun crew drove them off, but the secret was now out that the Confederates were on the river below Johnsonville. Even so, boats kept appearing. The next morning, October 30, the *Anna* came down. A few shots from the upper battery (Bell's) hit her and it appeared that she was going to surrender. A white flag appeared, and she nosed toward the Kentucky bank of the river. General Buford, expecting to enjoy some more captured liquor "threw his tobacco out and walked down to receive her." Suddenly, she threw on full steam and shot downstream. None of the rounds the *Anna* had taken were disabling, and she had edged so close to the bank that Lyon's Parrott guns could not depress their tubes enough to fire on her. When it was clear that she was going to escape, Buford, "with a look of disappointment," yelled, "Shoot hell out of her!" The cannons roared as the *Anna* disappeared from view, and Buford missed his morning toddy.[14]

The *Anna*'s escape was a nice piece of seamanship, for she emerged from the trap badly damaged. The Chicago *Tribune* said, "Her pilothouse, texas and cabin were completely riddled with shot of every size." Her machinery finally failed, so she had to be taken in tow by a gunboat and pulled into Paducah, where her officers and crew spread the report that Forrest was close by. The city went into a frenzy. A rumor spread with the speed that such rumors do that Forrest had twelve thousand men at Fort Heiman and Paris Landing and had a dozen artillery pieces. Brigadier General Solomon Meredith, commanding the District of Western Kentucky, yelped to department headquarters, "I need more assistance. All reports concur that he is to attack me soon. . . . I ought to at least have 2000 men for this place." He ended his dispatch on a brave note, saying, "Give me a sufficient force and I will drive him out of the country," but his alarm was unmistakable.[15]

In spite of the knowledge both upstream and down that the Confederates were in place, boats kept appearing. In quick succession after the *Anna* came the gunboat *Undine*, the troop transport *Venus*, and the *J. W. Cheeseman*. They steamed right into the trap and behaved with the desperate circling run of cornered animals. George said, "When they had passed the guns of Bell's brigade they opened fire on them, but damaged them but little. When they came within range of the guns with the Kentucky brigade they opened fire on them with such telling effect that they turned to make their escape up the river, past the guns they had passed coming down, but when they came in range of the guns with Bell's brigade they opened on them with such a fusillade of shot that they were afraid to attempt to pass them again. They were then between the two batteries, neither of which could reach them. At this time another steamer came down the river and was captured between the two batteries." The end came only after Colonel Rucker moved forward to a point where his guns could reach the enemy vessels. A few rounds persuaded them to surrender.[16]

The last boat the Confederates captured, the *J. W. Cheeseman*, was a supply boat, which "proved to be laden with sutler stores and furniture, and the candies, nuts, and good things were quickly loaded around and devoured by the hungry troopers, so long accustomed to hard-tack and lean beef." The *Cheeseman* was so badly damaged that she was subsequently burned. That left the *Undine* and the *Venus*, and Forrest had plans for them. He went to Captain Morton, his artillery chief, and asked, "John, how would you like to transfer your guns to these boats and command a gunboat fleet?" Morton did not like the idea at all. He said that land batteries were his forte and told Forrest he preferred "to say on *terra firma*."[17]

Forrest ended up giving command of the *Undine* to Captain Gracey, who had swum the river to make possible the retrieval of the *Mazeppa,* and who was himself a former riverboat pilot. He gave the *Venus,* soon to be armed with two Parrott guns, to Lieutenant Colonel W. A. Dawson, who accepted his new role reluctantly. He said to Forrest, "General, I will go with these boats wherever you order, but I tell you candidly that I know very little about managing gunboats. You must promise me that if I lose the fleet you won't give me a cussing when I wade ashore and come back on foot." Forrest is said to have laughed. He told Dawson not to worry, just ground the boat and burn it, if necessary.[18]

The two boats of Forrest's brown water fleet were taken for a practice run so that their crews could get some experience before they cruised into battle. The army officers were on board as guests. After a while, the officers were put back on shore, Confederate flags were run up the masts, and on November 1, the *Undine* and the *Venus* headed upstream. The cavalry marched parallel to the river on the west bank, Chalmers in the lead and Buford guarding the rear. On this occasion, at least, the horsemen may have envied the men on the boats, for a heavy rain had set in and made the going hard for the mounted element of Forrest's expedition. Both arms halted for the night at Danville. The second day was a repeat of the first, until two enemy vessels appeared in the afternoon. They were the *Key West* and the *Tawah* come down from Johnsonville. The *Undine* backed off, but the *Venus* could not get away. Her two Parrott guns and her inexperienced crew were no match for the superior guns and seasoned Union seamen. Colonel Dawson steered her into the bank, and the crew hurried away. They had not had time to follow Forrest's orders to burn the boat.

Now it was Forrest who was in the hotbox. Johnsonville was ahead of him; its gunboats were patrolling the river and its powerful garrison of infantry and artillery waited on shore; and a flotilla of six gunboats under the command of Lieutenant Commander LeRoy Fitch was coming up the Tennessee behind him. Another officer might have suspended the operation, with some justification for doing so, but Forrest had his sights on Johnsonville, and he would not be dissuaded. The next day, November 3, he arrived at his goal. He said, "All my troops having arrived, I commenced disposing of them with a view of bombarding the enemy." In this, he sought General Lyon's help. He said to the Kentuckian, "Lyon, you were an artillery officer, and I want you to ride with me to the Tennessee River, and tell me whether or not the Yankees can with their guns in Forts on the hills in rear of Johnsonville, hurt badly a command on this side of the river." That was the way Lyon remembered Forrest speaking to him.[19]

The two rode to where they could examine the enemy's gun placement, and Lyon answered Forrest that "the Yankees could not depress their guns as to hurt his command on that side of the river, for, if they did depress them, the recoil would dismount their guns."[20]

Forrest then said to Lyon, "Lyon, how many men would you want to sink a six gun battery tonight so that it cannot be seen from the other side of the river?" Lyon said, "One thousand men with all the picks and shovels that can be found in the country around here." Forrest answered, "All right, I will order the detail, and will order Morton to have one of his batteries placed at your command." Captain James C. Thrall's howitzer battery was assigned to Lyon.[21]

The ground was perfect for what Forrest and Lyon intended. A description of the immediate terrain was given years later in an article by E. G. Cowen in *Confederate Veteran*. Cowen said, "On the western side the bank rises twenty feet above the water and drops back abruptly to a bottom, thus forming a natural earthwork, at that time heavily timbered and overgrown with cane. . . . Under [Lyon's] direction, the guns were pushed forward to within a few feet of the river and sunk below the surface of the ground in pits, with embrasures cut through the bank." The guns were in position and masked with brush before daylight. Lyon's was the upper battery. A second battery was placed directly across from Johnsonville, and a third was placed below.[22]

Captain John W. Morton arrived the next morning, Friday, November 4, and did not like the placement of one of the batteries. One thinks that it must have been professional jealousy that made Morton so dissatisfied with the placement of the guns; Lyon had directed it and not himself, and he felt the need to reassert his supremacy as chief of artillery. He asked Forrest for permission to adjust the one battery's position. Forrest agreed to delay his attack, scheduled to begin at noon, for two hours to give Morton time to complete his arrangements. In the meantime, the Union gunboats had to be considered. Forrest was satisfied from what Lyon had told him that he was safe from the Johnsonville shore batteries, but the gunboats were another matter. They could come to him, and they must be removed as a threat. The previous afternoon he had tried and failed to lure them into range by a display from the *Undine*. On the morning of the 4th, while waiting for Morton to move his battery, Forrest ordered the *Undine* to repeat her earlier performance. She steamed to within sight of Johnsonville and tried by every trick her captain knew to decoy the Federal flotilla into the range of Forrest's masked batteries. This time, it worked. Captain Henry Howland, assistant quartermaster at Johnsonville, wrote, "Our gunboats immediately moved down, shelling the rebel sharpshooters along the shore as they advanced. When nearly within range of the *Undine* firing was heard below. . . . This proved to come from a number of gunboats that had just arrived from below." Lieutenant Commander LeRoy Fitch's fleet had come on the scene, and his six gunboats had engaged with one of Forrest's shore batteries. Meanwhile, the Rebel artillerists were doing well against Lieutenant Commander King's Johnsonville three-boat flotilla. The *Key West* was taking a pounding and some of her guns were disabled, the *Elfin* had sustained some injuries, and the *Tawah* was leaking and her crew discovered belatedly that a recently arrived issue of ammunition was of the wrong size for her guns. However, the *Undine* had sustained some damage as well, and those six boats coming up behind presented a threat that Captain Frank P. Gracey believed he could not meet.[23]

One observer said that Gracey "was sorely pressed by gunboats above and below, shells exploding all around him, and fast knocking the little boat to pieces. The result was inevitable. He saw that he would be compelled to abandon her. He ordered the guns to be charged and the mattresses cut open and pressed into the magazine." The stuffing from the mattresses was scattered around the deck and doused with oil. He ran the boat aground against a sandbar and then ordered his men off the boat. When he saw that they were on the bank, "he walked back and set fire to the mattresses; then going deliberately to the bow of the boat, where the bursting shells made the heavens lurid, and waving defiance at the enemy, he jumped into the river and swam ashore." A little after 11:00 AM, the boat's magazine exploded, and, as the C.S.S. *Undine* sank below the surface of the Tennessee River, the short, colorful history of Forrest's aquatic cavalry came to an end.[24]

The Federals convinced themselves that Forrest retreated after the destruction of the *Undine*. It was a misty autumn day. Sounds were muffled and visibility limited. The three gunboats returned to the Johnsonville wharf to see to their repairs. Watching from concealment, the Rebels could see the deckhands and the dock workers going about their duties, while the soldiers on shore visited with a party of visiting local ladies. The lull lasted until mid-afternoon, when the Yankees observed Morton's artillery crew working to adjust the position of that one battery, as the captain had ordered. The fort on the hill opened fire and, more seriously, so did the gunboats. Forrest did not reply for about twenty minutes. Then, at three o'clock, the Rebel guns opened up. Lyon seemed to claim in his late life memoir that his battery was the first to open fire, but Forrest said in his report, "The bombardment commenced by the section of Morton's battery commanded by Lieutenant [John W.] Brown. The other batteries joined promptly in the assault." Whoever was the first to respond to the Johnsonville gunners, the curtain had raised on one of the most dazzling performances of the war. The orchestration alone was sensational. Captain Howland said that the roar of the contending cannon "was the most terrific I have ever witnessed."[25]

Fifty Confederate and Federal guns were in deafening action for the next quarter hour. Then the gunboats, having fired most of their ammunition and having sustained disabling damage, were set afire by order of Lieutenant Commander Edward M. King. Forrest said, "My batteries next opened upon the transports." Lieutenant Commander King ordered Captain Howland to burn them, as well. The sparks from the burning transports flew against the boxes and bundles of commissary and quartermaster stores on the docks, and they began to burn. The fire spread from the docks to the warehouses. Things were getting out of control. Confederate sharpshooters kept back the Yankees who came forward to fight the fires, and the artillery shells kept falling "into the midst of the supply station." A reporter for the New York *Times* who was on the scene later said, "An immense conflagration was raging with unabated fury, the rebel batteries kept up one of the most terrific cannonading ever heard, shot and shell bursting from the mouths of over thirty twenty-pound Parrott guns. The scene during the entire Friday evening and to a late hour in the night, was grand and terrific, and baffles description." The whole panorama was never to be forgotten, but one detail of the scene was uniquely memorable. Shelby Foote relates that there "was a warehouse on high ground, which, when struck and set afire, turned out to be stocked with several hundred barrels of whiskey that burst from the heat and sent a crackling blue-flame river of bourbon running down the hillside."[26]

It was a fantasia, an extravaganza! The Confederates had a front row seat at the greatest entertainment most of them would see in their lifetimes. Even Forrest agreed that the show was spectacular. He said in his report, "By night the wharf for nearly one mile up and down the river presented one solid sheet of flame." He was so delighted with the thoroughness of the destruction he was dealing out to the enemy that he took a turn at a cannon and played artilleryman. As the amused officers and men around him watched, he sighted and fired the gun and "when a shot fell short, General Forrest would exclaim: 'A rickety-shay! A rickety-shay! I'll hit her next time!' He adjusted his aim by ordering the gunners, 'Elevate the breach of that gun lower!'"[27]

Two Federal transports survived the conflagration, and Forrest had plans for them. About dark, he went to General Lyon and asked if he "could cut the hawsers of the two transports, not burned, and let them float below Johnsonville where he could cotton clad them and run by the batteries at Johnsonville and run them to Florence, Alabama, and aid General John Bell Hood in crossing his army over [the] Tennessee River on his expedition to Nashville." General Hood had slipped away from Sherman at Atlanta and was leading the Army of Tennessee north toward Nashville and, perhaps, beyond, to Kentucky. He believed that Sherman could not allow him to operate unopposed along his lines of communication in North Georgia and Tennessee; he would be forced to follow. Forrest had this in mind when it occurred to him to send Lyon and the unburned transport boats to Hood. Lyon said that he would give it a try. He picked his crew and was about to start across the river when "fire burst out of the top of the two boats, and they with the others were burned to the water's edge."[28]

Night was falling. Satisfied that he had accomplished his purpose at Johnsonville, Forrest fell back six miles in the direction of Corinth, his way "lighted by the light of the enemy's burning property." He left Rucker's brigade and one section of artillery to cover the withdrawal. The next morning, November 5, Rucker's artillery fired on Johnsonville for about an hour, and Forrest came back to look over the scene of his great victory. There was "nothing to be seen but great piles of ashes from its ruins, save the fort, which stood out in bold relief with its great guns, which had been of so little value the day before." Forrest's spirits were high as he studied the ruins across the river, and he said to Captain Morton, "There is no doubt we could soon wipe old Sherman off the face of the earth, John, if they'd give me enough men and you enough guns."[29]

Forrest said that, at a cost to himself of only two men and nine wounded, he had destroyed "4 gunboats, 14 transports, 20 barges, 26 pieces of artillery." He added, "Brigadier General Buford, after supplying his own command, turned over to my chief quartermaster about 9,000 pairs of shoes and 1,000 blankets." Including everything, Forrest placed an estimate of $6,700,000 on the property damages done to the enemy.[30]

The Federals calculated the loss to be $2,200,000; about a third of Forrest's estimate. "Old Sherman" griped, "That devil Forrest was down about Johnsonville, making havoc among the gunboats and transports." It was a costly annoyance, but not crippling. Sherman said as much in a letter to General Grant, when he dismissed the raid as unimportant, since, "We now have abundant supplies at Atlanta, Chattanooga and Nashville with the Louisville and Nashville R. Road, and the Cumberland River unmolested." Sherman's comment would have sounded defensive, except that it was true. Forrest's destruction of Johnsonville had come too late to have any effect on Sherman's operations in Georgia, and it did not affect General George H. Thomas (who was making preparations in Nashville to meet and defeat John Bell Hood and the Army of Tennessee), except to make him send reinforcements to Colonel Thompson. The reinforcements were unnecessary; Forrest was falling back.[31]

The Confederates moved over "almost impassable roads" to Corinth. Beyond there, they continued to Iuka and to Florence. Forrest had nothing except praise for his division and brigade commanders. Of Lyon, he said, "Brigadier General Lyon, who has been assigned to another department, reported to me on this expedition and rendered much valuable service at Johnsonville and Fort Heiman." It was a fitting benediction to Lyon's service with the Kentucky Brigade. After Johnsonville, Lyon never commanded his Kentuckians again. He returned to his own department and was soon off on an expedition of his own; very few knew exactly where, except that it was off to the north. As Nannie Haskins wrote in her diary, "Lyon is somewhere in the woods."[32]

12

LYON'S KENTUCKY RAID

It was the intention of Lieutenant General John Bell Hood to drive hard into the heart of Tennessee, blow through General George H. Thomas's army at Nashville, and race through lightly defended Kentucky all the way to the Ohio River. Middle Tennessee would be freed of Federal occupation, and Kentucky, which had joined the Confederacy only on a provisional basis, would at last realize the promise that Henry C. Burnett, Willis B. Machen, and others had made at the Russellville convention back in 1861. At the same time, Georgia would be saved. The rear echelon troops would be insufficient to handle the Army of Tennessee as it racked up victories and destroyed Sherman's communications through Nashville, Bowling Green, and, perhaps, all the way to Louisville. Uncle Billy would be forced to turn his back on Georgia and come north to salvage what he could of Union military and political rule in the West. It was a daring plan, and Hood, the man Robert E. Lee had once compared to a lion, was confident that he could carry it off. He summoned Nathan Bedford Forrest from Mississippi to join him, and he gave General H. B. Lyon a role to play, as well.

Lyon found the orders waiting for him when he returned from Johnsonville to his Paris, Tennessee, headquarters on November 20, 1864. With a dateline of November 18, Florence, Alabama, they had come to Lyon via Forrest, and they said, "General Hood directs that you will move at once with your command, crossing the Tennessee and Cumberland Rivers between Paducah and Johnsonville, and then move up the north bank of the Cumberland to Clarksville, taking possession of that place, if possible. You will place all the mills within your reach on that side of the Cumberland in running order, and put them to grinding at once. You will also destroy the railroads between Nashville and Clarksville, and between Bowling Green and Nashville, taking care to keep all the telegraphic communications between these places constantly destroyed." With Lyon operating in the Yankees' rear. Hood would be able to move boldly against their front.[1]

In addition to destroying infrastructure to prevent intelligence and reinforcements from reaching General Thomas and repairing the mills and grinding corn in anticipation of Hood's arrival in Kentucky, Lyon had another purpose for his raid, and that was to enforce the Confederate conscription law. It went into effect in December 1864. The Federals inadvertently helped Lyon in this by instituting their own draft law. The Federal Writers' Project's *Military History of Kentucky* points out that when the Union draft began, "drafted men disappeared in great numbers . . . nearly 7000 men of the men drafted in Kentucky in November and December, 1864, failed to report for duty." Lowell Harrison adds, "Some men hid out in their own neighborhoods; others moved to states where they were not known, and a number fled to Canada or Europe. Some joined guerrilla bands, and a considerable number decided that if they had to fight, they would prefer to be on the Confederate side." Lyon expected to take advantage of the situation in Kentucky by adding Union draft evaders to Confederate enlistment rolls, and, up to a point, it worked. During the first half of his raid, from Hopkinsville to Elizabethtown, nearly six hundred men escaped the clutches of U.S. conscription officers and came to join Lyon.[2]

On December 6, 1864, Lyon left Paris, Tennessee, with eight hundred men divided into two brigades. Colonel J. J. Turner commanded the First Brigade, and Colonel James Q. Chenoweth commanded the Second Brigade. There were also two 12-pounder howitzers from Cobb's Battery, commanded by Captain Frank P. Gracey. General Lyon no doubt had confidence in his three subordinates, but he had misgivings about the men. He said that they were "undisciplined and but poorly organized . . . poorly equipped, except in arms, 100 of my men were dismounted, but few had blankets or overcoats, and many were destitute of shoes or clothing sufficient to make a respectable appearance."[3]

On December 9, the column reached Cumberland City on the Cumberland River a few miles south of Fort Donelson. Captain Gracey captured the U.S. troop transport *Thomas E. Tutt* by using the same trick the Confederates had used at Fort Heiman. Gracey placed one howitzer upstream and one down and created a hot box which blocked the boat from escaping on either end. She suffered only minor damage before she was captured. The *Tutt* proved to be "loaded with forage and provisions." Lyon's men robbed and paroled the crew, and then they clambered aboard the *Tutt* to be ferried across to the east bank. Presumably, Frank Gracey, the former riverboat pilot, took charge of the wheel. Once everyone was across, Lyon captured two more paddle wheelers and four barges, which he used to block the channel. He anchored them there and burned them, along with the *Tutt*. He also burned the trestle and the water tanks on the Memphis branch of the Louisville &

Nashville Railroad, and he tore down the telegraph wires. The raid was off to an impressive start. Lyon estimated the property damages at Cumberland City to be $1,000,000. The embarrassed Union officers found a small measure of comfort in the Kentuckian's destruction of the boats. It was a critical mistake, they believed. Rear Admiral Samuel P. Lee at Clarksville crowed, "Lyon has no visible means of recrossing." Typically, the Federals overestimated his strength at nine guns and up to five thousand men, but at least he was trapped.[4]

Lyon might be trapped on the wrong side of the Cumberland, but that still gave him a very large territory to roam. The Federals were not sure where he was going. Some informants said that he was heading toward Munfordville, Kentucky, to destroy the great L&N Railroad bridge over the Green River. Others believed that his target was either Henderson or Hopkinsville, Kentucky. Still others speculated that he was going to Fort Donelson. Colonel A. A. Smith at Clarksville was so convinced that Fort Donelson was Lyon's destination that he sent the 42nd Missouri Infantry down as reinforcements. Lyon had no intention of attacking Fort Donelson. Even Clarksville proved to be too well defended for an attack. Instead, Lyon turned north. Colonel Chenoweth said that after only a few hours at Cumberland City, "Lyon's entire division was in line for the winter's raid on Kentucky. By forced marches and through a driving snowstorm we reached Hopkinsville." When they approached the outskirts of the Christian County seat on December 11, the garrison of four hundred United States Colored Troops fled. Lyon and his men took possession of the town unopposed on the twelfth of December.[5]

Miss Fannie Keen was twenty-one years old and single on the morning General Lyon and his men rode into Hopkinsville. Fifty years later, when she was the widow of Edward C. Roach and a venerable member of the United Daughters of the Confederacy, she shared her recollections of that day. She said, "When he [Lyon] reached Hopkinsville, my father pleaded with him to spare the [courthouse] here, with all its old papers, but he could not be moved from his purposes." The courthouse had been used as a barracks for U.S. Colored troops, and Lyon insisted on burning it. He did allow the citizens to remove the county records before they put the building to the torch, however. It is an odd and seemingly contradictory facet of Lyon's behavior during his raid that he repeatedly allowed citizens to preserve their deeds and tax documents and their records of civil and criminal law while at the same time he would not be turned aside from his determination to burn their temples of justice. It is hard to reconcile, but that was the case. The ragged Confederates clothed themselves out of Hopkinsville's stores, and they robbed the bank, and some of the people began to wonder if a Confederate occupation was in any way preferable to having the Federals in town.[6]

Ruins of the Burned Christian County Courthouse, Hopkinsville, Kentucky, December 1864. Courtesy of the William T. Turner Collection, Museums of Historic Hopkinsville-Christian County.

Colonel Chenoweth said that Lyon decided to rest at Hopkinsville "until he could receive definite information concerning Hood's army of the Tennessee, which had fought the disastrous but glorious little battle at Franklin on the 30th day of November, and was now investing the city of Nashville." That did not mean that he needed all of his men to sit idle and wait for the latest intelligence from Tennessee. He granted some of the men furloughs, and, the next day, December 13, he took Colonel J. J. Turner's brigade toward Cadiz, Eddyville, and Princeton. Colonel Chenoweth was left to occupy Hopkinsville with his men.[7]

It was a relatively short ride from Hopkinsville to Cadiz, and Lyon and Turner arrived a few hours later on the same day, December 13. The black garrison of Cadiz fled at their approach, but several were captured and escorted back to town. The Trigg County courthouse had a cupola and a roof of wooden shakes. The prisoners were ordered to climb up top and tear them off to prevent the fire from spreading to nearby homes after the courthouse was put to the torch. Once they were finished with their precautions, the courthouse was fired, and the raiders proceeded to Eddyville. Lyon's return to his hometown was a dangerous move. The kidnapping of Mrs. Lyon in October showed how quickly a Union gunboat could appear and seize prisoners, and cavalry or mounted infantry from Paducah could very easily have surrounded him before he knew they were near. Furthermore, the excursion to Eddyville was not strictly within the parameters of his orders. Lyon may have been thinking of a military justification for going to Eddyville when he ordered Captain Gracey to place one of his howitzers at Kelly's Crossing on the Cumberland River, twelve miles below, to threaten Federal shipping. The gun did fire on the *Naugatuck* as she passed and placed three 12-pound balls through her pilothouse and smokestack. (The Yankees thought that there were eight guns at Kelly's Crossing.) When the artillery rounds failed to stop her, the men opened up with small arms fire, "and her upper works [were] thoroughly riddled." The *Naugatuck* escaped to spread the news of Confederate raiders on the Cumberland. The region was frightened by the reports of Lyon's proximity, and, as always, the rumors flew—he was marching on Evansville, Smithland, and Morganfield simultaneously, and he was "enforcing the conscription law to the very letter" every place he went and everywhere in between.[8]

While the people worked themselves into a frenzy and spread wild, unsubstantiated tales, Lyon was paying his wife and young son a quiet Christmas visit. They were staying at the Lyon County estate called "Martha's Vineyard," the home of John Washington and Martha Gracey Marshall. Laura O'Hara Lyon was Mrs. Marshall's niece. The rigors of war made the reunion a short one. As he prepared to leave Eddyville, Lyon ordered the courthouse to be burned, and then, before the torch was applied, he rescinded the order. Various stories are told as to why he changed his mind. Some say that it was because his own residence was nearby and would be threatened by the flames. Another often repeated story says that it was because of the intervention of a prominent citizen of the town named Skinner, either the same Frederick H. Skinner who had raised the orphaned boy who became the general or a kinsman of the man. On that December day, the citizen named Skinner asked Lyon "as a personal favor not to burn the building. He told him that a baby had that day been born in his residence next door to the courthouse and that the mother was in no condition to be frightened by a fire [or] moved from her bed. Gen. Lyon was moved by the plea thus made and gave orders to spare the building." In honor of the general and as a tribute to his consideration toward a mother and her newborn, the baby that was born that morning was named Hylan Lyon Skinner. The courthouse was saved from the torch, but the town did not escape destruction altogether. The raiders left "a corral, or a place of rendezvous for Negroes" burning behind them as they rode east.[9]

Lyon burned the courthouse at Princeton on December 15. The Federals in Paducah were keeping track of Lyon's movements. They reported that he was "robbing and conscripting" through the countryside, and yet they made no move to stop him. General Solomon Meredith said, "There is no force of ours after Lyon." Lyon's scouts undoubtedly knew that their party was not being hunted, and that gave the general a certain leisure to go about his work. As was the case in Hopkinsville and Cadiz, the courthouse in Princeton had been used as barracks for the U.S. Colored Troops. Lyon told the locals that the blacks were infested with smallpox and he was burning the building to prevent an epidemic. It was a fabrication, of course. In his post-raid report, he admitted forthrightly, "I destroyed the court-house at Hopkinsville, Cadiz, and Princeton as they were occupied as barracks and used as fortifications by the Negroes." The general made no mention at all of smallpox in his report of the raid. Lyon's small side adventure ended with the raid on Princeton, and he rode southeast for a rendezvous with Chenoweth.[10]

Approaching Hopkinsville from the west on December 16, Lyon met soldiers of Chenoweth's command streaming down the road. They had been attacked and defeated that morning by two Union brigades under Brigadier General Edward M. McCook. Chenoweth's brigade was shattered, and the men were escaping the best way they could.

In response to Lyon's operations behind the lines, General McCook had been detached from the cavalry forces at Nashville on December 11. He moved by special train to Bowling Green. The Federals were sure that Lyon's target was the L&N Railroad bridge at Munfordville. General McCook was ordered to rendezvous with the brigades of Brigadier General Louis D. Watkins and Colonel Oscar La Grange and, with this small division, meet and defeat Lyon and save the Green River bridge.

Upon his arrival at Bowling Green, McCook learned that Lyon was at Hopkinsville. Instead of continuing north to Munfordville, he moved west to Russellville. From there, his command took the road to Fairview, the birthplace of Jefferson Davis. The men began arriving about nine o'clock on the evening of December 15. They drove away Colonel Chenoweth's pickets and settled down for a few hours' rest before resuming the march very early on the morning of December 16. The going was hard. The roads were so icy that the men had to dismount and lead their horses. Two hours of travel brought them to within three miles of Hopkinsville where they paused and waited for the sun to rise. By that time, the Confederates were in position to meet them.

Chenoweth's men were at a ball at Hopkinsville's Phoenix Hotel when news first reached them that the Federals were advancing. Chenoweth had been unconcerned about his situation. He said, "There was no enemy of which we could hear nearer than Russellville, where Johnson's negro brigade was reported, but this gave us no concern. Johnson was held in great contempt." Not that his complacency made Chenoweth entirely careless. The young belle Fannie Keen, who was at the dance, remembered the loaded rifles with affixed bayonets leaning against the walls and said that "all danced with loaded pistols around their waists. . . . Guards were outside and inside the building."[11]

Even when word came that McCook was approaching, Chenoweth was not particularly alarmed. Fannie Keen heard Chenoweth say that the boys should be allowed to "finish their dance, that they had had such a hard time and no pleasure for so long, that they would get out of town safely." It was impossible to keep the news of the enemy's advance quiet, of course, and as it spread through the room, the ladies "begged the soldiers to leave quickly and let us go home alone. But, with Southerners' usual gallantry, they would see us safely home before they left town." The soldiers escorted the ladies to the home of a Mrs. Leavell and then took their leave, heading in the direction of Fairview to meet McCook's cavalrymen. The Nashville *Daily Times and True Union* later reported that Colonel Chenoweth allowed some looting of the stores in town before the Confederates went out. If what the paper reported was true, the men rode to the battle with pilfered ribbons tied to the manes and tails of their horses. They deployed across the turnpike a short distance from the campus of the state asylum.[12]

At dawn, Chenoweth tried to gauge the threat he faced by means of a ploy. He sent forward a rider under a white flag of truce with some "polite request." In his memoir chapter in the book *The Partisan Rangers of the Confederate Army*, Chenoweth was not specific about the nature of the request, but he got the information he needed. He said, "When the staff officer bearing the same returned, I readily gleaned from his haste and bulging eyes that I was in the midst of a fix." Chenoweth learned that two brigades were in front of him. They were just beginning to exchange shots with his pickets.[13]

McCook sent General Watkins "to the right, with instructions to make a detour, get in rear of the enemy, and cover all the roads," while he and Colonel La Grange attacked the Rebels from the front. From his vantage point on the Confederate line, Chenoweth observed Watkins's move. It did not look good. He said, "The dismounted cavalry were rapidly closing on my front. On my left a large body of cavalry was passing to my rear. It looked as if my command would soon be surrounded and overwhelmed, possibly destroyed, certainly captured."[14]

As the fight was developing between Chenoweth and McCook at the asylum, General Watkins gained the Confederate rear. He sent the 7th Kentucky Cavalry to block the Greenville Road and led his other two regiments, the 4th and 6th Kentucky Cavalry, into Hopkinsville. They encountered a few Confederates, whom they captured, and they fanned out to search the town for more. One of the first houses they entered was the home of Mrs. Leavell, where young Fannie Keen and the other women had gone for shelter after the dance at the Phoenix Hotel. They had been listening to the gunfire from the direction of the asylum; they had no idea that Northern soldiers were near their hiding place, and they were horrified when the Yankees came bursting in. Miss Keen said, "We were barely allowed time to drape bed clothes around us, before they came to search every nook and corner, large enough for a child to hide in. They even rammed their bayonets through the mattresses." And, as if their destructive rummaging were not upsetting enough, they ordered Mrs. Leavell to make their breakfast. She had to cook for forty men who "made themselves thoroughly at home, lounging and sprawling, smoking and chewing."[15]

While the soldiers at Mrs. Leavell's house loafed and waited for their breakfast, the fight at the asylum was reaching its peak. Colonel La Grange's brigade was pressing the Rebels hard. So far as McCook could see, the battle was unfolding perfectly, and the Confederates were beginning to waver. After two hours of fighting, they cracked. McCook said that the Rebels "ran away, abandoning their artillery, caisson, and ammunition, nearly all of them throwing away their guns and escaping by the Greenville road and through the woods. I expected, and from the disposition I had made of my force had a right to expect, that the morning's work would result in the capture and destruction of the entire force opposed to me."[16]

The Confederates broke into groups. They could not go back into Hopkinsville; Watkins was there. They had to find another way to safety. Chenoweth had with him "a soldier guide who understood the topographical surroundings." With the guide by his side to show the way, Chenoweth "led the column to a creek some distance on my right. It had been swollen by recent rains and snow, was sheeted with ice and was not at all inviting. With my staff I leaped in and crossed, swimming some distance and breaking the ice." Some men balked and huddled on the bank rather than brave the icy water, but Chenoweth said their hesitation lasted only a moment, "for the Federal cavalry now put in their savage appearance and were seen charging down upon them. It was a dilemma—sabre or water." Most of the men chose water. The Federals made prisoners of those who refused to swim and were satisfied with that. They did not cross to chase down the rest.[17]

Another group flared off to the northeast and made their way to the Greenville Road. McCook had anticipated such a move and had ordered Watkins to block that escape route. Watkins gave the assignment to Colonel John K. Faulkner and the 7th Kentucky Cavalry, and they were in position at the critical moment when the escaping Rebels appeared. Incredibly, Faulkner let them through. He said, "I discovered a column of cavalry moving on my left, which I estimated at about 300, and which I mistook for one of our regiments, they being dressed differently from rebels I had formerly seen." Too late, Faulkner realized the mistake he had made. He groused, "Their movements were in every way calculated to deceive."[18]

It was this bunch, or at least a part of it, that General Lyon met as he was returning from Princeton. He gathered them up and raced back toward Hopkinsville. They soon saw the Federals coming. A detachment of the 6th Kentucky Cavalry had been sent to join the chase for the three hundred escapees, but they found more than they had counted on. Lyon led his men in a headlong charge, hitting the enemy with such momentum that Watkins believed the general's "whole force" was attacking him. They chased the bluecoats back into Hopkinsville, and then broke off the attack. They swung around to the north and rode about sixteen miles in the direction of Madisonville before stopping to make camp. The fighting at Hopkinsville had cost the Confederates one of their artillery pieces, about sixty officers and men captured at the asylum and in Hopkinsville, two men killed, and about a dozen wounded (who were taken into the asylum and cared for there). It was a bad morning that could have been worse. Lyon was still free, and when Chenoweth's fugitives joined him later that night, his raiding column was restored to near full strength.[19]

For his part, McCook was satisfied with the morning's work. He reported to cavalry corps commander Brigadier General James H. Wilson at Nashville that he had routed Lyon, captured his artillery, and made a prisoner of the wounded Colonel Chenoweth, which was only about half true, and, in the case of Chenoweth, not true at all. McCook added that he thought Lyon had gone back toward Princeton, and it was in that direction that he led the Federal cavalry the next morning, December 17. When McCook discovered that Lyon had turned toward Madisonville, he divided his forces. He ordered Colonel La Grange to take his brigade and pursue Lyon, while he moved with Watkins and the artillery back to Hopkinsville. From Hopkinsville, McCook and Watkins could block Lyon's return to the Cumberland River, if he decided to double back.

General Lyon was not planning to double back. He continued north and east. He reached Madisonville on December 17, began conscripting all the able-bodied, draft age men and prepared to burn the brick courthouse. The county records were carried to the nearby home of his cousin Chittenden P. Lyon, the fires were set, and the Confederate column continued east.

La Grange was with the advance of his brigade when it finally caught up with Lyon at the steamboat landing of Ashbyburg (usually rendered in the historical documents as Ashbysburg) on the Green River in Hopkins County. Chenoweth said, "Green River, if not very wide, is deep, swift and forbidding at this point. We procured what boats could be had, the citizens about here very generally sympathizing with us and aiding us to the extent of their ability." Everyone had crossed except for General Lyon, his staff, and his escort when La Grange showed up. The Yankees did not attack immediately. Historian B. L.

Roberson thinks that La Grange did not want to appear impetuous. He "had been censured for a too rash attack at Dalton [Georgia] and was thus psychologically disposed toward erring in the other direction," Roberson says.[20]

Instead of attacking, La Grange sent forward a demand that Lyon surrender. He used the name of General McCook, a deception that Lyon did not immediately see through. Lyon read the message and said to the bearer of the demand, "Go tell General McCook that he knows me well enough to know that I will not surrender without a fight." The contentious exchange between the two commanders notwithstanding, there was not much fighting at Ashbyburg. The Federals fired a few artillery rounds in the direction of the river and the cavalry charged forward to take prisoners. The Louisville *Daily Journal* published a propaganda-filled fantasy of the moment La Grange opened fire. The article said that the Rebels burned their train, and "Lyon abandoned his men like a coward, telling his subordinate officers to get the men out the best they could, while he and his staff returned south and crossed the Cumberland River." Nothing of the sort occurred. Lyon, the few dozen men of his escort, and some citizens who had been helping the Rebels cross simply scattered into the trees. The Confederates made their way to a crossing about two miles down and rejoined the others on the east bank. That was all. The encounter cost Lyon one killed, an undetermined number drowned, and seven captured along with some small arms, four wagons and an ambulance. No subtractions from a force as small as Lyon's was welcome, but the bulk of his men and the howitzer were saved. La Grange had come up short, and he admitted that the fault was his. "I now think that waiting for the column was a serious mistake," he said.[21]

Lyon had destroyed all the small boats for ten miles up and down the river, and La Grange and his men could not cross. They had to wait until a river steamer, the *D. B. Campbell*, came by. It was two days before the Yankees were all ferried across to the east bank of Green River. From Ashbyburg, Lyon continued toward Hartford, destroying more boats and burning bridges all along the way. A comfortable gap opened between Lyon and the men who were pursuing him.

Hartford was on the Rough River in Ohio County. Lyon's raiders arrived there on the afternoon of December 20, 1864. Forty-eight officers and men of the 52nd Kentucky Mounted Infantry defended the town. A. L. Morton, the Ohio County Court Clerk, later said that the Rebels came into Hartford under fire. Some of the citizens, including Morton himself, had taken up arms to defend their homes and businesses against these rough looking horsemen. "I thought they were a band of guerrillas," he said.[22]

The 52nd Kentucky boys had barricaded themselves in the courthouse, and they put up a fight when the raiders came into view. Perhaps they still thought they were fighting guerrillas; Lyon's men were dressed in a variety of homespun, stolen, and captured clothing. In any case, the defenders did not give up easily. Citizens later remembered the sound of bullets smacking against the courthouse and the surrounding buildings. In the end, the men of the 52nd surrendered. They were escorted out of the courthouse, and the raiders spread out to see what Hartford had to offer them. One of the raiders, Lieutenant Henry Metcalf, happened to be a former resident of Hartford. Before the war he was known as "a businessman of character and honesty throughout the community." Recognizing Metcalf as their one-time neighbor, the people went to him and petitioned him to help protect their town and their personal property. Alexander B. Beard was the postmaster in Hartford as well as a merchant, and he was one of those who appealed to Metcalf "to try and save excesses among the soldiers as to my own goods and my neighbors." Beard was relieved to hear Metcalf say that "he would do everything he possibly could to shield the people from impressments, robberies, etc." Generally, Metcalf kept his word, though Beard did lose a wagonload of pork. There were others who commented that Lyon's men "were well behaved and paid for the supplies they took." The exception to the rule was horseflesh. In later years there were specific memories in Hartford of horses that were seized with no recompense to the owners, and Colonel Chenoweth himself confessed that "occasionally it happened sadly enough, that no consideration but good will was returned" when a citizen was made to give up a horse to Lyon's raiders.[23]

Lieutenant Metcalf's influence might have been one reason for the restraint of the raiders while they were in Hartford. However, not even Lieutenant Metcalf could persuade General Lyon to let the courthouse stand. As he had done in other towns during the raid, Lyon spared the county records, but the courthouse was torched. While the building burned, the raiders gathered their plunder and made ready to ride. Before leaving Hartford on the morning of December 21, Lyon let it be known that he was headed toward Elizabethtown, where he "expected to form a junction with Forrest." And that was not the only misinformation he spread. Some of the paroled prisoners of the 52nd Kentucky who later reported to Louisville stated definitely that Lyon was turning south in the direction of Bowling Green.[24]

It was 20° below zero and six inches of snow covered the ground when the raiders left Hartford. Lieutenant Metcalf had charge of the rear guard and prevented any last-minute mischief that might have been intended. Lyon led his men east toward Grayson County and the county seat of Leitchfield. Since Ashbyburg, the raid had been a lark. Colonel La Grange was far behind them, and the Federal garrisons at the various towns were no real threat, but on the way to Leitchfield they were given a reminder of just how dangerous a game they were playing. At a place called Devil's Gulch a band of bush-whackers fired upon them and killed one of the Confederates. The raiders chased their assailants and came back with one. The man was put under guard and made to ride in the back of the ammunition wagon. The man's wife requested to take a seat beside him, and she was permitted to do so. The presence of the wife is troubling; was she riding with the bushwhackers or was she scooped up when the Federals followed the man and arrested him at his own house? No one knows. Chenoweth, who told the story, did not reveal how she came to be on the scene. It was a minor detail, forgotten in light of what happened next. Chenoweth said, "The column halting for a while, one of the guards brought a live coal from a cabin by the roadside and proceeded to light his pipe for a smoke. The prisoner begged for the privilege of a smoke, and when fire for that purpose was given him, he deliberately dropped it through a hole in the powder keg from which he had already removed the stopper. The wagon, mules, and driver and the wife of the prisoner were in-stantly killed. One of the guards standing not far away was seriously injured. The prisoner himself was blown some ten or twelve feet and was still alive when the guard who had not been hurt by the explosion ran up to him and emptied his loaded gun into his head."[25]

Made somber by the suddenness of the suicide/murder on what had been a fine December day, the raiders continued to Leitchfield. The Union garri-son fled at their approach, and the Southerners went unopposed about their business of preparing the courthouse for burning. One detail seized some local boys and made them chop up the courthouse benches for kindling while others went through the town in search of clothes, food, medicines, and, as always, horses. Considering what had happened at Devil's Gulch, the men might have gone on a rampage of rape and pillage in Leitchfield, but they did not. The damage they inflicted on the town, estimated at $10,000, was not much worse than the destruction suffered by any other town along their route.

After a night in Leitchfield, the invaders headed toward Elizabethtown, the Hardin County seat. A few miles from the town, Lyon divided his col-umn. The Louisville & Nashville Railroad ran through Hardin County. The L&N had been a major supply line for all the Federal operations in Mid-dle Tennessee (and it fed the rail lines that extended from Nashville farther south, into Northern Alabama and Georgia), and it had been a torment to the Confederates. The Rebels struck at it continually. They had rarely been able to close it for long periods, but on one occasion a section of the L&N was so thoroughly wrecked as to terminate a major campaign. When John Hunt Morgan collapsed the L&N's Big South Tunnel and destroyed a long section of track near Gallatin, Tennessee in August 1862, it brought

General Don Carlos Buell's North Alabama Campaign to a complete stop and paved the way for the Confederate invasion of Kentucky the following October. Now, Hylan B. Lyon hoped to oversee an event of equal importance. He would break the L&N in multiple places to deny rations and arms to General George H. Thomas's army in Nashville. When that was accomplished, General Hood would move north, with no serious opposition facing him between Nashville and the Ohio River.

General Lyon went with his brigades toward the village of Nolin, where there was a small railroad bridge and a blockhouse. Meanwhile, Captain Echols of Lyon's staff and a detail of fifty men continued to Elizabethtown. They entered the town so quietly on the evening of December 23, that the townsfolk believed they were a column of returning Home Guards. They were thunderstruck when gunfire broke out between the group and the men of the 13th Kentucky Infantry who garrisoned the town. It was a nearly equal contest; forty-five Yankees opposed the Confederates, and they were behind barricades, yet it was the bluecoats who surrendered. The skirmish won, Echols's men went to work. They made the citizens of Elizabethtown carry all manner of combustibles down to the L&N Railroad trestle, which was soon ablaze, along with the depot and its half million dollars' worth of army supplies, a flatcar loaded with lumber, and the stockade where the Federal garrison lived. Echols spared the courthouse because it had not been turned into a U.S. barracks. As Captain Echols's men were finishing up, Colonel La Grange and his brigade came cantering in. Since Ashbyburg, La Grange had been trailing behind, delayed by burned bridges at every creek and river, but he pushed his men hard, reducing the miles between them and their prey, until he caught up with them at Elizabethtown. Though much had already been destroyed, La Grange boasted that his horse soldiers arrived "in time to drive the enemy from the bridge and turn his column from the direction of the trestle-work" at Muldraugh Hill.[26]

Protecting the twin railroad trestles at Muldraugh Hill between Elizabethtown and Louisville had been an obsession with the Federals ever since John Hunt Morgan destroyed them during the Christmas Raid of December 1862. Reports of General Lyon in Hardin County convinced the high command in Louisville that Muldraugh Hill was the intended target of the raid. Wild and false stories flew of Lyon's movements toward the great trestles. Railroad officials and Union officers turned back southbound passenger trains at Lebanon Junction, rather than send them on to certain capture, and reinforcements hurried from Louisville to the trestlework. Even so, as one officer said in a truncated message to concerned parties, "have fears will not be enough."[27]

The Yankees had worked themselves into a lather for nothing. Lyon's men were not coming toward Muldraugh Hill. Captain Echols had finished his work in Elizabethtown and left in the direction of Hodgenville, and Lyon was busy at Nolin. What occurred there guaranteed that the Confederates would not move north.

Lyon had sent a detail to burn the L&N depot at the tiny village of Glendale while the rest of his men went on to the more important target of Nolin. They captured and paroled the Nolin garrison, another detail of the 13th Kentucky, and proceeded to tear up railroad track and to set fire to the blockhouse and the railroad bridge it guarded. They may have thought their work was done until they heard a northbound train coming. It was Express No. 4, and it was carrying Captain Ely F. Scott (83rd Indiana Infantry) with a detachment of two hundred convalescents who had left General Thomas at Nashville and were on their way to New York. From there they would board a ship that would take them to General Sherman in time to join him for his campaign in the Carolinas. The engineer saw what was happening ahead and slowed the train to avoid a catastrophic crash. When the express agent heard the brakes on this straight and level stretch of track, he quickly decided that there was danger ahead, and he threw a sack containing $80,000 off the train into the weeds in the corner of a farm fence. A moment later, the train jumped the track at the place where Lyon's raiders had torn up the rails. The Confederates fired one round from their howitzer to persuade the Yankee passengers to surrender. They were formally captured, then paroled, and the train was set on fire.

It may have been from Captain Scott that Lyon first heard that General Hood had been defeated at Nashville on December 16. Surely, it took a dispatch or a newspaper to verify the story, but before the night was done, Lyon knew that it was true: Hood was not just defeated, he was destroyed. The ragged and bloody remnant of the Army of Tennessee was retreating toward Alabama. The purpose of Lyon's raid had been to aid General Hood and to prepare the way for him in Kentucky. Now, Hood was finished, and Lyon was two hundred miles behind enemy lines. Lyon said that the news of Hood's defeat "had a very demoralizing effect upon my command (which were all new recruits), and within two days after it was ascertained that the Confederate army had left Tennessee 500 of my men deserted and returned to their homes." Three of them returned to their homes richer than before; they spotted that sack of $80,000 in the fence corner and took it with them when they deserted. Some respectable, post-war family fortunes may have been founded on $80,000 of stolen Yankee loot.[28]

Elizabethtown, Glendale, and Nolin were the high-water marks of Lyon's raid. From Nolin, Lyon began his retreat from Kentucky. He rode southeast toward the designated rendezvous point at Hodgenville. The raiders spared the courthouse there and hurried on. Speed was important now. The Union

scouts were hot on their trail again, but only a short distance beyond Hodgenville Colonel La Grange called off the pursuit, citing the jaded condition of
his horses.

From Hodgenville, Lyon led his men toward Campbellsville. The column
was sloughing off deserters by the tens and twenties as it went along. They
were not good material in the first place. The men who had joined only because they wanted to avoid being drafted into the Union army or because they
were conscripted by Lyon skulked away as the opportunity presented. No
patriotic sentiments stirred them, and now they turned on their own people.
Over the next few weeks, Federal reports and the newspapers carried one
account after another of crimes committed by deserters from Lyon's division.
La Grange commented on the "conduct of the stragglers of the enemy, who
burned houses and forage, ravished women, and plundered indiscriminately."
Some of them operated as simple road agents, while others collected themselves into gangs or joined existing guerrilla bands. A week after Nolin, the
Louisville *Daily Union Press* said, "The country is full of stragglers from the
command of Brig. Gen. Hylan B. Lyon." It reported an incident in southwest
Hardin County where seven of them showed up in the yard of Mr. Samuel
Tabor. They demanded that he, his wife, and his nephew come out of the
house and surrender. Mr. Tabor and his nephew fired on them with shotguns
and killed three and mortally wounded another before the would-be maraud-
ers could escape. A larger gang of thirty-three of Lyon's deserters operated in
Grayson and Edmonson Counties, robbing, murdering and fighting Home
Guards. Captain Jake Bennett, a guerrilla chieftain from Western Kentucky,
accepted several of Lyon's stragglers into his gang. A Louisville paper from
late January 1865 carried an item about Bennett's attack on Albany, Kentucky. Bennett, "accompanied by a few of Brig. Gen. Hylan B. Lyon's men"
rode into Albany on January 20. They burned the courthouse, plundered the
stores, beat the county sheriff, killed two citizens, and seized two others as
prisoners before they rode out. As late as March, Lyon's stragglers were still
terrorizing the state. That month, another bunch of men who had left Lyon
stopped a train near Glasgow Junction on the L&N and robbed the passen-
gers. They wounded fourteen persons and they burned the train before they
disappeared. Their outrages began coming to an end only when the war did,
in April 1865.[29]

Lyon led his ever-diminishing column into Campbellsville on Christmas
Day, 1864. They rode in unopposed, robbed the stores and citizens and took
all the serviceable horses. They burned a storehouse, a hospital, and the courthouse, which the Yankees had used as a barracks. As was customary, Lyon
allowed the citizens to remove all the county records. They were carried by
civic volunteers to the residence of Mr. John P. Davis on Main Street, as the

black columns of smoke began to blanket the town. Lyon's raiders did not linger to enjoy the conflagration. They rode on and left Campbellsville burning behind.

The raiders only paused at Columbia long enough to burn the Green River bridge and pressed on to Burkesville, the seat of Cumberland County. They were in the foothills of the Appalachians now, the section of the state that was most fervent in its support for the Union. Three hard-fighting Federal regiments had been raised, in large part, in Cumberland County, the 1st and 5th Kentucky Cavalry and the 3rd Kentucky Infantry. The Confederates knew that they would find few friends here. Lyon was called a "desperado," and his men were called "just as bad as guerrillas," quite an indictment when it is remembered that Cumberland County was the long-suffering stamping ground of the notorious Champ Ferguson and his band of irregulars.[30]

The 13th Kentucky Cavalry had used the courthouse as storage for commissary and quartermaster supplies, and that use doomed it to be burned. Chenoweth defended the burning of this and the other courthouses by saying, "These court-houses were no longer needed by the citizens of Kentucky as houses of law and temples of justice, but as military barracks and stockades for Federal soldiers and prison-houses for unoffending Kentuckians who dared to entertain any sympathy for the Southern cause." The citizens of Cumberland County certainly would not have agreed with Chenoweth's explanation; their courthouse was new and had cost $10,000 to build. Nevertheless, Lyon's course was set, and he proceeded. The procedure was as usual. The county records were removed, the benches were broken up for kindling and piled inside and the torch applied. The fire was said to have been lit by Lyon's own hand while his men stood guard outside. They were near the end of their raid, but they still must subsist, so they took whatever supplies and horses they needed before they left Burkesville, heading south.[31]

On January 3, 1865, they crossed the ice-filed Cumberland River in boats that Captain Gracey built. It was the river that Lyon had known all his life, and on the other end of it was Eddyville. Lyon's wife and infant son were waiting for him there. Did he look downstream and think of them? The destruction at Nashville of the Army of Tennessee was a mortal blow to Confederate hopes. Prospects had never seemed so dim, and Lyon was insightful enough and realistic enough to know that the cause for which he had fought was finished. The men who died from this point on would die for nothing. Was Lyon tempted to turn the bow of his boat downstream and follow the current home? If the thought of home and family crossed his mind, he made no mention of it in his memoirs. His West Point education still informed his actions: duty, honor, country. His honor bound him to his duty, which was to stay with the men who remained with him and to lead them to the Confederate lines where they would turn and fight again, even if the country they served was gasping its last.

They were in the process of destroying the boats on the south bank of the Cumberland when "the advance vidette of our friends, the enemy, hove in sight on the other shore," as Chenoweth said. The Confederates waved them "a fond farewell" and continued south. It was only about ten miles to the Tennessee line, and they passed out of Kentucky with no further harassment. The Kentucky Raid was over.[32]

That the raid had failed in its greater purpose did not rest on General Lyon's shoulders; it was on General Hood's. Lyon had conducted his raid with considerable skill even while Hood was foolishly smashing his army to bits at Franklin and Nashville, unnecessary battles that showed an abysmal lack of understanding of what mortal men could do.

Lyon said, "When all things are considered pertaining to this expedition, it was a success beyond my most sanguine expectations. The men were all new recruits, but poorly organized, and armed for the first time only one day before they crossed the Tennessee River. They captured 3 valuable steamers; burned 8 fortified court-houses, several important railroad bridges, depots, stockades, and block-houses; captured and paroled 250 prisoners; and caused to be withdrawn from Nashville McCook's entire division of cavalry." He also said that they had tied up over one thousand enemy troops during Hood's retreat from Nashville.[33]

Most of what General Lyon said in his report was true, but perhaps it was not the entire truth. The raid was his most important mission at the head of an independent command, and it revealed both his strengths and his weaknesses as a leader. To begin with the positive: the speed with which he moved his column and the skill with which he evaded the pursuing Federals showed that he could apply the lessons of hit-and-run that he had learned at the side of Van Dorn, Wheeler, and Forrest and, one might suggest, from the Indians in the Northwest. He was quick to understand situations in the field and quick to respond. Also, aside from his admitted failure to prevent the desertion of numerous conscripts during the retreat from Kentucky, Lyon did not preside over a breakdown of discipline or demonstrate a willful neglect to keep his men under control. Both things had happened during the war. One thinks of the riotous behavior of General Sherman's men in Jackson, Mississippi, in May and again in July of 1863, John Hunt Morgan's men in Mt. Sterling, Kentucky, in June 1864, and the violent sacking of Athens, Alabama, by the troops of Union General Basil Turchin, the "Mad Cossack," in May 1862. Lyon's men did not go on a violent rampage in any town they visited, though they did rob stores and, in Hopkinsville, the bank. Even that, the bank robbery, could be justified by the need of an impoverished department commander to make the enemy pay for his raid. The requisitions of horses and clothing that Lyon's raiders made throughout the expedition were a commonplace occurrence with all raiding parties, and the men did not exceed the other limits of what was acceptable in such situations; indeed, as the citizens of Hartford attested, they were careful to pay for what they took, except horses, and they did not molest the citizens. At times, they were unexpectedly generous in their behavior. The Conklin family was made to shelter some of Lyon's men overnight while they were in Leitchfield, but Miss Bettie Conklin remembered all her life that the raiders allowed the family to keep its only horse and, more than that, left them an extra one when they left town. (Miss Conklin also remembered that La Grange's men stole both of them when they passed through a day later.)

Lyon's raiders did not set fire to private homes, as the Confederates retreating from Bowling Green maliciously did to the Underwood residence, Mt. Air, after promising to spare the house. In fact, Lyon took pains at Cadiz to protect private homes. Lyon's men did burn a number of courthouses, but the arson was committed in a manner that was orderly, almost formulaic. Furthermore, the burning of the courthouses did not seem to be motivated strictly by racial hatred. As noted earlier, Lyon said that he burned the courthouses in Hopkinsville, Cadiz, and Princeton because "they were used as fortifications by Negroes," but the garrisons that used the Hartford and Burkesville courthouses were white, and he burned those courthouses just the same. The garrisons were all U.S. troops; that was the point and it was more important than their race.

Before leaving the subject of racial animosity, one might also add that no atrocities were reported after Lyon captured the black garrison at Cadiz during his December raid. Just as had been the case with the twenty-seven black troopers of the 13th USCHT, who were captured at Eddyville in October, Lyon spared them the ultimate penalty. This is not to pretend that Lyon was not a racial bigot; as a slave owner and a Confederate officer he certainly was. Rather, it is merely to point out that no evidence exists that he, as an independent commander, ever ordered the execution of captured black Federals or stood by unconcerned while his men committed murder, as other officers had done.

Up to this point, one might argue that there was nothing atypical about Lyon's raid; raiding and burning were acts of war, and war was hard. However, there are other questions about Lyon's leadership during the Kentucky Raid that are more disturbing. First, although Kentucky had never left the Union and was technically the enemy, Kentucky was Lyon's native state (and Western Kentucky was his native *region*), and the burning of the courthouses there put a terrible financial burden on his fellow citizens. Lyon would have realized this, yet he persisted, and he set the last courthouse fire of the raid, at Burkesville, with his own hand.

Secondly, and more serious from a military standpoint, Lyon's instructions from General Hood were to put the gristmills in working order and begin grinding grain, and he was to destroy the rail and telegraph communications with Nashville. There was no mandate to burn courthouses. Why, then, did Lyon take it upon himself to make such destruction the trademark of his three weeks in Kentucky? There was no obvious advantage either tactical or strategic to be gained by these acts, even when Lyon believed that Hood was coming. In fact, the time and effort devoted to courthouse destruction might actually have been a factor in Lyon's failure to carry out his instructions to put the mills in good order and to set their wheels to grinding. Though specifically instructed to do so, Lyon later admitted that he had not accomplished this. Because General Hood was prevented from coming north, Lyon's failure to insure bread for the Army of Tennessee is easily overlooked, but one can imagine what General Hood's reaction would have been if he *had* gotten past Nashville and arrived in Kentucky with his hungry men to find that the mills had not been made serviceable and that no meal and flour had been ground for the army. In that case, Lyon would have found it harder to claim that the success of his raid exceeded his "most sanguine expectations."

Finally, Lyon's tendency to take unilateral action that was possibly detrimental to the goals of the mission was also seen in his side trip to Cadiz, Eddyville, and Princeton. Hood's orders to Lyon had been to destroy rail and telegraphic communications "between Nashville and Clarksville, and between Bowling Green and Nashville." His jaunt to visit his wife placed him too far north for the first and too far west for the second. It exceeded his orders, contributed nothing toward his aims, and, as it turned out, put Chenoweth at great risk when General McCook appeared in force on the outskirts of Hopkinsville. Lyon's side trip to Eddyville was an indulgence that came very close to costing him half of his command and which put the entire operation at risk.

Whatever questions General Lyon left for future historians to ponder, the raid was over. Now, retreat was all that was left to him. He was in Tennessee, but Tennessee was not what it once was to the Confederacy. The Federals had pushed the Confederate lines into Alabama. Lyon still had far to go. He must continue south and save his men, if he could.

13
"AN ILLUSIVE CUSS"

General Lyon and his men moved fast through Tennessee. Their route took them through McMinnville, Tullahoma, and Winchester. They had occasional brushes with the Federals and with bushwhackers, and the creeks and rivers were swollen from winter rains, but they faced no real obstacles until they crossed into Alabama north of Huntsville.

Brigadier General Thomas J. Wood was in command of the IV Corps, Army of the Cumberland at Huntsville. Like Lyon, he was Kentucky born, the son of a prominent slave-holding family; he was a pre-war graduate of West Point and a veteran of service on the Western frontier. The two seemed to have much in common, but Wood's loyalties had kept him in the Union army when the war began. Now General Wood was in command of the army corps that was athwart Lyon's escape route, and he was determined to catch his fellow Kentuckian. Wood learned on January 6, 1865, that Lyon had crossed the state line and was moving in the direction of Larkinsville. The raiders were "well mounted and had a large number of led horses." Wood mobilized his own forces and took command of others who were merely passing through his area, most notably the provisional division of Brigadier General Charles Cruft. Cruft was surprised to be detained on his way to Chattanooga, where he was going to join General James B. Steedman. It was Steedman who, along with General Lovell Harrison Rousseau, gave Forrest such a spirited chase during his Middle Tennessee Raid. Wood stopped Cruft and ordered him to send a brigade to the vicinity of Larkinsville "and to scout well thereabouts to find Lyon and destroy him if possible."[1]

There was initially some question as to whether General Wood had exceeded his authority when he seized for his own purposes Cruft's division, but when General Thomas sustained the order, Cruft sent out the brigade as Wood had ordered. Cruft himself soon followed "with all the troops for which transportation could be had." Arriving at his destination, Cruft sent out cavalry patrols in all directions. They could find no sign of Lyon. Cruft decided that it had all been a mistake. He wired Wood that the rumors of Lyon in the area were false, though bushwhackers did infest the hills. Wood insisted that Lyon "must certainly be in your neighborhood somewhere, either north or south of the railroad, as his course has been traced from Kentucky by McMinnville and Manchester to south of Winchester." He ordered the patrols to continue. On January 8, Cruft received intelligence that Lyon and five hundred men had been spotted moving toward Bellefonte Station. Cruft immediately sent Colonel Benjamin Harrison's brigade in that direction. At the same time, Colonel Adam G. Malloy was ordered to lead his brigade to Scottsboro.[2]

The garrison at Scottsboro was fifty-four soldiers of the 101st and the 110th U.S. Colored Infantry commanded by Lieutenant John Hull. At 5:30 PM on January 8, 1865, General Lyon attacked and drove in Hull's pickets. Thirty minutes later, he massed his dismounted men on the north side and charged the brick Memphis & Charleston Railroad depot where Hull and his men had barricaded themselves. Hull repulsed the attack after ten minutes in a fight the lieutenant characterized as "almost hand-to-hand." The Confederates regrouped and made a second attempt, this time on the south side of the depot. They made it to the wall, "coming up and laying hold of the muzzles of my men's guns, attempting to wrest them through the loop-holes of the depot building, in which we were stationed," Hull said. After fifteen minutes, Lyon's men fell back. A half hour passed before they assaulted the depot from the south and west in "the most severe and closely contested of all, lasting some thirty minutes before they were driven back." Retiring beyond the range of the Federal muskets, the Confederates for the first time employed their howitzer. It was the artillery fire pounding the depot walls that finally succeeded in driving out Hull and his men. They fell back with the Confederates pursuing for about 450 yards. There, they turned, "intending to renew the fighting," when Hull learned that Colonel Malloy had arrived by rail and was only about a mile away. Hull marched his men down to meet them. Colonel Malloy ordered Lieutenant Hull to report with his command to Brigadier General Cruft at Larkinsville. They had sustained six wounded; two of them had had legs shot off by Lyon's artillery.[3]

At about the same time that Malloy's brigade arrived, a detachment of Harrison's brigade came in from Bellefonte. With the numbers stacked against them by these arriving trainloads of Yankees, Lyon retreated into the hills. Scottsboro was the first setback he had suffered since Hopkinsville. Lyon left no report of the action, so there is no official accounting of his casualties. Union reports claimed that the Rebels had lost eighteen killed and an unspecified number of wounded. The newspapers reported that the wounded totaled forty to fifty, a number that can be safely cut by half to reach something like an accurate figure.

General Wood was not finished with Lyon. On January 9, the day after the fight at Scottsboro, he said, "If my directions are vigorously and promptly carried out, I trust we will give Mr. Lyon a hard time." The Federals increased their chances of success two days later when General Thomas asked Lieutenant Moreau Forrest, U.S.N., to "have your gun-boats carry on a lively patrol of the [Tennessee] river from Bridgeport to Decatur." Lieutenant Forrest agreed to the request and dispatched his tinclads, the *General Grant* and the *General Thomas*, to churn the waters of the upper Tennessee and watch for Lyon. Wood soon allowed General Cruft's division to proceed to General Steedman in Chattanooga, since "infantry can do nothing more in the pursuit," and he gave the assignment of chasing Lyon to Colonel William J. Palmer and the 15th Pennsylvania Cavalry. Wood's orders to Palmer were "to scour the country well between Flint River and Paint Rock Creek. . . . Go without any weapons; take such rations as you can on your horses, and depend on the country for the rest."[4]

The gray column reached the Tennessee River in a blizzard on January 9. A blockhouse, "one of those pestiferous interferences which had interrupted our peaceful progress throughout our extended raid," threatened their successful crossing of the river. Chenoweth said, "General Lyon was compelled to resort to the same means which all along proved so persuasive," this was to say, his howitzer. One round was all that was needed to intimidate the defenders in the blockhouse, and Lyon's men prepared to cross, unmolested. They dismantled the field piece and gathered logs for rafts since there was no bridge at this point. The howitzer crossed on one of the frail rafts and was reassembled on the high bank of the southern shore to cover the rest of the men as they paddled over. General Lyon and Turner's brigade made it across and Chenoweth's was in the process of doing so when the *General Grant* steamed into view. The howitzer crew began firing at the gunboat. The one round they put through her had no effect. Chenoweth was watching from the north bank. He and his men were cut off. The *General Grant*'s five guns were booming in their direction. Chenoweth and his men scattered. The next day, he got an old swamper to carry a note over to General Lyon naming the hour that he would attempt to cross. Lyon was ready with the howitzer when the hour came, and Chenoweth was crossing when the *General Grant* again made an appearance. The gun on shore and the guns of the tinclad exchanged fire, and Chenoweth was able to get across with eighty-three men, "but in as woeful a condition as men ever found themselves."[5]

Frozen, hungry, and tired, Chenoweth was escorted by his surgeon to a nearby farmhouse, and he settled down for a desperately needed rest. General Lyon and his staff were quartered about half a mile way, in the home of Mr. Tom Noble at Red Hill, and his brigades were in camp about a half a mile from there. Lyon intended to remain for several days. He later admitted that once he was across the Tennessee River he was "feeling perfectly safe from Federal interference. I had passed through so many dangers unscathed that I had become exceedingly incautious, and to some extent reckless."[6]

About four o'clock on the morning of January 15, 1865, Colonel William J. Palmer and the 15th Pennsylvania Cavalry discovered the Confederate camp. They came up and surrounded them in the dark. J. B. Waller later said, "The enemy was upon us before we were aware of their nearness to us." Somehow, the pickets had allowed the Yankees to catch the camp completely off guard. Some of the men escaped in the dark, but the Pennsylvanians bagged about one hundred of them and their horses and also the reliable little howitzer that had served them so well. Palmer's advance guard went ahead to the house where General Lyon was staying. They surrounded the house, and Sergeant Arthur P. Lyon (no known relation to the general) went up to the porch and knocked on the door.[7]

Lyon had heard the riders approach. He believed that they were couriers from his pickets. Unsuspecting of the danger he was in, he went in his nightclothes to answer the door. Some months later, in a letter to his sister-in-law, Lyon wrote a more complete and detailed account of the next few minutes than he did of any other single episode of the war, including battles. As he told it, Sergeant Lyon burst in, introduced himself, and pronounced the astonished General to be his prisoner. "I replied very cooly, 'Very well, will you let me put on my clothes?' for I was not yet dressed." Sergeant Lyon agreed to let the general get dressed, and he followed him into the bedroom. The general said, "He very foolishly did not ask me for my arms but was so much rejoiced at capturing a General, believing that thereby his reputation was made that he forgot the small details necessary to hold a General after he is captured." The room was dark, and Sergeant Lyon demanded more light. As the quartermaster stirred up the coals in the fireplace and General Lyon fumbled with his clothes, stalling for time, one of the patrol outside shouted, "Here comes the Cavalry! Here comes the Cavalry!" The general said, "I knew this would throw them into some confusion as they thought it was some of my command and I said to myself, 'now is your time.'" General Lyon grabbed his pistols from their holsters under his pillow and shot his captor Sergeant Lyon through the head.[8]

Lyon and his quartermaster could have dashed out the back door and made their escape, but the general was still feeling reckless. The two Confederates charged out the front of the house, firing their pistols, and they had the fifty horsemen who had been waiting outside cowed until the riders that had been announced came on the scene—more Yankees! Lyon and his quartermaster ducked back inside the house and ran to the back door. It was hard to open, and Lyon said, "I was delayed a second or two, which I thought was hours in opening it (the soldiers firing at us all the while) and made our escape in different directions." The soldiers spotted Lyon and shouted, "There he goes, shoot him shoot him!" Their bullets did not touch him. He made his escape into the woods, and the bluecoats did not follow.[9]

The Federals were outraged at the killing of Sergeant Lyon. Their gunboats were dispatched on a punitive expedition to Guntersville, which they pounded into rubble with explosive shells. A shore party of more than one hundred sailors from the *General Sherman* went into the battered town after the shelling stopped and burned what was left. When they finished, only seven buildings remained standing in Guntersville. The Union high command took the wider view of the action at Red Hill. It had succeeded in breaking up a large portion of Lyon's forces. General Thomas considered it the "last blow" of the Nashville Campaign and gave all credit to Colonel William J. Palmer. General Thomas J. Wood, who had directed the manhunt for Lyon's Confederates from Huntsville, also congratulated Palmer and his men and gave them his thanks for "giving this party of raiders a finishing touch after they had succeeded in crossing the Tennessee River and considered themselves safe. The blow you struck him probably used up his command 'as a command.'"[10]

It was a shattering blow to Lyon's raiders as an organization, but Lyon himself had escaped. In the hours after his killing of Sergeant Lyon, the general threaded his way through the woods north toward where he had his last intelligence of Colonel Chenoweth. The weather was frigid, and he was poorly dressed. After sunrise, he came to a creek too deep to ford. He crossed by clinging to a log and discovered too late that he had only come to an island. He found a second log and was crossing to the far bank when he heard riders on the shore behind him. Believing them to be the enemy, the general "plunged into the water and increased my speed." He later learned that he had taken a soaking for nothing; the riders were Confederates. He rested until "after the excitement which I had undergone, had somewhat subsided," and continued toward the Tennessee River, where he hoped to find what remained of his command. He described his condition, in a flurry of commas, as "without a hat or coat, and with only one sock on, and on foot, all my horses, three in number, having been captured by the enemy."[11]

He reached Chenoweth's camp later that day. In borrowed clothes (which Chenoweth said were not in "any recognized military style") and riding a horse that he purchased, Lyon led his remaining men southwest to Tuscaloosa. He gave his men several days of rest there, and he dined with the CSA president's brother, Joseph Davis, who charmed him with his intelligence and his affection for Kentucky. Chenoweth said that the men, those "bruised and battered relics of that splendid band of rangers who had bravely ridden out with Lyon from Paris, Tennessee, in November, and who had passed through the hardships of a long, fierce winter campaign inside the enemies' lines . . . were properly housed in hospitals" to recover from their ordeal. Lyon and his staff and officers rested in the hotel operated by a Mrs. Steel before they continued through Meridian to Aberdeen, Mississippi. There, Lyon reported to General Forrest.[12]

Stephen A. Forbes writes, "A cavalry raid at its best is essentially a game of strategy and speed, with personal violence as an incidental complication. It is played according to more or less definite rules, not inconsistent, indeed, with the players' killing each other if the game cannot be won in any other way; but it is commonly a strenuous game rather than a bloody one." Lyon had played the game exactly as Forbes describes, and he was generally pleased with the results. Admittedly, some killings had occurred during the raid, but bloodshed had not been the object, and the deaths on both sides had been relatively few. Lyon employed the strategy and speed that Forbes references, and earned the sobriquet that Union cavalry chief General James Wilson applied to him, "an illusive cuss." Wilson was deeply frustrated that the mounted forces that had been committed to the pursuit of Lyon through Kentucky had weakened him and prevented him from delivering the finishing blow to Hood's army at Nashville.[13]

In his post-action report, Lyon cited Colonel Chenoweth and Captain Gracey for their contributions to the raid, and he thanked by name the various members of his staff. The notable omission in the list is Colonel J. J. Turner, who was probably the man responsible for the embarrassing surprise at Red Hill. His careless placement of the pickets, or his failure to impress upon them the need to keep alert, had let the Yankees in, and Lyon seems to have held the mistake against him.[14]

General Lyon's desire now was to return to his department headquarters in Paris, Tennessee. General Taylor had asked on January 30, that Lyon's command be assigned to him, saying, "Present conditions of affairs prevents his accomplishing anything now in the department to which he was ordered by the War Department." Two days later Lyon was ordered to report to Taylor. Lyon resisted the reassignment. On February 4, he wrote a long letter to Secretary of War Seddon in which he argued his case. He reviewed events since his appointment to command the Department of Western Kentucky the previous fall. He told how he had organized the men and, through his own efforts, had "procured arms, ammunition, and equipments" for them. Then, before he could build upon on this successful start, General Hood ordered him to make his Kentucky raid. "The Department of [Western] Kentucky has not yet had a fair trial," he said.[15]

He continued, "I know that Lieutenant General Taylor, commanding the Department of Mississippi, Alabama, and East Louisiana [*sic*], has applied to have the Department of Western Kentucky broken up, and asks that I be ordered to report to him for duty. Against this I enter my earnest protest, because I believe the service will be greatly benefitted by the department where men coming from Kentucky can be organized, and after being drilled and disciplined can be made serviceable anywhere in the Confederate States." He was suggesting that trained Kentuckians might be sent east to help defend Richmond, a matter of keen interest to President Davis and all the members of his cabinet. Furthermore, he warned that the dissolution of his department would mean that "that portion of Kentucky and Tennessee, which I have undisputed possession of will be abandoned to roving bands of guerrillas, no more recruits received from Kentucky, and the Confederate lines as now established in my department on the Tennessee and Ohio be retired to their old position, 200 miles south."[16]

The matter was not immediately resolved. It was nearly two months before the War Department replied to Lyon's concerns, and even then the answer did not come directly to him. The message went to General Taylor's adjutant general, and it said, "Inform General Lyon that no action is at present contemplated looking to the abolishing of his department. Whilst in General Taylor's limits he should report to him as a matter of course." Lyon was in an official limbo; his department remained intact, yet he, its commander, was expected to stay until further notice in Mississippi. General Taylor having no particular orders for him, Lyon made his bivouac with General Forrest.[17]

Forrest had been with Hood in Middle Tennessee. He commanded the familiar divisions of Buford and Chalmers, as well as the division of Brigadier General William H. "Red" Jackson. Forrest fought at Franklin, but not at Nashville, having been detached to go to Murfreesboro to keep General Lovell H. Rousseau's Federals pinned down. Forrest had not had any luck against Rousseau at Pulaski the previous fall, and he did not have any against Rousseau at Murfreesboro. The Kentuckian and his eight thousand soldiers were well protected inside the largest earthen fort of the war, Fortress Rosecrans. Forrest's main attack against Rousseau failed, and before another attempt could be made, Hood was defeated at Nashville and began falling back toward Alabama. Forrest was summoned to join Hood and take charge of the rear guard. He covered the retreat to the Tennessee River and then returned to Mississippi. Lyon's former command, the Kentucky Brigade, had done its share and more. George said, "During all the campaign the Kentucky Brigade was always in the forefront and was relied upon, and did do its duty under all trying circumstances." They returned to Mississippi exhausted and burdened with the knowledge that, after Nashville, "there was but the least hope that the Confederacy could finally succeed." Forrest gave them a furlough so that they could go home for a rest and to get new clothes and fresh saddle mounts. When they returned at the end of a month, Colonel Edward Crossland was made commander of the Kentucky Brigade.[18]

While in Forrest's camp, Lyon had the chance to become reacquainted with the Kentuckians. They forced him to become involved in a matter of military justice that began with the forcible exchange of two jaded CSA horses for some Mississippi farmer's fresh ones. Charges were filed, and the two culprits, Sergeant B. F. Brown (Company L, 3rd Kentucky) and Private T. J. Milner (Co. I, 12th Kentucky), were arrested and taken to the stockade. When their comrades heard of it, they immediately began to make plans to liberate them. Two men were sent from Forrest's camp at West Point to reconnoiter. They visited their friends who were in custody and confided the plan to them; they should be ready to break out at eleven o'clock that night. Fourteen men with two revolvers each took part in the jailbreak. The men guarding the prisoners put up a brief struggle, but they were soon subdued and warned to be quiet. The prisoners were freed. Their mission accomplished, the Confederates returned to their camp with no further trouble, hid the rescued men, rubbed down the horses, and turned in. Word of the nocturnal rescue of Brown and Milner spread through the camp next day, and General Lyon ordered the whole of Company L, 3rd Kentucky, and the whole of Company I, 12th Kentucky, to be jailed. They were taken to the same calaboose that some of them had raided only hours before. Generals Forrest, Lyon, and Jackson convened a court of inquiry. It was a frustrating and futile exercise. None of the witnesses called, all of whom were Kentuckians, would admit to knowing anything about the crime. Since not a single man of the rescue party could be identified, no action could be taken. "We outgeneraled the generals," they boasted. All were released except for three who were detained merely on suspicion that they had been involved, and they, too, were soon set free. The two sprung jailbirds continued to hide out, their comrades provided for them, and the story of what had really happened did not come out until after the war.[19]

The whole episode has the tone of a prank to it, the kind of crude mischief that one would expect from high school boys near the end of their senior year, but the war was still on, and there was one more Yankee threat to attend to before they would be dismissed to go home. On March 22, 1865, Major General James H. Wilson began a raid to destroy the industrial capability of central Alabama. His target was Selma, the great rail center and manufacturing hub, home of a Confederate States arsenal, a foundry, and numerous smaller, privately owned workshops that produced cannon tubes and carriages, caissons, and tons of ammunition, as well as "swords, bayonets, gear for horses and wagons, ammunition boxes, shovels, knapsacks, and every imaginable article of clothing." Selma was also "a production and repair center for locomotives and rolling stock."[20]

Wilson marched with three divisions, those of Brigadier Generals Edward M. McCook and Eli Long and of Brevet Major General Emory Upton. They were experienced campaigners, and their men were armed with sabers and seven-shot Spencer carbines. Henry George said, "This was perhaps the best-armed and all-around best equipped force sent out by the Federal government during the war." Forrest did not know of this threat from the north until March 26, four days after the expedition set out. His attention had been focused to the south. General Frederick Steele had led a bluecoat column out from Pensacola, and it was thought that *he* was the one who was going to attack Selma. Now, intelligence reached Forrest that the real threat was coming from the north. General William H. "Red" Jackson's division was best poised to be the first line of defense against Wilson's raiders. Forrest ordered Jackson to move with his division and Lyon's unspecified command toward Tuscaloosa. General Richard Taylor approved. He wrote Forrest, "Your order for Jackson to move via Tuscaloosa is right. Jackson, with his own and Lyon's command, should meet, whip, and get rid of the enemy soon as possible."[21]

On March 31, Forrest ordered Jackson, and his subordinate, Lyon, to move to Scottsville "without halting," and to continue to Centreville. Later that same day, a more urgent message arrived from Forrest, saying that the bluecoats "are moving right on down the railroad with their wagon train and artillery" and ordering Jackson to turn and follow them, "taking the road behind them from Montevallo down."[22]

At about the same time, General John T. Croxton's brigade of McCook's division veered away from the main column by order of General Wilson. Wilson had instructed McCook to detach one of his brigades "to proceed rapidly by the most direct route to Tuscaloosa to destroy the bridge, factories, mills, university (military school), and whatever else may be of benefit to the rebel cause." Wilson singled out one man of whom the expedition leader should beware. General Wilson said to McCook, "Caution him to look out for Lyon." McCook chose General Croxton to lead the mission. While he was on his was to Tuscaloosa, the main column would continue the march to Selma, and Croxton was to rejoin his division there as soon as possible.[23]

Croxton moved out at dawn on March 31, the start of an escalating game of back and forth. That afternoon, he learned that "Lyon's brigade, under Crossland, had passed the evening previous; that Forrest had passed at daybreak that morning, and Jackson's division, with part of Chalmers,' numbering in the aggregate of 5000 men, had passed during the day." Croxton was behind Jackson. The Rebels had left Tuscaloosa vulnerable, but Croxton decided to let it wait. He saw more importance in "disposing of Forrest's command, which would leave not only Tuscaloosa but every vital point open to us." He decided to follow the Confederate column. In the morning, he would be close enough to help catch Forrest in a pincer; he would attack the Confederates from the rear while the main Federal column assailed him from the front. Croxton halted to feed his horses before the long nighttime ride, while an advance guard forged ahead to keep an eye on the rear guard of Jackson's Rebel division.[24]

The Yankee scouts dogged Jackson for only two miles before their presence was discovered. Jackson turned and slammed into them. They rode back to their general to report that they had been found out and attacked. Croxton became convinced that Jackson's scouts were reconnoitering for a way to "envelop my position preparatory to an attack at daylight. . . . I determined, therefore, to avoid an engagement with a force of unknown strength by moving directly west." He left behind two companies of the 6th Kentucky Cavalry to watch and report on Jackson's movements. The Federals had not yet completed their evasive action the next morning, April 1, when the Confederates attacked. They hit the detachment of the 6th Kentucky hard and shoved them back on the main column. Their own regiment happened to be the rear guard. Major William H. Fidler commanded them, and he turned back with a battalion to oppose the charging Confederates. It became a running fight of several miles. Fidler held them until Jackson broke off the attack and took a side road that would place him between Croxton and Tuscaloosa. With the Confederates on the defensive, Croxton was free to roam wherever he pleased. He said, "I determined, therefore, to effect by stratagem what I could not hope to accomplish directly." He moved north and then west to get around Jackson's flank and approach Tuscaloosa from an unexpected direction. He and his brigade arrived near their target that evening. They began crossing the Black Warrior River immediately.[25]

That same day, April 1, Wilson's men had captured a Confederate dispatch rider carrying papers that described the scattered locations of Forrest's command. Jackson was on the other side of the Cahawba River near Tuscaloosa and Chalmers was twenty miles away between Randolph and Selma. Wilson believed if he moved quickly, he could defeat the Confederates in detail. To contain Jackson and Lyon, he sent McCook and the brigade of Colonel Oscar La Grange. McCook had heard of the previous night's fight between Croxton and Jackson, so he did not tarry. He and La Grange had a brush with Jackson's men that afternoon and a more serious one on the morning of April 2. McCook said, "A short and severe skirmish ensued, when my forces were withdrawn." Colonel La Grange said that McCook was convinced "that Jackson commanded more than double" his own number of men. This, plus the information that Croxton had moved beyond immediate danger, made him decide to fall back to the Cahawba River. If he could not defeat the Rebels, he could at least lure them away from Tuscaloosa. Jackson took the bait. He followed in full force, but McCook and La Grange got across the river and burned the bridge. McCook said that "as this was the only bridge on the stream, Jackson was never able to cross any portion of his command in time to interfere with the operations of the main body of General Wilson's corps, then moving against Selma."[26]

Jackson and Lyon had intimidated two Union brigades, convinced them that they had superior numbers, and forced each of them to fall back in fear of a full-fledged attack, and yet the Confederate commanders had failed in their two great responsibilities. They had allowed themselves to be pulled away from Tuscaloosa, which Croxton destroyed on April 3–4, and they had allowed themselves to be cut off from Forrest at the time when they were most needed to help defend Selma. Jackson and General Lyon were out of the campaign.

Without the help of Jackson and Lyon (as well as Chalmers, who was likewise unable to reach Forrest), the Confederates had been driven steadily back. On April 1, Forrest turned to meet the enemy at Ebenezer Church. Brian Wills says that he had been given critical time to prepare the position by Crossland and his Kentuckians, "who used alternating retiring lines to slow down Wilson's advance." The Federals arrived at 4:00 PM to find Forrest ready and waiting. The Rebels fought well at first and repulsed an attack that hit them with such force that the Yankees actually penetrated the line. In the even harder attack that followed, Forrest's right flank collapsed and then the whole line. Leaving behind three hundred captured, an unknown number killed and wounded, and three field pieces, Forrest fell back nearly twenty miles into the defenses of Selma. Slave labor had produced three and a half miles of works around the city, but Forrest did not have the numbers necessary for its defense. He took the city's factory workers and made them into soldiers for the day. Lieutenant General Taylor was in Selma, and he and Forrest consulted about the fight that was coming. They did not have long to wait.[27]

At 2:00 PM, April 2, Wilson's advance appeared. An hour later General Eli Long sent his skirmishers forward and his artillery crews began to exchange fire with the Rebel gunners. The ground shook with the concussion of cannon fire for the next two hours, and then, a little before five o'clock, Long threw his division forward. They took heavy losses coming across the flat, open ground, but they reached the barricades, planted their flag, and poured over. Inside, the defenders and the attackers grappled hand-to-hand. The Rebels soon had all they could take and streamed back toward the city center. General Emory Upton's division had joined the attackers by now and the collapse of the defense was eminent. Forrest hurried to General Taylor and advised him to leave Selma immediately. Taylor boarded a train, and, as he recalled, "My engine started toward Meridian, and barely escaped. Before headway was attained the enemy was upon us and capture seemed inevitable. Fortunately, the groups of horsemen near prevented their comrades from firing, so we had only to risk a fusillade from a dozen, who fired wild. The driver and the stoker, both negroes, were as game as possible, and as we thundered across the Cahawba bridge, all safe, raised a loud 'Yah! yah!' of triumph."[28]

Inside the city, the defense had broken apart. Selma was won, and the surviving defenders tried to escape into the night. Whole squads of men in butternut and gray were captured by Union patrols. Henry George and his friends tried to escape by going west toward the Alabama River. They were "attacked by a column of the enemy with drawn sabers . . . the squad was surrounded, compelled to surrender, and marched to a stockade constructed by the Confederates for Federal prisoners." Forrest, his staff, and escort were luckier that night. The bluecoats harassed them and added some more prisoners to their total of 2700, but the general made good his escape. George says that the skirmish that Forrest and his escort fought on their way to freedom "was the last engagement in which he or any of his men participated." They broke through to the east, worked their way north to Plantersville, then turned west to cross the Cahawba. Forrest reached Marion, Alabama, on April 4, where he found Chalmers and Jackson.[29]

Lyon was not with Jackson when Forrest arrived. He had headed north sometime before the campaign ended, perhaps in response to an urgent summons from his family in Kentucky. If Eddyville was in fact his destination, he started too late. He was "on the bank of the Tennessee River" when he received a letter from his sister-in-law, Florence O'Hara, announcing an "irreparable loss." His wife, Laura O'Hara Lyon, had died on April 4, 1865, and he was not there.[30]

They had waited for years to marry while Lyon was in the West. They had finally exchanged vows when he returned from the Mullan Road expedition, but their marriage had barely started before he went south in 1861. They saw each other only sporadically during the years of the Rebellion. She suffered in a hell of nervous dread at the news of every battle. She suffered without the comfort of her husband during her first pregnancy and suffered in silence during his imprisonment at Fort Warren. She suffered without the comfort of her husband when their infant son died in 1863. In 1864, she suffered without the comfort of her husband a second pregnancy and the birth of another son. Shortly after, she was taken hostage by a Federal gunboat crew, and she suffered without the comfort of her husband in her final illness and her moment of death. Suffering was the byword of her marriage to General Lyon, a marriage that lasted only four years. In reviewing her life, there is no question that Mrs. Lyon, like so many thousands of Southern women, was also a victim of the war. Lyon called Laura "my darling angel wife, the only woman and the only person whom I have ever or can ever truly love," and he must have grieved more deeply knowing that his sense of professional duty had kept them apart for so much of their short marriage.[31]

General Lyon reached Paris, Tennessee, on April 6. A few days later at Humboldt, he read in a Memphis newspaper that Robert E. Lee had surrendered. Southern loyalists through the region were stunned. In nearby Clarksville, Nannie Haskins wrote in her diary, "Surely this must be a dark dream: Is there no South. No army to avenge our wrongs. Has our beautiful Dixie been overrun by the vile and ruthless Yankee." Lyon knew that it was no dark dream. He had seen the thin ranks of ragged Confederates swept from the field by the enemy. Even the invincible Forrest had been powerless to stop them in the end. It is hard to imagine the depth of Lyon's despair in the first weeks of April 1865. Desolation was all around him. The Confederacy was dead, hundreds of thousands of her young men were dead, slavery was dead, his wife was dead. Maybe Lyon was thinking, too, about the U.S. Army officers he had known during his early career in Washington Territory, of their treachery and especially of Colonel George Wright's nonchalant execution of Qualchan, who had come in peaceably. In his experience, officers wearing the Union blue had proven that they could be capricious and cruel. How would they treat their defeated enemies in gray? General Lee had surrendered; the ones in the West soon would. The Confederacy was finished. There was nothing left to do. Lyon said to his trusted lieutenant, "It's all over, Chenoweth. I shall go to Mexico and cast my fortunes with Maximilian."[32]

14
MEXICO

In his late-life autobiographical sketch, the general said, "Lyon refused to sur-render, and with his servant, commenced his journey to Mexico. At Grenada Miss he learned from Genl [Marcus J.] Wright, in command at that place, that Gov. Isham G. Harris of Tennessee was at a farm house, near there, in hid-ing under the assumed name of Major Green and was anxious to join some one going to Mexico." Harris's fellow Tennessean and personal enemy Andrew Johnson had succeeded Abraham Lincoln as president, and Tennessee Gover-nor W. G. "Parson" Brownlow, another Unionist, had put a price on Harris's head. It was prudent for him to leave the country. Lyon went to Governor Harris and they made a plan. Lyon would go to Fort Pemberton on the Yazoo (where he had helped turn back a Federal expedition when there was still hope for the Confederacy), and arrange to have a boat built that would carry him and Harris and their two servants to the Mississippi River and across to the Arkansas side. When the general returned from Fort Pemberton, he discovered that Harris had added another member to the party. The fifth man was a cousin of Gover-nor Harris, and he could guide them through the backwaters in the direction they wanted to go. They set out on May 14, 1865. Cousin Harris took them first to his house, where they rested for several days. Other guides got them across the river to a spot near Napoleon, Arkansas, on May 21. They continued as far as they could by boat in swampy East Arkansas, and then they bought horses and pack mules. Lyon remembered that he was in charge of the packing, "as he had seen service of that kind in the U.S. army on the plains."[1]

The "illusive cuss" had evaded the Federals through Mississippi and Ar-kansas; now Texas was before him. Lyon and Harris crossed into Texas near Clarksville, in Red River County, on June 7. Back in 1862, Harris had sent some of his slaves and livestock to a farm he owned a short distance outside of Clarksville. They could hide there in safety and comfort before continuing their journey south. They had not been at the farm long before the gover-nor fell ill. Texas was practically lawless as the Confederacy collapsed, and

Lyon discovered that gangs of civilian toughs were scouting about for Harris in hopes of collecting the reward for his capture. Some of them were near Clarksville. Lyon carried the news to Harris, who felt that he was too ill to move. In the last episode he described in his memoir, Lyon told what happened next. Harris said,

> "Lyon I cannot move I suppose I will have to surrender, but you make your escape" to which Lyon replied "No they don't want me, but you had better if possible make your escape" Harris answered "it is impossible I cannot leave my bed"[ʰ]
> Reports came to Lyon continuously and it was reported late in the evening that the Bushwhackers were in Clarksville, two miles distant, and Lyon reported this to Harris. Harris said "well have one saddled, and send, Ran, his servant, to me. I will make an effort to get up." When the horses were saddled & mules packed, Ran had dressed Harris, & he & Lyon helped him to mount his horse, and the party rode four or five miles, and encamped in the woods and, next morning continued their journey, without further complaint of sickness on Harris' part. The scare to [the] report of the movement of the Bush-whackers had given him entirely cured him.[2]

Lyon and Harris hoped to catch up to General Jo Shelby in San Antonio. Shelby, a native Kentuckian who had won a great reputation as a cavalry leader in the trans-Mississippi, was another Rebel who decided that he could not tolerate living in a land under Yankee rule. He and his men had stopped in San Antonio for a rest on their journey to Mexico. Shelby took rooms in the Menger Hotel. The best food and liquor were served there in a setting of unexpected elegance in such a raw frontier town. Everyone who was on his way to Mexico seemed to have found his way to the Menger. One could lean against the mahogany bar and rub elbows with General John "Prince John" Magruder and Edmund Kirby Smith and an impressive collection of Southern governors. Shelby biographer Daniel O'Flaherty says that the Menger was "expatriate headquarters."[3]

Joining Shelby's "brigade" was a desirable thing. The company was distinguished, and there was safety in traveling with a large number of men. O'Flaherty says that "the countryside was alive with bandits and cutthroats of every description . . . murder, looting, and raping were the order of the day." Houston, Tyler, and Waxahachie were each occupied at times by gangs of outlaws armed with military grade weapons that they retained from their service or stole from more honorable men, and when Shelby and his men first rode into San Antonio they had to clear out a similar band of villains before they could have any peace. Some of the bad men were shot, some were hanged, and some took the wiser course and fled to the countryside where they waited like wolves just beyond the firelight.[4]

Shelby and his brigade would likely be able to defend themselves against any sort of assault by the thieves and killers they would find on the trail to Mexico. Lyon and Harris, however, were a very small party and vulnerable. Attaching themselves to Shelby's column would insure their safety. Unfortunately, when they arrived in San Antonio on June 26, they found that they were too late. Shelby had been gone for ten days or more. Lyon and Harris remained at the Menger only one night. The next morning, they continued toward Eagle Pass on the Rio Grande. En route, their small party divided. Somewhere between San Antonio and Eagle Pass, Harris's servant killed a sandhill crane. He planned to cook it, but Harris said that sandhill cranes were not good eating and told him to throw it away. Lyon disagreed; he said that he had known sandhill cranes to make a fine meal, and he told the servant to proceed with cooking supper. When the crane was served, Lyon found that Harris was right. The bird got tougher the longer he chewed. Finally, he could bear it no more. He spit it out. Harris made sport of it and kept insisting on giving Lyon another serving, bullyragging him until he became irritated. A few days later, Lyon and Harris came upon another traveler, a Kentuckian like Lyon, and they continued toward the Rio Grande together. To make conversation as they traveled, Harris began relating the story of Lyon and the sandhill crane. Harris seems to have been one of those supposedly humorous men who take such delight in another's embarrassment that they never know when to stop the hazing. As he had done the night of the meal, Harris practiced his ridicule until Lyon's annoyance boiled over. He said, "I have traveled thus far with you, governor, because I thought you deserved and needed my company and assistance . . . but I don't propose to be made fun of in this matter about this damned sandhill crane any longer."[5]

Harris replied that "if Gen. Lyon fancied for a moment that his company was either agreeable to him personally, or essential to the success of the journey, he was making a most outrageous mistake," and he invited him to pitch camp in another place, which Lyon did. They traveled separately but within sight of one another for several days. Harris portrayed himself as the bigger man, claiming later that he sent food over to Lyon's camp at night, and that he made more than one attempt to repair the breech between them. At last, they did begin riding together again, even though Lyon's demeanor showed that he had not forgotten Harris's earlier ridicule. They crossed the Rio Grande together on June 30, 1865, and at the Mexican town of Piedras Negras, Lyon and Harris parted ways, and each made his own trek to Mexico City.[6]

Harris may or may not have exaggerated the help he provided to Lyon when they were on the trail to Eagle Pass, but it appears that he rendered genuine aid to the general a few weeks later in Mexico City. Soon after Lyon left Piedras Negras, his camp was raided by bandits. They stole his animals and most of his gear, and he had to continue to Mexico City on foot. He never revealed how he survived; one supposes he begged. Lyon entered Mexico City destitute, and it was there and in that condition that he met Harris again. Harris had caught up with another distinguished expatriate party at Monterey on July 9. General Sterling Price and ex-Governor Trusten Polk of Missouri were traveling with an escort of twenty armed Missourians, and Harris joined them. They arrived in Mexico City on August 9. Harris described the trip as "one of the longest, most laborious, and hazardous of my life."[7]

It was no doubt true that Harris's trip was a hard one, but how much more so for the "woe-begone, bedraggled, dirty, footworn individual" he saw before him now on the sidewalk in Mexico City. Harris later said that he thought the down-on-his-luck man looked familiar, and then he knew. It was General Lyon. He was dressed in rags and nearly starved. Harris sent him to a bath house and a barber shop and lent him money to buy some clothes. He invited him to come back for a meal at his hotel after he was properly cleaned up. Over the dinner table, Harris offered to help Lyon find work. The general is said to have replied, "I want to work—I am ready to do anything, if it is to hoe corn in the fields—anything to get money to get along." It sounds a little out of character, a bit too slavish for a man of Lyon's pride, and a West Pointer, no less, but maybe he was brought down to a state of humility by his misfortunes. Whatever tone the conversation took, in a few days Harris had found Lyon a $6 a day job on the Mexican National Railroad. Lyon was properly grateful for Harris's timely help, and, when he was able, he paid back the loan for the clothes.[8]

Lyon had had time to reconsider his future plans during the long journey to Mexico City, and, despite what he had said to Colonel Chenoweth in Tennessee, he apparently never offered his services as a soldier to the Emperor Maximilian. Many of the expatriate Southerners did. General Shelby had an interview with Maximilian at the National Palace shortly after he arrived in Mexico City, and he told the emperor that he could "recruit a corps of 40,000 Americans" and subdue the Mexican insurgents "with a strong and well organized force." Maximilian listened patiently and politely to the scheme and then said no. As O'Flaherty puts it, Maximilian "was not willing to trust the Americans in an organization so large and so complete . . . he found the thought of such an army in his midst disturbing."[9]

Still, the Americans were in his country and more were coming—by the spring of 1866, 2500 Confederates had settled in Mexico—and some accommodation must be made for them. Colonization was the answer, and the government was generous. On September 5, 1865, the emperor decreed that all of Mexico was open "to immigration and colonization." He held out "very liberal inducements," including 640 acres to each head of a household and 320 acres to each single man. The land was tax free for five years, and the men were exempt from military conscription for the same period of time. The guarantee was made that their Protestant faith would be tolerated, and they could even bring laborers "of any race whatever" into the country. They would be peons, officially, since slavery was illegal in Mexico. The land that Maximilian offered was part of fifty thousand acres in the Cordova Valley, east of Mexico City and sixty-five miles from Veracruz on the coast. The land had originally been confiscated from the Catholic Church by the forces of Benito Juarez for debt, and the Maximilian government had confiscated it from the Juaristas. It was public land, and Maximilian offered it to the Americans. They liked what they saw—good climate, adequate rainfall, and "extremely fertile soil." Historian George Harmon says, "A more ideal location for planting a permanent colony could hardly have been found in Mexico."[10]

By the spring of 1866, as many as 250 Confederates—one-tenth of the total number of Southern expatriates—had taken up land in the *Tierrias de Colonizacion*, as General Lyon called it. They grew coffee and tobacco, various vegetables and root crops, grain, fruit, and, of course, animal husbandry was common among these natives of Kentucky and Virginia. Rank fields of sugarcane were testimony to the once important sugar industry in the valley, and there was no reason that it could not be revived at a profit, as well. The leading figures in the colony included Generals Sterling Price and "Prince John" Magruder, Governor Harris, and Admiral Matthew F. Maury, who was named by the emperor to be "honorary counselor of state and imperial commissioner of colonization." General Magruder became "chief of the land office of colonization." To further Maury's and Magruder's work and to promote the national government's policies, an English language newspaper, the *Mexican Times*, was published with the emperor's financial support in Mexico City. Former Confederate brigadier general and Louisiana Governor Henry Watkins Allen was the editor, and Major John Newman Edwards was assistant editor.[11]

There were two expatriate towns in the valley. Carlotta, the new town, was named for the empress, whose beauty dazzled the Confederates. A New York *Herald* reporter who visited in the spring of 1866 said that the village was laid out in the traditional manner, around a large plaza "which is covered with a natural growth of trees, among which is a grove of mangoes, the most beautiful shade trees, whose interlacing boughs and thick, glossy foliage exclude completely the sun's rays, affording a delightful retreat during the heat of the day." The reporter predicted, "In a few years, Carlotta will be the most pleasant town in Mexico . . . and the society there will be formed from the best educated families of the South and West." General Price and Governor Harris made their home in Carlotta, and they promoted the colony by speaking of the bright prospects there. Price told the correspondent that he had made $25,000 solely on his coffee crop.[12]

The other town was Cordova, nine miles to the northwest. General Lyon made his home near here. Cordova sat in surroundings of great natural beauty. To the east was a splendid view of the Sierra Madre Oriental, and a few miles to the west was Orizaba, a dormant volcano that was the highest mountain in Mexico. Its snowy peak must have reminded Lyon of Mt. Hood. General Shelby lived in Cordova. He ran a freight service and brought into the valley all manner of goods in ten-mule wagons, each carrying loads of three tons or slightly more. Shelby's wagons brought the merchandise from the railhead of the Mexican National Railroad at Paso del Macho. In a letter that was reprinted in the New York *Herald* in December 1865, Governor Harris spoke with pride and optimism of the rail service to this second American colony. He said, "The railroad is now in operation to within eighteen miles of this place, and all the balance to the city of Mexico is under contract and the work rapidly progressing. It is a few hours' run by rail from here to Vera Cruz." It was on this railroad that General Lyon found work as a chief surveyor, along with General John McCausland, a graduate of Virginia Military Institute and a veteran of Confederate service in both the Eastern and Western theaters.[13]

Supervising the work of a survey crew was not as demanding, nor as reminiscent of slave labor, as that of breaking the soil and building a farm from the ground up. It took advantage of Lyon's West Point education, and he liked it well enough. He wrote to his sister-in-law, Florence O'Hara, "My salary is now $1800.⁰⁰ a year or $150.⁰⁰ per month. I am now in excellent health, but have about forty pounds less flesh than when I last saw you, which loss, I fancy, has improved my personal appearance." He added that if "Americans or Europeans can be induced to emigrate here, this can be made a splendid country."[14]

Life in Mexico had only one drawback—at least, only one that the general mentioned in his letter—and that was being separated from Hylan F., his young son. Lyon wrote to Florence, "I am almost dying to hear one word from my boy. I have not heard from him or home since the reception of your letter on the bank of the Tennessee River last April. . . . Write dear Florence everything about my boy and all about the family." He told her that he intended to return to the United States in the spring to settle any unresolved affairs and get his son and return to Mexico, or, perhaps, he might go on to join the Confederado colony in Brazil. Lyon made no mention of a permanent return to the United States. And yet, he had already begun taking tentative steps to do just that.[15]

In early spring 1866, Lyon was still at work with his surveyors along the line of the national railroad. The long news item that was written on March 30 from Cordova and published in the New York *Herald* on April 19, 1866, said, "Brigadier General Lyon is at the head of a surveying party near Tuxpan."[16]

Months earlier, Lyon had begun to reconsider his plans in a fundamental way, perhaps because of what he observed happening in the *Tierrias de Colonizacion*. Despite a great potential, there were weaknesses that caused the eventual failure of the Confederate colonization efforts, not only in the Cordova Valley, but also in Chihuahua, Jalisco, Sonora, and San Luis Potosi. To begin with, the establishment of viable colonies in a practically undeveloped region required more physical labor than many of the expatriates were willing or knew how to put forth. These were men of the planter class. They were members of the Confederate congress and governors and generals, when what were needed were mechanics, carpenters, and small farmers. The aristocrats were unaccustomed to working with their hands, the military men were broken down by the hardships of war, and the efforts of both groups were insufficient to the task. Others who might have worked arrived destitute and were not able to buy the tools and seeds they needed to make a success of their experiment.

The colonies faced hostilities on all sides. The Southern press in the United States was against the colonists and editorialized against them, with information both true and false. They condemned the expatriates for taking their energy and talents into a foreign land when they were needed to help rebuild their own. The colonists' neighbors, the native population of Mexico, were hostile, as well. They remembered that a mere twenty years before the United States had invaded Mexico and precipitated a war that had cost them the northern half of their nation. They remembered how the invaders had treated them, and they knew how the conquerors had treated their kinsmen who ended up on the U.S. side of the new border. In addition to resentments from the recent past, there was the fact that the American colonists immediately alienated half the population by siding with Maximilian. Then, they foolishly offended the emperor who had been so open-handed in his generosity by exceeding the limits of their land grants and squatting on the lands of the peaceful local Indians, expelling people who had a far greater right to the land than themselves. The Americans were always grasping for more, and they managed to outrage all of Mexican society, from the people who lived in huts to the people who lived in palaces. And they were fully aware of the hostile atmosphere that surrounded them.

Also, the struggle between Maximilian and Juarez was bloody and the outcome uncertain. The Confederates had just come out of a war, and most of them had no appetite for more. Furthermore, if Juarez should win, what guarantee was there that any of Maximilian's promises would be honored? Would even their lives be safe?

Finally, there was the most basic factor of all that contributed to the colonists' dissatisfaction—they were homesick for the counties and states where they had ties stretching back to the Revolution and, in some cases, even earlier. The familiar customs and the loyalties that they had grown up with were not easily forgotten.

Ignoring the disgust of the stick-tights like the one who compared any Southern colonist who abandoned Mexico to a miserable dog "returning to its vomit," many did, in fact, go home. Within a relatively short number of years, over half of the expatriates returned to the United States. Hylan B. Lyon was one of them.[17]

As early as September 1865, Lyon had begun laying the groundwork for his return to the United States. From Orizaba, on the 25th of that month, he wrote a letter to President Andrew Johnson to request a pardon. He said:

> I have the honor to request of his Excellency, the President of the United States, a pardon for my participation in the War waged by the insurrectionary States of the South against the United States government. I am a graduate of the United States Military Academy at West Point New York and was an officer of the United States Army at the beginning of the War. My resignation of my commission as 1st Lieutenant of the 3rd Regiment of Artillery U.S.A. was accepted by President Lincoln on the 3rd of April [sic] 1861. I am a native of Kentucky.
>
> All my act during the War were governed by humane and civilized principles. I desire to return to my home in Kentucky and if permitted to do so, I will take the oath of allegiance to the United States Government and will conduct myself as a quiet and loyal citizen.[18]

He concluded by asking that Johnson send his reply to Judge F. H. Skinner in Eddyville, and he signed his request, "H. B. Lyon, Late Brigadier General, Provisional Army of the Confederate States." The general's designated go-between, County Judge Frederick H. Skinner, was the same man who had taken in the orphaned Hylan B. Lyon and at least some of his siblings in 1844, before he was a judge and was still a humble hosteler. Skinner had come to Lyon's rescue in the mid-forties, and twenty years later he was called on once again to play a similar role. He was going to help bring Lyon home.[19]

Lyon returned to Kentucky in May before the presidential pardon was granted. He almost certainly traveled by rail to Veracruz and took passage on a ship to New Orleans. He had not been on the Gulf since his early days as a young U.S. Army officer going west to his assignment at Fort Yuma. It was as if he was turning back through the pages of his life, all the way back to where the story began. From New Orleans, he would have taken a paddle wheeler up the Mississippi to the mouth of the Ohio, thence to the mouth of the Cumberland at Smithland, thence to the familiar landing at Eddyville.

The pardon came not long after his return. Dated June 11, 1866, it said that General Lyon was given "a full pardon and amnesty for all offences by him committed, arising from participation direct or implied, in the said rebellion." Some conditions were attached to the pardon. The most substantial of them was that he would take the loyalty oath prescribed by the presidential decree of May 29, 1865. Lyon signed the receipt of the pardon and returned it on October 25, 1866. H. B. Lyon was home.[20]

15
KENTUCKY

The Kentucky to which Lyon returned was different from the one he had left in 1861. Kentucky had remained loyal to the Union, and many more of her sons wore the blue than the gray. But, she was a slave state, and her loyalty was always doubted by the Federal government and by the district and departmental officers who commanded there. Jeremiah Boyle, Stephen G. "The Butcher" Burbridge, and John M. Palmer had all been harsh in their treatment of Kentuckians, and Kentuckians were pushed into greater sympathy with the South by what they considered abuse by their Union rulers. That was one cause of Kentucky's change of attitude. The second was the Emancipation Proclamation. Kentuckians entered the Federal service with the understanding that they were fighting to save the Union; for most, an end to slavery did not enter into their thinking. When President Lincoln issued the Emancipation Proclamation in mid-war, Kentuckians realized that the aim of the war had shifted. A Northern victory now would very likely mean the end of slavery and cost them tens of millions of dollars in chattel property. Their attitude hardened against the administration.

The Emancipation Proclamation was a signpost to the future, but it did not pertain to the Border States when it went into effect in 1863, and Kentucky took political action to make sure that the freedom it promised would *never* change the status of the slaves who lived inside her borders when her voters rejected the Thirteenth Amendment. Kentucky's Unionist leaders were dismayed. Former Union General Lovell Harrison Rousseau, a native of Lincoln County who now represented Louisville in the U.S. House of Representatives, bemoaned the fact that "In the whole Christian world there remain but three slave states: Cuba, Brazil, and Kentucky."[1]

Kentuckians' conservatism continued to assert itself in the months to come. Anne E. Marshall says, "For some, voting Democratic was retaliation for the tight reign of martial law during the war, for the perceived injustice of Reconstruction further south, and, most of all, for the violation of racial order in their own state." Voting Democratic "was for many whites not simply an attempt to redress the past but rather to seize control of the present." In the elections for the General Assembly in August 1865, the citizens gave another early warning that they intended to guide their destiny in a conservative direction when they handed control of both the House and the Senate to the Democrats. Once seated, they "proceeded to repeal all the 1862 wartime measures which deprived Confederates and their supporters of political and civil rights. . . . Repeal of these measures left the popular ex-Confederates free to participate in Kentucky politics." With their civil rights fully restored and a sympathetic voting public eager to support them, many former Confederates "hastened to groom themselves for public office."[2]

H. B. Lyon was not among those who hoped for a career in politics. He returned to Eddyville and kept his promise to President Johnson to live quietly. He was satisfied to devote himself to restoring his neglected farm in a world without slave labor, to attend to business at his mill, and to become acquainted with the young son he barely knew. Lyon was a conservative, though, and a Democrat, and he must have watched with approval as his native state became more intransigent in its opposition to the liberal social changes which the Union had fought for and which he had fought against. It appeared that he and his fellow Confederates were vindicated in each ensuing election.

In a special Congressional election in the spring of 1867, Democrats won all nine House seats. Also that year, John LaRue Helm became governor. Helm was the father of General Ben Hardin Helm, who had died at the head of the Orphan Brigade on the second day at Chickamauga. Helm defeated his Republican opponent by a margin of almost three to one. The lieutenant governor and others on the Democratic ticket were also Southern men. Marshall quotes the eminent Kentucky historian Lowell H. Harrison as saying, "If you wanted to be elected, it was by far best to be an ex-Confederate. If you had lost one or two limbs for public display, you were almost a shoo-in."[3]

Some Kentuckians used violence as another way to guarantee that nothing significant had changed in the Bluegrass State. They wanted to show the country that Reconstruction meant nothing; the ante-bellum social order would endure. They intended to make sure that blacks understood they were still subservient to even the lowest white man. The Ku Klux Klan and groups calling themselves Regulators began to be a presence in the state soon after the end of the war. The terrorist groups targeted not only the freedmen, but also the whites who tried to register blacks to vote or attempted in any way to live in cooperation with the former slaves. Marshall says, "Near Owensboro, in Western Kentucky, one group threatened to burn the property of white farmers who rented land to African Americans and warned the black tenants to leave by the next day," and, "In 1866, regulators in Daviess, Marion [and other] counties burned housing farmers had built for laborers." In late 1865, a Freedman's Bureau investigator reported after touring the state that he had found twenty-three instances of shootings, whippings, rapes, and arson. This was the record of only a few weeks' time, and the violence went on for years. It was more virulent in the Bluegrass Region than in Western Kentucky, though its presence was known from the mountains to the Mississippi. A former slave named Mary Wright remembered that in Trigg County, which bordered Lyon County on the southeast, the Klan decapitated the blacks they murdered and put the heads on pikes along the Cadiz Road. She said the "buzzards would eat them until nuthin' was left but the bones," and the signs on the posts beneath the skulls said, "Look out Nigger You are next."[4]

Some communities made an effort to suppress the terroristic violence. The Hickman *Courier* was outspoken in its disapproval of the Klan in an April 1868 item called "The Hickman Ku-Klux." It said, "We regret to observe that some indiscreet persons are amusing themselves by posting order about town emanating from the Ku Klux Klan. One, to which our attention has been called, orders 'all the negroes to leave town,' and another is addressed to an enterprising and worthy citizen, ordering him 'not to employ any negroes.' . . . This is all wrong, and extremely foolish, and calculated to do the community serious injury." The newspaper urged calm and advised the black people "to pursue their daily employment quietly and industriously, and to pay no regard to these orders from thoughtless and inconsiderate persons. There is no such thing as a Ku-Klux Klan in Hickman or Fulton County." Klansmen were occasionally seen riding in Fulton County, it is true; but they were not local. They came across the border from Tennessee.[5]

Where Hylan B. Lyon came down on the pro-Klan/anti-Klan conundrum is not known, for a certainty, but the question deserves consideration. Lyon was a well-traveled, educated man, and such sophistication was often death to the crude and violent expressions of racial prejudice for which the Klan was infamous. He had shown a certain measure of sympathy for people of another race during the Coeur d'Alene War, when he condemned Colonel George Wright's behavior toward the hostiles, and, so far as is known, he did not mistreat black prisoners during either of his raids into Kentucky in 1864. A clue about Lyon's racial attitudes in later life might be seen in a news item that appeared in the Iron County [Missouri] *Register* in June 1904. Titled "Negro Confederate Is Dead," the brief items said, "Ike Copeland, 78 years old, died Saturday at Eddyville, Ky. He was said to have [been] the only negro confederate living in the state. He lived in a home given him by Gen. H. B. Lyons [*sic*]."[6]

Furthermore, Lyon's residence, Eddyville, like Hickman, was a busy river town, the first being on the Mississippi and the second on the Cumberland.

The river traffic brought to these and other towns a broader interchange of ideas. Travelers from other regions were frequent, and commercial ties with the North tended to engender a less provincial attitude among townspeople than was observed among those who lived in the rural areas more distant from the navigable rivers and the railroads. This was true even in the Deep South. Vicksburg, Mississippi, for instance, which became a symbol of Confederate militarism, had opposed secession in 1860.

There is no evidence that H. B. Lyon was in sympathy with the Klan and certainly none that he put on a white hood and rode by night. All the available information indicates that his sole concern for years after his return to Eddyville was to restore his fortune and reunite with his family. On the other hand, Lyon was a Southerner, a former slave owner, and a Confederate officer who had renounced his oath and his career in the U.S. Army to serve in the rebellion. Added to these was the fact that his beloved commander, Nathan Bedford Forrest, had spoken publicly in favor of the KKK, may have been a member, and, more than that, may have been the Grand Wizard. The whole question of Forrest's exact connection with the Klan is shadowy. Despite his endorsement of the Klan's goals, Forrest insisted that he was not even a member of the group, much less its leader. However, it appears that Forrest traveled from Memphis to Nashville in the spring of 1867 to meet with his old artillery chief, John W. Morton, who had become the Grand Cyclops of the Klan, and that Morton presided over his swearing in at the Maxwell House. In addition, in a long interview that first appeared in the Cincinnati *Commercial* (and reprinted in the Athens [Tennessee] *Post*), Forrest stated authoritatively that there were forty thousand Klansmen in Tennessee and perhaps as many as half a million across the South. He offered to show the reporter the constitution of the group; demonstrated that he knew its organizational structure; and said that, though there "was no doubt" that the Klan had been of benefit to Tennessee, orders had gone out to the "foolish young men" to stop riding through the country with masks over their faces. Forrest said that three members of the Ku Klux Klan had been "court-martialed and shot" for violating orders and said that he had sent a man to investigate a murder in Franklin. He had investigated other offenses, as well.[7]

As the biographer Brian Steel Wills observes, "If he did not actually command the Ku Klux Klan, Bedford Forrest certainly acted like a commander. He exercised the same stern discipline he had formally demanded of his soldiers, punished violators in a similar fashion, and attempted to maintain the same element of control over their actions." It may very well be that the Wizard of the Saddle became the Wizard of the Klan by the late 1860s. The question is, did Lyon follow the example of his old chieftain and become a Klansman? Again, one can only say that there is no evidence that he did. He displayed little interest in public life of any kind; just the opposite, in fact. He seemed to be intensely focused on his private life. Romance had even reentered the picture. He had begun to court Grace Machen, who was eight years younger. They married on August 28, 1869.[8]

Grace Machen was the niece of Willis B. Machen, one of the Confederate representatives from Kentucky, whose home, Mineral Mound, overlooked the Cumberland River in Lyon County. The passing Federal gunboats had made a practice of firing at the Confederate flag he defiantly flew outside his house. His brother, Francis B. "Frank" Machen, was Grace Machen's father. Hylan B. and Grace Machen Lyon became the parents of three children: Grace (born in 1872), Frank (born in 1874), and Ernest (born in 1880). With Grace, Lyon found a new stability in his domestic life, and his finances, too, were on a respectable footing. In the 1870 Federal Census, his real estate was valued at $2500 and his personal property at $800. He listed his occupation as "surveyor," but surveying probably contributed little to his financial well-being. His main interests were his store, his mill, and farming. Agriculture was experiencing something of a boom in Kentucky because of the advent of new and improved farm machinery in the 1870s. Those who could afford machinery found it to be an efficient substitute for human labor. Corn, tobacco, and hemp were the primary crops, and hogs, mules, cattle, and chickens the principal farm animals.[9]

In 1880, Lyon identified himself to the federal census takers as a farmer. His status changed that year, however, when Governor Luke P. Blackburn named him to be one of the three-man commission to study prison reform and select a location for a new prison in the commonwealth. Kentucky's prison dated back to 1799, when a useless lot of five acres of swampy ground was selected as the site for the state's house of corrections. Separate facilities were built for the male and female convicts. The larger of the two was for the men. Prison historian Bill Cunningham described it as "poorly ventilated, inadequately heated and filthy." Worse than the cells, perhaps, were the workhouses. The inmates made such items as chairs and tables and rope. Cunningham says that the hemp house, where hemp plants were broken and pounded in the first step of the rope-making process, was "the most despised assignment," so much so that in a span of just two years, "a prison physician reported that three men chopped off their hands with hatchets, five cut off one or more fingers, and two slashed their arms—all to escape the hemp house."[10]

The state exercised little control over the prison, other than furnishing the "accommodations of the inmates, the workshops, machinery, tools, etc." Day to day operations were the responsibility of a lessee, who paid the state $8000 for a bond and used the prison thereafter as a private manufactory with the inmates as the labor force. The lessee was appointed by the legislature and his bond was good for a period of four years. Cunningham says that the les-see "had complete control over the prisoners—feeding, clothing, and housing them. He also hired guards and maintained order. . . . The profits, after cov-ering the costs of the prison operation, went into the keeper's pocket. Natu-rally, the lessee increased his profits by cutting corners."[11]

Lyon was associated in some official capacity with the prison system in the early 1870s, and he showed himself to be a reformer. In January 1872, after the legislature appropriated $500 for reading material for the inmates, Lyon was one of a group who selected "suitable educational, moral, historical and religious books." He helped secure funds to erect a new stable for the horses which were essential to the work of the inmates. During the same period, the dirt floors of the prison cell-houses were paved with asphalt. Lyon made a tentative step toward a higher public profile in 1874 when his name was put forth as a candidate for lessee of the penitentiary. He had four competitors for the appointment, and when the vote was taken on January 15, Lyon came in third.[12]

Despite losing the appointment, Lyon's progressive view of penology was undoubtedly one reason that Governor Blackburn asked him to help reform Kentucky's prison system in 1880. Certainly his Confederate credentials did not hurt him in the governor's eyes. Blackburn himself was an ex-Confederate and also a physician. He was elected governor in 1879 and let little time pass before he made the legislators understand that he intended to address con-ditions in the state penitentiary in a major way, and he wanted the funds to proceed. He told the lawmakers in his 1880 New Year's Day address, "A Kentuckian myself, native to the manor born, I almost feel the blush of shame when I think of the accumulated horrors to be witnessed in our state prison. I regard our present penitentiary as a stigma upon the fair name of the Com-monwealth." He told them that there were 953 prisoners, 173 more than the number of cells available. The cells were only 3'9" wide, 6'8" long, and 6'3½" tall, and many of them contained two prisoners. Blackburn said, "The Black Hole of Calcutta, so abhorred in history, was not much worse than this. Only think of it: two human beings crammed together in these dark unwholesome little dens. To what beastliness may it not lead; yes, to what beastliness has it not already led . . . shuddering delicacy will turn away and avert its head at the disgusting recital."[13]

Blackburn cited the unacceptable death rate among prisoners and con-demned the high rate of recidivism. He said, "The object of all punishment should be the prevention of crime and the reformation of the offender; but our great prison degrades and brutalizes and is a nursery of crime—indeed, as has been well and truthfully said, it is the great college and university of crime." Then, having outlined the problem, Blackburn named the solution.

He wanted a new prison to be built "remote from this," where young inmates could be separated from the old. He urged that a warden system be adopted to replace the lessee system. He said that the prisoners should be properly fed and clothed and receive religious instruction. He called for the hiring of a full-time physician and for the inmates to be taught a trade. He quoted prison system experts from around the country to support the need for reform, and, to soften the financial blow to the tight-fisted lawmakers, he insisted that a well-run prison could be self-supporting.[14]

Blackburn had laid out a broad program of reforms for the legislators to consider. To study the issues and make specific recommendations, the legislature approved a committee of three men. They were Judge William M. Beckner of Clark County, former Congressman R. H. Stanton of Maysville, and Hylan B. Lyon of Eddyville. The penitentiary commissioners met for the first time on May 25, 1880, and chose Stanton to be their chairman. Though Stanton held the title, Lyon was the motivating force of the commission. Cunningham says, "Unquestionably the dominating member of this group, by reputation and personality, was General Lyon."[15]

They were not chimney-corner reformers. They traveled in June 1880 to the Ohio State Penitentiary, followed by visits to prisons in Massachusetts, New York, Tennessee, Indiana, and Illinois. They also attended the Conference of Charities and Correction in Cleveland, Ohio. They came away from their investigations impressed by the "Irish System" of corrections, which Governor Blackburn also favored. This was a system of graduated levels of punishment ranging from hard labor to work-release. In work-release the inmate lived and worked (under supervision) outside the prison walls. The committee also emphasized education as a curative for crime.

In its report to the legislature, the committee said, "We unhesitatingly recommend an immediate repeal of the law establishing the leasing system, that the contracts with lessees, violated in every particular, be immediately annulled, and the convicts withdrawn." They pointed out the brutalities of the present system, the prevalence of scurvy among the inmates (nearly eight hundred of the state's one thousand prisoners "had been treated for scurvy in 1879"), and the cruel culture of discipline ("one prisoner had been given 150 lashes as punishment").[16]

With the supporting testimony from his prison commission, Governor Blackburn got, if not all, nearly everything he wanted in the field of penal reform. The Irish System would be adopted, a warden would replace the lessee, and, as the committee also recommended, a new prison would be built as an adjunct to the old one in Frankfort, its location to be decided. According to newspaper reports, four cities were initially considered for the new prison site. They were Paducah, Bowling Green, Owensboro, and Henderson. A less likely contender was little Eddyville, which was eager to secure the new prison as a replacement for the "now defunct iron industry and diminishing river trade." The same three commissioners who studied prisons around the country and reported back to the legislature were charged with selecting a site, and in this, Lyon's influence was all-important. Cunningham says, "General Hylan B. Lyon was king in this far western community." His ally in the promotion of Eddyville as the prison site was the one-legged ex-Confederate, and now state senator, William Stone. They pointed out that Eddyville had stone and coal and a "mild and healthy climate." Practically every town in Western Kentucky had easy access to the same mineral resources and enjoyed the same salubrious climate, but Eddyville showed its sincerity by pledging money toward the purchase of the land, and that secured the hoped for result. It was announced that the new prison would be built in Eddyville.[17]

A different board of commissioners was assembled to buy the necessary acreage, select the architect, and oversee the construction. General Lyon was named as one of the new commissioners. He was joined by Wilhite Carpenter of Bullitt County and J. M. Thomas of Bourbon County. One of their first tasks was to procure the land. Here again, Lyon's influence was evident. They selected was eighty-seven acres that had once belonged to Robert Cobb, the commander of Cobb's Battery during the war. His two-story mansion still stood on the grounds of the estate. Cobb had suffered financial reversals, and Willis B. Machen bought it for taxes at a courthouse auction. Now, Machen sold it to the state for $4000. Eddyville paid $1400 of the price.

The General Assembly appropriated $150,000 to begin construction (a second appropriation of $112,500 was later made), McDonald Bros. of Louisville was the architectural firm selected to design the penitentiary, and ground was broken on October 18, 1884. Fifty-one convicts made up the crew for the heavy work (a number later increased to over 160), and Italian masons were brought in to cut and dress the stone.

The stone came from Hylan B. Lyon's own quarry and was brought to the worksite by a "small gauge railway built for the purpose." As would also be the case in the present day, there were questions about the propriety of buying stone from the quarry that Lyon owned for the building project that he was overseeing, and accusations were made. Suspicions of overpayment and kickbacks arose. The Louisville *Commercial* launched a full investigation. In the end, it concluded that General Lyon's conduct was completely proper and above board. The *Commercial* said, "A careful examination of the books show [sic] that he has conducted his business systematically and honestly . . . his charges were moderate, and in many instances lower than were asked by others." Tipton A. Miller, the state representative from Calloway County wrote to the Murray *News* that the "old general stands fully and honorably acquitted. Not the least stigma rests on his noble and gallant brow. He stands vindicated in full."[18]

The progress of the work was followed closely by the state's newspapers, and Lyon used the press to tamp down false rumors of malfeasance, both his own and the state's. In an interview that appeared in the Hickman *Courier* on August 30, 1885, he said that the "wild statements of enormous expenditures" had no foundation in fact. He said, "The appropriation made for the work is $150,000, with expenditures limited to $5,000 per month, and so far, we have been unable to get even that much. We are working 145 convicts and 18 stone cutters. We have drawn a little less than $35,000 up to date, and have vouchers for indebtedness out amounting to about $12,000. In other words, we have expended about $47,000 to date."[19]

Lyon insisted that the rumors of convict escapees were exaggerated, and he reported that the health of the convict laborers was good. He also revealed a bit of frustration that the work was taking so long and identified the cause as the legislature's extreme frugality and short-sightedness. He said, "Yes, the work is very slow and tedious. . . . You see, 300 convicts and 50 stonecut-ters could be worked just as well and without costing the state any more for guards and overseers. According to the limit it will require twenty months yet to complete the work."[20]

That Lyon was able to continue his duties at all was testimony to the strength of his character and his belief in the importance of the work, for he had suffered a crippling double loss in his personal life. His second wife, Grace, died at age forty on March 22, 1885, leaving motherless three children, the youngest only five years old. Barely two weeks later, on April 4, his oldest son, Hylan F. Lyon, died accidentally by his own hand. He was killed by a shotgun blast which the newspapers assured readers was unintentional. They added that "Young Lyon was just entering his twenty-first year, and was one of the most popular and promising young men." With the death of H. F., all trace of Lyon's life with his great love, Laura, vanished from the earth, and with the death of Grace, he lost his second love and was thrust once again into the role of that tragic stereotype, the widower father.[21]

In spite of his private grief, his oversight of the state's Eddyville project went on. As the new penitentiary neared completion, observers approved of what they saw. One newspaper article said, "From an architectural standpoint it is undoubtedly the handsomest building of its kind in the country." Above the administration building, an impressive clock tower was underway, and, the description continued, "The exterior of the entire structure is of rough gray limestone, with dressed trimmings. Over the structure is sprung a mas-sive arch, surmounted by the keys of the authority, with the names of the three commissioners cut in stone."[22]

Lyon's 1885 prediction that the job would not be complete for twenty months turned out to be overly optimistic. The prison was not ready to accept inmates until the winter of 1889. The first prisoner moved in on Christmas Eve. The project had cost $275,000. The warden's job was offered to Lyon at a salary of $2000 per year, but he turned it down. One probable consideration in his decision to refuse the post was the fact that he and the other commissioners had already been forced to sue the state for $4000 in back pay that was due them. The issue dragged on until July 1901, when their legal counsel collected a sum of $12,000 to be divided among H. B. Lyon, J. M. Thomas, and the estate of Wilhite Carpenter, minus the lawyer's fee.

Lyon's refusal of a job with a good salary, one that would not even require him to leave home, was a sign that his finances had more than recovered from his neglect during the war years and the months of exile in Mexico. Had it been otherwise, he surely would have accepted the job offer, for, by the time the prison was completed and the warden's office needed to be filled, Lyon had remarried and fathered a daughter, and an additional income would have been welcome. On January 5, 1887, he married Miss Ruth Wolfe. The Hopkinsville *Semi-Weekly South Kentuckian* made a little jest in its announcement of the Lyon-Wolfe nuptials, "That good time of universal peace foretold in the Bible must be drawing near. Just look at those names." Miss Wolfe was twenty-one years old and Lyon was fifty-four, but still vital. Their first child, Maybelle, was born on June 7, 1889, and their second daughter and last child, Lorraine, was born June 27, 1894.[23]

Like the Lyon family, Eddyville was showing signs of new life. The town had five lawyers; shoe, broom, and wagon manufacturers; mills; a hotel; and a variety of stores where just about every necessity could be satisfied. Lyon could have lived comfortably there, had the fires of his ambition burned lower. Outside interests were increasingly on his mind. He had begun identifying himself as a capitalist, and he had expanded his interests beyond farming, milling, and his mercantile. He was, for example, a founding investor of a new railroad, the Paducah, Nashville, & Charleston. It was incorporated in March 1900. A contemporary news item said that the P.N.&C. was "intended to be an extension of the Ohio Valley road to Nashville. . . . The Ohio Valley is completed to Princeton, and is projected to Nashville, via Clarksville and Ashland, Tenn. . . . The proposed line runs through magnificent coal beds."[24]

Also, General Lyon was becoming more politically active. As early as 1886 his name was mentioned as a possible gubernatorial candidate. He was, said one newspaper, "the very kind of material of which to make an ideal Governor." Nothing came of that. The next year he was offered the post of state adjutant general by the new governor, Simon Bolivar Buckner. This, too, he refused. By 1897, however, he found the idea of life as a politician to be more attractive. He was elected permanent chair of a Democratic convention that met in Murray that year to nominate candidates out of the First District for judicial vacancies. The Hopkinsville *Kentuckian* said, "Gen. Lyon made a most acceptable and impartial chairman and presided with easy dignity and soldierly discipline."[25]

The following spring, Lyon announced that he would be a candidate for the state House of Representatives in the next year's election. The Paducah *Daily Sun* commented on what some considered a premature announcement, saying, "Gen. H. B. Lyon, of Lyon county, believes in the early bird theory." Lyon defeated his Democratic opponent in the primary in July 1899 and won the general election in the fall. That December, before he had even taken his seat, he was being touted, apparently with his consent, as a candidate for Speaker of the House. He was not elected to the post and did not gavel the House to order when the legislature convened on January 2, 1900, but he was chosen to be one of the three-man House committee who, acting in concert with an identical committee from the Senate, called on the governor to "inform him that the General Assembly is now organized and ready to receive any communication he may desire to make."[26]

The members got down to serious business on January 4, when they began selecting by lot the members of the committees that would determine the elections in the various counties. Lyon was chosen to serve on the board to affirm the outcome of the contest for the representative from the city of Louisville. Four days later, Lyon was appointed to four standing committees, at least two of which complimented his interests and experience. They were: State Prisons and House of Reform, Printing, Propositions and Grievances, and Military Affairs. The House had a great many bills to consider in the session just starting. They ran the gamut from a measure to regulate the sale of kerosene to promoting the creation of a national military park at Perryville. However, the most significant work by far that Lyon did during the legislative session of 1900–1901 was to help decide, as part of an eleven-man joint committee, the outcome of the contested gubernatorial election between the Republican William Sylvester Taylor and the Democrat William Goebel.

Taylor was a native of Butler County, Kentucky. He had worked his way up from a poor beginning to school teacher, lawyer, and Butler County Clerk. He joined the Republican Party in 1882 and was elected Butler County Judge in 1884. In 1895, he became state attorney general. It was Attorney General Butler who gave Hylan B. Lyon and the other prison commissioners a hard time over collecting the back pay that was due them. At the end of this term, Butler was chosen to be the GOP gubernatorial candidate. A newspaper, referring to Taylor by the unflattering nickname "Hogjaw," said he was a "slouch in gait, a boor in his manners, and the butt of the entire bar of Kentucky. . . . Taylor knows nothing of social or political amenities." The Western

Kentucky humorist and newspaperman Irvin S. Cobb characterized Taylor as "a poor enough creature" who was easily molded and shaped by the stronger personalities around him.[27]

Taylor's Democratic opponent was William Goebel. Born in Pennsylvania, Goebel grew up in Covington, Kentucky, where the family had moved during the Civil War. He absorbed the liberalism of his German immigrant parents and, after he earned his law degree in 1877, made himself the enemy of the monied interests of the state. He supported unions and striking railroad workers, and this work continued when he became a state senator in 1887. He formed a commission to regulate the railroads and fought endlessly with the railroad lobby. Naturally, the directors of the Louisville & Nashville Railroad and other influential capitalists despised him. A great many people loved him, though. He fought for expanded rights for women and blacks, and he wanted all the power he could hold in order to accomplish his goals. His enemies called him "Boss Bill," and said of him that he "loved power as drunkards love their bottle." Irvin S. Cobb said that Goebel had "audacity, ruthlessness, a genius for leadership, a perfect disregard for other men's rights or their lives where his own wishes were concerned; the brain to plan and the will to execute."[28]

Hogjaw and Boss Bill kicked off their campaigns in August 1899. Through the summer and into the fall, each candidates' remarks toward the other became increasingly personal. Feelings on both sides were running high. Election day violence was expected. Governor William O. Bradley ordered the militia to be prepared to maintain order, and some cities, like Louisville, hired special police to prevent disturbances.

To everyone's relief, election day passed quietly, but, at its end, no clear winner had emerged in the gubernatorial contest. There was confusion about the outcome until the first week in December, when the election board declared the Republican Taylor the winner by a tiny plurality of about four hundred votes. On December 12, 1899, Taylor was inaugurated.

The state's Democratic Central Committee was not willing to let the election board's decision stand. They planned to challenge the outcome when the legislature convened in January. They wasted no time; the legislature was called to order on January 1, and the next day, January 2, the Democrats filed a notice of contest. They specified nine grounds for their challenge. They included some mountain counties' use of tissue-thin ballots, which were so transparent that they violated the citizen's right to cast a secret vote. They claimed that the militia interfered with U.S. marshals in some counties, including populous Jefferson County. They claimed intimidation by management of the employees of the L&N Railroad in favor of Taylor, and they claimed that the Republican Party itself had provided the L&N and some other corporations the funds with which to bribe voters.

Democrats controlled the legislature, and they created an ad hoc committee of four senators and seven House members to investigate the charges of election day manipulation and intimidation and to invalidate the decision of the election board, if necessary. Names were written on slips of paper and drawn from a box. When it was over, ten of the eleven committeemen selected were Democrats. The freshman House member Hylan B. Lyon, who did not particularly care for either Goebel or Taylor, was one of them. The Republican raised a loud cry of trickery, but in the end a resolution was adopted which exonerated the clerk of any wrong doing and the results were allowed to stand. The joint committee held its first meeting on January 15, 1900. With only a single Republican on the committee, there was practically no doubt as to what the ultimate outcome of the investigation would be. A similar committee was looking into the lieutenant governor's race, with expectations that its decision would also favor the Democrats.

With little legislative power available to them, the Republicans "tried to put pressure on the General Assembly and brought in a 'Mountain Army' of supporters, a move suggesting that force might be used." The Democrats charged that the Republicans conspired with the Louisville & Nashville Railroad to carry the mountaineers into the capital free of charge. By the morning of January 25, nearly one thousand Eastern Kentuckians had gathered in Frankfort, and hundreds of them were camped on the capitol lawn. The Republicans in the General Assembly arranged for them to be fed in their camp. Rumors abounded that the Taylor forces were also smuggling into Frankfort quantities of ammunition and arms and hiding them around the city for the use of their mountain friends. The stories of clandestine arsenals and the presence of the menacing, gun-toting strangers unnerved the citizens of Frankfort, and many of them began to arm themselves with pistols and even shotguns. The presence of so many guns seen and unseen meant that "another volatile element was added to an already combustible political mix."[29]

The atmosphere was so tense that the Republicans turned to fighting one another. Even before the majority of the mountaineers arrived, there had been a shooting scrape between two prominent Republicans who were visiting Frankfort. David G. Colson and Ethelbert Scott had a pistol duel in the lobby of the Capital Hotel. As the gunmen circled and fired, two bystanders were killed and three wounded; of the two adversaries, Scott was killed, and Colson was wounded. The police had their hands full keeping the peace, and they were almost overwhelmed when the hordes of mountaineers piled off of the train cars. Robert Elkin Hughes, who wrote about these events the year they occurred, said that the grim, bearded men wandering Frankfort's streets sometimes "ran afoul of the local police [and] a half-dozen of the Republican strangers were lugged off to jail on the charge of carrying concealed or deadly weapons and fined heavily." Governor Taylor began issuing pardons. Seeing that their friends were only being charged with carrying concealed weapons, the mountaineers started wearing their pistols outside their coats in plain view, a precaution that kept them out of jail, but which did nothing to settle jangled nerves in the capital city.[30]

If William Goebel's nerves were jangled, he refused to let it show. On the morning of January 25, he arrived at the statehouse grounds, and, ignoring the advice of his handlers, he walked directly into the crowd of hostile men. Hughes said "by an almost imperceptible movement, a pathway opened through the crowd, and hundreds of curious, scrutinizing glances were turned upon the man who was the head and front of the movement to which the assembled ones were opposed." He continued into the capitol unruffled and unmolested. Goebel had shown his nerve, which was admirable, and had also shown that he would not avoid being seen on the sidewalks outside of the state capitol, and that proved to be a critical mistake.[31]

The joint committee was nearing the end of its work by January 30, 1900. A little after eleven o'clock that morning, Goebel and two of his friends were seen strolling toward the capitol building. The crowd that had been milling around for the past week had dispersed. The capitol grounds were practically deserted, and Goebel came up the sidewalk unimpeded. He walked fast; the General Assembly was in session and the Senate Democrats were waiting for him. Things seemed calmer than they had for days. When he was about one hundred feet from the building, gunfire rang out. Goebel groaned and bent over, clutching his right side. His friend Eph Lillard glanced around and thought he saw an open window in the ground floor secretary of state's office in the executive office building, just a few steps east of the capitol. Goebel was falling, and as he went down, his other friend, Jack Chinn, said to him, "My God! Goebel, they have killed you." Goebel said, "I guess they have." Goebel struggled to rise, and Chinn said, "Lie still, Goebel, or they might shoot you again," and the wounded man lay back on the ground.[32]

The capitol grounds began filling up with people who came running at the sound of the gunfire, and the legislators inside were watching the confusion from the windows. Some of them rushed out and joined the crowd. A black man in the jostling knot of men pushed up against a white man, who pulled a pistol and shot the black man dead. Hughes said, "Very little attention was paid to this matter." Most were focused on getting the wounded Goebel to a place of comfort and safety, but some went toward the executive office building and the secretary of state's office from which the shot seemed to have been fired. A company of militia arrived and threw a cordon around the scene, and order was restored.[33]

Some of the gawkers who had gathered helped to carry Goebel back to his rooms at the Capital Hotel. The examining doctors found that the rifle bullet had passed diagonally through the senator's body in a slightly downward trajectory from the point it entered in the upper right chest to the point where it exited just left of the spine. It had pierced the right lung and shattered some ribs, and Goebel was bleeding profusely. Still, the doctors believed that there was a chance that he would recover, and Goebel, who was conscious during the examination, vowed that he would.

The ad hoc committee was scheduled to meet that afternoon, and now there was a new sense of urgency. Since the militia had all entrances to the capitol sealed off, they had to assemble in the Frankfort city hall. Emotions were running high, and shortly after they were called to order the members had to adjourn to calm themselves. They came back in an hour to vote. They submitted their report the next day. When the flowery official language was excised, the pertinent parts said:

> The undersigned, the Board appointed and selected by the General Assembly to determine the contest of the election for the office of Governor of this Commonwealth between William Goebel, contestant, and W. S. Taylor, contestee, beg leave to report that we have heard all the evidence offered by both parties, and . . . in our opinion William Goebel was legally elected Governor of the Commonwealth of Kentucky on the 7th day of November 1899, and that he then and there received the highest number of legal votes cast for anyone for the office of Governor. . . . We decide that the said William Goebel has received the highest number of legal votes and is adjudged to be the person elected to said office of Governor for the term prescribed by law.[34]

The members signed and dated the report, and it was decided. William Goebel was sworn in as governor that evening, January 31, 1900. A newspaper report said, "Mr. Goebel was propped up with pillows and was unable [sic] to raise his hand only with the greatest difficulty. . . . When the oath had been given, Mr. Goebel sank back exhausted, the effort having been almost too much for his strength." As his first act, he ordered the militia out of Frankfort. All other groups were also instructed "to disband and desist from terrorizing and intimidating" the members of the legislature and all other citizens.[35]

Goebel's condition worsened over the days that followed, and the death watch began. He died on the evening of February 3, 1900. Within an hour of Goebel's death, Lieutenant Governor J. C. W. Beckham was sworn in at the Capital Hotel, which was serving as the temporary statehouse for as long as the militia blocked entry to the capitol. The militia had remained loyal to

Taylor and were still on duty despite the dead governor's January 31 instructions for them to return home. They stood sentry outside the capitol, and they guarded the door to Taylor's office, where he had barricaded himself. The militiamen showed no sign of standing down, and Taylor did little to defuse the situation. From inside his *sanctum sanctorum* he issued a statement that said in part, "I have concluded to allow this controversy to take its due course, vigorously contesting every inch of ground and upholding the rights of the people to the uttermost."[36]

The legislature reconvened on February 19. From the start, the day's session was a parliamentary muddle. The Democrat, L. H. Carter, and Taylor's Republican lieutenant governor, John Marshall, each claimed to be the president of the Senate, and both tried to preside. They were frustrated when they were recognized only by members of their own party. The chaotic meeting adjourned, having decided nothing.

This is how it was for the rest of the legislative term. The Republicans would gather for the roll call and then adjourn, leaving the Democrats to debate and pass legislation, which the absent Republicans maintained was completely illegal. The Democratic majority pressed on, nonetheless. They considered a bill making it a misdemeanor for any corporation licensed to operate in Kentucky to contribute to a political party or to reimburse any person or persons who did. General Lyon voted in favor of this bill, as he did the bill which required citizens of cities of the second class (that is, smaller cities) to appropriate money annually for the support of their public libraries. The yearly stipend was to be not less than $5000. Lyon favored the bill that mandated a salary for commissioners in counties with a population of 75,000, and which required the commissioners to keep accurate account books. He approved of the resolution that called for two senators and three representatives to be appointed to a board whose duty would be to see that the Senate and House journals were printed. Lyon voted "aye" for a bill to reorganize and equip the state militia and to recover "the possession and control of all cannon, gatling guns, small fire arms and other munitions of war belonging or entrusted to the control and custody of the Commonwealth of Kentucky now in possession or under the control of W. S. Taylor," and he lent his support to a bill to establish a "uniform series of text books to be used in public schools."[37]

While the Democrats in the halls of the General Assembly attempted to maintain a semblance of normalcy, the investigation into the Goebel shooting continued. In a classic campaign of disinformation, Republicans spread the rumor that Goebel's friend, Chinn, had shot Goebel himself; shot him in the back accidentally when the plan was to shoot him in the arm or through the flap of his coat. But, said the rumor mongers, Chinn's aim was off, and he inflicted a mortal wound rather than a minor one. The theory went on to explain that an attempted assassination would rally those in the legislature who were on the fence about accepting the joint committee's pro-Goebel report. Two ladies of Frankfort asserted that they had seen Chinn shoot Goebel. Chinn sued them for slander. One lady recanted and the other denied that she had ever made such a statement, and that particular effort lost its momentum, leaving the way open for others to begin. A second theory was that Goebel had shot himself, for the same reason given above, and another tale that sprang up later was that Goebel had not died at all; he was hiding in some secret mountain location while looking for the man who had shot him.

Investigators had to sift through testimony that was often contradictory. They finally concluded that a total of five shots were fired. The first was believed to have been a rifle shot, while the others were pistol shots. A rifle slug was eventually found in a hackberry tree and was shown to have flown in a straight line connecting the Secretary of State's office to the spot where Goebel fell.

In a separate case, the issue of whether the Taylor ticket or the Goebel ticket was the winner of the gubernatorial election was working its way through the courts. It reached the Court of Appeals in Louisville in April. That court decided in favor of Goebel. The Republicans appealed the decision to the U.S. Supreme Court. On May 21, 1900, the high court refused to hear the case, which meant that the decision of the Court of Appeals stood, the January report of the joint committee was upheld, and the Goebel-Beckham ticket was declared, once and for all, the lawful winner in the election of 1899.

Sixteen people were eventually indicted for having played a role in the assassination of William Goebel. William S. Taylor was one of them. He and others fled the state. Taylor went to Indianapolis and practiced law there until the end of his life. Five of those who were indicted actually went to trial, and three of them were convicted. Jim Howard of Clay County was convicted as the actual trigger-man. His life sentence was commuted in 1908 by Governor Augustus E. Willson, a Republican.

General H. B. Lyon watched these final events unfold from his home in Eddyville. The term of office for a state representative was two years, but the legislature met only every other year. That meant that when the House of Representatives ended its session on March 13, 1900, Lyon's term was effectively over. There had been no session like it since the time of Kentucky statehood in 1792, and he had played an important part. Nevertheless, he seems to have decided that holding public office was an unfulfilling use of his time, for he did not run for a second term. Instead, he returned home to stay.

16
THE FINAL REUNION

Lyon spent the last seven years of his life in pursuit of his private interests, and the interest that attracted him with increasing force was attending reunions with his aging comrades from the years 1861 to 1865. His military career, including his time as a West Point cadet, had lasted thirteen years. For only four of those years had he been a Confederate, yet it was that period of four years that wrote the denouement of his long life.

Lyon had shown some interest in the Confederate reunions and veterans organizations back in the 1890s. He was elected commander of the United Confederate Veterans group at Eddyville in 1897, and he was also an officer in the group Forrest's Cavalry Veterans. The U.C.V. camp in neighboring Calloway County was called the H. B. Lyon Camp. Calloway County had sent more than one thousand young men to the Confederate Army.

However, it was after the turn of the century that Lyon's interest in his Confederate past seemed to be most intense. He attended the reunion of Forrest's Cavalry Veterans at Brice's Crossroads in June 1900. Brice's Crossroads was the site of Forrest's greatest victory, but the Wizard was not there among his old comrades in 1900 except in memory; he had died in 1877.

Lyon did not have to travel so far when he attended the reunion of the veterans of Cobb's Battery in Kuttawa, Kentucky, in 1901. At the October 1903 reunion of the Second Brigade, Kentucky Division, U.C.V. in Paducah, Lyon did the unusual and delivered a speech to the 650 aging veterans who attended. The Hopkinsville *Kentuckian* said that the two-day reunion "proved the most successful in the memory of the West Kentucky survivors of the lost cause."[1]

That same year, 1903, Lyon was inspired to an even more extraordinary effort when he began to write his memoirs. Except for his detailed letters home during his United States and Confederate States service, Lyon had shown that he took no pleasure in writing. His after-action reports as they appear in the *OR*s are few, and the ones that do appear are a bare recital of the facts, short on detail and barren of style. The longest report he is known to have written is that of his 1864 Kentucky Raid, and even this account of his greatest independent command is not as thorough as it could have been. But, in 1903, he sat down and began to write his life story with special attention paid to his military service. He filled page after page with tight, neat script. It was plainly a first draft, a mere sketch, and one regrets that he did not finish the account of his adventurous life and flesh it out with more details. He ended the narrative with his rescue of Governor Harris from the bounty hunters in North Texas during their escape to Mexico in 1865. What he did choose to emphasize in his memoir reveals something of his personality—his strong condemnation of Colonel George Wright's summary execution of Qualchan, for example—and he obviously revered Nathan Bedford Forrest and took pride in relating instances when the general turned to him for counsel and advice. His asides provide a glimpse of his attitudes, as well. He veers from the narrative at one point to criticize the *Confederate Veteran* monthly. He says, "By the way, this periodical, the *Confederate Veteran*, is mainly conspicuous for incorrect statements made in many of its publications." The memoir is an honest account of Lyon's life and is, for the most part, accurate as to detail. The few mistakes that do appear arise from an old man's forgetfulness about what happened when. They were excusable in a first draft and so insignificant in nature that they plainly were not meant to deceive. They would have been easily corrected if Lyon had not lost interest. He laid his memoir aside, however, and never returned to it. It lay unseen and unknown until the summer of 1951, when scholar Edward M. Coffman visited Lyon's widow Ruth and his married daughter, Mrs. Maybelle Faxon, in Eddyville. They lent him the memoir. Coffman copied it, and history is grateful that he did, for after Mrs. Lyon died in November 1952, the original manuscript disappeared.[2]

Veterans who gathered in Paducah in January 1904 to commemorate the birth of Robert E. Lee used the occasion to award Lyon the Confederate Cross of Honor. In the summer and fall of 1906, he attended two of the last great reunions of the veterans of Forrest's cavalry. The first was in Washington Artillery Hall in New Orleans. *Confederate Veteran*, the periodical he disparaged, said, "Gen. H. B. Lyon, of Kentucky, a gentleman of noble appearance, erect, of fine countenance, in every line of which is written determination tempered with kindness . . . spoke eloquently of the comrades who are gone into the brighter life, as well as to those who were gathered here among the living mementos of a glorious if unsuccessful struggle." The speech went over well, and he was "frequently interrupted with bursts of prolonged applause."[3]

He spoke again at a reunion of the Second Brigade, Kentucky Division, United Confederate Veterans in Fulton, Kentucky, late that summer, and in October he attended a parade of the "mounted survivors of Forrest's Cavalry."

They "formed in line of march, as they were formed so often in the stirring days of yore, going forward to do their duty." No "frills or furbelows," no "maids of honor" were allowed, just the aged horse soldiers pretending one last time to ride forward to the sound of the guns. There were only four surviving division or brigade commanders of the old cavalry corps. They were Colonel Edmund W. Rucker, Colonel D. C. Kelley, General Frank C. Armstrong, and General Hylan B. Lyon. For the last time, each one was at the head of his own column as the hoary knights from a different century passed by and faded into memory. It was perhaps Lyon's final appearance on horseback.[4]

Not that he was recusing himself from life. The old general still had an active mind and physical vigor, as he demonstrated when he announced his decision to put his name forward for the office of mayor of Eddyville in October 1906. The next month, he was elected. He had barely begun his term of office when, on April 25, 1907, he went to his farm outside of Eddyville. Lyon had some matters he wanted to discuss with his farmhands. He found them in one of the fields, and there they conferred. He turned to walk away and had gone only a few steps when he was seized with a massive heart attack. His hired men saw him fall and they rushed to his side, but he had died instantly and there was nothing they could do. Lyon had never been wounded in battle, and he died without apparent suffering. He was seventy-one years old.

The obituaries were filled with respect for General Lyon. The Paducah *Evening Sun* called him "One of the prominent politicians and Confederate veterans in the South," and the Crittenden *Record Press* said, "He was probably the most prominent man of his section of the State for many years." In its December 1907 issue, *Confederate Veteran* summarized his career and said, "General Lyon was a true, courageous man in all the walks of life. As a soldier, legislator, and citizen, he was without hypocrisy or guile. A blunt, honest man, and totally without fear, he spoke his mind on all occasions."[5]

Lyon's funeral was scheduled for 10:00 AM on April 28, 1907. It had to be postponed until 3:30 that afternoon because his oldest surviving son, Captain Frank Lyon of the United States Navy, was unable to complete the trip from Norfolk, Virginia, in time for the morning service. When the eulogies were done, the general's casket was carried to Riverview Cemetery, where generations of the Lyon family rested. He was buried there among them for the reunion that has no end. Lyon had served three national governments and his native state, but he honored only one of them on his grave marker. On the massive piece of granite was an engraved panel showing pyramidal stacks of cannonballs and the battle flag of the C.S.A. Hylan B. Lyon wanted the world to know that he had no remorse. He was a Confederate to the end.

NOTES

Preface

1. Vince Staten, "Is Kentucky Southern?" *Courier-Journal Magazine* Nov. 29, 1987, 4, 8.

2. Lowell H. Harrison and James C. Klotter, *A New History of Kentucky* (Lexington: University Press of Kentucky, 1997), 195.

3. William C. Davis, *Breckinridge: Statesman, Soldier, Symbol* (Baton Rouge: Louisiana State University Press, 1992), 490.

4. Hughes, Nathaniel Cheairs, Jr., *Brigadier General Tyree H. Bell, CSA* (Knoxville: University of Tennessee Press, 2004), 248; James Q. Chenoweth, "The Rangers' Last Campaign," in *The Partisan Rangers of the Confederate States Army*, ed. William J. Davis (Utica, KY: Cook & McDowell Publications, 1979), 183.

1. Far From Home

1. James Fairfax McLaughlin, *Matthew Lyon: The Hampden of Congress* (New York: Wynkoop Hallenbeck Crawford Company, 1900), 418–19.

2. Ibid., 420–21.

3. Elizabeth Lyon Roe, *Recollections of Frontier Life* (Rockford, IL: Gazette Publishing House, 1885), 7.

4. Christopher Waldrep, "Kentucky's Slave Importation Law in Lyon County: A Document," *The Filson Club History Quarterly*, Oct. 1991, 505.

5. Ibid., 505–6.

6. Edgar S. Dudley, "Discipline at the United States Military Academy," in *Personal Recollections of the War of the Rebellion: Addresses Delivered Before the New York Commandery of the Loyal Legion of the United States, Third Series*, ed. A. Noel Blakeman (New York: G. P. Putnam's Sons, 1907), 397.

7. Edward C. Boynton, *History of West Point* (London: Sampson, Low, Son, & Marsten, 1864), 258.

8. Douglas Southall Freeman, *R. E. Lee: A Biography* (New York: Charles Scribner's Sons, 1934), 1:320.

9. Boynton, 266–267.

10. Freeman, 1:320; John M. Schofield, *Forty-Six Years in the Army* (New York: The Century Co., 1897), 15.

11. Freeman, 1:341.

12. "Affairs in Washington," *New York Herald*, Apr. 14, 1857.

13. Hylan B. Lyon. Letter to Laura O'Hara, Apr. 27, 1857. Hylan B. Lyon Papers, MS 69–03, Box 1, File 1. Courtesy of Pogue Special Collections and Archives Library, Murray State University Libraries, Murray, KY. Hereafter cited as Hylan B. Lyon Papers, M.S.U.

14. Ibid. Laura O'Hara was the daughter of Reuben O'Hara and Mary Ann Lyon. Mary Ann Lyon was the daughter of Hylan's Uncle Chittenden Lyon, which means that Mary Ann was Hylan's first cousin and her daughter Laura was Hylan's first cousin, once removed.

15. "The Overland Mail Route," *Washington (DC) Union*, July 30, 1857.

16. Hylan B. Lyon. Letter to Laura O'Hara, Oct. 13, 1857. Lyon–O'Hara Papers, SC 107. Courtesy of Manuscript and Folklife Archives, Kentucky Museum and Library, Western Kentucky University, Bowling Green, KY.

17. Ibid.

18. Ibid.

19. Laura O'Hara. Letter to Hylan B. Lyon, Dec. 8, 1857. Hylan B. Lyon Papers, M.S.U., MS 69–03, Box 1, File 1.

2. The Coeur d'Alene War

1. Hubert Howe Bancroft, *History of Washington, Idaho, and Montana: 1845–1889* (San Francisco: The History Company, Publishers, 1890), 182.

2. "The Indian Hostilities," *New York Herald*, July 16, 1858.

3. Lawrence Kip, *Army Life on the Pacific: A Journal of the Expedition Against the Northern Indians* (New York: Redfield, 1859), 11–12.

4. "Army News from the Pacific," *New York Herald*, July 16, 1858.

5. Kip, 16.

6. Ibid., 25.

7. Hylan B. Lyon, "Memoirs of Hylan B. Lyon," ed. Edward M. Coffman, *Tennessee Historical Quarterly*, Vol. XVIII, No. 1 (May 1959): 37. Hereafter cited as Lyon, "Memoirs."

8. Bancroft, 186; Kip, 55.

9. Kip, 56–57; Benjamin F. Manring. *The Conquest of the Coeur d'Alenes, Spokanes and Palouses* (Spokane, WA: John W. Graham Co., 1912), 193.

10. "The Indian War in Washington Territory," *Washington (DC) Union*, Oct. 30, 1858.

11. Ibid.; Kip, 64.

12. Kip, 64–65.

13. Lyon, "Memoirs," 36; Manring, 205.

14. Kip, 67–68.

15. "Indian War," *Washington Union*, Oct. 30, 1858.

16. Erasmus D. Keyes, *Fifty Years' Observation of Men and Events* (New York: Charles Scribner's Sons, 1884), 273.

17. "Indian War," *Washington Union*.

18. Ibid.

19. Kip, 84.

20. Ibid., 85.

21. Ibid., 93.

22. A. J. Splawn, *Ka-mi-akin: The Last Hero of the Yakimas* (Portland, OR: Kilham Stationery & Printing Co., 1917), 119. Kamiakin did not return to his home country until 1861. The authorities knew that he had returned, but they did not bother him. He died in 1877.

23. Lyon, "Memoirs," 37–38.

24. Ibid., 37. Latah Creek, where Qualchan was executed, was known ever afterward as Hangman Creek. This account of the hanging of Qualchan is drawn from Lyon's "Memoirs." Different accounts from the time differ only slightly. They add only a few unimportant details and contradict Lyon's account only slightly. One point of disagreement is which officer it was who told Colonel Wright that Qualchan had come into camp. Lyon positively asserted that it was he; some others claim that it was his immediate superior, Captain Keyes.

25. Kip, 116–17.

26. Ibid., 106.

27. Keyes, 279.

28. Kip, 124.

29. Robert M. Utley, *Frontiersmen in Blue: The United States Army and the Indians, 1848–1865* (Lincoln: University of Nebraska Press, 1981), 208; "Results of Gen. Clarke's Operations," *Washington Union*, Nov. 14, 1858.

30. Kip, 143–44.

3. The Mullan Road

1. Lyon, "Memoirs," 38. Mullan simply referred to Lyon as the acting assistant quartermaster.

2. Keyes, 284.

3. "News from Oregon," *New York Herald*, May 30, 1859.

4. "The Mullan Road: John Mullan's Report of 1863," www.narhist.ewu.edu /mullan_report/mullan_report_home.html, 14. Accessed Aug. 25, 2016. Hereafter referred to as Mullan's Report.

5. Ibid., 15.

6. Ibid.; John Mullan, *Miners and Travelers' Guide to Oregon, Washington, Idaho, Montana, Wyoming, and Colorado* (New York: Wm. M. Franklin, 1865), 24.

7. "Summary of the News," *New York Daily Tribune*, Aug. 29, 1859; "Army and Navy Intelligence," *New York Daily Tribune*, Sept. 13, 1859.

8. Mullan's Report, 18.

9. "The Northern Pacific Military Road Expedition," *New York Herald*, Dec. 12, 1859; Hylan B. Lyon. Letter to Laura O'Hara, Feb. 19, 1860. Hylan B. Lyon Papers, M.S.U., MS 69–03, Box 1, File 3.

10. Mullan's Report, 21.

11. Hylan B. Lyon. Letter to Laura O'Hara, Mar. 9, 1860. Hylan B. Lyon Papers, M.S.U., MS 69–03, Box 1, File 3.

12. Ibid.

13. Hylan B. Lyon. Letter to Laura O'Hara, Apr. 5, 1860. Hylan B. Lyon Papers, M.S.U., MS 69–03, Box 1, File 3.

14. Ibid.

15. Ibid.

16. Mullan's Report, 23.

17. Ibid., 25–27; Mullan, *Miners and Travelers' Guide*, 17. Travelers on today's I-15 will cross Lyon's Creek between Helena and Craig.

18. Mullan's Report, 28.

19. Ibid.

4. The War between the States Begins

1. Lowell H. Harrison, *The Civil War in Kentucky* (Lexington: University Press of Kentucky, 1975), 5.

2. United States War Department, *The War of the Rebellion: A Compilation of the Official Records of the Union and Confederate Armies.* 129 Volumes. (Washington, DC: Government Printing Office, 1880–1901) series 4, volume 1, 12. Here-

after cited as *ORA*, series number, volume number, part number (if applicable), page number.

3. Lyon, "Memoirs," 39. The fact that Hylan B. Lyon and Laura O'Hara married in Jefferson County no doubt explains why there has been so much mystery about the date of their wedding. The marriage record was hard to find because researchers were very naturally looking in Lyon County. With no record to be found in Western Kentucky, researchers had to estimate the year of their marriage and some, dating from the birth of their second child (not knowing of the first), guessed that Hylan and Laura married in 1863. This is wrong. Hylan referred to Laura as his wife in letters written in the winter of 1861/62. They seem to have eloped, which was not particularly unusual even in that era. The wedding trip was easily accomplished by steamboat and let them enjoy their honeymoon in Kentucky's largest and most exciting city. At times during the war, Laura O'Hara Lyon returned to Louisville to live.

As for Lyon's decision to resign his commission on Apr. 30, 1861, one might simply point out that he was not alone in feeling that Lincoln's Apr. 15 call for volunteers was the proverbial straw that broke the camel's back. He and the others perceived Lincoln's call as an intolerable act of aggression on the part of an overreaching Federal government and a mortal threat to their region. Some well-known men did not join the Confederacy until after Lincoln's request for volunteers forced them into it, as they believed. They included E. P. Alexander and Joseph Wheeler of Georgia, James Longstreet of South Carolina, and Albert Sidney Johnston and John Bell Hood of Texas. Many Arkansans, Tennesseans, North Carolinians, and Virginians hesitated until after Lincoln's call, but they might be considered to have decided more on account of the secession of their states (which, of course, was a statewide response to the Lincoln's call) than the President's perceived aggression. The Virginians who delayed their decision included John C. Pemberton, Joseph E. Johnston, J. E. B. Stuart, and the Lees of Virginia: Robert E., George Washington Custis, William Fitzhugh, and their cousin (and Lyon's West Point classmate) Fitzhugh. Among Lyon's fellow Kentuckians who did not decide to join the Confederacy until after President Lincoln's call for volunteers were Ben Hardin Helm, Joseph H. Lewis, and Simon Bolivar Buckner.

4. Harrison, 9.

5. "Troops Concentrating in Tennessee," *Memphis Daily Appeal*, July 17, 1861.

6. Ibid.

7. William C. Davis, *The Orphan Brigade: The Kentucky Confederates who Couldn't Go Home* (Garden City, NY: Doubleday & Company, Inc., 1980), 20–21.

8. T. D. Wardlaw, "Mr. Editor," *Clarksville Chronicle*, Aug. 9, 1861.

9. Untitled, *Clarksville Chronicle*, Aug. 16, 1861.

10. *ORA*, series 1, vol. 4, 367.

11. Ibid., 374; 389.

12. Ibid., 407.

13. Arndt M. Stickles, *Simon Bolivar Buckner: Borderland Knight* (Chapel Hill: University of North Carolina Press, 1940), 68.

14. *ORA*, series 1, vol. 4, 410.

15. Davis, 38; Untitled, *Confederate Veteran* (July 1915): 309.

16. *ORA*, series 1, vol. 52, part 2, 151.

17. Josie Underwood, *Josie Underwood's Civil War Diary*, ed. Nancy Disher Baird (Lexington: University Press of Kentucky, 2009), 99–102. Mr. Warner Underwood, a lawyer and former U.S. Congressman, was one of the richest men in Warren County, the owner of twenty-eight slaves. At the same time, like many slave owners in Kentucky, he was a Unionist. However, it was his daughter Josie who was the real fire breather of the family. The belles of the Deep South were legendary for the passion of their patriotism for the Confederacy, but they had nothing on Josie Underwood. About a week after the Confederates occupied Bowling Green, Josie went into town and saw there an old schoolmate named Terah Freeman. He was wearing a Confederate uniform, and theirs was not a happy reunion. When Freeman asked if he could call at Mt. Air, Josie answered, "Not in that uniform." Freeman was taken aback. He said that he had supposed that she was a Rebel. She snapped, "Why should you have supposed that? Did you ever in the old school days hear me express great admiration for Benedict Arnold?" (Underwood, *Diary*, page 102)

18. Ibid., 103.

19. Hylan B. Lyon. Letter to Laura O'Hara Lyon, Dec. 22, 1861. Hylan B. Lyon Papers, M.S.U., MS 69–03, Box 1, File 4; Letter to Laura O'Hara Lyon, Jan. 7, 1862. Hylan B. Lyon Papers, M.S.U., Box 1, File 5.

20. *ORA*, series 1, vol. 7, 358; Benjamin Franklin Cooling, *Forts Henry and Donelson: The Key to the Confederate Heartland* (Knoxville: University of Tennessee Press, 1989), 132.

21. Cooling, 132.

22. *ORA*, series 1, vol. 7, 360; 375.

23. Lyon, "Memoirs," 40.

24. J. M. Hoppin, *Life of Andrew Hull Foote, Rear Admiral, United States Navy* (New York: Harper, 1874), 223; *ORA*, series 1, vol. 7, 255.

25. *ORA*, series 1, vol. 7, 265–266.

26. Ibid., 360–361. Simonton disagreed with Johnson's recollection that the assignment to command the Second Brigade came when the men went on line. He says that he received the order to relieve Davidson from General Pillow at 1:00 AM.

27. Ibid., 361; 373.

28. Ibid., 373; Cooling, 169; *ORA*, series 1, vol. 7, 189–190.

29. *ORA*, series 1, vol. 7, 373; Shelby Foote, *The Civil War, A Narrative: Fort Sumter to Perryville* (New York: Random House, 1986), 207.

30. *ORA*, series 1, vol. 7, 372; 374.

31. Ibid., 332.

32. Ibid.; 343–44.

33. Ibid., 332; 338–39.

34. Ulysses S. Grant, *Personal Memoirs of U. S. Grant* (New York: Library of America, 1990), 205.

35. *ORA*, series 1, vol. 7, 618; Cooling, 185.

36. *ORA*, series 1, vol. 7, 332–33.

37. Ibid., 333.

38. Ibid., 334.

39. Brian Steel Wills, *A Battle from the Start: The Life of Nathan Bedford Forrest* (New York: HarperCollins Publishers, 1992), 64.

40. *ORA*, series 1, vol. 7, 160; 362–63.

41. Ibid., 161.

42. Cooling, 212.

43. *ORA*, series 1, vol. 7, 43. Private Head continued to serve in the Confederate army until he was wounded in the Battle of Kennesaw Mountain in 1864. General Johnson made good his escape and went on to fight in the battles of Shiloh, Perryville, and in the Knoxville Campaign. In East Tennessee, he transferred to General Longstreet's corps in the Army of Northern Virginia, fought through the rest of the war in the Eastern Theater, and was present at the surrender at Appomattox Courthouse in 1865.

44. *ORA*, series 1, vol. 7, 625; Cooling xi, xiii.

5. *Prisoner*

1. Untitled, *Holmes County (OH) Republican*, Feb. 27, 1862.

2. Ibid.

3. Cooling, 222.

4. Charles W. Sanders, Jr., *While in the Hands of the Enemy: Military Prisons of the Civil War* (Baton Rouge: Louisiana State University Press, 2005), 61.

5. Hylan B. Lyon. Letter to Laura O'Hara Lyon, Mar. 15, 1862. Hylan B. Lyon Papers, M.S.U., MS 69–03, Box 1, File 6; Lawrence Sangston, *The Bastiles of the North* (Baltimore: Kelly, Hedian & Piet, 1863), 61.

6. Sanders, 61.

7. Ibid.

8. Hylan B. Lyon. Letter to Cousin Jim, Mar. 9, 1862. Hylan B. Lyon Papers, M.S.U., MS 69–03, Box 1, File 6.

9. Stickles, 181.

10. Sangston, 67.

11. Hylan B. Lyon. Letter to Cousin Jim, Mar. 9, 1862. Hylan B. Lyon Papers, M.S.U., MS 69–03, Box 1, File 6.

12. Hylan B. Lyon. Letter to Laura O'Hara Lyon, Mar. 15, 1862. Hylan B. Lyon Papers, M.S.U., MS 69–03, Box 1, File 6.

13. Hylan B. Lyon. Letter to Laura O'Hara Lyon, Apr. 13, 1862. Hylan B. Lyon Papers, M.S.U., MS 69–03, Box 1, File 7.

14. Hylan B. Lyon. Letter to Laura O'Hara Lyon, May 6, 1862. Hylan B. Lyon Papers, M.S.U., MS 69–03, Box 1, File 8. Lieutenant Colonel Neff was George Washington Neff, who was captured at the Battle of Scary Creek in what is now West Virginia.

15. Hylan B. Lyon. Letter to Laura O'Hara Lyon, July 27, 1862. Hylan B. Lyon Papers, M.S.U., MS 69–03, Box 1, File 10.

16. Hylan B. Lyon. Letter to sister, Jan. 13, 1866. Hylan B. Lyon Papers, M.S.U., MS 69–03, Box 1, File 16; Letter to Laura O'Hara Lyon, July 27, 1862. Hylan B. Lyon Papers, M.S.U., MS 69–03, Box 1, File 11.

17. *ORA,* series 1, vol. 17, part 1, 377.

18. Foote, *Fort Sumter to Perryville,* 722.

19. *ORA,* series 1, vol. 17, part 1, 405; 168; 386.

20. Ibid., 405; 379.

21. Ibid., 169; 387; 171.

22. Ibid., 406.

23. Foote, *Fort Sumter to Perryville,* 725.

24. James W. Rabb, *Confederate General Lloyd Tilghman: A Biography* (Jefferson, NC: McFarland and Co., 2006), 128; *ORA,* series 1, vol. 17, part 2, 728–29.

6. The Vicksburg Campaigns

1. Terrence J. Winschel, "A Tragedy of Errors: The Failure of the Confederate High Command in the Defense of Vicksburg," *North and South* (Jan. 2006), 45.

2. John Keegan, *The American Civil War: A Military History* (New York: Alfred A. Knopf, 2009), 142, 177.

3. *ORA,* series 1, vol. 17, part 1, 469, 467; Grant, *Personal Memoirs,* 286; *ORA,* vol. 17, part 1, 469.

4. *ORA,* series 1, vol. 17, part 2, 732, 734.

5. Ibid., 755.

6. Ibid., 768; 770.

7. Ibid., 903.

8. *ORA,* series 1, vol. 17, part 1, 504.

9. Ibid., 504–5.

10. Ibid., 494–95.

11. Ibid., 505; Phineas O. Avery, *History of the Fourth Illinois Cavalry Regiment* (Humboldt, NE: The Enterprise: A Print Shop, 1903), 91.

12. Ibid., 496; Lyman B. Pierce, *History of the Second Iowa Cavalry* (Burlington, IA: Hawk-Eye Steam Book and Job Printing Establishment, 1865), 44.

13. *ORA,* series 1, vol. 17, part 1, 505.

14. Ibid., 506.

15. Ibid., 473.

16. Steven W. Woodworth, *Nothing but Victory: The Army of the Tennessee: 1861–1865* (New York: Alfred A. Knopf, 2005), 257; 258; Lucius Barber, *Army Memoirs of Lucius W. Barber, Company "D," 15th Illinois Volunteer Infantry* (Chicago: J. M. W. Jones Stationery and Printing Co., 1894), 91–92.

17. Bruce Catton, *Grant Moves South* (Boston: Little, Brown and Company, 1960), 336; Foote, *Fort Sumter to Perryville,* 170.

18. Grant, 290; "Letter from Mississippi," *Winchester (TN) Daily Bulletin,* Jan. 13, 1863; *ORA,* series 1, vol. 17, part 1, 503.

19. John M. Adair, *Historical Sketch of the Forty-Fifth Illinois Regiment* (Lanark, IL: Carroll County Gazette Print, 1869), 9; James W. Rabb, *Confederate General Lloyd Tilghman: A Biography* (Jefferson, NC: McFarland and Co., 2006), 141.

20. Catton, *Grant Moves South,* 342.

21. *ORA,* series 1, vol. 24, part 3, 643.

22. Rabb, 153–154.

23. *ORA,* series 1, vol. 24, part 1, 412.

24. Ibid., 415, 417.

25. United States Naval Records Office, *Official Records of the Union and Confederate Navies in the War of the Rebellion,* 27 Volumes (Washington, DC: Government Printing Office, 1894–1917), series 1, vol. 24, 285. Hereafter cited as *ORN.*

26. *ORA,* series 1, vol. 24, part 1, 417.

27. Ibid., 419.

28. Grant, *Personal Memoirs,* 301.

29. *ORN,* series 1, vol. 24, 479.

30. *ORA*, series 1, vol. 24, part 1, 570.

31. Ibid., 251.

32. Henry Ewell Hord, "Her Little Flag," *Confederate Veteran* (Oct. 1915): 473.

33. Ibid., 474.

34. *ORA*, series 1, vol. 24, part 3, 783. Van Dorn's assignment to Tennessee was his last. Though he was a married man with two children, he was a habitual adulterer. In Spring Hill, Tennessee, he seduced Mrs. Jessie McKissack Peters, the young wife of Dr. George Peters. Their affair was a poorly kept secret; they met at his headquarters, the Cheairs mansion in Spring Hill, and it was there that Dr. Peters came to make Van Dorn pay for his misbehavior. On May 7, 1863, the cuckolded husband shot Van Dorn in the back of the head with a small caliber pistol. Van Dorn died four and a half hours later. The doctor turned himself in, but the killing was considered justified and he was never prosecuted for the shooting. Van Dorn's reputation was such that he was not grieved, even in his home state of Mississippi. During his visit to the state, Captain Arthur Fremantle found that Van Dorn's death "does not seem to be much regretted, as it appears he was always ready to neglect his military duties for an assignation. In the South it is not considered necessary to put yourself on an equality with a man in such a case as Van Dorn's by calling him out. His life belongs to the aggrieved husband, and 'shooting down' is universally esteemed the correct thing." (Arthur James Lyon Fremantle, *The Fremantle Diary: A Journal of the Confederacy*, ed. Walter Lord [Short Hills, NJ: Burford Books, Inc., 1954], 116).

35. *ORA*, series 1, vol. 24, part 1, 254; "The War in Mississippi," *Memphis Daily Appeal*, Apr. 24, 1863.

36. *ORA*, series 1, vol. 24, part 1, 656, 657.

37. S. H. Lockett, "The Defense of Vicksburg," *Battles and Leaders*, 487.

38. *ORA*, series 1, vol. 24, part 3, 821.

39. Joseph E. Johnston, "Jefferson Davis and the Mississippi Campaign," *Battles and Leaders*, 478.

40. *ORA*, series 1, vol. 24, part 1, 271.

41. Ibid., 273.

42. *ORA*, series 1, vol. 24, part 2, 397.

43. J. J. Kellogg, *War Experiences and the Story of The Vicksburg Campaign* (N.p.: by the author, 1913), 28.

44. *ORA*, series 1, vol. 24, part 2, 398; Sherman, 351; Lockett, 489.

45. Foote, *Fredericksburg to Meridian*, 381.

46. *ORA*, series 1, vol. 24, part 3, 892; Lyon, "Memoirs," 41.

7. The Army of Relief

1. Lyon, "Memoirs," 41.

2. "Federal Army in Jackson," *Canton (MS) American Citizen*, May 22, 1863.

3. Ibid.; Grant, 338.

4. Samuel C. Jones, *Reminiscences of the Twenty-second Iowa Volunteer Infantry* (Iowa City, IA: by the author, 1907), 45–46.

5. Arthur James Lyon Fremantle, *The Fremantle Diary: A Journal of the Confederacy*, ed. Walter Lord (Short Hills, NJ: Burford Books, Inc., 1954), 81.

6. Ibid; 96–97.

7. Ibid., 87–89.

8. Ibid., 93. After leaving Johnston's headquarters, Fremantle traveled through Mobile and Montgomery to Chattanooga, thence to Atlanta, Charleston, Petersburg, and Richmond. He was looking for the Army of Northern Virginia. He found it at Berryville, Virginia. The Gettysburg Campaign had begun. He attached himself to General Longstreet and continued with him through Maryland and Pennsylvania and was with him at the Battle of Gettysburg. Fremantle left the army on July 7, traveled to New York City, and from there he returned home to England.

9. *ORA*, series 1, vol. 24, part 2, 212.

10. *ORA*, series 1, vol. 24, part 3, 943.

11. William C. Davis, *Breckinridge: Statesman, Soldier, Symbol* (Baton Rouge: Louisiana State University Press, 1974), 366.

12. *ORA*, series 1, vol. 24, part 2, 215.

13. Ibid., 217–18.

14. *ORA*, series 2, vol. 5, 761.

15. *ORA*, series 1, vol. 24, part 3, 393; *ORA*, vol.24, part II, 221.

16. *ORA*, series 1, vol. 24, part 3, 960–61; Lyon, "Memoirs," 41.

17. Joseph E. Johnston, *Narrative of Military Operations During the Late War Between the States* (New York: D. Appleton and Company, 1874). 191; *ORA*, series 1, vol. 24, part 3, 828.

18. Untitled, *Nashville Daily Union*, July 2, 1863; Lyon, "Memoirs," 41. Port Hudson surrendered on July 8, 1863.

19. *ORA*, series 1, vol. 24, part 2, 224.

20. *ORA*, series 1, vol. 24, part 1, 227–28.

21. W. O. Dodd, "Recollections of Vicksburg During the Siege." *Southern Bivouac, Volume I: September 1882–August 1883* (Wilmington, NC: Broadfoot Publishing Company, 1992), 3; Johnston, *Narrative*, 202.

22. Lockett, 492.

23. *ORA*, series 1, vol. 24, part 1, 281; Johnston, *Narrative*, 203.

24. Lyon, *Memoir*, 41.

25. "Fall of Vicksburg," *Lancaster (SC) Ledger*, July 15, 1863.

26. "A.B." "The Eighth Kentucky at Pearl River," *Southern Bivouac, Volume IV: June 1885–May 1886* (Wilmington, NC: Broadfoot Publishing Company, 1993), 313; "The Eighth Kentucky at Jackson," *Confederate Veteran* (Dec. 1913): 592.

27. "The Eighth Kentucky Regiment at Jackson," *Confederate Veteran* (Dec. 1913): 592.

28. "From Mississippi," *Yorkville (SC) Enquirer*, July 13, 1863. The gallantry of Cobb's Battery during the battle of July 12 was rewarded afterward when it was presented a new banner by the wives of General Breckinridge, General Buckner, and Colonel H. B. Lyon. The ladies had sewn it from swatches taken from their dresses. After the war, the bullet-torn flag was presented to Frank P. Gracey, the last commander of the battery. It is said to still be in the possession of his descendants.

29. Foote, *Fredericksburg to Meridian*, 623; Winschel, 48.

30. *Richmond (VA) Daily Dispatch*, July 18, 1863.

31. William T. Sherman, *Sherman's Civil War: Selected Correspondence of William T. Sherman, 1860–1865*, ed. Brooks D. Simpson and Jean V. Berlin (Chapel Hill: University of North Carolina Press, 1999), 507.

32. Grant, *Personal Memoirs*, 387–388; Sherman, *Sherman's Civil War*, 508.

8. The War Child and the Wizard

1. *ORA*, series 1, vol. 31, part 3, 675.

2. *ORA*, series 1, vol. 31, part 3, 720–21.

3. Ibid., 722, 733.

4. Lyon, "Memoirs," 42. Late 1864 was a time of change for Cobb's Battery. Captain Robert H. Cobb was assigned to the staff of General Breckinridge after the Battle of Chickamauga. His successor was Lieutenant Frank P. Gracey. In his first battle as commander of the battery, Gracey found his guns surrounded on Missionary Ridge and lost them all, including the "Lady Breckinridge" and the "Lady Buckner." He took some chaffing for the loss, but went on to prove himself to be a skillful commander. Supplied with replacements, Gracey's Kentucky Battery continued in active service with the Army of Tennessee until the end of the Atlanta Campaign. As will be seen, Gracey and his battery served with Lyon in some of his late war adventures. The battery ended the war in the Department of Alabama, Mississippi, and East Louisiana.

5. John Witherspoon DuBose, *General Joseph Wheeler and the Army of Tennessee* (New York: Neale Publishing Company, 1912), 265.

6. W. C. Dodson, *Campaigns of Wheeler and His Cavalry, 1862–1865* (Atlanta: Hudgins Publishing Company, 1899), 156; Edward G. Longacre, *A Soldier to the Last: Maj. Gen. Joseph Wheeler in Blue and Gray* (Washington, DC: Potomac Books, 2007), 140, 138.

7. Hodding Carter, *Lower Mississippi* (New York: Farrar & Rinehart, Inc., 1942), 271; Brian Steel Wills, *A Battle from the Start: The Life of Nathan Bedford Forrest* (New York: HarperCollins Publishers, 1992), 16.

8. Wills, 145; John Allen Wyeth, *Life of Lieutenant-General Nathan Bedford Forrest* (New York: Harper & Brothers, 1908), 400.

9. Wyeth, 243.

10. Sherman, *Sherman's Civil War*, 584.

11. Mercer Otey, "Story of Our Great War," *Confederate Veteran* (Mar. 1901): 110; Marshall D. Krolick, "Brig. Gen Abraham H. Buford," in *Kentuckians in Gray*, ed. Bruce S. Allardice and Lawrence Lee Hewitt (Lexington: University Press of Kentucky, 2008), 50.

12. Henry Ewell Hord, "Brice's X Roads From a Private's View," *Confederate Veteran* (Nov. 1904): 529.

13. James Dinkins, "The Battle of Brice's Crossroads," *Confederate Veteran* (Oct. 1925): 380; Edwin C. Bearss, *Forrest at Brice's Cross Roads and in North Mississippi in 1864* (Dayton, OH: Press of Morningside Bookshop, 1979), 77.

14. George, 89, 87.

15. Stewart L. Bennett, *The Battle of Brice's Crossroads* (Charleston, SC: History Press, 2012), 53.

16. Jack Hurst, *Nathan Bedford Forrest: A Biography* (New York: Knopf Doubleday Publishing Group, 2011), 187.

17. *ORA*, series 1, vol. 39, part 1, 223.

18. Ibid., 93.

19. Bennett, 68.

20. *ORA*, series 1, vol. 39, part 1, 208.

21. Edwin C. Bearss, "The Battle of Brice's Cross Roads," *Blue & Gray*, Aug. 1999, 45; *ORA*, series 1, vol. 39, part 1, 223.

22. George, 91.

23. Bennett, 96.

24. *ORA*, series 1, vol. 39, part 1, 224; Wills, 212.

25. Ibid., 93; Bearss, 47. John Watson Morton, *The Artillery of Nathan Bedford Forrest's Cavalry* (Nashville: Publishing House of the M.E. Church, South, 1909), 176.

26. *ORA*, series 1, vol. 39, part 1, 125; D. B. Castleberry, "Lyon's Brigade at Brice's Crossroads," *Confederate Veteran* (Jan. 1926): 7; W. D. Brown, "Guntown or

Brice's X Roads Fight," *Confederate Veteran* (Dec. 1901): 556; Robert Cowden, *A Brief Sketch of the Organization and Services of the Fifty-Ninth Regiment of United States Colored Infantry* (Dayton, OH: United Brethren Publishing House, 1883), 116.

27. Noah Andre Trudeau, *Like Men of War: Black Troops in the Civil War: 1862–1865* (Edison, NJ: Castle Books, 1998), 176; Bearss, 48; Bennett, 46–47.

28. Trudeau, 177; Jordan and Pryor, 476; Cowden, 199.

29. George, 91.

30. *ORA,* series 1, vol. 39, part 1, 224, 221; George, 92.

31. Brown, 556.

32. Young, 16.

33. Hylan B. Lyon. Letter to Laura O'Hara Lyon, June 16, 1864. Hylan B. Lyon Papers, M.S.U., MS 69–03, Box 1, File 12.

34. Henry Ewell Hord, "Pursuit of Gen. Sturgis," *Confederate Veteran* (Jan. 1905): 17.

35. Jordan and Pryor, 483; Young, 2.

9. *The Federals Take Their Turn*

1. Samuel A. Agnew, "Battle of Tishomingo Creek," *Confederate Veteran* (Sept. 1900): 402; Samuel A. Agnew, "Diary, September 27, 1863–June 30, 1864," in "Documenting the American South." docsouth.unc.edu/imls/agnew/agnew .html. Accessed Dec. 2, 2016, 309–12.

2. Hylan B. Lyon. Letter to Laura O'Hara, June 19, 1864. Lyon–O'Hara Papers, SC 107. Courtesy of Manuscript and Folklife Archives, Kentucky Museum and Library, Western Kentucky University, Bowling Green, KY.

3. Lyon, "Memoirs," 45. Lyon was mistaken in saying that he was assigned command of Morgan's cavalry because Morgan had been killed. The reason that Lyon was ordered to assume command of his cavalry was that Morgan was under a cloud for the behavior of his men during his last Kentucky Raid in June 1864. They robbed stores and banks and generally showed themselves to be beyond the control of the man who had once been considered one of the South's greatest cavalry commanders. Shortly after the end of the raid Morgan was relieved of command. He had not restored his reputation at the time he was killed, Sept. 4, 1864, in Greeneville, Tennessee.

4. *ORA,* series 1, vol. 38, part 4, 480.

5. Cowden, 122.

6. Ibid., 104–5.

7. Morton, 198.

8. *ORA*, series 1, vol. 39, part 1, 96; Cowden, 102. Sturgis never held another field command.

9. W. H. Tucker, *The Fourteenth Wisconsin Vet. Vol. Infantry (General A. J. Smith's Command) in the Expedition and Battle of Tupelo* (Indianapolis: F. E. Engle & Son, 1892), 8.

10. Shelby Foote, *The Civil War, A Narrative: Red River to Appomattox* (New York: Random House, 1986), 510; Henry Ewell Hord, "Personal Experiences at Harrisburg, Miss.," *Confederate Veteran* (Aug. 1905): 361; *ORA* series 1, vol. 39, part 1, 321.

11. Thomas E. Parson, "The Battle of Tupelo (or Harrisburg)," *Blue & Gray*, Volume XXX, Number 6, 23.

12. *ORA*, series 1, vol. 39, part 1, 321.

13. Tucker, 10; Parson, 23.

14. Parson, 24.

15. Foote, *Red River to Appomattox*, 511; Wills, 233.

16. Morton, *The Artillery of Nathan Bedford Forrest's Cavalry*, 207–8.

17. George, 100; Hord, "Personal Experiences at Harrisburg, Miss.," 362.

18. Parson, 44.

19. *ORA*, series 1, vol. 39, part 1, 331; Hord, "Personal Experiences at Harrisburg, Miss.," 362.

20. *ORA*, series 1, vol. 39, part 1, 337.

21. Parson, 43; *ORA*, series 1, vol. 39, part 1, 331.

22. George, 101; G. J. Puryear, "No Man's Battle," *Confederate Veteran* (Nov. 1914): 510.

23. *ORA*, series 1, vol. 39, part 1, 336, 323.

24. Parson, 47. Forrest continued to refuse to accept any responsibility in the days following the battle. Thomas E. Parson quotes Forrest going around saying to his men, "Boys, this was not my fight, and I take no responsibility for it" (Parson, 49).

25. Foote, *Red River to Appomattox*, 512.

26. Henry Ewell Hord, "Campaigning Under Forrest," *Confederate Veteran* (Jan. 1904): 6–7.

27. George, 103; *ORA*, series 1, vol. 39, part 1, 332, 323–24.

28. Bearss, *Forrest at Brice's Cross Roads and in North Mississippi*, 37.

29. Foote, *Red River to Appomattox*, 513.

10. Forrest Resurgent

1. *ORA*, series 1, vol. 39, part 2, 763, 766.

2. Wills, 237; *ORA*, series 1, vol. 39, part 1, 400.

3. George, 113.

4. *ORA*, series 1, vol. 39, part 1, 469, 400.

5. Ibid., 470.

6. *ORA*, series 1, vol. 39, part 2, 296.

7. Ibid., 796–97.

8. Richard Taylor, *Destruction and Reconstruction*, ed. Richard B. Harwell (New York: Longmans, Green and Co., 1955), 242.

9. Ibid.

10. Ibid., 243.

11. Ibid.

12. George, 119.

13. William E. Merrill, "Block-Houses for Railroad Defense in the Department of the Cumberland," in *Sketches of War History, 1861–1865: Papers Prepared for the Ohio Commandery of the Military Order of the Loyal Legion of the United States*, ed. Robert Hunter (Cincinnati: Robert Clarke & Co., 1890), 396. John E. Clark, Jr., *Railroads in the Civil War: The Impact of Management on Victory and Defeat* (Baton Rouge: Louisiana State University Press, 2004), 23.

14. Lyon, "Memoirs," 44.

15. George, 120.

16. *ORA*, series 1, vol. 39, part 1, 543.

17. Ibid., 524; Morton, 229; "Operations During the Late Raid," *Nashville Daily Union*, Oct. 15, 1864.

18. *ORA*, series 1, vol. 39, part 1, 544.

19. Ibid.

20. Lyon, "Memoirs," 44; Jordan and Pryor, 569.

21. *ORA*, series 1, vol. 39, part 1, 545; Wills, 254–55. As had been the case after the surrender of the works at Athens, the black prisoners were sent to Mobile, Alabama.

22. Ibid., 545.

23. Ibid.

24. Ibid., 505.

25. Ibid., 545; "Operations During the Late Raid," *Nashville Daily Union*, Oct. 15, 1864; *ORA*, series 1, vol. 39, part 1, 546.

26. *ORA*, series 1, vol. 39, part 1, 545.

27. Lyon, "Memoirs," 44–45.

28. *ORA,* series 1, vol. 39, part 1, 506–7.

29. Ibid., 546.

30. Ibid., 547.

31. Ibid.; George, 125.

32. *ORA,* series 1, vol. 39, part 1, 548.

33. Ibid., 548; Merrill, 400. George S. Burkhardt points to another aspect of the raid that Forrest did not mention, namely, the treatment of the U.S. Colored Troops whom he took prisoner at the various blockhouses. Burkhardt says the fact that Forrest spared the blacks, and took hundreds of them with him as prisoners during his retreat across the Tennessee River, shows that Forrest *could* control his men when he wanted and simply had chosen not to at Fort Pillow and Brice's Crossroads. George S. Burkhardt, *Confederate Rage, Yankee Wrath: No Quarter in the Civil War* (Carbondale: Southern Illinois University Press, 2013), 189.

34. Henry Ewell Hord, "Scouting About Memphis," *Confederate Veteran* (May 1912): 208.

35. George, 127; Foote, *Red River to Appomattox,* 601.

36. *ORA,* series 1, vol. 39, part 1, 549.

11. Johnsonville

1. *ORA,* series 1, vol. 39, part 2, 874, 819.

2. James Q. Chenoweth, "The Rangers' Last Campaign," in *The Partisan Rangers of the Confederate States Army,* ed. William J. Davis (Utica, KY: Cook & Mc-Dowell Publications, 1979), 183.

3. *ORA,* series 1, vol. 39, part 1, 876.

4. Ibid.

5. Chenoweth, 184.

6. Steven L. Wright, compiler, *Kentucky Soldiers and Their Regiments in the Civil War: Abstracted from the Pages of Contemporary Kentucky Newspapers,* 5 vols. (By the editor, 2009), 4:167; 296–97. Hereafter cited as Wright, *Kentucky Soldiers.*

7. Ibid.

8. J. M. Stevens, Untitled, *Confederate Veteran* (Jan. 1897): 159.

9. Ibid.

10. Nannie Haskins Williams, *The Diary of Nannie Haskins Williams: A Southern Woman's Story of Rebellion and Reconstruction: 1863–1890,* ed. Minoa D. Uffelman, Ellen Kanervo, Phyllis Smith, and Eleanor Williams (Knoxville: University of Tennessee Press, 2014), 80.

11. *ORA*, series 1, vol. 39, part 1, 861.

12. "Capture of the Mazeppa: H. B. Lyon to Julian F. Gracey," *Confederate Veteran* (Dec. 1905): 567.

13. George, 129; "From Cairo and Below," *Chicago Tribune*, Nov. 2, 1864; Morton, 246–47.

14. George, 129.

15. "From Cairo and Below," *Chicago Tribune*, Nov. 2, 1864; *ORA*, series 1, vol. 39, part 1, 867.

16. George, 129.

17. Young, 113; Morton 248.

18. Davidson, 98.

19. Lyon, "Memoirs," 46.

20. Ibid.

21. Ibid.

22. E. G. Cowen, "The Battle of Johnsonville," *Confederate Veteran* (Apr. 1914): 175.

23. *ORN*, series 1, vol. 26, 622.

24. "Capture of the Mazeppa: H. B. Lyon to Julian F. Gracey," *Confederate Veteran* (Dec. 1905): 566.

25. *ORA*, series 1, vol. 39, part 1, 871; *ORN*, series 1, vol. 26, 622.

26. *ORA*, series 1, vol. 39, part 1, 871; Young, 292; "The War in Tennessee," *New York Times*, Nov. 13, 1864; Foote, *Red River to Appomattox*, 620.

27. *ORA*, series 1, vol. 39, part 1, 871; Morton, 256.

28. Lyon, "Memoirs," 47.

29. *ORA*, series 1, vol. 39, part 1, 871; George F. Hager, "Second Tennessee Cavalry," in *The Military Annals of Tennessee, Confederate*, ed. John Berrien Lindsley (Nashville: J. M. Lindsley & Co., Publishers, 1886), 621; Morton, 257.

30. *ORA*, series 1, vol. 39, part 1, 871.

31. *ORA*, series 1, vol. 39, part 2, 659; Sherman, *Sherman's Civil War*, 750.

32. *ORA*, series 1, vol. 39, part 1, 871; Nannie Haskins Williams, 101.

12. Lyon's Kentucky Raid

1. *ORA*, series 1, vol. 45, part 1, 1221.

2. Federal Writers Project, *Military History of Kentucky* (Frankfort: The State Journal, 1939), 223; Harrison, 88.

3. *ORA*, series 1, vol. 45, part 1, 803–4.

4. *ORA*, series 1, vol. 45, part 1, 804; *ORA*, series 1, vol. 45, part 2, 181. Admiral S. P. Lee was a cousin of General Robert E. Lee.

5. Chenoweth, 187.

6. Fannie K. Roach, "Mrs. Fannie K. Roach's Interesting War Paper," *Hopkinsville Kentuckian*, Oct. 8. 1914. Hereafter cited as Roach, "War Paper."

7. Chenoweth, 107.

8. Wright, *Kentucky Soldiers*, 4:321, 317.

9. "The Convicts Bridge," *Hopkinsville Kentuckian*, Nov. 26, 1895; *ORA,* series 1, vol. 45, part 1, 804.

10. *ORA,* series 1, vol. 45, part 2, 245. Caldwell County historian Sam Steger writes, "The county paid dearly for the destruction of the [Princeton] courthouse by General Lyon. For each $100 of assessed value, the following levies were made for the construction of a new hall of justice: $0.15 for the year 1865, $0.20 for the year of 1866, and finally $2.50 for the year of 1867." He points out that this was "very steep for the economy that existed after the War Between the States," and the people were not quick to forget. Steger says that, after the war, Lyon "was always cautious to never be caught in Princeton after dark." Sam Steger, "Historical Notebook: Caldwell County's Fourth Courthouse," Caldwell County *Times*, no date.

11. Chenoweth, 187; Roach, "War Paper." Chenoweth's reference to Johnson being at Russellville with a "negro brigade" is mysterious. The Union officer at Russellville was Lieutenant Colonel Samuel F. Johnson, who commanded the 17th Kentucky Cavalry, a white regiment. The 17th joined Watkins' brigade at Russellville and accompanied it into the Dec. 16 fight at Hopkinsville. Perhaps racial animosity affected Chenoweth's thinking, or perhaps he was using the adjective "negro" as a euphemism for Yankee.

12. Roach, "War Paper."

13. Chenoweth, 188.

14. *ORA,* series 1, vol. 45, part 1, 792; Chenoweth, 188.

15. Roach, "War Paper."

16. *ORA,* series 1, vol. 45, part 1, 792.

17. Chenoweth, 188.

18. *ORA,* series 1, vol. 45, part 1, 798.

19. Ibid., 796.

20. Chenoweth, 189; B. R. Roberson, "The Courthouse Burnin'est General," *Tennessee Historical Quarterly* 23 (4) (Dec. 1964): 375.

21. Chenoweth, 189; Untitled, *Louisville Daily Journal*, Dec. 26, 1864; *ORA,* series 1, vol. 45, part 1, 794–95. Five of those captured at the crossing of Green River at Ashbyburg were Captain Edward B. Ross and four of his men. They were sent as prisoners to Camp Chase, Ohio. Eventually, more than eighty of Lyon's raiders would end up in Camp Chase.

22. Steven L. Wright, compiler, *On Trial for Their Lives: Kentucky's Guerrillas and Military Justice in the Civil War* (by the author, 2012), 33. Hereafter cited as Wright, *On Trial*.

23. Wright, *On Trial*, 37; Chenoweth, 191. Henry Metcalf's behavior in Hartford paid off in the end. Just before Lyon crossed into Tennessee, he sent a captain and a few men, including Metcalf, back into Kentucky in a final effort to try to gather conscripts. The captain was subsequently killed in a fight with some Federals near Bardstown and the rest of the men scattered. For the next several weeks, Metcalf was part of no command. He fell in with two guerrillas who were going south to join General Lyon's command. They were Henry Magruder and Jerome M. Clarke, who is better known by his alias, Sue Mundy. Their attempt to reach Tennessee was a tale of woe from start to finish. The three were discovered hiding in a Meade County barn, arrested, and taken to Louisville for military trials. Magruder and Mundy were hanged, but Metcalf's fate was different. A number of people from Hartford came to Louisville during his trial as witnesses for the defense. They described at some length his protection of their lives and property, and their testimony saved his life. Though Metcalf was convicted and initially sentenced to die, his sentence was almost immediately commuted to five years in the state penitentiary in Frankfort, and he ended up serving only a fraction of his term.

24. *ORA*, series 1, vol. 45, part 2, 345.

25. Chenoweth, 190.

26. *ORA*, series 1, vol. 45, part 1, 795.

27. *ORA*, series 1, vol. 45, part 2, 330.

28. *ORA*, series 1, vol. 45, part 1, 805.

29. Roberson, 376; Wright, *Kentucky Soldiers*, 4:335; Wright, *Kentucky Soldiers*, 5:21.

30. J. W. Wells, *History of Cumberland County* (Louisville: The Standard Printing Co., 1947), 213; Ernest M. Lawson, *Awakening of Cumberland County* (Burkesville, KY: Cumberland County Publishing Company, 1973), 131.

31. Chenoweth, 191.

32. Ibid. The newspapers were not very forgiving of the Federals who had allowed General Lyon to escape Kentucky. The Louisville *Daily Journal* said, "The affair is not very creditable to those who have been engaged in the pursuit. They might as well have remained in camp. Lyon moved where he pleased, and at his leisure. Our cavalry was content to follow in his rear and pick up a few stragglers. The escape of the raiders is disgraceful." (*Louisville Daily Journal*, Dec. 31, 1864)

33. *ORA*, series 1, vol. 45, part 1, 805.

13. "An Illusive Cuss"

1. *ORA*, series 1, vol. 45, part 2, 527; 531–32.

2. Ibid., 545; *ORA*, series 1, vol. 45, part 1, 513–14.

3. *ORA*, series 1, vol. 45, part 1, 802.

4. *ORA*, series 1, vol. 45, part 2, 555, 568, 571.

5. Chenoweth, 192.

6. Hylan B. Lyon. Letter to Florence O'Hara, Jan. 13, 1866. Hylan B. Lyon Papers, M.S.U., MS 69–03, Box 1, File 16.

7. J. B. Waller, "War Reminiscences," in *The Partisan Rangers of the Confederate States Army*, ed. William J. Davis (Utica, KY: Cook & McDowell Publications, 1979), 424.

8. Hylan B. Lyon. Letter to Florence O'Hara, Jan. 13, 1866. Hylan B. Lyon Papers, M.S.U., MS 69–03, Box 1, File 16.

9. Ibid.

10. *ORA*, series 1, vol. 45, part 1, 46; *ORA*, series 1, vol. 45, part 2, 611.

11. Hylan B. Lyon. Letter to Florence O'Hara, Jan. 13, 1866. Hylan B. Lyon Papers, M.S.U., MS 69–03, Box 1, File 16.

12. Chenoweth, 193–94.

13. Forbes, 6; James H. Wilson, *Under the Old Flag*, 2 vols. (New York: D. Appleton and Company, 1912), 1:144.

14. *ORA*, series 1, vol. 45, part 1, 806.

15. *ORA*, series 1, vol. 49, part 1, 959.

16. Ibid., 959–60.

17. Ibid., 960.

18. George, 137–38.

19. "Dare of Some of Forrest's Men," *Confederate Veteran* (Nov. 1907): 501.

20. James Pickett Jones, *Yankee Blitzkrieg: Wilson's Raid Through Alabama and Georgia* (Lexington: University Press of Kentucky, 2015), 78–79.

21. *ORA*, series 1, vol. 49, part 2, 1160.

22. Ibid., 1181–82.

23. *ORA*, series 1, vol. 49, part 1, 419.

24. Ibid., 420.

25. Ibid., 421.

26. Ibid., 417. The modern spelling is Cahaba River.

27. Wills, 308.

28. Taylor, 268–269.

29. George, 142–43.

30. Hylan B. Lyon. Letter to Florence O'Hara, Jan.13, 1866. Hylan B. Lyon Papers, M.S.U., MS 69–03, Box 1, File 16.

31. Ibid.

32. Williams, 113; Chenoweth, 194. Taylor surrendered his department on May 4, 1865; Forrest issued his farewell address to his troops on May 9.

14. Mexico

1. Lyon, "Memoirs," 52.

2. Ibid., 53. Lyon's adventures continued, and one wishes that his memoir did, as well. Why he decided to end his account mid-journey is a mystery. Perhaps he was just old and tired. The last paragraph he wrote, as can be seen, was uncharacteristically careless of punctuation and capitalization. Whatever the cause, Lyon ended his narrative at June 1865, and interested parties must rely on other sources to learn what happened to Lyon and Harris as they proceeded to San Antonio and beyond.

3. Daniel O'Flaherty, *General Jo Shelby: Undefeated Rebel* (Chapel Hill: University of North Carolina Press, 2000), 242.

4. Ibid., 236.

5. "Harris' Flight to Mexico," *Galveston Daily News*, July 14, 1897.

6. "Isham G. Harris' Flight to Mexico," *Covington (TN) Leader*, Apr. 14, 1921.

7. Robert Adamson, "Gov. Harris at the Close of the War," *Confederate Veteran* (Aug. 1897): 405.

8. "Harris' Flight to Mexico"; "Isham G. Harris' Flight to Mexico."

9. O'Flaherty, 286–88.

10. Adamson, 404; George D. Harmon, "Confederate Migration to Mexico," *The Hispanic American Historical Review* (Nov. 1937): 460.

11. Harmon, 461.

12. "Our Cordova Correspondence: The American Colony at Cordova," *New York Herald*, Apr. 19, 1866.

13. Isham G. Harris, "The Rebels in Mexico," *New York Herald*, Dec. 18, 1865.

14. Hylan B. Lyon. Letter to Florence O'Hara, Jan. 13, 1866. Hylan B. Lyon Papers, M.S.U., MS 69–03, Box 1, File 16.

15. Ibid.

16. "Our Cordova Correspondence: The American Colony at Cordova," *New York Herald*, Apr. 19, 1866.

17. Harmon, 475.

18. Andrew Johnson, *The Papers of Andrew Johnson: September 1865–January 1866*, ed. Paul H. Bergeron (Knoxville: University of Tennessee Press, 1967), vol. 9: 130.

19. Ibid.

20. Andrew Johnson, Pardon of Hylan B. Lyon, 11 June 1866. Hylan B. Lyon Papers, M.S.U., MS 69–03, Box 1, File 16.

15. Kentucky

1. "General Rousseau on the Stump," *New York Times*, July 14, 1865. The Emancipation Proclamation created a crisis for many of Kentucky's Union soldiers when it went into effect on January 1, 1863. Kentucky was a slave state that had never left the Union, and the goal of most Kentuckians in the Federal service was to preserve both the Constitution and slavery. That is, they were not fighting to achieve any sort of social reform, they were fighting for a return to the *status quo antebellum*. When Lincoln proclaimed that emancipation was now a goal of the war, many Kentuckians in the Union army felt betrayed, and they had to decide what their future course would be. Soldiers in the ranks and junior officers who could not abide the emancipation policy showed their disapproval by various means, including desertion, resignation, or refusing to re-enlist. Some general officers, like Major General Lovell Harrison Rousseau, a slave owner himself, came to accept the new reality. In a speech at Shelbyville, Tennessee, on Apr. 4, 1864, "he boldly declared himself in favor of the abolition of slavery. He stated that a severe conflict had been going on between his prejudices and his judgment, but the former were finally conquered, and now he believes in all sincerity, that slavery not only was the cause of the war, but its removal from the land is a necessity to permanent national peace." (*Chicago Journal*, Apr. 12, 1864). Another Kentucky slave owner serving in the Army of the Cumberland was Brigadier General Thomas J. Wood, the officer who shuffled men and resources all over North Alabama during the search for Lyon's command in Alabama in early 1865. Like Rousseau, Wood overcame his prejudices to accept the emancipation policy. Until that day came, he remained in the army and saved his career by the simple expedient of keeping private his views on the subject of slavery. Then there is the case of Colonel Frank Wolford, commander of the 1st Kentucky Volunteer Cavalry, who was so bitterly opposed to the Emancipation Proclamation that he could not restrain himself. His hateful speeches against the policy and against the President himself resulted in his expulsion from the army and, when he would not desist, his arrest. The Emancipation Proclamation did not create a similar crisis among Kentuckians in the Confederate service—it only confirmed what they had believed from the start about President Lincoln and his agenda—but it did result in a rage that sometimes boiled over when blacks in uniform were seen on the battlefield. The killing of blacks after the Battle of Brice's Crossroads is an example.

2. Anne E. Marshall, *Creating a Confederate Kentucky: The Lost Cause and Civil War Memory in a Border State* (Chapel Hill: University of North Carolina Press, 2013), 33; Hambleton Tapp and James C. Klotter, *Kentucky: Decades of Discord, 1865–1900* (Lexington: University Press of Kentucky, 1977), 13–14.

3. Marshall, *Creating a Confederate Kentucky*, 43.

4. Ibid., 59; 65.

5. "The Hickman Ku-Klux," *Hickman Courier*, Apr. 18, 1868.

6. "Negro Confederate Is Dead," *Iron County (MO) Register*, June 23, 1904. The Iron County *Register* and various other Southern newspapers called Ike Copeland a "Confederate" because of his wartime tenure as a body servant to his master, who was a Rebel officer. John C. Espie of Kuttawa, Kentucky, verified this in the 1940s. When he was a boy, Espie knew the aged Ike Copeland, and he shared some of his memories in Allan Trout's popular column "Greetings!" which appeared in the Louisville *Courier-Journal*. Espie said, "Ike had been servant to Capt. Thomas Copeland, of Tennessee. At the death of his master, Ike drifted over to Eddyville, my boyhood home." Espie added that Eddyville was "also the home of Gen. H. B. Lyon of the Confederate Army. The General took care of him" ("Greetings!" *Courier-Journal*, Feb. 25, 1946).

7. "The Crisis at Home: Views of Gen. Forrest and Others," *Athens (TN) Post*, Sept. 11, 1868.

8. Wills, 337.

9. "1870 United States Federal Census," database, Ancestry.com (http:// www .ancestry.com: accessed 5 Aug. 2017), entry for Lyon County, Kentucky. Willis B. Machen, Lyon's double kinsman by marriage, continued to have a political career after the war. Considering the prevailing mood, his service for the Confederacy may actually have worked in his favor. He served a truncated term as U.S. Senator from Kentucky, 1872–1873, and he was appointed to the Kentucky Railway Commission in 1880. After his term ended, he retired to his plantation. He died in Sept. 1893 at the state asylum in Hopkinsville, where Chenoweth's brigade of Lyon's division had fought the Federals in Dec. 1864. His home, Mineral Mound, is gone, but the grounds are now a Kentucky State Park. Incidentally, Willis B. Machen was the grandfather of Zelda Sayre, who became the jazziest of Jazz Age personalities. She was most famous for being the wife F. Scott Fitzgerald.

10. Bill Cunningham, *Castle: The Story of a Kentucky Prison* (Kuttawa, KY: McClanahan Publishing House, 1995), 8.

11. *Journal of the Regular Session of The House of Representatives, of the Commonwealth of Kentucky* (S. I. M. Major, Public Printer, 1873), 45; Cunningham, 8–9.

12. *Journal of the Regular Session of The House of Representatives, of the Commonwealth of Kentucky* (S. I. M. Major, Public Printer, 1871), 399.

13. *Journal of the Regular Session of the House of Representatives, of the Commonwealth of Kentucky* (Frankfort: E. H. Porter, Public Printer, 1880), 43.

14. Ibid.

15. Cunningham, 13.

16. Tapp and Klotter, 182.

17. Cunningham, 17.

18. Ibid., 23; "Gen. Lyon's Case," *Hickman Courier* Sept. 9, 1887; Untitled, *Hickman Courier*, Mar. 2, 1888. The newspaper stories also indicated that Carpenter and Thomas were frequently absent, and that Lyon was performing most of the work of the commission alone.

19. "The Branch Penitentiary," *Hickman Courier*, Aug. 28, 1885.

20. Ibid.

21. "Notes of Current Events," Stanford [Kentucky] *Semi-Weekly Interior Journal*, Apr. 7, 1885.

22. "The Eddyville Penitentiary," *Hopkinsville Semi-Weekly South Kentuckian*, Feb. 8, 1887.

23. Untitled, *Hopkinsville Semi-Weekly South Kentuckian,* Jan. 11, 1887.

24. "The O.V.'s Intentions," *Hopkinsville Kentuckian*, Mar. 28, 1900.

25. "Cook and Howell," *Hopkinsville Kentuckian*, Apr. 13, 1897.

26. Untitled, *Paducah Daily Sun*, Mar. 27, 1898; *Journal of the Regular Session of the House of Representatives, of the Commonwealth of Kentucky* (Louisville: Geo. G. Fetter, 1900), 23. Hereafter cited as House *Journal*, 1900.

27. Tapp and Klotter, 426. Irvin S. Cobb, the author of more than sixty books and hundreds of short stories, was among America's most popular writers between 1907 and 1944. He was the grandson of the Confederate artillerist Robert Cobb, the commander of Cobb's Kentucky Battery.

28. Ibid., 413–414.

29. Lowell H. Harrison and James C. Klotter, *A New History of Kentucky* (Lexington: University Press of Kentucky, 1997), 271.

30. Robert Elkin Hughes, Frederick William Schaefer, and Eustace Leroy Williams, *That Kentucky Campaign: or, The Law, the Ballot, and the People in the Goebel-Taylor Contest* (Cincinnati: Robert Clarke Company, Publishers, 1900), 188. Hereater cited as Hughes.

31. Ibid., 194.

32. Ibid., 202–4.

33. Ibid., 204.

34. House *Journal,* 1900, 297–98.

35. "Goebel Sworn In," Maysville *Daily Public Ledger*, Feb. 1, 1900; Hughes, 227.

36. Hughes, 259; 266–67.

37. House *Journal,* 1900, 704–6.

16. The Final Reunion

1. "'Vets' Reunion," *Hopkinsville Kentuckian*, Oct. 20, 1903.

2. Lyon," Memoirs," 47.

3. "Forrest's Cavalry Corps Elects Officers," *Confederate Veteran* (June 1906): 253.

4. "Attention Forrest's Cavalry!" *Union City (TN) Commercial*, Oct. 5, 1906.

5. "Brave Heart Stilled in Death," *Paducah Evening Sun*, Apr. 26, 1907; "Gen. H. B. Lyon Dead," Crittenden *Record Press*, May 2, 1907; "Gen. H. B. Lyon Dies Suddenly," *Confederate Veteran* (Dec. 1907): 560.

BIBLIOGRAPHY

Unpublished Sources

Hylan B. Lyon Papers, Pogue Special Collections and Archives Library, Murray State University Libraries, Murray, KY.

Lyon File. Glenn E. Martin Genealogy Library, Princeton, KY.

Lyon–O'Hara Papers (SC 107), Department of Library Special Collections, Western Kentucky University, Bowling Green, KY.

Wright, Steven L. *The Georgian Renegade and His Kentucky Troops: Louis D. Watkins and the Sixth Kentucky Cavalry*. Unpublished manuscript.

Published Sources

"A. B." "The Eighth Kentucky at Pearl River." Southern Bivouac, Volume IV: June 1885–May 1886. Wilmington, NC: Broadfoot Publishing Company, 1993.

Adair, John M. *Historical Sketch of the Forty-Fifth Illinois Regiment*. Lanark, IL: Carroll County Gazette Print, 1869.

Adamson, Robert. "Gov. Harris at the Close of the War." *Confederate Veteran* (Aug. 1897).

Adams, George Rollie. *General William S. Harney: Prince of Dragoons*. Lincoln: University of Nebraska Press, 2005.

Agnew, Samuel A. "Battle of Tishomingo Creek." *Confederate Veteran* (Sept. 1900).

———. "Diary, September 27, 1863–June 30, 1864." In "Documenting the American South." docsouth.unc.edu/imls/agnew/agnew.html. Accessed December 2, 2016.

Allardice, Bruce S. *Confederate Colonels: A Biographical Register*. Columbia: University of Missouri Press, 2008.

Avery, Phineas O. *History of the Fourth Illinois Cavalry Regiment*. Humboldt, NE: The Enterprise: A Print Shop, 1903.

Badgett, J. Chester. *Campbellsville Baptist Church: A Two-Hundred Year History.* N.P.: Taylor Publishing Co., 1993.

Ballard, Michael B. "Misused Merit: The Tragedy of John C. Pemberton." In *Confederate Generals in the Western Theater: Classic Essays on America's Civil War,* edited by Lawrence L. Hewitt and Arthur W. Bergeron, Jr. Knoxville: University of Tennessee Press, 2010.

———. *Vicksburg: The Campaign that Opened the Mississippi.* Chapel Hill: University of North Carolina Press, 2004.

Bancroft, Hubert Howe. *History of Washington, Idaho, and Montana, 1845–1889.* San Francisco: History Company, Publishers, 1890.

Barber, Lucius W. *Army Memoirs of Lucius W. Barber, Company "D," 15th Illinois Volunteer Infantry.* Chicago: J. M. W. Jones Stationery and Printing Co., 1894.

Baskett, George W. "Incidents of Grierson's Raid." *Confederate Veteran* (June 1914).

Battle, J. H., W. H. Perrin, and G. C. Kniffin. *Kentucky: A History of the State.* Louisville: F. A. Battey Publishing Company, 1885.

Bearss, Edwin C. "The Battle of Brice's Cross Roads." *Blue & Gray,* Summer 1999.

———. *Forrest at Brice's Cross Roads and in North Mississippi in 1864.* Dayton, OH: Press of Morningside Bookshop, 1979.

———. *Protecting Sherman's Lifeline: The Battles of Brice's Cross Roads and Tupelo, 1864.* Washington, DC: Office of Publications, National Park Service, 1971.

Bennett, Stewart L. *The Battle of Brice's Crossroads.* Charleston, SC: History Press, 2012.

Bentley, W. H. *History of the 77th Illinois Volunteer Infantry.* Peoria: Edward Hine, Printer, 1883.

Berard, Augusta Blanche, ed. *Reminiscences of West Point in the Olden Time.* East Saginaw MI: Evening News Printing and Binding House, 1886.

Berg, Gordon. "Signals Crossed." *America's Civil War,* May 2017.

Bergeron, Arthur W., Jr. "Lt. Gen. Richard Taylor." In *Kentuckians in Gray,* edited by Bruce S. Allardice and Lawrence Lee Hewitt. Lexington: University Press of Kentucky, 2008.

———. "Mansfield Lovell." In *Confederate Generals in the Western Theater: Classic Essays on America's Civil War,* edited by Lawrence L. Hewitt and Arthur W. Bergeron, Jr. Knoxville: University of Tennessee Press, 2010.

Blackwell, Robert Lee. "Matthew Lyon: A Forgotten Patriot Recalled." *The Filson Club History Quarterly* (July 1972).

Boynton, Edward C. *History of West Point.* London: Samson, Low, Son, & Marston, 1864.

Bradley, Michael R. *They Rode With Forrest.* Gretna, LA: Pelican Publishing Co., 2012.

Brown, W. D. "Guntown or Brice's X Roads Fight." *Confederate Veteran* (Dec. 1901).

Burkhardt, George S. *Confederate Rage, Yankee Wrath: No Quarter in the Civil War.* Carbondale: Southern Illinois University Press, 2013.

Burns, W. S. "A. J. Smith's Defeat of Forrest at Tupelo." In *Battles and Leaders of the Civil War: Retreat with Honor*, edited by Robert Underwood Johnson and Clarence Clough Buel. Edison, NJ: Castle Books, 1995.

Campbell, Tom W. *Two Fighters and Two Fines: Sketches of the Lives of Matthew Lyon and Andrew Jackson.* Little Rock: Pioneer Publishing Company, 1941.

"Capt. Ed. B. Ross." *Confederate Veteran* (Apr. 1912).

"Capture of the Mazeppa." *Confederate Veteran* (Dec.1905).

Carter, Hodding. *Lower Mississippi.* New York: Farrar & Rinehart, Inc., 1942.

Casseday, Morton M. "The Surrender of Fort Donelson." *Southern Bivouac, Volume VI: January 1887–May 1887.* Wilmington, NC: Broadfoot Publishing Company, 1993.

Castleberry, D. B. "Lyon's Brigade at Brice's Crossroads." *Confederate Veteran* (Jan. 1926).

Catton, Bruce. *Grant Moves South.* Boston, MA: Little, Brown and Company, 1960.

———. *This Hallowed Ground: The Story of the Union Side of the Civil War.* Garden City, NY: Doubleday & Company, Inc., 1956.

Chenoweth, James Q. "The Rangers' Last Campaign." In *The Partisan Rangers of the Confederate States Army*, edited by William J. Davis. Utica, KY: Cook & McDowell Publications, 1979.

Clark, John E., Jr. *Railroads in the Civil War: The Impact of Management on Victory and Defeat.* Baton Rouge: Louisiana State University Press, 2004.

Cleveland, Henry Whitney. "Old Scipio." *Southern Bivouac, Volume VI: January 1887–May 1887.* Wilmington, NC: Broadfoot Publishing Company, 1993.

Collins, Lewis. *History of Kentucky.* Lexington: Henry Clay Press, 1968.

"Commander of the Famous Cobb's Battery." *Confederate Veteran* (July 1915).

Cooling, Benjamin Franklin. *Forts Henry and Donelson: The Key to the Confederate Heartland.* Knoxville: University of Tennessee Press, 1989.

Coombe, Jack D. *Thunder Along the Mississippi: The River Battles that Split the Confederacy.* Edison, NJ: Castle, 2005.

Corle, Edwin. *The Gila: River of the Southwest.* New York: Rinehart & Company, Inc., 1951.

Covington, James. "The Indians Scare of 1849." *Tequesta*, 1961.

Cowden, Robert. *A Brief Sketch of the Organization and Services of the Fifty-Ninth Regiment of United States Colored Infantry.* Dayton, OH: United Brethren Publishing House, 1883.

Cowen, E. G. "The Battle of Johnsonville." *Confederate Veteran* (Apr. 1914).

Cullum, George W. *Biographical Register of the Officers and Graduates of the United States Military Academy at West Point*, New York, Since Its Establishment in 1802. Saginaw, MI: Seeman & Peters, 1910.

Cunningham, Bill. *Castle: The Story of a Kentucky Prison*. Kuttawa, KY: McClanahan Publishing House, 1995.

Cutler, Donald L. *"Hang Them All": George Wright and the Plateau Indian War, 1858*. Norman: University of Oklahoma Press, 2016.

"Dare of Some of Forrest's Men." *Confederate Veteran* (Nov. 1907).

Davidson, Donald. *The Tennessee: Civil War to TVA*. New York: Rinehart & Company, Inc., 1948.

Davis, Edwin Adams. *Fallen Guidon: The Saga of Confederate General Jo Shelby's March to Mexico*. College Station, TX: Texas A&M University Press, 1962.

Davis, William C. *Breckinridge: Statesman, Soldier, Symbol*. Baton Rouge: Louisiana State University Press, 1974.

———. *The Orphan Brigade: The Kentucky Confederates who Couldn't Go Home*. Garden City, NY: Doubleday & Company, Inc., 1980.

Denney, Robert E. *Civil War Medicine: Care and Comfort of the Wounded*. New York: Sterling Publishing Co., Inc., 1994.

Dinkins, James. "The Battle of Brice's Crossroads." *Confederate Veteran* (Oct. 1925).

Dodd, W. O. "Recollections of Vicksburg During the Siege." *Southern Bivouac, Volume I: September 1882–August 1883*. Wilmington, NC: Broadfoot Publishing Company, 1992.

Dodge, Grenville M. "Personal Recollections of General Grant, and His Campaigns in the West." In *Personal Recollections of the War of the Rebellion: Addresses Delivered Before the New York Commandery of the Loyal Legion of the United States, Third Series*, edited by A. Noel Blakeman. New York: G. P. Putnam's Sons, 1907.

Dodson, W. C. *Campaigns of Wheeler and His Cavalry, 1862–1865*. Atlanta: Hudgins Publishing Company, 1899.

Dooley, Michael J. *Joint Operations During the Vicksburg Campaign of 1863: The Yazoo Pass Expedition*. Carlisle Barracks, PA: U.S. Army War College, 2000.

Dossman, Steven Nathaniel. *Vicksburg 1863: The Deepest Wound*. Santa Barbara, CA: ABC-CLIO, LLC, 2014.

Douglas, Marjorie Stoneman. *The Everglades: River of Grass*. New York: Rinehart & Company, Inc., 1947.

DuBose, John Witherspoon. *General Joseph Wheeler and the Army of Tennessee*. New York: Neale Publishing Company, 1912.

Dudley, Edgar S. "Discipline at the United States Military Academy." In *Personal Recollections of the War of the Rebellion: Addresses Delivered Before the New York Commandery of the Loyal Legion of the United States, Third Series*, edited by A. Noel Blakeman. New York: G. P. Putnam's Sons, 1907.

"The Eighth Kentucky Regiment at Jackson." *Confederate Veteran* (Dec. 1913).

Elliott, Isaac H. *History of the Thirty-Third Regiment Illinois Veteran Volunteer Infantry*. Gibson City, Illinois: The [Regimental] Association, 1902.

Elliott, Sam Davis. *Isham G. Harris of Tennessee: Confederate Governor and United States Senator*. Baton Rouge: University of Louisiana Press, 2010.

Esposito, Vincent J., ed. *The West Point Atlas of American Wars*. New York: Praeger, 1978.

Evans, Clement A., ed. *Confederate Military History: A Library of Confederate States History, Written by Distinguished Men of the South*. Twelve Volumes. Honolulu, HI: University Press of the Pacific, 2004.

Federal Writers Project. *Military History of Kentucky*. Frankfort: The State Journal, 1939.

Feis, William B. "Charles S. Bell, Union Scout." *North and South* (June 2001).

———. *Grant's Secret Service: The Intelligence War from Belmont to Appomattox*. Lincoln: University of Nebraska Press, 2004.

Fogle, McDowell A. *Fogle's Papers: A History of Ohio County, Kentucky*. Utica, KY: McDowell Publications, 1981.

Foote, Shelby. The Civil War, A Narrative: Fort Sumter to Perryville. New York: Random House, 1986.

———. *The Civil War, A Narrative: Fredericksburg to Meridian*. New York: Random House, 1986.

———. *The Civil War, A Narrative: Red River to Appomattox*. New York: Random House, 1986.

Forbes, Stephen A. *Grierson's Cavalry Raid*. Springfield: Illinois State Historical Society, 1907.

Force, M. F. "Personal Recollections of the Vicksburg Campaign." In *Sketches of War History, 1861–1865: Papers Read Before the Ohio Commandery of the Military Order of the Loyal Legion of the United States, Volume I*, edited by Robert Hunter and William Henry Chamberlin. Cincinnati: R. Clarke & Co., 1888.

"Forrest's Guntown Victory." *Confederate Veteran* (Dec. 1905).

Freeman, Douglas Southall. *R. E. Lee: A Biography*. Four Volumes. New York: Charles Scribner's Sons, 1934.

Fremantle, Arthur James Lyon. *The Fremantle Diary: A Journal of the Confederacy*, edited by Walter Lord. Short Hills, NJ: Burford Books, Inc., 1954.

George, Henry. *History of the 3d, 7th, 8th and 12th Kentucky C.S.A.* Lyndon, KY: Mull-Wathen Historic Press, 1970.

George, Henry, and J. W. Hollingsworth. "Gen. H. B. Lyon." *Confederate Veteran* (Dec. 1907).

Glassley, Ray Hoard. *Pacific Northwest Indian Wars.* Portland, OR: Binford & Mort, 1953.

Glazier, Jack. *Been Coming Through Some Hard Times: Race, History, and Memory in Western Kentucky.* Knoxville: University of Tennessee Press, 2013.

Godbey, Jack. "Inmates Endured Horrid Conditions in First Kentucky State Penitentiary." *Kentucky Explorer* (Oct. 2017).

Goebel, Robert. "'Misunderstood and Misrepresented': Beriah Magoffin and the 1859 Kentucky Gubernatorial Election." *Ohio Valley History* (Winter 2016).

Gott, Kendall D. *Where the South Lost the War: An Analysis of the Fort Henry–Fort Donelson Campaign, February 1862.* Mechanicsburg, PA: Stackpole Books, 2003.

Grabau, Warren E. *Ninety-Eight Days: A Geographer's View of the Vicksburg Campaign.* Knoxville: University of Tennessee Press, 2000.

Grant, Ulysses S. *Personal Memoirs of U. S. Grant.* New York: Library of America, 1990.

Grecian, Joseph. *History of the Eighty-third Regiment, Indiana Volunteer Infantry.* Cincinnati: J. F. Uhlhorn, Printer, 1865.

Greif, J. V. "Baker's Creek and Champion Hill." *Confederate Veteran* (Oct. 1896).

Grierson, Benjamin H. *A Just and Righteous Cause: Benjamin H. Grierson's Civil War Memoir,* edited by Bruce J. Dinges and Shirley A. Leckie. Carbondale: Southern Illinois University Press, 2008.

Groom, Winston. *Vicksburg, 1863.* New York: Vintage Books, 2009.

Hager, George F. "Second Tennessee Cavalry." In *The Military Annals of Tennessee, Confederate,* edited by John Berrien Lindsley. Nashville: J. M. Lindsley & Co., Publishers, 1886.

Hall, Thomas O. "The Key to Vicksburg." *Southern Bivouac, Volume II: September 1883–August 1884.* Wilmington, NC: Broadfoot Publishing Company, 1992.

Hancock, R. R. *Hancock's Diary: or, A History of the Second Tennessee Confederate Cavalry.* Nashville: Brandon Printing Company, 1887.

Hanson, E. Hunn. "Forrest's Defeat of Sturgis at Brice's Cross-Roads." In *Battles and Leaders of the Civil War: Retreat with Honor,* edited by Robert Underwood Johnson and Clarence Clough Buel. Edison, NJ: Castle Books, 1995.

Harmon, George D. "Confederate Migration to Mexico." *Hispanic American Historical Review* (Nov. 1937).

Harp, Beth Chinn. *Torn Asunder: Civil War in Ohio County and the Green River Country*. Georgetown, KY: Kinnersley Press, 2003.

Harrison, Lowell H. *The Civil War in Kentucky*. Lexington: University Press of Kentucky, 1975.

Harrison, Lowell H., and James C. Klotter. *A New History of Kentucky*. Lexington: University Press of Kentucky, 1997.

Hattaway, Herman. *General Stephen D. Lee*. Jackson: University Press of Mississippi, 1976.

Heafford, George H. "The Army of the Tennessee." In *War Papers Read Before the Commandery of the State of Wisconsin, Military Order of the Loyal Legion of the United States, Volume I*. Milwaukee: Burdick, Armitage, & Allen, 1891.

Heintzelman, Samuel P., and E. D. Townsend. "Official Report of Samuel P. Heintzelman." *Journal of California and Great Basin Anthropology* 28 (1): 2008.

Henry, Robert Selph. *As They Saw Forrest: Some Recollections and Comments of Contemporaries*. Jackson, TN: McCowat-Mercer Press, 1956.

———. *"First with the Most" Forrest*. Indianapolis, IN: Bobbs-Merrill, 1944.

Holt, Joseph, compiler. "Military Road from Fort Benton to Fort Walla-Walla." www.narhist.ewu.edu/mullan_road/mullan_michigan.html. Accessed Apr. 23, 2017.

Hoppin, J. M. *Life of Andrew Hull Foote, Rear Admiral, United States Navy*. New York: Harper, 1874.

Hord, Henry Ewell. "Brice's X Roads From a Private's View." *Confederate Veteran* (Nov. 1904).

———. "Campaigning Under Forrest." *Confederate Veteran* (Jan. 1904).

———. "Her Little Flag." *Confederate Veteran* (Oct. 1915).

———. "Personal Experiences at Harrisburg, Miss." *Confederate Veteran* (Aug. 1908).

———. "Pursuit of Gen. Sturgis." *Confederate Veteran* (Jan. 1905).

———. "Scouting About Memphis." *Confederate Veteran* (May 1912).

Howard, Richard L. "The Vicksburg Campaign." In *War Papers Read Before the Commandery of the State of Maine, Military Order of the Loyal Legion of the United States, Volume II*. Portland: LeFavor-Tower Company, 1902.

Hughes, Nathaniel Cheairs, Jr. *Brigadier General Tyree H. Bell, CSA*. Knoxville: University of Tennessee Press, 2004.

Hughes, Robert Elkin, Frederick William Schaefer, and Eustace Leroy Williams. *That Kentucky Campaign: or, The Law, the Ballot, and the People in the Goebel-Taylor Contest*. Cincinnati: Robert Clarke Company, Publishers, 1900.

Hurst, Jack. *Nathan Bedford Forrest: A Biography*. New York: Knopf Doubleday Publishing Group, 2011.

Irwin, Richard B. "The Capture of Fort Hudson." In *Battles and Leaders of the Civil War: The Tide Shifts*, edited by Robert Underwood Johnson and Clarence Clough Buel. Edison, NJ: Castle Books, 1995.

Ives, Joseph C. *Report Upon the Colorado River of the West*. Washington, DC: Government Printing Office, 1861.

Jackson, Andrew. *The Papers of Andrew Jackson, 1770–1803*, vol. 1. Edited by Sam B. Smith, Harriet Fason Chappell Owsley, and Harold D. Moser. Knoxville: University of Tennessee Press, 1980.

Jackson, Jane Ann, and Thomas H. Wortham. *Eighty-Six Madisonville Historic Homes*. Madisonville, KY: Sprint Print, 2013.

Jackson, W. Turrentine. *Wagon Roads West: A Study of Federal Road Surveys and Construction in the Trans-Mississippi West, 1846–1869*. Berkeley: University of California Press, 1952.

Jenney, William L. B. "Personal Recollections of Vicksburg." In *Military Essays and Recollections: Papers Read Before the Commandery of the State of Illinois, Military Order of the Loyal Legion of the United States, Volume III*. Chicago: Dial Press, 1899.

Johnson, Andrew. *The Papers of Andrew Johnson: September 1865–January 1866*, vol. 9. Edited by Paul H. Bergeron. Knoxville: University of Tennessee Press, 1991.

Johnson, L. F. *Famous Kentucky Trials and Tragedies*. Lexington: Henry Clay Press, 1972.

Johnston, Joseph E. "Jefferson Davis and the Mississippi Campaign." In *Battles and Leaders of the Civil War: The Opening Battles*, edited by Robert Underwood Johnson and Clarence Clough Buel. Edison, NJ: Castle Books, 1995.

———. *Narrative of Military Operations During the Late War Between the States*. New York: D. Appleton and Company, 1874.

Jones, Archer. "Tennessee and Mississippi, Joe Johnston's Strategic Problem." In *Confederate Generals in the Western Theater: Classic Essays on America's Civil War*, edited by Lawrence L. Hewitt and Arthur W. Bergeron, Jr. Knoxville: University of Tennessee Press, 2010.

Jones, James Pickett. *Yankee Blitzkrieg: Wilson's Raid Through Alabama and Georgia*. Lexington: University Press of Kentucky, 2015.

Jones, Reinette F. "African American Shoemakers in Kentucky Prisons." nkaa.uky.edu/nkaa/items/show/3113. Accessed July 2, 2017.

Jones, Samuel Calvin. *Reminiscences of the Twenty-second Iowa Volunteer Infantry*. Iowa City, IA: by the author, 1907.

Jordan, Thomas, and J. P. Pryor. *The Campaigns of Lieut.-Gen. N. B. Forrest, and of Forrest's Cavalry*. New Orleans: Blelock & Company, 1868.

Journal of the House of Representatives of the United States. Washington, DC: Government Printing Office, 1878.

Journal of the Regular Session of the House of Representatives, of the Commonwealth of Kentucky. Frankfort: S. I. M. Major, Public Printer, 1871.

Journal of the Regular Session of the House of Representatives, of the Commonwealth of Kentucky. Frankfort: S. I. M. Major, Public Printer, 1873.

Journal of the Regular Session of the House of Representatives, of the Commonwealth of Kentucky. Frankfort: E. H. Porter, Public Printer, 1880.

Journal of the Regular Session of the House of Representatives, of the Commonwealth of Kentucky. Louisville: Geo. G. Fetter, 1900.

Keegan, John. *The American Civil War: A Military History*. New York: Alfred A. Knopf, 2009.

Keenan, Jerry. *Wilson's Cavalry Corps: Union Campaigns in the Western Theatre, October 1864 through Spring 1865*. Jefferson, NC: McFarland & Company, Inc., 2006.

Kellogg, J. J. *War Experiences and the Story of the Vicksburg Campaign*. N.p.: by the author, 1913.

Kentucky State Gazetteer and Business Directory, 1896. Detroit: R. L. Polk & Co., 1896.

Keyes, Erasmus D. *Fifty Years' Observation of Men and Events*. New York: Charles Scribner's Sons, 1884.

Kip, Lawrence. *Army Life on the Pacific: A Journal of the Expedition Against the Northern Indians*. New York: Redfield, 1859.

Kiper, Richard L. *Major General John Alexander McClernand: Politician in Uniform*. Kent, OH: Kent State University Press, 1999.

Krolick, Marshall D. "Brig. Gen. Abraham H. Buford." In *Kentuckians in Gray*, edited by Bruce S. Allardice and Lawrence Lee Hewitt. Lexington: University Press of Kentucky, 2008.

Larned, Charles W. "West Point." In *Personal Recollections of the War of the Rebellion: Addresses Delivered Before the New York Commandery of the Loyal Legion of the United States, Third Series*, edited by A. Noel Blakeman. New York: G. P. Putnam's Sons, 1907.

Lawson, Ernest M. *Awakening of Cumberland County*. Burkesville, KY: Cumberland County Publishing Company, 1973.

Lee, Dan. *The Civil War in the Jackson Purchase, 1861–1862*. Jefferson, NC: McFarland & Company, Inc., 2014.

Lee County, Mississippi: A Pictorial History. Paducah, KY: Turner Publishing Company, 2001.

———. *The L&N Railroad in the Civil War.* Jefferson, NC: McFarland & Company, Inc., 2011.

Leeson, Michael. *History of Montana, 1739–1885.* Chicago: Warner, Beers and Company, 1885.

Lockett, S. H. "The Defense of Vicksburg." In *Battles and Leaders of the Civil War: The Opening Battles,* edited by Robert Underwood Johnson and Clarence Clough Buel. Edison, NJ: Castle Books, 1995.

Longacre, Edward G. *A Soldier to the Last: Maj. Gen. Joseph Wheeler in Blue and Gray.* Washington, DC: Potomac Books, 2007.

Lucas, Scott J. "'Indignities, Wrongs, and Outrages': Military and Guerrilla Incursions on Kentucky's Civil War Home Front." *The Filson Club History Quarterly* (Oct. 1999).

Lyon, Hylan B. "Memoirs of Hylan B. Lyon," edited by Edward M. Coffman. *Tennessee Historical Quarterly* (May 1959).

Lyon, Matthew. "Letters from Matthew Lyon, 1818–1819. *Western Kentucky Journal* (Winter 2002).

"Lyon County (KY) Slaves, Free Blacks, and Free Mulattoes, 1860–1880." nkaa.uky .edu/nkaa/items/show/2443. Accessed Apr. 5, 2018.

Manring, Benjamin F. *The Conquest of the Coeur d'Alenes, Spokanes and Palouses.* Spokane, WA: John W. Graham Co., 1912.

Marshall, Anne E. *Creating a Confederate Kentucky: The Lost Cause and Civil War Memory in a Border State.* Chapel Hill: University of North Carolina Press, 2013.

Marshall, Thomas B. *History of the Eighty-third Ohio Volunteer Infantry.* Cincinnati: The Eight-third Ohio Volunteer Infantry Association, 1912.

Martin, W. W., and E. F. McNeill. *The Tale of Two Cities: A History of Kuttawa-Eddyville, and Lyon County, Kentucky.* Kuttawa, KY: McClanahan Publishing House, 1992.

McLain, Minor H. "The Military Prison at Fort Warren." In *Civil War Prisons,* edited by William B. Hesseltine. Kent, OH: Kent State University Press, 1972.

McLaughlin, James Fairfax. *Matthew Lyon: The Hampden of Congress.* New York: Wynkoop Hallenbeck Crawford Company, 1900.

McPherson, James M. *The Negro's Civil War: How American Blacks Felt and Acted During the War for the Union.* New York: Knopf Doubleday Publishing Group, Inc., 2008.

Meacham, Charles Mayfield. *A History of Christian County, Kentucky from Oxcart to Airplane.* Nashville, TN: Marshall & Bruce Co., 1930.

Memorial Record of Western Kentucky. Two Volumes. Chicago, IL: Lewis Publishing Company, 1904.

Merrill, William E. "Block-Houses for Railroad Defense in the Department of the Cumberland." In *Sketches of War History, 1861–1865: Papers Prepared for the Ohio Commandery of the Military Order of the Loyal Legion of the United States,* edited by Robert Hunter. Cincinnati, OH: Robert Clarke & Co., 1890.

Morgan, George W. "The Assault on Chickasaw Bluffs." In *Battles and Leaders of the Civil War: The Tide Shifts.* edited by Robert Underwood Johnson and Clarence Clough Buel. Edison, NJ: Castle Books, 1995.

Morton, John Watson. *The Artillery of Nathan Bedford Forrest's Cavalry.* Nashville: Publishing House of the M.E. Church, South, 1909.

Morton, Joseph W., ed. *Sparks from the Camp Fire, or, Tales of the Old Veterans.* Philadelphia, PA: Keeler and Kirkpatrick, 1899.

Mulesky, Raymond. "Brig. Gen. Adam Rankin Johnson." In *Kentuckians in Gray,* edited by Bruce S. Allardice and Lawrence Lee Hewitt. Lexington: University Press of Kentucky, 2008.

Mullan, John. *Miners and Travelers' Guide to Oregon, Washington, Idaho, Montana, Wyoming, and Colorado.* New York: Wm. M. Franklin, 1865.

"The Mullan Road: John Mullan's Report of 1863." www.narhist.ewu.edu/mullan _report/mullan_report_home.html. Accessed Aug. 25, 2016.

Myers, Marshall. "An Alabama Commissioner Tried to Convince Ky. to Secede." *The Kentucky Explorer* (Dec. 2012/Jan. 2013).

Nesbitt, Robert Lee. *Early Taylor County History.* Campbellsville, KY: The News-Journal, 1941.

O'Flaherty, Daniel. *General Jo Shelby: Undefeated Rebel.* Chapel Hill: University of North Carolina Press, 2000.

Orr, J. F. "The Captured Undine and Mazeppa." *Confederate Veteran* (July 1910).

Otey, Mercer. "Story of Our Great War." Confederate Veteran (Mar. 1901).

Parson, Thomas E. "The Battle of Tupelo (or Harrisburg)." *Blue & Gray Magazine,* vol. XXX, no. 6.

Pierce, Lyman B. *History of the Second Iowa Cavalry.* Burlington: Hawk-eye Steam Book and Job Printing Establishment, 1865.

Puryear, G. J. "No Man's Battle." *Confederate Veteran* (Nov. 1914).

Quisenberry, A. C. "The Alleged Secession of Kentucky." *Register of the Kentucky Historical Society* (May 1917).

Rabb, James W. *Confederate General Lloyd Tilghman: A Biography.* Jefferson, NC: McFarland and Co., Inc., 2006.

Reavis, L. U. *The Life and Military Services of Gen. William Selby Harney.* St. Louis: Bryan, Brand & Co., 1876.

Roberson, B. L. "The Courthouse Burnin'est General." *Tennessee Historical Quarterly* (Dec. 1964).

Roe, Elizabeth A. Lyon. *Aunt Leanna, or, Early Scenes in Kentucky.* Auburn, IL: Miller, Orten & Mulligan, 1855.

———. *Recollections of Frontier Life.* Rockford, IL: Gazette Publishing House, 1885.

Rolle, Andrew F. *The Lost Cause: The Confederate Exodus to Mexico.* Norman: University of Oklahoma Press, 1965.

Russell, Sinclair Merrell. "Sidelights on the Assassination of Governor William Goebel." Reprinted in *The Kentucky Explorer* (Feb. 2013).

Sanders, Charles W., Jr. *While in the Hands of the Enemy: Military Prisons of the Civil War.* Baton Rouge: Louisiana State University Press, 2005.

Sangston, Lawrence. *The Bastiles of the North.* Baltimore, MD: Kelly, Hedian & Piet, 1863.

Schlicke, Carl P. *General George Wright: Guardian of the Pacific Coast.* Norman: University of Oklahoma Press, 1988.

Schofield, John M. *Forty-Six Years in the Army.* New York: Century Co., 1897.

Scott, Reuben B., compiler. *The History of the 67th Regiment Indiana Infantry Volunteers.* Bedford, IN: Herald Book and Job Print, 1892.

Sherman, William T. *Memoirs of General W. T. Sherman.* New York: Library of America, 1990.

———. *Sherman's Civil War: Selected Correspondence of William T. Sherman, 1860–1865,* edited by Brooks D. Simpson and Jean V. Berlin. Chapel Hill: University of North Carolina Press, 1999.

Shunk, William A. "The Vicksburg Campaign." In *War Papers Read Before the Commandery of the State of Wisconsin, Military Order of the Loyal Legion of the United States, Volume IV.* Milwaukee: Burdick & Allen, 1914.

Smith, Frank E. *The Yazoo River.* New York: Rinehart & Company, Inc., 1954.

Smith, Myron J., Jr. *The Timberclads in the Civil War: The Lexington, Conestoga, and Tyler on the Western Waters.* Jefferson, NC: McFarland and Co., Inc., 2008.

———. *Tinclads in the Civil War: Union Light-Draught Gunboat Operations on Western Waters, 1862–1865.* Jefferson, NC: McFarland and Co., Inc., 2010.

Smith, Timothy B. *Champion Hill: Decisive Battle for Vicksburg.* Havertown, PA: Casemate Publishers, 2004.

Smith, Zachariah Frederick. *The History of Kentucky: From Its Earliest Discovery and Settlement to the Present Date.* Louisville: Courier-Journal Job Printing Company, 1892.

Soley, James Russell. "Naval Operations in the Vicksburg Campaign." In *Battles and Leaders of the Civil War: The Opening Battles,* edited by Robert Underwood Johnson and Clarence Clough Buel. Edison, NJ: Castle Books, 1995.

Splawn, A. J. *Ka-mi-akin: The Last Hero of the Yakimas.* Portland, OR: Kilham Stationery & Printing Co., 1917.

Staten, Vince. "Is Kentucky Southern?" *Courier-Journal Magazine*, Nov. 29, 1987.

Stevens, J. M. Untitled. *Confederate Veteran* (Jan. 1897).

Stevenson, Thomas M. *History of the 78th O.V.V.I.* Zanesville, OH: H. Dunne, 1865.

Stickles, Arndt M. *Simon Bolivar Buckner: Borderland Knight.* Chapel Hill: University of North Carolina Press, 1940.

Strong, William E. "The Campaign Against Vicksburg." In *Military Essays and Recollections: Papers Read Before the Commandery of the State of Illinois, Military Order of the Loyal Legion of the United States, Volume II.* Chicago, IL: A. C. McClurg and Company, 1894.

Sutherland, George E. "The Negro in the Late War. " In *War Papers Read Before the Commandery of the State of Wisconsin, Military Order of the Loyal Legion of the United States, Volume I.* Milwaukee, WI: Burdick, Armitage, & Allen, 1891.

Symonds, Craig L. *Joseph E. Johnston: A Civil War Biography.* New York: W. W. Norton & Company, 1994.

Tapp, Hambleton, and James C. Klotter. *Kentucky: Decades of Discord, 1865–1900.* Lexington: University Press of Kentucky, 1977.

Taylor, Richard. *Destruction and Reconstruction,* edited by Richard B. Harwell. New York: Longmans, Green and Co., 1955.

Thompson, Edwin Porter. *History of the Orphan Brigade.* Louisville, KY: Lewis N. Thompson, 1898.

Thompson, Jerry D. *Civil War to the Bloody End: The Life and Times of Major General Samuel P. Heintzelman.* College Station: Texas A&M University Press, 2006.

Tilford, John E., Jr. "The Delicate Track: The L&N's Role in the Civil War." *The Filson Club History Quarterly* (July 1962).

Trudeau, Noah Andre. *Like Men of War: Black Troops in the Civil War, 1862–1865.* Edison, NJ: Castle Books, 1998.

Tucker, W. H. *The Fourteenth Wisconsin Vet. Vol. Infantry (General A. J. Smith's Command) in the Expedition and Battle of Tupelo.* Indianapolis, IN: F. E. Engle & Son, 1892.

Tyler, Robert O. *Memoir of Brevet Major-General Robert Ogden Tyler, U.S. Army.* Philadelphia, PA: J. B. Lippincott & Co., 1878.

Underwood, Josie. *Josie Underwood's Civil War Diary,* edited by Nancy Disher Baird. Lexington: University Press of Kentucky, 2009.

"1860 United States Federal Census." Database. Ancestry.com. http://www .ancestry.com: 2017.

"1870 United States Federal Census." Database. Ancestry.com. http://www .ancestry.com: 2017.

"1880 United States Federal Census." Database. Ancestry.com. http://www
.ancestry.com: 2017.

"1900 United States Federal Census." Database. Ancestry.com. http://www
.ancestry.com: 2017.

United States Military Academy. *Official Register of the Officers and Cadets.* West
Point, NY: United States Military Academy Printing Office, 1855.

United States Naval Records Office. *Official Records of the Union and Confederate
Navies in the War of the Rebellion, Series I.* 27 Volumes. Washington, DC:
Government Printing Office, 1894–1917.

United States War Department. *The War of the Rebellion: A Compilation of the Official Records of the Union and Confederate Armies.* 129 Volumes. Washington,
DC: Government Printing Office, 1880–1901.

Utley, J. Harold. "The Civil War in Hopkins County." In *Historical Society of
Hopkins County Twenty-Sixth Annual Yearbook.* Madisonville, KY: Historical Society of Hopkins County, 2000.

Utley, Robert M. *Frontiersmen in Blue: The United States Army and the Indians,
1848–1865.* Lincoln: University of Nebraska Press, 1981.

Vilas, William Freeman. *A View of the Vicksburg Campaign: A Paper read before the
Madison Literary Club, October 14, 1907.* N.p.: Wisconsin History Commission, 1908.

Wahlstrom, Todd W. *The Southern Exodus to Mexico: Migration Across the Borderlands
After the American Civil War.* Lincoln: University of Nebraska Press, 2015.

Walker, Odell. "How Eddyville Was Named County Seat of Three Counties." *The
Kentucky Explorer,* June 2016.

———. *In Lyon County, Saturday Was Town Day.* Kuttawa, KY: McClanahan
Publishing House, 2002.

———. *Profiles of the Past.* Kuttawa, KY: McClanahan Publishing House, 1994.

Wallace, Lew. "The Capture of Fort Donelson." In *Battles and Leaders of the Civil
War: The Opening Battles,* edited by Robert Underwood Johnson and Clarence Clough Buel. Edison, NJ: Castle Books, 1995.

Waller, J. B. "War Reminiscences." In *The Partisan Rangers of the Confederate States
Army,* edited by William J. Davis. Utica, KY: Cook & McDowell Publications, 1979.

Ward, Andrew. *River Run Red: The Fort Pillow Massacre in the American Civil War.*
New York: Penguin, 2006.

Warner, Ezra J. *Generals in Blue.* Baton Rouge: Louisiana State University Press,
2006.

———. *Generals in Gray.* Baton Rouge: Louisiana State University Press, 2008.

Weber, Lawrence. "Sealing Vicksburg's Fate." *Civil War Quarterly* (Early Fall, 2014).

Wells, J. W. *History of Cumberland County.* Louisville: Standard Printing Co., 1947.

Wennersten, John R. *Leaving America: The New Expatriate Generation.* Westport, CT: Greenwood Publishing Group, 2008.

Wiley, Bell Irvin. *The Life of Johnny Reb: The Common Soldier of the Confederacy.* Baton Rouge, Louisiana State University Press, 1978.

Williams, Frances Leigh. *Matthew Fontaine Maury, Scientist of the Sea.* New Brunswick, NJ: Rutgers University Press, 1963.

Williams, Kenneth H., and James Russell Harris. "Kentucky in 1860: A Statistical Overview." *Register of the Kentucky Historical Society* (Autumn 2005).

Williams, Nannie Haskins. *The Diary of Nannie Haskins Williams: A Southern Woman's Story of Rebellion and Reconstruction, 1863–1890.* Edited by Minoa D. Uffelman, Ellen Kanervo, Phyllis Smith, and Eleanor Williams. Knoxville: University of Tennessee Press, 2014.

Wilkes, John S. "First Battle Experience—Fort Donelson." *Confederate Veteran* (Nov. 1906).

Wills, Brian Steel. *A Battle from the Start: The Life of Nathan Bedford Forrest.* New York: HarperCollins Publishers, 1992.

———. "Brig. Gen. Hylan Benton Lyon." In *Kentuckians in Gray,* edited by Bruce S. Allardice and Lawrence Lee Hewitt. Lexington: University Press of Kentucky, 2008.

Wilson, James Harrison. *Under the Old Flag.* Two volumes. New York: D. Appleton and Company, 1912.

Winschel, Terrence J. "Brig. Gen. Lloyd Tilghman." In *Kentuckians in Gray,* edited by Bruce S. Allardice and Lawrence Lee Hewitt. Lexington: University Press of Kentucky, 2008.

———. "A Tragedy of Errors: The Failure of the Confederate High Command in the Defense of Vicksburg." *North and South* (Jan. 2006).

Wood, Frank. "Brice's Crossroads and After." *Confederate Veteran* (Nov. 1925).

Wood, Wales W. *A History of the Ninety-Fifth Regiment Illinois Infantry Volunteers.* Chicago, IL: Tribune Company's Book and Job Printing Office, 1865.

Woodrick, Jim. *The Civil War Siege of Jackson, Mississippi.* Charleston, SC: History Press, 2016.

Woodworth, Steven E. *Nothing But Victory: The Army of the Tennessee, 1861–1865.* New York: Alfred A. Knopf, 2005.

Wright, Steven L., ed. *Kentucky Soldiers and Their Regiments in the Civil War: Abstracted from the Pages of Contemporary Kentucky Newspapers.* Five volumes. By the editor, 2009.

————, compiler. *On Trial for Their Lives: Kentucky's Guerrillas and Military Justice in the Civil War.* By the author, 2012.

Wyeth, John Allan. "Gen. N. B. Forrest in 1864." *Confederate Veteran* (Aug. 1895).

————. *Life of Lieutenant-General Nathan Bedford Forrest.* New York: Harper & Brothers, 1908.

Wynne, Ben. *A Hard Trip: A History of the 15th Mississippi, CSA.* Macon, GA: Mercer University Press, 2010.

————. *Mississippi's Civil War: A Narrative History.* Macon, GA: Mercer University Press, 2006.

Yeary, Mamie, compiler. *Reminiscences of the Boys in Gray, 1861–1865.* Dallas, TX: Smith & Lamar, 1912.

Young, Bennett. *Confederate Wizards of the Saddle.* Nashville, TN: J. S. Sanders & Company, 1914.

Young, John Preston. *The Seventh Tennessee Cavalry, Confederate, A History.* Nashville, TN: Publishing House of the M.E. Church, 1890.

INDEX

www.ingramcontent.com/pod-product-compliance
Lightning Source LLC
Chambersburg PA
CBHW031937090426
42811CB00002B/209